WITHDRAWN

THE
UNIVERSITY
CRISIS
READER

The Liberal
University Under Attack

THE
UNIVERSITY
CRISIS
READER

VOLUME I

The Liberal
University Under Attack

Edited by

IMMANUEL WALLERSTEIN
and PAUL STARR

RANDOM HOUSE
New York

Acknowledgment is gratefully extended to the following for permission to
reprint from copyrighted works:

The New Yorker: From an editorial in the March 22, 1969 issue. Copyright
© 1969 by The New Yorker Magazine, Inc.

Atlantic-Little, Brown and Co.: "Rebels Without a Program" from
Democracy and the Student Left, by George F. Kennan. Copyright ©
1968 by George F. Kennan.

Beacon Press: From *The Ideal of the University*, by Robert Paul Wolff,
Chapter 3. Copyright © 1969 by Robert Paul Wolff.

Harvard University Press: Excerpts from *The Uses of the University* by
Clark Kerr. Copyright © 1963 by the President and Fellows of Harvard
College.

Dedicated to the memory of
C. Wright Mills

Acknowledgments

This book originated out of our involvement in the intellectual debates at Columbia and our awareness of the vast flow of interesting documents that emerged from those debates. We could not, however, have put together this book had not many persons throughout the United States made available to us their own collections of material and in some instances assisted us in tracking down elusive documents.

We collected so much material that we could only use a fraction of it and some very interesting cases had to be omitted altogether. We apologize both to those who helped acquire the unused material and to the readers who will not see it. We can only say that the university crisis has surely been a prodigiously verbal one.

We offer especial thanks to Harry Alderman, James Bowen, D. Michael Collins, David Elesh, William H. Friedland, Nathan Glazer, Ruth Goldman, Richard M. Gummere, Jr., Richard Hill, Milton Himmelfarb, Serge Lang, Otto McClarrin, John Meyer, Chandler Morse, Rae A. Moses, Leslie Rubin, Edward E. Sampson, Howard Schless, Jay Schulman, Richard D. Schwartz, William Scott, Philip Shapiro, Richard Sklar, Richard Strassberg, Judith Wallerstein, Robert S. Wallerstein, David Wiley, M. Crawford Young, Aristide Zolberg.

Summary of Contents

Contents

Introduction

The student revolt on American campuses in the late 1960s, though in some respects similar to student rebellions elsewhere in the world and at other times in history, served as the point of confluence of three distinctively American social movements.

One was the movement of America's Black minority, first for civil rights and integration, and then for power and institutional autonomy. Significantly, the initial impetus for the Black movement came from the efforts to implement the Supreme Court's desegregation decision in 1954. The Black college students who sought to desegregate lunch counters in southern towns were perhaps the first in recent U.S. history, besides the factory workers, to use confrontation tactics. With the Montgomery Bus Boycott, civil disobedience became legitimate in the eyes of many people. White students became increasingly involved through the Freedom Rides and voter registration campaigns.

However, 1964 and 1965, the years Congress passed the two major civil rights acts that capped the movement's efforts, were also the years of the Watts riots in Los Angeles, the assassination of Malcolm X, and the spurning of the Mississippi Freedom Democratic Party by the Democratic National Convention. It was not long before the movement for civil rights became a movement for Black power and Black liberation.

A second movement, which fed into the student revolt and became intertwined with it, was the peace movement—originally concerned with banning nuclear weapons and subsequently with stopping the war in Vietnam. During the height of the Cold War period, the movement limped along under grievous suspicion, gaining momentum only in the late 1950s. Organizations like SANE (the Committee for a Sane Nuclear Policy) and Women's Strike for Peace played a leading role during that time. When their immediate objective was achieved in 1963 with the signing of the test-ban treaty, the peace movement seemed very respectable and in the mainstream of American life. But two years later, in 1965, President Johnson's decisions to make a large-scale commitment of troops to Vietnam and to send Marines into the Dominican Republic led to a new and much more radical thrust within the peace movement. It began to question the very premises of American foreign policy as well as the wisdom of particular strategies.

The third movement was the drive for cultural liberation. In a sense, its presence in the United States had been evident since the end of World War I, but only among intellectuals, artists, and writers. In the 1950s, a particular kind of unorthodox withdrawal centered around a group of novelists and poets who called themselves the "beat generation." Antagonistic to the bureaucratic pressures of industrial society, hostile to the hypocrisies and easy optimism of the American middle class, they took up Zen Buddhism and pot, venerated the "open road," revived folk singing, and explained to each other their anger at American society. This movement passed through many stages, from rock music and LSD, to hippies and long hair and flower children, to a directly political mutation in 1968, the Youth International Party or Yippies. In the process the movement brought about enormous changes in clothing styles and personal accoutrements. It legitimized nudity, unconventional sex, and pornography in the American arts to an extent never before tolerated.

The first great outburst on a modern American campus, the Berkeley Free Speech Movement of 1964, foreshadowed the upheavals to come later in the decade. In its political content, howver, the Berkeley episode marked the close-out of an era rather than the beginning of a new one. Started by students who had returned from the Mississippi Summers and Peace Corps assignments, nurtured in the still moderate forms of cultural rebellion, the Berkeley students centered their demands for reform around the greatest of liberal themes: free speech. In "An end to history," Mario Savio declared: "Last summer I went to Mississippi to join the struggle there for civil rights. This fall I am engaged in another phase of the same struggle, this time in Berkeley. The two battlefields may seem quite different to some observers, but this is not the case. The same rights are at stake in both places—the right to participate as citizens in a democratic society and the right to due process of law."

The turning point came in 1965 when the Vietnam war and the Watts riot raised new kinds of questions about the viability of the great American compromise—the liberal welfare state. The protest movement slowly began to turn against liberalism and those who embodied it—the government, the Democratic Party, and eventually college professors. The protesters began to develop a theory about universities that viewed their liberal ideology as a camouflage for society's corporate and military structure. The universities were seen as reflections of the larger society, mirroring its institutionalized racism, its support for the recolonization of the Third World, its repression of new life styles. Furthermore, to the new radicals, the universities were not just miniature replicas of society, they were one of its main pillars. Hence an attack on the university was seen as more than a symbolic gesture of protest; it was an effective act of resistance to a corrupt society. To what degree the struggle within the university was in fact effective enough to change society became a tactical issue within the left. But at least in the beginning, radical students shared the belief that the university was a relevant arena for their activity.

The forces of the attack were disparate and their ideology not always coherent. But beneath the welter of issues and viewpoints a fundamental theme emerged. The society under attack was not merely a capitalist society or a bureaucratic society; it was a liberal society. And the university was a liberal university. Not only did the dissenters insist that there was no fundamental difference between liberalism and contemporary conservative ideologies; they also charged that liberalism represented a dangerous deception, a way of deflecting criticism of the social order without making significant changes, a way of sapping the morale and the energy of potentially revolutionary forces. Thus, it was important to attack the principles of liberalism in their stronghold, the liberal university, in order to clear the underbrush, in order to radicalize the forces of opposition, in order to create a situation in which revolution could become a serious possibility.

This book is the story of the radical attack on the liberal university and its defense. What we the editors have done is to collect the original documents—the pamphlets, leaflets, articles and reports, letters and speeches—that have appeared between 1965 and 1970, with emphasis on the later years. Some of these documents discuss the problems at the national level. Some come from the campuses—principally those on the firing line: Columbia, Harvard, San Francisco State, Cornell, Berkeley, Stanford, Wisconsin, etc. These are primary documents, in the sense that they were written by those who were committed, by those who wished to persuade. They are generally not the secondary analyses of disinterested observers.

This book is not a history of the confrontations on American campuses, although many incidents are covered. It is, rather, an attempt to clarify the debates that underlay the conflicts by bringing together diverse sources and allowing the reader to view directly the contending arguments. We do this on one assumption: that the attack on the liberal university is historically important and intellectually serious.

Our method is simple. We start with a prologue, consisting of a set of general statements, famous in their own right, which reveal the tone of the debates and present, in a broad sweep, some of the arguments.* Then, we lay out the issues under discussion. We believe that six main issues were raised by the movement about the liberal university: its functions for society as an educational institution, the actions of the university as a firm, its links to the government and the war, racism, the distribution of power within the university, and the nature of the educational process. Under each heading, we seek to present both the challenge made by the movement and the response of the establishment. Occasionally we include the views of the so-called New Right, who share some of the movement's criticisms of the liberal university, while standing quite clearly for a third set of values.

* We regret we are unable to reprint one of the readings originally chosen for this section, "Education and Revolution," by Eldridge Cleaver. The essay may be found in *The Black Scholar*, November 1969.

These debates have not been purely academic. What has distressed the establishment most is that the student movement has acted on its beliefs and acted in a style that challenged one of the fundamental tenets of liberalism—the primacy of rational discussion as a method of resolving conflicts. Thus the second volume of this reader is entitled *Confrontation and Counterattack*. It outlines the debate over the legitimacy of confrontation tactics and the effectiveness of disruption and violence, and explores the tactical debates on each side: within SDS as to how to build a movement, within the faculty as to its role, and within the establishment as to how to respond to turmoil.

Next we present the ideological counterattack that the adversaries of the student movement made against the values they claimed the movement represented.

Finally, we conclude with our own assessments of the situation.

I.W.
New York City   P.S.

THE
UNIVERSITY
CRISIS
READER

The Liberal
University Under Attack

Prologue

The five following selections are important in their own right, as presentations of an overall outlook on student discontent, as influential writings. They set the stage for the more specific debates that make up the bulk of this volume.

George Wald's March 4 address, given on the occasion of a nation-wide protest against the use of science for military purposes, was one of those rare speeches which establish a man's reputation as a public figure overnight. Wald, a Harvard biology professor and Nobel laureate, tried to diagnose the "profound uneasiness" besetting his students. He found the source partly in the Vietnam war, partly in the expansion of the military, partly in the draft, but mostly in vast insecurity caused by nuclear weaponry. His students, he said, were a generation uncertain that it had a future. Wald, like them, was ready to be intemperate, and he shared their demand for new priorities: "Our business is with life, not death."

George Kennan, the diplomat and foreign policy analyst, has been one of the most outspoken opponents of the student movement. His sentiments are evident in the very title of his article: "Rebels without a program." He accused the students of two unforgivable sins: "violence for violence's sake" and "an extraordinary degree of [moral] certainty." To their demand for a new university, he restated the classical "ideal of the association of the process of learning with a certain remoteness."

But that "remoteness" is not true of the university itself today, according to the authors of the Columbia Statement, a declaration adopted by the Columbia University chapter of Students for a Democratic Society in the fall of 1968. According to SDS, the university is deeply implicated in the violence of American imperialism. In a denunciation of military research and counter-insurgency work, the Columbia Statement declared: "The most heinous crimes of our century are not the crimes of passion; they are the crimes of intellect." And the radicals added, "We believe that a university should have nothing to do with human subjugation, except the overthrowing of it."

The Amherst College Statement was one of the few major collective declarations to emerge from the university crisis. Signing as individuals, the president and a majority of the faculty and students of Amherst sent an open letter to President Richard Nixon in May 1969 outlining their consensus on the causes and significance of the student revolt. They observed that there would continue to be turmoil on American campuses "until political leadership addresses itself to the major problems of our society." While Kennan maintained that the student left had no program to deal with the nation's problems, Amherst suggested the government had none.

President Nixon never replied directly to the Amherst Statement. He did, however, give a formal address on student unrest the following month at General Beadle State College in South Dakota—one campus where he could be sure of not meeting any demonstrators. In his speech, the President implicitly rejected the views of the Amherst Statement, asserting that the nation's fundamental principles were under attack, that American society was not immoral, and that the country had to rise to the defense of traditional values.

Speech given at MIT, on March 4, 1969, by Nobel Laureate George Wald, Professor of Biology at Harvard University.

A Generation in Search of a Future

All of you know that in the last couple of years there has been student unrest, breaking at times into violence, in many parts of the world: in England, Germany, Italy, Spain, Mexico, Japan, and, needless to say, many parts of this country. There has been a great deal of discussion as to what it all means. Perfectly clearly, it means something different in Mexico from what it does in France, and something different in France from what it does in Tokyo, and something different in Tokyo from what it does in this country. Yet, unless we are to assume that students have gone crazy all over the world, or that they have just decided that it's the thing to do, it must have some common meaning.

I don't need to go so far afield to look for that meaning. I am a teacher, and at Harvard I have a class of about three hundred and fifty students—men and women—most of them freshmen and sophomores. Over these past few years, I have felt increasingly that something is terribly wrong—and this year ever so much more than last. Something has gone sour, in teaching and in learning. It's almost as though there were a widespread feeling that education has become irrelevant.

A lecture is much more of a dialogue than many of you probably realize. As you lecture, you keep watching the faces, and information keeps coming back to you all the time. I began to feel, particularly this year, that I was missing much of what was coming back. I tried asking the students, but they didn't or couldn't help me very much.

But I think I know what's the matter. I think that this whole generation of students is beset with a profound uneasiness, and I don't think that they have yet quite defined its source. I think I understand the reasons for their uneasiness even better than they do. What is more, I share their uneasiness.

What's bothering those students? Some of them tell you it's the Vietnam war. I think the Vietnam war is the most shameful episode in the whole of American history. The concept of war crimes is an American invention. We've committed many war crimes in Vietnam—but I'll tell you something interesting about that. We were committing war crimes in World War II, before the Nuremberg trials were held and the principle of war crimes was stated. The saturation bombing of German cities was a war crime. Dropping those atomic bombs on Hiroshima and Nagasaki was a war crime. If we had lost the war, it might have been *our* leaders who had to answer for such actions. I've gone through all that history lately, and I find that there's a gimmick in it. It isn't written out, but I think we established it by precedent. That gimmick is that if one can allege that one is repelling or retaliating for an aggression, after that everything goes.

And, you see, we are living in a world in which all wars are wars of defense. All War Departments are now Defense Departments. This is all part of the doubletalk of our time. The aggressor is always on the other side. I suppose this is why our ex-Secretary of State Dean Rusk went to such pains to insist, as he still insists, that in Vietnam we are repelling an aggression. And if that's what we are doing—so runs the doctrine—everything goes. If the concept of war crimes is ever to mean anything, they will have to be defined as categories of *acts,* regardless of alleged provocation. But that isn't so now.

I think we've lost that war, as a lot of other people think, too. The Vietnamese have a secret weapon. It's their willingness to die beyond our willingness to kill. In effect, they've been saying, You can kill us, but you'll have to kill a lot of us; you may have to kill all of us. And, thank heaven, we are not yet ready to do that.

Yet we have come a long way toward it—far enough to sicken many Americans, far enough to sicken even our fighting men. Far enough so that our national symbols have gone sour. How many of you can sing about "the rockets' red glare, the bombs bursting in air" without thinking, Those are *our* bombs and *our* rockets, bursting over South Vietnamese villages? When those words were written, we were a people struggling for freedom against oppression. Now we are supporting open or thinly disguised military dictatorships all over the world, helping them to control and repress peoples struggling for their freedom.

But that Vietnam war, shameful and terrible as it is, seems to me only an immediate incident in a much larger and more stubborn situation.

Part of my trouble with students is that almost all the students I teach were born after World War II. Just after World War II, a series of new and abnormal procedures came into American life. We regarded them at the time as temporary aberrations. We thought we would get back to normal American life someday.

But those procedures have stayed with us now for more than twenty years, and those students of mine have never known anything else. They think those things are normal. They think that we've always had a Pentagon, that we have always had a big Army, and that we have always had a draft. But those are all new things in American life, and I think that they are incompatible with what America meant before.

How many of you realize that just before World War II the entire American Army, including the Air Corps, numbered a hundred and thirty-nine thousand men? Then World War II started, but we weren't yet in it, and, seeing that there was great trouble in the world, we doubled this Army to two hundred and sixty-eight thousand men. Then, in World War II, it got to be eight million. And then World War II came to an end and we prepared to go back to a peacetime Army, somewhat as the American Army had always been before. And, indeed, in 1950—you think about 1950, our international commitments, the Cold War, the Truman Doctrine, and all the rest of it—in 1950, we got down to six hundred thousand men.

Now we have three and a half million men under arms: about six hundred thousand in Vietnam, about three hundred thousand more in "support areas" elsewhere in the Pacific, about two hundred and fifty thousand in Germany. And there are a lot at home. Some months ago, we were told that three hundred thousand National Guardsmen and two hundred thousand reservists—so half a million men—had been specially trained for riot duty in the cities.

I say the Vietnam war is just an immediate incident because as long as we keep that big an Army, it will always find things to do. If the Vietnam war stopped tomorrow, the chances are that with that big a military establishment we would be in another such adventure, abroad or at home, before you knew it.

The thing to do about the draft is not to reform it but to get rid of it.

A peacetime draft is the most un-American thing I know. All the time I was growing up, I was told about oppressive Central European countries and Russia, where young men were forced into the Army, and I was told what they did about it. They chopped off a finger, or shot off a couple of toes, or, better still, if they could manage it, they came to this country. And we understood that, and sympathized, and were glad to welcome them.

Now, by present estimates, from four to six thousand Americans of draft age have left this country for Canada, two or three thousand more have gone to Europe, and it looks as though many more were preparing to emigrate.

A bill to stop the draft was recently introduced in the Senate

(S. 503), sponsored by a group of senators that runs the gamut from McGovern and Hatfield to Barry Goldwater. I hope it goes through. But I think that when we get rid of the draft we must also drastically cut back the size of the armed forces.

Yet there is something ever so much bigger and more important than the draft. That bigger thing, of course, is the militarization of our country. Ex-President Eisenhower, in his farewell address, warned us of what he called the military-industrial complex. I am sad to say that we must begin to think of it now as the military-industrial-labor-union complex. What happened under the plea of the Cold War was not alone that we built up the first big peacetime Army in our history but that we institutionalized it. We built, I suppose, the biggest government building in our history to run it, and we institutionalized it.

I don't think we can live with the present military establishment, and its eighty-billion-dollar-a-year budget, and keep America anything like the America we have known in the past. It is corrupting the life of the whole country. It is buying up everything in sight: industries, banks, investors, scientists—and lately it seems also to have bought up the labor unions.

The Defense Department is always broke, but some of the things it does with that eighty billion dollars a year would make Buck Rogers envious. For example, the Rocky Mountain Arsenal, on the outskirts of Denver, was manufacturing a deadly nerve poison on such a scale that there was a problem of waste disposal. Nothing daunted, the people there dug a tunnel two miles deep under Denver, into which they have injected so much poisoned water that, beginning a couple of years ago, Denver has experienced a series of earth tremors of increasing severity. Now there is grave fear of a major earthquake. An interesting debate is in progress as to whether Denver will be safer if that lake of poisoned water is removed or is left in place.

Perhaps you have read also of those six thousand sheep that suddenly died in Skull Valley, Utah, killed by another nerve poison—a strange and, I believe, still unexplained accident, since the nearest testing seems to have been thirty miles away.

As for Vietnam, the expenditure of firepower there has been frightening. Some of you may still remember Khe Sanh, a hamlet just south of the Demilitarized Zone, where a force of United States Marines was beleaguered for a time. During that period, we dropped on the perimeter of Khe Sanh more explosives than fell on Japan throughout World War II, and more than fell on the whole of Europe during the years 1942 and 1943.

One of the officers there was quoted as having said afterward, "It looks like the world caught smallpox and died."

The only point of government is to safeguard and foster life. Our government has become preoccupied with death, with the business of killing and being killed. So-called defense now absorbs sixty per cent of the national budget, and about twelve per cent of the Gross National Product.

A lively debate is beginning again on whether or not we should deploy antiballistic missiles, the ABM. I don't have to talk about them—everyone else here is doing that. But I should like to mention a curious circumstance. In September, 1967, or about a year and a half ago, we had a meeting of M.I.T. and Harvard people, including experts on these matters, to talk about whether anything could be done to block the Sentinel system—the deployment of ABMs. Everyone present thought them undesirable, but a few of the most knowledgeable persons took what seemed to be the practical view: "Why fight about a dead issue? It has been decided, the funds have been appropriated. Let's go on from there."

Well, fortunately, it's not a dead issue.

An ABM is a nuclear weapon. It takes a nuclear weapon to stop a nuclear weapon. And our concern must be with the whole issue of nuclear weapons.

There is an entire semantics ready to deal with the sort of thing I am about to say. It involves such phrases as "Those are the facts of life." No—there are the facts of death. I don't accept them, and I advise you not to accept them. We are under repeated pressure to accept things that are presented to us as settled—decisions that have been made. Always there is the thought: Let's go on from there. But this time we don't see how to go on. We will have to stick with these issues.

We are told that the United States and Russia, between them, by now have stockpiled nuclear weapons of approximately the explosive power of fifteen tons of TNT for every man, woman, and child on earth. And now it is suggested that we must make more. All very regrettable, of course, but "those are the facts of life." We really would like to disarm, but our new Secretary of Defense has made the ingenious proposal that now is the time to greatly increase our nuclear armaments, so that we can disarm from a position of strength.

I think all of you know there is no adequate defense against massive nuclear attack. It is both easier and cheaper to circumvent any known nuclear-defense system than to provide it. It's all pretty crazy. At the very moment we talk of deploying ABMs, we are also building the MIRV, the weapon to circumvent ABMs.

As far as I know, the most conservative estimates of the number of Americans who would be killed in a major nuclear attack, with everything working as well as can be hoped and all foreseeable precautions taken, run to about fifty million. We have become callous to gruesome statistics, and this seems at first to be only another gruesome statistic. You think, Bang!—and next morning, if you're still there, you read in the newspapers that fifty million people were killed.

But that isn't the way it happens. When we killed close to two hundred thousand people with those first, little, old-fashioned uranium bombs that we dropped on Hiroshima and Nagasaki, about the same number of persons were maimed, blinded, burned, poisoned, and otherwise doomed. A lot of them took a long time to die.

That's the way it would be. Not a bang and a certain number of corpses to bury but a nation filled with millions of helpless, maimed, tortured, and doomed persons, and the survivors huddled with their families in shelters, with guns ready to fight off their neighbors trying to get some uncontaminated food and water.

A few months ago, Senator Richard Russell, of Georgia, ended a speech in the Senate with the words "If we have to start over again with another Adam and Eve, I want them to be Americans; and I want them on this continent and not in Europe." That was a United States senator making a patriotic speech. Well, here is a Nobel laureate who thinks that those words are criminally insane.

How real is the threat of full-scale nuclear war? I have my own very inexpert idea, but, realizing how little I know, and fearful that I may be a little paranoid on this subject, I take every opportunity to ask reputed experts. I asked that question of a distinguished professor of government at Harvard about a month ago. I asked him what sort of odds he would lay on the possibility of full-scale nuclear war within the foreseeable future. "Oh," he said comfortably, "I think I can give you a pretty good answer to that question. I estimate the probability of full-scale nuclear war, provided that the situation remains about as it is now, at two per cent per year." Anybody can do the simple calculation that shows that two per cent per year means that the chance of having that full-scale nuclear war by 1990 is about one in three, and by 2000 it is about fifty-fifty.

I think I know what is bothering the students. I think that what we are up against is a generation that is by no means sure that it has a future.

I am growing old, and my future, so to speak, is already behind me. But there are those students of mine, who are in my mind always; and there are my children, the youngest of them now seven and nine, whose future is infinitely more precious to me than my own. So it isn't just their generation; it's mine, too. We're all in it together.

Are we to have a chance to live? We don't ask for prosperity, or security. Only for a reasonable chance to live, to work out our destiny in peace and decency. Not to go down in history as the apocalyptic generation.

And it isn't only nuclear war. Another overwhelming threat is in the population explosion. That has not yet even begun to come under control. There is every indication that the world population will double before the year 2000, and there is a widespread expectation of famine on an unprecedented scale in many parts of the world. The experts tend to differ only in their estimates of when those famines will begin. Some think by 1980; others think they can be staved off until 1990; very few expect that they will not occur by the year 2000.

That is the problem. Unless we can be surer than we now are that this generation has a future, nothing else matters. It's not good enough to give it tender, loving care, to supply it with breakfast foods, to buy it expensive educations. Those things don't mean anything unless this generation has a future. And we're not sure that it does.

I don't think that there are problems of youth, or student problems. All the real problems I know about are grown-up problems.

Perhaps you will think me altogether absurd, or "academic," or hopelessly innocent—that is, until you think of the alternatives—if I say, as I do to you now: We have to get rid of those nuclear weapons. There is nothing worth having that can be obtained by nuclear war—nothing material or ideological—no tradition that it can defend. It is utterly self-defeating. Those atomic bombs represent an unusable weapon. The only use for an atomic bomb is to

keep somebody else from using one. It can give us no protection
—only the doubtful satisfaction of retaliation. Nuclear weapons
offer us nothing but a balance of terror, and a balance of terror is
still terror.

We have to get rid of those atomic weapons, here and everywhere. We cannot live with them.

I think we've reached a point of great decision, not just for our
nation, not only for all humanity, but for life upon the earth. I tell
my students, with a feeling of pride that I hope they will share,
that the carbon, nitrogen, and oxygen that make up ninety-nine
per cent of our living substance were cooked in the deep interiors
of earlier generations of dying stars. Gathered up from the ends of
the universe, over billions of years, eventually they came to form,
in part, the substance of our sun, its planets, and ourselves. Three
billion years ago, life arose upon the earth. It is the only life in the
solar system.

About two million years ago, man appeared. He has become
the dominant species on the earth. All other living things, animal
and plant, live by his sufferance. He is the custodian of life on
earth, and in the solar system. It's a big responsibility.

The thought that we're in competition with Russians or with
Chinese is all a mistake, and trivial. We are one species, with a
world to win. There's life all over this universe, but the only life in
the solar system is on earth, and in the whole universe we are the
only men.

Our business is with life, not death. Our challenge is to give
what account we can of what becomes of life in the solar system,
this corner of the universe that is our home; and, most of all, what
becomes of men—all men, of all nations, colors, and creeds. This
has become one world, a world for all men. It is only such a world
that can now offer us life, and the chance to go on.

Speech given by George F. Kennan at Swarthmore College in December 1967.

Rebels Without a Program

There is an ideal that has long been basic to the learning process
as we have known it, one that stands at the very center of our
modern institutions of higher education and that had its origin, I

suppose, in the clerical and monastic character of the medieval university. It is the ideal of the association of the process of learning with a certain remoteness from the contemporary scene—a certain detachment and seclusion, a certain voluntary withdrawal and renunciation of participation in contemporary life in the interests of the achievement of a better perspective on that life when the period of withdrawal is over. It is an ideal that does not predicate any total conflict between thought and action, but recognizes that there is a time for each.

No more striking, or moving, description of this ideal has ever come to my attention than that which was given by Woodrow Wilson in 1896 at the time of the Princeton Sesquicentennial.

"I have had sight," Wilson said, "of the perfect place of learning in my thought: a free place, and a various, where no man could be and not know with how great a destiny knowledge had come into the world—itself a little world; but not perplexed, living with a singleness of aim not known without; the home of sagacious men, hardheaded and with a will to know, debaters of the world's questions every day and used to the rough ways of democracy; and yet a place removed—calm Science seated there, recluse, ascetic, like a nun, not knowing that the world passes, not caring, if the truth but come in answer to her prayer. . . . A place where ideals are kept in heart in an air they can breathe; but no fool's paradise. A place where to hear the truth about the past and hold debate about the affairs of the present, with knowledge and without passion; like the world in having all men's life at heart, a place for men and all that concerns them; but unlike the world in its self-possession, its thorough way of talk, its care to know more than the moment brings to light; slow to take excitement, its air pure and wholesome with a breath of faith; every eye within it bright in the clear day and quick to look toward heaven for the confirmation of its hope. Who shall show us the way to this place?"

There is a dreadful incongruity between the vision and the state of mind—and behavior—of the radical left on the American campus today. In place of a calm science, "recluse, ascetic, like a nun," not knowing or caring that the world passes "if the truth but come in answer to her prayer," we have people utterly absorbed in the affairs of this passing world. And instead of these affairs being discussed with knowledge and without passion, we find them treated with transports of passion and with a minimum,

I fear, of knowledge. In place of slowness to take excitement, we have a readiness to react emotionally, and at once, to a great variety of issues. In place of self-possession, we have screaming tantrums and brawling in the streets. In place of the "thorough way of talk" that Wilson envisaged, we have banners and epithets and obscenities and virtually meaningless slogans. And in place of bright eyes "looking to heaven for the confirmation of their hope," we have eyes glazed with anger and passion, too often dimmed as well by artificial abuse of the psychic structure that lies behind them, and looking almost everywhere else but to heaven for the satisfaction of their aspirations.

I quite understand that those who espouse this flagrant repudiation of the Wilsonian ideal constitute only a minority on any campus. But tendencies that represent the obsession of only a few may not be without partial appeal, at certain times, and within certain limits, to many others. If my own analysis is correct, there are a great many students who may resist any complete surrender to these tendencies, but who nevertheless find them intensely interesting, are to some extent attracted or morally bewildered by them, find themselves driven, in confrontation with them, either into various forms of pleasing temptation, on the one hand, or into crises of conscience, on the other.

If I see them correctly (and I have no pretensions to authority on this subject), there are two dominant tendencies among the people I have here in mind, and superficially they would seem to be in conflict one with the other. On the one side there is angry militancy, full of hatred and intolerance and often quite prepared to embrace violence as a source of change. On the other side there is gentleness, passivity, quietism—ostensibly a yearning for detachment from the affairs of the world, not the detachment Woodrow Wilson had in mind, for that was one intimately and sternly related to the real world, the objective, external world, whereas this one takes the form of an attempt to escape into a world which is altogether illusory and subjective.

What strikes one first about the angry militancy is the extraordinary degree of certainty by which it is inspired: certainty of one's own rectitude, certainty of the correctness of one's own answers, certainty of the accuracy and profundity of one's own analysis of the problems of contemporary society, certainty as to the iniquity of those who disagree. Of course, vehemence of feeling and a conviction that right is on one's side have seldom been absent from the feelings of politically excited youth. But somehow or other they seem particularly out of place at just this time. Never has there been an era when the problems of public policy even approached in their complexity those by which our society is confronted today, in this age of technical innovation and the explosion of knowledge. The understanding of these problems is something to which one would well give years of disciplined and restrained study, years of the scholar's detachment, years of readiness to reserve judgment while evidence is being accumulated. And this being so, one is struck to see such massive certainties already present in the minds of people who not only *have not* studied very much but presumably *are not* studying a great deal, because it is hard to imagine that the activities to which this aroused portion of our student population gives itself are ones readily compatible with quiet and successful study.

The world seems to be full, today, of embattled students. The public prints are seldom devoid of the record of their activities. Photographs of them may be seen daily: screaming, throwing stones, breaking windows, overturning cars, being beaten or dragged about by police and, in the case of those on other continents, burning libraries. That these people are embattled is unquestionable. That they are really students, I must be permitted to doubt. I have heard it freely confessed by members of the revolutionary student generation of Tsarist Russia that, proud as they were of the revolutionary exploits of their youth, they never really learned anything in their university years, they were too busy with politics. The fact of the matter is that the state of being *enragé* is simply incompatible with fruitful study. It implies a degree of existing emotional and intellectual commitment which leaves little room for open-minded curiosity.

I am not saying that students should not be concerned, should not have views, should not question what goes on in the field of national policy and should not voice their questions about it. Some of us, who are older, share many of their misgivings, many of their impulses. Some of us have no less lively a sense of the dangers of the time, and are no happier than they are about a great many things that are now going on. But it lies within the power as well as the duty of all of us to recognize not only the possibility that we might be wrong but the virtual certainty that on some occasions we are bound to be. The fact that this is so does not absolve us from the duty of having views and putting them forward. But it does make it incumbent upon us to recognize the element of doubt that still surrounds the correctness of these views. And if we do that, we will not be able to lose ourselves in transports of moral indignation against those who are of opposite opinion and follow a different line; we will put our views forward only with a prayer for forgiveness for the event that we prove to be mistaken.

I am aware that inhibitions and restraints of this sort on the part of us older people would be attributed by many members of the student left to a sweeping corruption of our moral integrity. Life, they would hold, has impelled us to the making of compromises, and these compromises have destroyed the usefulness of our contribution. Crippled by our own cowardice, prisoners of the seamy adjustments we have made in order to be successfully a part of the American establishment, we are regarded as no longer capable of looking steadily into the strong clear light of truth.

In this, as in most of the reproaches with which our children shower us, there is of course an element of justification. There is a point somewhere along the way in most of our adult lives, admittedly, when enthusiasms flag, when idealism becomes tempered, when responsibility to others and even affection for others compels greater attention to the mundane demands of private life. There is a point when we are even impelled to place the needs of children ahead of the dictates of a defiant idealism, and to devote ourselves, pusillanimously, if you will, to the support and rearing of these same children—precisely in order that at some future date they may have the privilege of turning upon us and despising us for the materialistic faintheartedness that made their maturity possible. This, no doubt, is the nature of the compromise that millions of us make with the imperfections of government and society in our time. Many of us could wish that it might have been otherwise—that the idealistic pursuit of public causes might have remained our exclusive dedication down into later life.

But for the fact that this is not so I cannot shower myself or others with reproaches. I have seen more harm done in this world by those who tried to storm the bastions of society in the name of utopian beliefs, who were determined to achieve the elimination of all evil and the realization of the millennium within their own time, than by all the humble efforts of those who have tried to create a little order and civility and affection within their own intimate entourage, even at the cost of tolerating a great deal of evil in the public domain. Behind this modesty, after all, there has been the recognition of a vitally important truth—a truth that the Marxists, among others, have never brought themselves to recognize; namely, that the decisive seat of evil in this world is not in social and political institutions, and not even, as a rule, in the ill will or iniquities of statesmen, but simply in the weakness and imperfection of the human soul itself, and by that I mean literally every soul, including my own and that of the student militant at the gates. For this reason, as Tocqueville so clearly perceived when he visited this country 130 years ago, the success of a society may be said, like charity, to begin at home.

So much, then, for the angry ones. Now, a word about the others: the quiescent ones, the hippies and the flower people.

In one sense, my feeling for these people is one of pity, not unmixed, in some instances, with horror. I am sure that they want none of this pity. They would feel that it comes to them for the wrong reasons. If they feel sorry for themselves, it is because they see themselves as the victims of a harsh, hypocritical and unworthy adult society. If I feel sorry for them, it is because I see them as the victims of certain great and destructive philosophic errors.

One of these errors—and it is one that affects particularly those who take drugs, but not those alone—is the belief that the human being has marvelous resources within himself that can be released and made available to him merely by the passive submission to certain sorts of stimuli: by letting esthetic impressions of one sort or another roll over him or by letting his psychic equilibrium be disoriented by chemical agencies that give him the sensation of experiencing tremendous things. Well, it is true that human beings sometimes have marvelous resources within themselves. It is also true that these resources are capable, ideally, of being released and made available to the man that harbors them and through him to others, and sometimes are so released. But it is not true that they can be released by hippie means.

It is only through effort, through doing, through action—never through passive experience—that man grows creatively. It is only by volition and effort that he becomes fully aware of what he has in him of creativity and becomes capable of embodying it, of making it a part of himself, of communicating it to others. There is no pose more fraudulent—and students would do well to remember this when they look at each other—than that of the individual who pretends to have been exalted and rendered more impressive by his communion with some sort of inner voice whose revelations he is unable to describe or to enact. And particularly is this pose fraudulent when the means he has chosen to render himself susceptible to this alleged revelation is the deliberate disorientation of his own psychic system; for it may be said with surety that any artificial intervention of this sort into the infinitely delicate balance that nature created in the form of man's psychic make-up produces its own revenge, takes its own toll, proceeds at the cost of the true creative faculties and weakens rather than strengthens.

The second error I see in the outlook of these people is the belief in the possibility and validity of a total personal permissiveness. They are misjudging, here, the innermost nature of man's estate. There is not, and cannot be, such a thing as total freedom. The normal needs and frailties of the body, not to mention the elementary demands of the soul itself, would rule that out if nothing else did. But beyond that, any freedom *from* something implies a freedom *to* something. And because our reality is a complex one, in which conflicts of values are never absent, there can be no advance toward any particular objective, not even the pursuit of pleasure, that does not imply the sacrifice of other possible objectives. Freedom, for this reason, is definable only in terms of the obligations and restraints and sacrifices it accepts. It exists, as a concept, only in relationship to something else which is by definition its opposite, and that means commitment, duty, self-restraint.

Every great artist has known this. Every great philosopher has recognized it. It has lain at the basis of Judaic-Christian teaching. Tell me what framework of discipline you are prepared to accept and I will attempt to tell you what freedom might mean for you. But if you tell me that you are prepared to accept no framework of discipline at all, then I will tell you, as Dostoevski told his readers, that you are destined to become the most unfree of men; for freedom begins only with the humble acceptance of membership in, and subordination to, a natural order of things, and it grows only with struggle and self-discipline, and faith.

To shun the cruelty and corruption of this world is one thing. It is not always unjustifiable. Not everyone is made to endure these things. There is something to be said for the cultivation, by the right people, and in the right way, of the virtues of detachment, of withdrawal, of unworldliness, of innocence and purity, if you will.

That, as a phase of life, is just what Wilson was talking about. In an earlier age, those who are now the flower children and the hippies would perhaps have entered monastic life or scholarly life or both. But there, be it noted, they would very definitely have accepted a framework of discipline, and it would normally have been a very strict one. If it was a monastic order, their lives would have been devoted to the service of God and of other men, not of themselves and their senses. If it was the world of scholarship, their lives would have been devoted to the pursuit of truth, which never comes easily or without discipline and sacrifice. They would have accepted an obligation to cultivate order, not chaos; cleanliness, not filth; self-abnegation, not self-indulgence; health, not demoralization.

Now I have indicated that I pity these people, and in general I do. But sometimes I find it hard to pity them; because they themselves are sometimes so pitiless. There is, in this cultivation of an absolute freedom, and above all in the very self-destructiveness with which it often expresses itself, a selfishness, a hardheartedness, a callousness, an irresponsibility, an indifference to the feelings of others, that is its own condemnation. No one ever destroys just himself alone. Such is the network of intimacy in which every one of us is somehow embraced, that whoever destroys himself destroys to some extent others as well. Many of these people prattle about the principle of love; but their behavior betrays this principle in the most elementary way. Love—and by that I mean the receiving of love as well as the bestowal of it—is itself an obligation, and as such is incompatible with the quest for a perfect freedom. Just the cruelty to parents alone, which is implicit in much of this behavior, is destructive of the purest and most creative form of love that does exist or could exist in this mortal state.

And one would like to warn these young people that in distancing themselves so recklessly not only from the wisdom but from the feelings of parents, they are hacking at their own underpinnings—and even those of people as yet unborn. There could be no greater illusion than the belief that one can treat one's parents unfeelingly and with contempt and yet expect that one's own children will some day treat one otherwise; for such people break the golden chain of affection that binds the generations and gives continuity and meaning to life.

One cannot, therefore, on looking at these young people in all the glory of their defiant rags and hairdos, always just say, with tears in one's eyes: "There goes a tragically wayward youth, striving romantically to document his rebellion against the hypocrisies of the age." One has sometimes to say, and not without indignation: "There goes a perverted and willful and stony-hearted youth by whose destructiveness we are all, in the end, to be damaged and diminished."

These people also pose a problem in the quality of their citizenship. One thing they all seem to have in common—the angry ones as well as the quiet ones—is a complete rejection of, or indifference to, the political system of this country. The quiet ones turn their backs upon it, as though it did not concern them. The angry ones reject it by implication, insofar as they refuse to recognize the validity of its workings or to respect the discipline which, as a system of authority, it unavoidably entails.

I think there is a real error or misunderstanding here. If you accept a democratic system, this means that you are prepared to put up with those of its workings, legislative or administrative, with which you do not agree as well as with those that meet with your concurrence. This willingness to accept, in principle, the workings of a system based on the will of the majority, even when you yourself are in the minority, is simply the essence of democracy. Without it there could be no system of representative self-government at all. When you attempt to alter the workings of the system by means of violence or civil disobedience this, it seems to me, can have only one of two implications: either you do not believe in democracy at all and consider that society ought to be governed by enlightened minorities such as the one to which you, of course, belong; or you consider that the present system is so imperfect that it is not truly representative, that it no longer serves adequately as a vehicle for the will of the majority, and that this leaves to the unsatisfied no adequate means of self-expression other than the primitive one of calling attention to themselves and their emotions by mass demonstrations and mass defiance of established authority. It is surely the latter of these two implications which we must read from the overwhelming majority of the demonstrations that have recently taken place.

I would submit that if you find a system inadequate, it is not enough simply to demonstrate indignation and anger over individual workings of it, such as the persistence of the Vietnam war, or individual situations it tolerates or fails to correct, such as the condition of the Negroes in our great cities. If one finds these conditions intolerable, and if one considers that they reflect no adequate expression either of the will of the majority or of that respect for the rights of minorities which is no less essential to the success of any democratic system, then one places upon one's self, it seems to me, the obligation of saying in what way this political system should be modified, or what should be established in the place of it, to assure that its workings would bear a better relationship to people's needs and people's feelings.

If the student left had a program of constitutional amendment or political reform—if it had proposals for the constructive adaptation of this political system to the needs of our age—if it was this that it was agitating for, and if its agitation took the form of reasoned argument and discussion, or even peaceful demonstration accompanied by reasoned argument and discussion—then many of us, I am sure, could view its protests with respect, and we would not shirk the obligation, either to speak up in defense of institutions and national practices which we have tolerated all our lives, or to join these young people in the quest for better ones.

But when we are confronted only with violence for violence's sake, and with attempts to frighten or intimidate an administration into doing things for which it can itself see neither the rationale nor the electoral mandate; when we are offered, as the only argument for change, the fact that a number of people are themselves very angry and excited; and when we are presented with a violent objection to what exists, unaccompanied by any constructive concept of what, ideally, ought to exist in its place—then we of my generation can only recognize that such behavior bears a disconcerting resemblance to phenomena we have witnessed within our own time in the origins of totalitarianism in other countries, and then we have no choice but to rally to the defense of a public authority with which we may not be in agreement but which is the only one we've got and with which, in some form or another, we cannot conceivably dispense. People should bear in mind that if this—namely noise, violence and lawlessness—is the way they are going to put their case, then many of us who are no happier than they are about some of the policies that arouse their indignation will have no choice but to place ourselves on the other side of the barricades.

These observations reflect a serious doubt whether civil disobedience has any place in a democratic society. But there is one objection I know will be offered to this view. Some people, who accept our political system, believe that they have a right to disregard it and to violate the laws that have flowed from it so long as they are prepared, as a matter of conscience, to accept the penalties established for such behavior.

I am sorry; I cannot agree. The violation of law is not, in the moral and philosophic sense, a privilege that lies offered for sale with a given price tag, like an object in a supermarket, available to anyone who has the price and is willing to pay for it. It is not like the privilege of breaking crockery in a tent at the county fair for a quarter a shot. Respect for the law is not an obligation which is exhausted or obliterated by willingness to accept the penalty for breaking it.

To hold otherwise would be to place the privilege of lawbreaking preferentially in the hands of the affluent, to make respect for law a commercial proposition rather than a civic duty and to deny any authority of law independent of the sanctions established against its violation. It would then be all right for a man to create false fire alarms or frivolously to pull the emergency cord on the train, or to do any number of other things that endangered or inconvenienced other people, provided only he was prepared to accept the penalties of so doing. Surely, lawlessness and civil disobedience cannot be condoned or tolerated on this ground; and those of us who care for the good order of society have no choice but to resist attempts at its violation when this is their only justification.

Now, being myself a father, I am only too well aware that people of my generation cannot absolve ourselves of a heavy responsibility for the state of mind in which these young people find themselves. We are obliged to recognize here, in the myopia and the crudities of *their* extremism, the reflection of our own failings: our smugness, our timidity, our faintheartedness and in some instances our weariness, our apathy in the face of great and obvious evils.

I am also aware that, while their methods may not be the right ones, and while their discontent may suffer in its effectiveness from the concentration on negative goals, the degree of their concern over the present state of our country and the dangers implicit in certain of its involvements is by no means exaggerated. This is a time in our national life more serious, more menacing, more crucial, than any I have ever experienced or ever hope to experience. Not since the civil conflict of a century ago has this country, as I see it, been in such great danger, and the most excruciating aspect of this tragic state of affairs is that so much of this danger comes so largly from within, where we are giving it relatively little official attention, and so little of it comes, relatively speaking, from the swamps and jungles of Southeast Asia into which we are pouring our treasure of young blood and physical resources.

For these reasons, I do not mean to make light of the intensity of feeling by which this student left is seized. Nor do I mean to imply that people like myself can view this discontent from some sort of smug Olympian detachment, as though it were not our responsibility, as though it were not in part our own ugly and decadent face that we see in this distorted mirror. None of us could have any justification for attempting to enter into communication with these people if we did not recognize, along with the justification for their unhappiness, our own responsibility in the creation of it, and if we did not accompany our appeal to them with a profession of readiness to join them, where they want us to, in the attempt to find better answers to many of these problems.

I am well aware that in approaching them in this way and taking issue as I have with elements of their outlook and their behavior, it is primarily myself that I have committed, not them. I know that behind all the extremisms—all the philosophical errors of the egocentricities and all the oddities of dress and deportment—we have to do here with troubled and often pathetically appealing people, acting, however wisely or unwisely, out of sincerity and idealism, out of the unwillingness to accept a meaningless life and a purposeless society.

Well, this is not the life, and not the sort of society, that many of us would like to leave behind us in this country when our work is done. How wonderful it would be, I sometimes think to myself, if we and they—experience on the one hand, strength and enthusiasm on the other—could join forces.

Political interpretation of the Columbia strike, written by Paul Rockwell and adopted by the Columbia SDS, on September 12, 1968.

The Columbia Statement

When we seized five buildings at Columbia University, we engaged the force of wealth, privilege, property—and the force of state violence that always accompanies them—with little more than our own ideals, our fears, and a vague sense of outrage at the injustices of our society. Martin Luther King had just been shot, his name demeaned by Columbia officials who refused to grant a decent wage to Puerto Rican workers, and who had recently grabbed part of Harlem for a student gym, offering a back door to blacks in the be-grateful way that liberals do.

For years Columbia Trustees had evicted tenants from their homes, taken land through city deals, and fired workers for trying to form a union. For years they had trained officers for Vietnam who, as ROTC literature indicates, killed Vietnamese peasants in their own country. In secret work for the IDA* and the CIA, in chemical-biological war research for the Department of War, the Trustees implicated their own University in genocide. They had consistently, as the record shows, lied to their own constituents and published CIA books under the guise of independent scholarship. The military colossus, which the Universities themselves helped to build (in 1965 Columbia was getting $15,835,000 in Military Prime Contract awards), had become a clear and present danger to large sectors of our society. The draft, through the fear which it engendered, controlled the character even of our civilian lives. And now it was picking us off one by one. We lived in an institution that channeled us, marked us, ranked us, failed us, used us, and treated masses of humanity with class contempt.

We felt helpless in the history of our times. For years we had gone to frantic parties, read esoteric poetry, smoked pot, or clothed ourselves in ornaments. We tried to stay aloof from the contiguous disasters of the world—fascism in Greece, starvation in India, ruin in Vietnam, and riots in America. Like the Indian rain dance, which never brings more rain but makes the Indians feel better about the drought, our own sorceries did not really work. The war continued, the riots spread, and capitalism decayed before our eyes.

The collegiate wing of privilege could not shield us from the decay and violence in our society. The University was not, as we first believed, a sanctuary from the world; it was, in fact, a proponent of the most violent system the centuries have created—the system of capital. It was that system that led to fascism in Greece, starvation in India, ruin in Vietnam, and racism in America.

Columbia, standing at the top of a hill, looked down on Har-

* Institute for Defense Analyses.

lem. At dusk, from Morningside Drive, one could even see the dust, the appalling exhaust of human affairs, hanging over the ghetto. People who survived in Harlem had been evicted by the Trustees from Morningside or still paid rent to Columbia. 116th Street between Broadway and Amsterdam, which was once public land, had been purchased from the City by the Trustees for $2,000. We walked to our classrooms across land that had been privatized; we studied in buildings that had once been homes in a city that is underhoused; and we listened to the apologies for Cold War and capital in our classes.

The incongruity between what we saw and what professors told us was, for a time, only vaguely felt. But as the Draft hovered over the University, we saw that capitalism exploited others by exploiting us, that the Trustees who ruled Columbia were part of the class that oppresses the world. The men who ran the monstrous corporations, whose interests were allied with war and empire, were the same men who ran the Universities. In spite of the divisions within the University, the expertise that blames the general understanding, we began to perceive connections. Hilsman and Brzezinski, who helped to set up concentration camps in Vietnam, also taught students at Columbia. The military that bombed entire cities, uprooted populations, ruined crops, co-opted revolutions, and blackmailed tiny nations, was the same military that confronted us at the University in the form of IDA, CIA, NROTC, and war research.

A University that so consistently made war on people could not remain immune from popular discontent. Our insurrection was directed to the destructive character of the institution. It was ironic that those who desired the process of genocide to operate with impunity called us destructive for fighting back. They never considered *what* we wanted to destroy.

Jefferson once said that a people who loses its capacity for resistance loses its capacity for democracy. In that sense, our actions were not negative. Like the Black struggle in America, we affirmed the right to live. It was only through struggle that we could overcome our helplessness.

Before the insurrection, before we established the communes, our education was systematically oriented towards isolating the individual, inducing him to follow the lonely track of material interest—getting a better grade from a superior, getting a degree, impressing the Dean for a letter of recommendation, taking on a useless subject for a lifetime in order to avoid the draft for two years.

In the communes, distances were broken down. Our collective life released creative capacities in individuals and we began to glimpse the outlines of a new society. One communard described the Math Commune: "The delegated clean-ups and night watches were important in our society, but much more integral were the seemingly endless discussions which formed our collective thinking. News came to us through these meetings not in faceless broadcasts or as cool sheets of newsprint; we received news by voice and gesture . . . Everything seemed tangible in that small society, events were close and real; duties were meaningful and human. We constantly touched one another with comfortableness born not only out of constant proximity, but also because we shared our political thoughts and our common danger. If we were led, we could touch our leaders. If we were in constant strain, we were not alone. If we were physically constrained in rooms, we were freer in our relations with one another . . . Perhaps our small society was limited in scope; certainly it was temporary and probably unrealistic in relation to the great amorphous society around us . . . But in the end, the lingering experience we still feel and yearn for is the experience of a society in which alienation is abnormal rather than normal. Briefly we smelled, tasted, and touched a society which needed each of us totally, a society in which we were not fragmented, to which each of us was vital, a society in which our minds and our bodies equally were required of us, a society in which we were whole."

In the communes we took up what Che once called, "the most important revolutionary aspiration: to see man liberated from alienation. Man under socialism is more complete. His opportunities for expressing himself and making himself felt in the social organism infinitely greater."

We knew that the Commune would be short-lived. To hope that we could establish a local democracy while the rest of society remained oppressive was naive. Columbia could not of itself become a democratic institution, while capitalism remained intact; for the character of local institutions depends on the operation of the entire system. The finance of Columbia, the material basis of organization, lay in the hands of an entire class. We realized that we could not gain a part of our society except by winning the whole. That is why many of us became revolutionaries, and not reformists.

It seemed perhaps that we had lost our common sense to conceive of a revolution in America. For most of our lives no idea had been more taboo, or seemed more absurd, than social revolution. To be sure, the insurrection was not a revolution. "Revolution" explicitly refers to a process in which one class, joined by intermediate strata of society, takes away the control of production by force from another class. The insurrection, however, was touched with a revolutionary consciousness. New developments in the world had changed our modes of thought. The war in Vietnam, which first disillusioned us about America, finally dramatized man's capacity for revolution. In Vietnam, the punji stick somehow triumphed over the cluster bomb and jet. History was more than odds. Blacks in America, peasants in Asia, had chosen to liberate themselves or die, and that very choice was the beginning of a victory for mankind. Nothing is so terrifying, nor so heroic, as an entire people fighting against great odds for their survival and independence.

The Tet offensive was a major event in history. It seemed to transform our consciousness. We began to feel that, if the U.S. military were to win in Vietnam by force or forced negotiations, if the struggle for liberation were crushed or compromised, something in us would die as well. Our rights and the Vietnamese struggle became inseparable.

In Cuba racism and illiteracy had disappeared. In China, starvation had been conquered; in Vietnam the people's war seemed indefatigable. A period of continuous revolution had come upon us, and men all over the world began to envision the new society. World history had somehow formed the ineffable motivations of the Columbia insurrection.

We did not abandon our student interests, but we defined our interests in relation to the historic struggle that manifested itself throughout the world. Vast populations, which had lived in poverty for centuries, had begun to demand an equal share in the resources of the world. Students in Spain, Mexico, and Italy had begun to expropriate their Universities from the ruling elite, and simultaneous to the Columbia insurrection, fought heroically against the State police.

There is an historic scope to the events of our times—the massive black rebellions in the cities, the constant strikes, the gigantic

demonstrations against the war, the heroic acts of individuals, the
Draft resistance, the liberation of Cubans from foreign dominance, the cultural revolution of 700 million people, and to be
sure, the supreme fortitude of the National Liberation of Vietnam. Though these events are separate in time and place, they
were part of a general movement directed against militarism and
capitalist control of human material. In special times in history,
and because of their special status in society, students become the
precursors of social change and liberation.

If the Vietnamese could withstand the force of bombs, if the
Blacks could withstand the onslaught of modern police, if Cubans
could triumph over Imperialism, could we not also, in some tiny
way, join the struggle for liberation? We thought we could.

The Strike did not follow the lines of civil disobedience. The
Strike at Columbia was an insurrection.

We refused to be tried by our accusers, who were responsible,
we thought, for the murder of Vietnamese, the ruin of local tenants, and the plight of blacks in Harlem. We demanded amnesty,
not so much from the enemy, as from people who might become
our friends. Amnesty was to become a test of understanding.
Many professors claimed to agree with our ends, and even admitted the necessity of our acts (privately), yet refused to advocate
amnesty for the students. We had learned through hard experience that such professors are just as slippery as the Administration. They 'agreed' with our goals only to deprive us of the right
of winning them—like demented liberals who believe the Vietnamese should be independent, but on no conditions should take
arms against foreign occupation.

For years, the Left had wrecked itself through martyrdom, and
we desired to break the trend of voluntary punishment. We would
not submit to reprisals without a fight. We were convinced that
capitalism could not be overcome by speech alone, that those who
are in the right should not be punished, and that those who, like
the Trustees, are criminal should not go free. That belief was so
crucial to our cause, that we could not compromise on amnesty.

Actually, the demand for amnesty is a normal procedure in a
Strike or confrontation. It is natural to demand that bargaining
occur under equal terms. As long as the Trustees had the power of
reprisal over us, negotiations would have been rigged on their behalf. The same principle worked itself out on a far vaster scale in
Vietnam. The North demanded a bombing halt prior to negotia-

tions in order that the bombing would not be used as a weapon within negotiations.

At Cornell University, Stanford, Boston, Northwestern, Long Island, and Ohio, demonstrating students were granted amnesty. Unions on strike very often demand amnesty prior to negotiations; for victories cannot be maintained if the management has the power to wipe out labor leaders after the bargaining is over.

To be sure, we did not understand the explosive character of our demands at first. The revolutionary meaning of the seizure was perceived only as the Strike developed. The Trustees, unable to grant concessions, appealed to the billy club against the manifestation of popular discontent. The repeated use of police brutality revealed the savagery to which the ruling class is prone as soon as students assert their rights in conjunction with blacks, workers, and the dispossessed. Hence, the strike became far more than a fight for student power or local reform. As on a ship where sailors first ask the captain to change his course (as we asked the Administration many times), and where the captain turns on his own sailors and becomes a danger to the ship, the sailors of necessity take away the helm—so too the conflict at Columbia turned into mutiny. We did not seize buildings to change current policy, only to leave a corrupt administration, representing the privileges of an entire class, in the seat of power. Rather, we challenged the capacity of the Trustees to run the University at all.

The right to rebel against unjust authority has been recognized by philosophers, jurists, and populations from the most ancient times. The city states of Greece, the philosophers of ancient India, theologians from Aquinas to Luther, proclaim that when a power degenerates into tyranny, subjects are released from obligation to obey their laws. The French Declaration of the Rights of Man proclaims that "When the government violates the rights of the people, insurrection is for them the most sacred of rights and the most imperative of duties."

Men should not have to fight in order to be free. Yet a social order that has outlived itself rarely yields to a successor without resistance. Social justice does not come as a gift from those in power; it comes through organized struggle against the class that controls the material of life. "Liberty," as Fidel Castro said, "is not begged but is won."

That we must acquire our rights at the hazard of civil peace is the fault, not of radicals, but of a social system that is already violent and creates the necessity of resistance. The ghettoes, the appalling conditions in Morningside and Harlem, are not accidents. They are inevitable results of absentee ownership, whereby the wealthy dictate to the poor over the brute necessities of life, as Columbia strongmen "bargain" with tenants just before eviction.

The land which Columbia took in Morningside was by proximity, by need, and by a certain natural right in things, the property of the people of Harlem. Having taken over the land, the Trustees tried to bribe Harlem into accepting a back-door entrance. But why should Harlem take partial use of land that should be wholly theirs? And how could Harlem respond to such an exercise of power except by fighting back?

That Columbia's city deals were "legal" did not becalm us; it alarmed us about the class character of the laws in our society. We did not attack the Trustees as individuals; we attacked the very existence of Trusteeship, whereby a wealthy elite buy, sell, and administer the resources of a vast population. Andrew Carnegie explained the essence of Trusteeship this way:

"Thus is the problem of rich and poor to be solved. The laws of accumulation will be left free; the laws of distribution free. Individualism will continue, but the millionaire will be a trustee of the poor; entrusted for a season with a great part of the increased wealth of the community, but administering it for the community far better than it could or would have done for itself."

We claimed that Columbia was a racist *institution,* that Trusteeship was inherently elitist. The conflict at Columbia is not between those who believe in law and those who disbelieve in it. Rather, the Columbia crisis pits two conceptions of law against each other: the law of Andrew Carnegie whereby a class of financiers freely administers the resources and lives of a working population; and the law of a socialist society, under which neither millionaires nor poverty exist, and through which the working population controls the wealth which it produces for the liberation of itself.

We do not want to replace the present Trustees with new Trustees. It is not for us to create better individual men. Not men themselves, but the relationships that force them to act in the ways of inhumanity, are at fault at Columbia, as in America. Trusteeship should be eliminated altogether. Forms and forces that men took for granted for decades, and once seemed to be in the very nature of things, have now become repressive and must be abolished. Relations of landlord to tenant, debtor to creditor, employer to employee, Trustee to student—relations that are inherently coercive—are some of the fetters which our movement has begun to break. Those who would postpone the struggle only make change more violent when it comes.

Our times, we realize, are fraught with desperate romantics, bourgeois anarchists, and moralistic individuals who, rather than build a revolutionary movement collectively, attempt to purge the body politic by some mad, dramatic act. Capitalism has its sorcerers.

But we are not sorcerers. The Columbia insurrection was not romantic; it was revolutionary. We did not use sabotage or gimmicks to stop the University, the kind of activism that is not only wrong, but futile. Any individual could shut down the University by stealth. But only a radical mass struggle can advance the cause of a new society. The Columbia insurrection was a collective act, which represented many strata of society—blacks from Harlem (who took over Hamilton with SAS*), tenants from the community in Morningside (who took over a building at 114th street), and High School students from the city (who lived with us in the communes). Out of our mass struggle came a Liberation School, a Community Action Committee, a Strike Committee representing thousands of people, and a sense of dedication that no repression can overcome.

It was the essence of the insurrection, and it will be the theme of our future activity, to include the vast unrepresented masses of humanity in the definition of the University. The words of Che aptly express our view:

> Let it be clear
> that we have measured the scope
> of our actions,
> and consider ourselves
> no more than elements in the great army
> of the proletariat.
> What do the dangers or sacrifices
> of a man
> matter
> when the destiny of humanity is at stake?

* Students Afro-American Society.

The Locus of Anarchy and Violence

The rulers of the Universities, with the rulers of America, give the name "anarchy" to almost any attack upon their own authority. Such people envision no other order of things than their own power and privilege.

Yet it is clear that, where there are constant convulsions in the State, as there are in America today, some social want lies in the background, which outworn institutions cannot satisfy. The repression of a need only makes it seethe below the surface of daily life, until it overthrows its repressor.

Up to a certain point, a society can re-adjust its social forms in a gradual, peaceful way. Its changes are quantitative and do not alter the foundations of society. Interest on surplus may decline or rise; profits on capital or land may be taxed a little more or little less. The landlords and financiers, with their forms of property, remain intact.

However, after a period of long development, productive forces and social pressures can no longer contain themselves within the established forms of property. A radical change in the social order becomes inevitable, and the society passes through a period of strife and shock.

Whatever we may wish, we live in such an extraordinary period today. The responsibility for violence does not lie in the urge to release social potentials that have grown over many years. It lies in the intransigence of the older order, wherein one class of men —landlords, financiers, the owners of production and property with their Trustees—appropriates the wealth produced by society.

A class, or a form of organization, that has outlived its usefulness, but which refuses to relinquish its control of social wealth, becomes a violent order. We desire to overcome the anarchy and violence that already exist in capitalism.

Capitalism has reached a desperate stage. Its military moves about the world like a wild beast that has received a mortal wound, and knowing that it is doomed, strikes out indiscriminately at the hostile elements, as if rage could hide its impotence. Imperialism begins to prey upon itself; the ghettoes become colonies; the standard of living of the working population begins to decline, as financiers maintain their rate of profit at the expense of the whole society. Today our physical livelihood deteriorates before our eyes, as major lakes and waterways become contaminated, the air polluted, the housing overcrowded. In 1962, two-fifths of the nation still lived in a state of economic deprivation ("Poverty and Deprivation in the U.S.", Conference on Economic Progress, Wash. D.C., April 1962), and conditions have worsened in the last few years. The economic "miracles" of the post-war decade are over. The inventions by which they were achieved—easy credit, government deficit, military spending—like the monstrosities of science fiction, have returned to haunt their own inventors.

Imperialism abroad naturally turns into civil wars at home. Imperialism does not represent a nation going to war. It represents a class using another class to do the dirty work of Empire. The British drafted the Irish to fight their foreign enterprises, and the Irish in time arose against their oppressors. Today, American rulers draft the Blacks and the sons of the working class to perform the filthy tasks of American rule abroad. Resistance is an inevitable result.

Imperialism leads normally to a stage of intense civil strife. For instance, at the turn of the century, Imperial Britain, "the richest nation in the world," rested on a foundation where one third of its population lived in "chronic poverty, unable to satisfy the primal needs of life." The English economy, like ours today, seemed prosperous. "Yet," as Barbara Tuchman notes, "the gap in the distribution of profits was growing not less but greater . . . The purchasing power of wages was falling and human material deteriorating."

Such anarchy, which we call Imperialism, laid a burden upon mankind heavier than it had ever borne before. In 1914, the Imperialist Powers went to war. Their rulers, reigning violence and anarchy over the entire world, claimed to be the champions of Law and Order.

It is in the name of law and order that American Imperialism has reached its most voracious stage. Though its rulers claim to be "the richest nation in the world," real wages have begun to fall, and human material deteriorates. Every phase of capitalism is in complete disintegration.

We live in cities where hospitals are overcrowded, lines of pregnant women stand for hours at clinic doors; where masses of people with rotten teeth, faulty eyes, and malnutrition cannot receive medical attention; where the entire saving of a middle-class family is liquidated by a single illness or a single operation; where thousands of black families rotate day and night for the use of a single room; where old ladies never leave their single rooms except to pick up the social security that fifty years of wage-drudgery has earned them; where blacks, after 300 years of slavery are drafted into a white man's war ten thousand miles away; where millions of youths are subjected to involuntary servitude and trained to kill; where police, with total impunity, gas, beat, and kill the very people who try to free themselves; where the courts are loaded with bureaucratic judges who evict tenants, render landlords immune, punish workers for striking to get a decent wage, uphold the legality of any war by any method, and sanction all policies of Imperialism and the draft; we live in cities where millions of apartments have peeling walls, sagging floors, busted plumbing, heaped-up garbage, subject to roaches and fantastic rents; where dirt and soot are ubiquitous, the cases of cancer, asthma, and emphysema, the bronchial maladies caused by polluted air, almost double every year; in short, we live in a state of anarchy, and capitalism is its name.

Under such conditions, the desire to do away with the present forms of social life, to overcome the anarchy that already exists in capitalism, is a creative force. Notwithstanding the bloodshed and the sacrifices of thousands of brave Americans, resistance signifies that many Americans are no longer reconciled to Imperialist wars, oppressive ghettoes, government corruption, Trustee control of entire institutions, a class system of law, and the predatory character of capitalism as a whole.

Violence and the University

Though it maintains a physical distance from the harm it inflicts on men, the University under Imperialism has become an especially violent institution. We cannot separate the modern forms of violence—the Green Berets, CIA, nerve gases, mace, chemical inventions, world strategies, and psychological techniques—from the cerebral character of modern Imperialism. The most heinous crimes of our century are not the crimes of passion; they are the crimes of intellect.

In *A Sign for Cain,* Frederic Wertham, M.D., notes that: "In trial after trial of men who committed mass murder during the Nazi regime, it has now been ascertained, some fifteen or twenty years after the crime, that the perpetrators were educated, respected citizens who lived typical, ordinary, successful lives with their wives and happy children . . . To label them psychopathic personalities merely serves to obscure the issue."

"Our problem," Robert Scheer has said, "has been that we expect the voice of terror to be frenzied, and that of madness irrational. It is quite the contrary in a world where genial, middle-aged Generals consult with precise social scientists about the parameters of the death equation and the problem of its maximation. The most rational, orderly, disciplined minds of our time are working long hours in our most efficient laboratories, at the task of eliminating us."

The "death equation" is not a histrionic term. There is a sense in which murder has become a science. The man who wrote the following report for the Institute of Defense Analysis was probably normal for our society:

> A model is developed for predicting the expected number of attacks to be made as a function of the target kill assessment (TKA) probabilities, the single attack kill probability, the confidence on the level of kill desired, and the maximum number of attacks available. The expected number of attacks is compared with the expected number of attacks required if no TKA data are available. Finally, the maximum number of attacks that might be required to achieve the desired kill confidence is computed.*

Columbia University, we already know, trains troops for the American Empire (NROTC), provides a base for the 432nd Military Intelligence Detachment under the Department of the Army. It is contracted to the Army Chemical Center at Edgewood Arsenal for research in biological warfare (Contract DA-18-035-AEC-269 A). Entire branches of the School for International Affairs are financed and controlled by lawless organizations like the CIA, as it is contracted to the IDA. Such contracts may not seem concrete if we divorce the wars abroad from the antecedents in civilian institutions. Yet if we view the Imperial processes as a whole, we see that NROTC, that trains at Columbia, actually kills peasants in Vietnam; the CIA, contracted to Columbia, actually helps to rig

---

* *U.S. Government Research and Development Reports,* June 10, 1966, p. 61.

elections in Latin America and overthrow elected governments; chemicals researched in the Universities actually destroy crops and limbs in Asia.

The violence in our society is far more grave than liberal professors, who chastise students for seizing buildings, realize. Many academics would rather see a million Vietnamese die from new inventions than interrupt the academic "civil liberties" of two professors involved in war research. Liberals refuse to take severe measures against the *de facto* violence of the University, but willingly take police measures against popular discontent.

Therein lies the moral of the liberal view of violence. *Liberals renounce violence when it comes to introducing changes in what already exists. But in defense of the existing order they will not stop at the most ruthless acts.*

The term "defense," as it is used by the Universities and the Department of War, is a euphemism. Much of what men call "defense" today is violative, not only of provisions of the Constitution (Article I, section 8; Article VI, section 2), but of the codified opinions of mankind. Overthrow of elected governments, contamination of food, rigging of elections, bribes, coups, political blackmail, secret use of troops, secret aid to dictators, undeclared war, indiscriminate bombing, the political use of medicine, scorched earth programs, forced transfers—the entire complex of anti-revolutionary wars in distant lands—goes by the name of "defense" in America. That is why defense science in American Universities can be part of a criminal, violent process, and why some professors are implicated in the general crime. Thirty-eight Universities have done chemical-biological war research. Defense expenditures for research and development leaped from $652 million in 1950 to $7 billion in 1965.

Those who lay responsibility for anarchy and violence on SDS have entirely missed the point. To purport that a small outside group wants to wreck "the University" is absurd. Under the Trustees, the University wrecked itself.

Of course, if by "University" one means war research, military training, elitist channeling, real estate deals, and all the other oppression that Trustees deal in,—then we *do* intend to destroy that University.

However, if one means by University a body that applies its labor and intelligence to the collective good, which affirms life and liberty, then we do not desire to destroy the University; we intend to build it.

The ruling class disposition to war is so great that professors who use our social resources to work out methods of counter-insurgency are, by some twist of language, considered lawful and constructive; while those who affirm life, and who fight against institutional war-making, are called destructive.

We believe that a University should have nothing to do with human subjugation, except the overthrowing of it. A University's labor, research, and knowledge should release the creative capacities of our society and advance the liberation of oppressed peoples of the world.

Intelligentsia and Revolution

Who Uses the University? For What Ends Is It Used? What Does Neutrality Mean?

Many people claim that we do not want to reform Columbia in a local way, but that we desire to change society as a whole and use the University to advance a revolutionary cause. In his letter to the parents, Dr. Kirk warned: "The leaders of SDS . . . are concerned with local or parochial University issues only as they serve as a means to a larger end."

That claim, though proposed by the Administration, is entirely true. We are not parochial. We do not see ourselves merely as students, and we do not accept the demeaning role which the rule of capital puts upon us.

The Political World-Wide Character of the American University

There is no group—neither the Trustees, nor their School of International Affairs, nor NROTC, nor SDS—that does not use the University for political ends. Columbia is *already* a world-wide institution involved in a world-wide struggle. Columbia would be an active political force regardless of SDS. Its Institute of Defense Analysis, for instance, devoted to counter-insurgency and riot control, serves the political ends of the rulers of America; it quells the uprisings of the Blacks and pre-empts revolutions abroad. Hence, SDS, among many other groups, demanded an end to

IDA. The gym affair also transcended the issue of local student power. For Columbia's seizure of Morningside represented a case of absentee control of Harlem's land.

True, the question is not whether we use the University—for who does *not* use it?—but for what ends and whose interests the University should be used. Should it remain the whore of Imperialism and corporate enterprise? Or should it begin to create a new society? The Trustees say that they will not allow the University to become an "agent of revolt." What that signifies is that the University will continue to be an agent of Imperialism. For it is clear that, without a sustained struggle in the University, it will not change its present role.

At Columbia, we measure the scope of our activity by the scope of Columbia's repressive operations. We believe that we cannot be free until the general exploitation of our society is overcome. Our personal struggles transcend local bounds, not because we are subversives, nor because we are missionaries, but because the unified system of Empire can be overcome in no other way than massive, international struggle. To the extent that a ruling class extends its power over others, others rise against that class. Columbia created its own opposition.

The Trustees are giants of corporate enterprise. Their businesses—from Allied Chemical to Socony Mobil—envelop more than half the world. Radicals who refuse to be parochial are subversive to the Trustees because, while the Trustees can manipulate local struggles (playing one off against the other), a mass struggle, welding many strata of society, threatens the very fabric of their privilege.

The Trustees are shrewd. They induce students to dissent only in a local way; while they, giants of Empire, transform the University into a bastion of Imperialism. "Our Colleges and Universities," said John A. Hannah, President of Michigan State University in 1961, "must be regarded as bastions of our defense, as essential to the preservation of our country and our way of life as supersonic bombers, nuclear-powered submarines, and intercontinental ballistic missiles." The "bastions of defense"—Michigan State, Columbia, MIT, Pennsylvania, Stanford, among many others—are not financed by local groups, any more than Saigon is run by the people of Saigon. The class that turns Universities into bastions of defense is not rooted in any single city, nor any single country—so ubiquitous is its wealth, property, and power.

Consequently, student power, faculty unions—localized forms of organization—are simply no match for Imperialism. A thousand parochial struggles are impotent against the unified control of the market and production. That is why the Ford Foundation, among many other wealthy corporations, gives millions of dollars away to "radical" groups; why, for instance, Ford gave $20,000 to a local organization at Columbia, notwithstanding the participation of its membership in the insurrection. Ford will donate to almost any organization, no matter how radical, if its localized approach inhibits a class struggle against capitalism. Just as SDS had begun to form a mass base around Columbia, Ford chose to donate $20,000 to a new organization that had no base at all, and which would inevitably come into conflict with SDS. The money would be a substitute for people, and in time the organization might draw in people who might otherwise join SDS. If the potential forces of revolution—the blacks in the ghettos, radicals on campus, disenchanted workers in the factories—can be isolated from each other, if they can be induced into parochial fights, Imperialism can remain supreme. Though local struggles as a means to larger victories may at times be useful, local control as an end is futile.

Just as it is illegal in America for labor unions to strike politically, to strike with other unions outside their locale, so at the University, students who work with forces outside the immediate area are called "subversive." Capitalism can maintain its power, its forms of exploitation through any form of organization (even those that radicals establish) except one—mass struggle on the basis of a class as a whole. That is why general strikes are outlawed. They work.

We maintain that Columbia cannot *of itself* become a democratic institution, while capitalism as a whole remains intact. What some people call local control, or participatory democracy, does not—we have found from our own experience in the civil rights movement—advance the cause of freedom. For the conduct of local institutions depends on the operation of the entire market system.

Mojo, the militant voice of the Black Student Congress, makes the same consideration with regards to black liberation. "As long as the black community exists within the capitalist community, it is impossible for blacks to control it. The Establishment has reached the point where it will allow blacks to run the black community . . . To administrate, however, is not to control. And in the end, it is irrelevant who controls the black community as long as that community exists within a capitalist structure."

We are trying to avoid at Columbia the kind of mistake which local trade unions make in labor struggles. Each union fights separately for itself, and tries to win a better standard of life through its local organization. At first the unions seem to get a better wage, only to discover that prices in the country go up, taxes rise, the power of the dollar declines, and all the so-called local victories, in the end, come to naught. Not able to control the market or the system of production, labor unions cannot even direct their private fate. In a vast market system, there is no such thing as local control of wages or of living standards. The capitalist system as a whole mediates our relation to the part.

"Participatory democracy," "sharing in decision-making," and "local control" are really trade-union forms of politics applied to the University. Democracy cannot be established formally or locally because the question of freedom is a material, not a formal question. Control of the University is exercised, not through faculty councils or student unions, but through the mode of production in society, through capitalism. The resource which we call the University is produced by a vast working population, and the issues of democracy must ultimately refer to it.

The material basis of American education, like American production, lies in the hands of an entire class. The Universities are entirely dependent on general finance, which no local group can dominate. Suppose, for a moment, that radical student and faculty groups were to gain a share in decision-making *at Columbia* (116th and Broadway). Does anyone believe that they could actually decide to use the resources in an anti-capitalist way? Could they take the School of International Affairs out of the hands of the Imperialists and turn it over to the graduates of, say, Brandeis High School? Obviously, Columbia's present financiers would simply cut off funds and then reconstitute their bastions under another name.

The University is a pluralist institution in this sense: that studies are divided into departments, courses, which in turn are chopped into tests and grades. Pluralism, whereby the domains of thought are isolated from each other, is a method of control. The University is constructed in such a way as to prevent comprehensive understanding.

Columbia is an anti-socialist force, not merely because of war research or racist deals, or anti-communist ideology in the courses. The University is anti-socialist in its very modes of thought. It presupposes that the measure of human achievement is individual, not collective. Hence, it grades individuals. Yet people create and produce socially. A group of twenty-five "C"-students working together on a common task may produce more wealth and value than twenty-five "A"-students working separately from each other.

The lack of generality is another anti-socialist aspect of the University. The University is an aggregate of experts. Yet socialism cannot be created without an overview of history. At Columbia, as at most Universities, each scholar may know and teach a part; but no one may see the whole. Capitalism cannot be overthrown except by men who understand its general operations. The Sears-and-Roebuck Bulletins of the schools are not wholly accidental. Expertise is simply the mental form of "keeping people in their place."

We believe that anything less than a socialist struggle is doomed to fail. In a sense, the whole society must be won before we can win the part.

The political significance of the Universities lies in one fundamental fact: that the class that controls production also controls the forms of consciousness. Keynesian economics, positivist philosophy, behaviorist psychology—these anti-humanities of the schools—are the mental forms of corporate enterprise. What J. A. Hobson wrote in 1909 is no less true today: "The actual teaching is none the less selected and controlled, wherever it is found useful to employ the arts of selection and control, by the business interests playing on the vested academic interests. No one can follow the history of political and economic history during the last century without recognizing that the selection and rejection of ideas, hypotheses, and formulae, the moulding of them into schools of thought, and the propagation of them in the intellectual world, have been plainly directed by the pressures of class interests."

At Columbia, Keynesian economics counsels us to place the burden of debt on the posterity of working men. Behaviorist psychology amoralizes the social sciences and makes advertising possible. A behaviorist view of human affairs naturally expects people to behave. Positivist philosophy blames the intellect that might otherwise dare to speak of general developments, and which could grasp the similitudes that interlock entire civilizations. As Tom Hayden notes: "With administrators ordering the institution, and faculty the curriculum, the student learns by his isolation to accept elite rule within the University, which prepares him to accept later forms of minority control."

The fragmentation within the curriculum of the University is based on world-wide concerns and interests.

The world-wide character of Columbia, the ease by which the University has been turned into a bastion of Imperialism, is reflected even in symbolic performances. Every year the Trustees, in the name of Columbia University, give its highest honorary degrees to anti-communists, dictators and reactionaries. These high honors are completely political. On November 5th, 1955, Columbia awarded a Doctor of Laws to Carlos Castillo Armas, who, with the CIA, had just overthrown the elected government of Guatemala. Their tribute to the new military dictator read as follows:

> He is a "soldier who inspired his fellow citizens to overthrow the rule of a despot; a statesman who is their leader as they re-establish Constitutional and democratic government built firmly upon principles of liberty. The alien communist regime which would have smothered freedom in his native Guatemala found in him a resolute foe. In armed strife he was a gallant warrior. With peace restored, the free ballots of a grateful electorate made him his people's guide . . . staunch advocate of inter-American friendship, he merits the honor of our constituents . . . This University, where many of his young countrymen have come to study, delights to honor him today for his dedication."

Actually Armas had disenfranchised *all* illiterate Guatemalans, 80% of the population. In May, 1955, Field Marshal P. Pibul Songgram, the Prime Minister of Thailand (a ruthless, military dictator who took away the new franchise of the Thais), received this acclaim from Columbia, with faculty acquiescence:

> He has been a "dynamic leader of an ancient people; trained . . . in the military sciences . . . fought and vanquished foes within and without . . . resolute in answer, with his battal-

ions, to the U.N. call against aggression in Korea . . . His nation became the first to ratify the SEATO; stalwart friend in this day of the Free World as people of his area gird against those who would by stealth disunite and then enslave them."

On June, 1, 1955, Allen Welsh Dulles received this charming Honor:

"He is a citizen whom his fellow Americans may never duly appreciate because they may never know the full extent of his service."

We cannot review the long, sorry record of reactionary honors —the degrees which, with the acquiescence of the liberal faculty, were bequeathed to Rusk, McNamara, Rockefeller, Premier Sato (1968), among many others. Most of the leading financiers, dictators and reactionaries of the world exploit their own countries under a halo bequeathed to them by an American University. The University is a sanctioning institution—making, grading, passing, failing, providing degrees and credits. Such "honors" are not superficial aspects of the learning process. They provide it a focus, a glass through which the world must be viewed. They perpetuate falsehoods, as we see in the content of the degrees. They give an ideal glow to activities that are substantially inhumane. It was just after the Bay of Pigs that Dean Rusk received the highest honor Columbia awards. If at first you don't succeed, try, try, again. Most important, sanctions coerce. University awards are crucial to winning or keeping a job. In the University, in the struggles for tenure, in fights for a grade in political science, the mere instinct for self-preservation guides students and faculty into reactionary channels. We cannot forget (especially when the faculty tries to re-establish its credibility after the Strike) that Columbia professors listened to the official lies of their University President, allowed the University to poison the forms of public thought, and remained silent for two decades. The University is corrupt today because in part liberal professors in the fifties submitted to the intimidation of the Trustees, whose McCarthyism reigned supreme. Professors were expelled while fellow teachers sat by and watched. The President maintained openly that Communists had no right to work in the University. The faculty was intimidated into silence. We shall not make the same mistake again. The

Strike is not made of the same malleable stuff that liberals are.

The present University does for Imperialism and corporate enterprise what the Church used to do for the feudal state. It protects it from effective attack, provides its inquisitions with the glow of divinity, and makes real change impossible. Classified research, training of troops, defense analysis, reactionary honors, are but some of the defenses within the University for interests that lie outside its bounds.

In America, with a military budget of $80 billion, the war machine owns American Universities. It buys minds, buys research, determines subject matters and allocates the means of communication and influence to those men who support the Cold War. The material basis of intellectual output lies in the hands of a small elite. As long as their power exists, we shall not be free.

Insofar as the American University has become a means of production—producing the mechanisms, the weapons, the research, the sanctions, and the reactionary modes of thought that all maintain the class character of capitalist society, and insofar as the University is controlled by a single class of men, the University cannot avoid the great political struggles of our age. Capitalism has reached a stage so desperate, so Imperial, so consistently repressive, that few institutions can remain aloof from the necessity to create a new society. And we repeat that a University that so consistently makes war on people cannot expect to remain immune from popular discontent.

Neutrality and the Class Character of Academia

A few professors, proud of their expertise and despondent of manual labor, claim that 1,000 people arrested by Columbia Trustees represent a minority of the University. However, these professors place themselves in the majority only by defining the University in an elitist way. Their definition of the University excludes the maids that clean their offices, the workers that build the buildings, the tenants that pay the rent, and the countless millions who endure the effects of their imperial research. Such people are part of the University only as victims. If the vast millions who build or endure the University were to control its uses and operations, many of the professors who now claim to be a majority, and whose studies, paid out of the public till, are superfluous to the necessities of life, might be expelled, so useless are they to the public good. Mr. Herbert Deane, as head of the Graduate Faculties, was quite correct when he said: "When this University becomes democratic, I won't be around."

Few men leech off society more than an academic elite which defines the University in terms of itself. Within an elitist definition of the University, the elite does stand in the majority. But within a democratic University, a classless University devoted to the needs of the people who labor to build the whole society, the present intelligentsia constitutes a petulant fragment of mankind.

For many years liberal and reactionary intelligentsia conceived themselves as a kind of sanctuary, divorced from the petty squabbles of mankind, though somehow in a position to influence them. They lived in a quiet dream about themselves. The most heinous crimes of our century were not the crimes of passion; they were crimes of intellect.

Today the American intelligentsia is still an elitist group. It is ironic that academia believes that, through the University, they transcend the class prejudices of capitalist society, when their very concept of the University is a prejudice.

Columbia professors often claim that the University is a neutral institution. But actually what most professors call neutrality is ignorance of the class basis of their own sciences. The intelligentsia is a social stratum within the framework of bourgeois society. Their status, their caste, their privileges, the very divisions of labor implied by "intelligentsia," are bound up with the existing mode of production, wherein one class appropriates the value produced by another class. Thus the American intelligentsia tends to preserve the present mode of production rather than transform it. At Berkeley, Chicago, and Columbia the faculties turned against their own students when they asserted their rights in a radical way. The status of faculty originates from the appropriation of wealth produced by labor in its broadest sense. Thus, we cannot expect the faculty to be radical. A socialist society would take away its privilege.

We believe, as one revolutionary put it a century ago, that "There can be no impartial social science in a society based on class struggle. In one way or another, all official and liberal science defends wage slavery . . . To expect science to be impartial in a wage-slave society is as foolishly naive as to expect impartiality from manufacturers on the question of whether workers' wages ought not to be increased by decreasing the profits of capital."

Many professors pursue all sides of a question as an end in itself. They find a certain refuge in the difficulty of defining good and evil. The result is a clogging of their moral sense, their capacity for collective justice. Dante could have been thinking of academic liberals when he said: "The hottest places in hell are reserved for those who, in a time of moral crisis, maintain their own neutrality." What liberals call neutrality is really one of the ways by which the faculty protects its special status in society.

We believe that it is absurd to talk of neutrality in a period of intense class struggle, when the nation is beset by wars, resistance, and riots; when, in short, the vast exploited masses are rising to assert their historic rights.

Our critique of war research does not mean that scientists cannot be disinterested in their methods. As a method of research, the scientific method is not in question here. It is the public choice of science, the institutionalization of defense perspective, that must be accounted for.

A University could not, even if it wanted, choose to be really value-free. It can choose good values; it can choose bad values; or it can remain ignorant of the values on which it acts. The notion of value-free inquiry, of social research without reference to social ends, is the bugaboo of escapist science. A social institution should at least articulate its own perspective, so that its own values may be consciously applied or modified. It is a typical fallacy of American teaching, that to remain silent on crucial issues is to be objective with your own constituents.

Actually a "neutral" institution is far more manipulative than a University committed to avowed goals and tasks. That is why the Strike Liberation School did not hide its own revolutionary aspirations. Through the Strike, we raised a major question for American Universities: whether the institution will openly express an integrated vision of science and society, or whether it will remain departmentalized into channels for corporate enterprise.

Columbia avoids responsibility for its own war-making sciences by using a phraseology that conceals, rather than enlightens, the members of the University. Officials defend classified research, military training, CIA liaisons, on the grounds that the University is a politically neutral institution. It would be "partial," David

Truman says, to sever relations with the Department of Defense. We have here a case of an official language that signifies the opposite of what it means. The entire conception of impartial secrecy is absurd. A University classifies its work precisely to deter special groups from access to the facts. The products of secret research are offered only to reactionary groups.

Suppose, for a moment, that another University espoused anti-Communism as official policy, proclaiming open support for the war in Southeast Asia. What would be the concrete forms of its support? How would a biased University help the government? A pro-war University would administer a draft system for defense, train officers for defense, and provide secret research for defense as well. Thus, how does any University support a war, except by the same programs Columbia now pursues? The term "neutrality" refers to projects which, in more truthful times, would be known as bias.

It is not that University officials lie directly (although they often do); their language is so perverted that it does the lying for them. Whereas the humane purpose of language is to relate men to men, to make sciences cognizant of each other, the language of institutions is devised to separate and departmentalize human achievement. American defense science is value-free only in this sense, that scientists are not accountable to the people whom they may kill or send to war. It is largely because social scientists have neutralized the language of social science that Americans do not recognize Empire for the sordid thing it is.

Actually, it is far more objective, certainly more fair, to espouse a real position than to act one out without defending it. Columbia University has refused to explain its use of power, to submit its views to public scrutiny, or to become accountable to the people over whom it exercises so much control.

The debate is not between activists and intellectuals. It is between those people who demand that the intellect be applied to humanity, which labors to produce the University, and those academics who refuse to use their resources for the collective good.

Statement by faculty, students, and administration of Amherst College, sent by President Calvin H. Plimpton to the President of the United States on May 2, 1969.

The Amherst College Statement

The faculty and students of Amherst College have just experienced an extraordinary two days. Our usual educational activities were replaced by debate, discussion and meditation, which have given shape to our beliefs about the nature of higher education and the governance of educational institutions.

It is clear that we have much to do to set our own house in order. We are convinced, and have shown during these days, that changes, even fundamental ones, can take place without physical duress.

It will require all our care and energy in the months ahead to combine change with continuity, to provide students with a real and regular role in influencing their education and the college's government, and to honor both intellectual discipline and creativity.

We have as a college emerged from these two days with a renewed sense of the urgency and seriousness with which we must attend to our primary purpose.

We have also as a college embraced a new sense of urgency of another kind. We believe that we must speak out to make clear that much of the turmoil among young people and among those who are dedicated to humane and reasoned changes will continue.

It will continue until you and the other political leaders of our country address more effectively, massively, and persistently the major social and foreign problems of our society. Part of this turmoil in universities derives from the distance separating the American dream from the American reality.

Institutions dedicated to the nurture, husbanding, and growth of critical intelligence, and to inquiry into basic problems cannot but open people's eyes to the shoddiness of many aspects of our society.

In yesterday's *New York Times* it is reported that five officers in your Cabinet "seemed to agree that the disorder was caused by a small minority of students."

Our conviction is that such a view is seriously in error if it is taken to mean that no legitimate and important reasons exist for the anger and sense of impotence felt by many students and faculty.

The pervasive and insistent disquiet on many campuses throughout the nation indicates that unrest results, not from a conspiracy by a few, but from a shared sense that the nation has no adequate plans for meeting the crises of our society. To name only one issue of special concern to the students: since the Kerner Commission's report, there has been no decisive response to its recommendations.

We do not say that all the problems faced by colleges and universities are a reflection of the malaise of the larger society. That is not true. But we do say that until political leadership addresses itself to the major problems of our society—the huge expenditure of national resources for military purposes, the inequities practiced by the present draft system, the critical needs of America's 23,000,000 poor, the unequal division of our life on racial issues—until this happens, the concern and energy of those who know the need for change will seek outlets for their frustration.

We realize that in writing this letter we have taken the unusual step of speaking publicly for our community on pressing issues of the moment. We do this out of an urgent concern to question the widely held view that university unrest is merely an internal problem, or at most fomented by an outside influence.

More, we believe that if political leaders act on this mistaken assumption, their actions will serve only to widen the separations within the university and between the universities and society at large.

If, however, this important element in student unrest is understood, it would be possible for you, Mr. President, to redirect youthful energy toward those more idealistic, creative and generous actions which reflect a concern for others. Your influence can provide that hope which encourages those visions to which young men so gladly dedicate themselves, and we will support those efforts.

I send this letter to you on behalf of an overwhelming majority of Amherst students, faculty and administration who attended the closing meeting of our days of inquiry tonight. Copies of this letter with the signatures of all those who wish to subscribe will follow as soon as possible.

Speech by President Richard M. Nixon, delivered at General Beadle State College, Madison, South Dakota, June 3, 1969.

Campus Revolutionaries

THE RIGHTS OF STUDENTS

FREEDOM. A condition and a process. As we dedicate this beautiful new library, I think this is the time and place to speak of some basic things in American life. It is the time, because we find our fundamental values under bitter and even violent attack; it is the place, because so much that is basic is represented here.

Opportunity for all is represented here.

This is a small college: not rich and famous, like Harvard or Yale; not a vast state university like Berkeley or Michigan. But for almost 90 years it has served the people of South Dakota, opening doors of opportunity for thousands of deserving young men and women.

Like hundreds of other fine small colleges across the nation, General Beadle State College—has offered a chance to people who might not otherwise have had a chance.

The pioneer spirit is represented here, and the progress that has shaped our heritage.

In South Dakota we still can sense the daring that converted a raw frontier into part of the vast heartland of America.

The vitality of thought is represented here.

A college library is a place of living ideas—a place where timeless truths are collected, to become the raw materials of discovery. In addition, the Karl E. Mundt Library will house the papers of a wise and dedicated man who for 30 years has been at the center of public events. Thus, more than most, this is a library of both thought and action, combining the wisdom of past ages with a uniquely personal record of the present time.

As we dedicate this place of ideas, therefore, let us reflect on some of the values we have inherited, which are now under challenge.

We live in a deeply troubled and profoundly unsettled time. Drugs, crime, campus revolts, racial discord, draft resistance—on every hand we find old standards violated, old values discarded, old precepts ignored. A vocal minority of the young are opting out of the process by which a civilization maintains its continuity: the passing on of values from one generation to the next. Old and young across a chasm of misunderstanding—and the more loudly they shout, the wider the chasm grows.

As a result, our institutions are undergoing what may be their severest challenge yet. I speak not of the physical challenge: the forces and threats of force that have wracked our cities, and now our colleges. Force can be contained.

We have the power to strike back if need be, and to prevail. The nation has survived other attempts at this. It has not been a lack of civil power, but the reluctance of a free people to employ it, that so often has stayed the hand of authorities faced with confrontation.

The challenge I speak of is deeper: the challenge to our values, and to the moral base of the authority that sustains those values.

At the outset, let me draw one clear distinction.

A great deal of today's debate about "values," or about "morality," centers on what essentially are private values and personal codes: patterns of dress and appearance, sexual mores; religious practices; the uses to which a person intends to put his own life.

These are immensely important, but they are not the values I mean to discuss here.

My concern today is not with the length of a person's hair, but with his conduct in relation to his community; not with what he wears, but with his impact on the process by which a free society governs itself.

I speak not of private morality but of public morality—and of "morality" in its broadest sense, as a set of standards by which the community chooses to judge itself.

Some critics call ours an "immoral" society because they disagree with its policies, or they refuse to obey its laws because they claim that those laws have no moral basis. Yet the structure of our laws has rested from the beginning on a foundation of moral purpose.

That moral purpose embodies what is, above all, a deeply humane set of values—rooted in a profound respect for the individual, for the integrity of his person and the dignity of his humanity.

At first glance, there is something homely and unexciting about basic values we have long believed in. We feel apologetic about espousing them; even the profoundest truths become clichés with repetition. But they can be like sleeping giants: slow to rouse, but magnificent in their strength.

Let us look at some of those values—so familiar now, and yet once so revolutionary:

Liberty: recognizing that liberties can only exist in balance, with the liberty of each stopping at that point at which it would infringe the liberty of another.

Freedom of conscience: meaning that each person has the freedom of his own conscience, and therefore none has the right to dictate the conscience of his neighbor.

Justice: recognizing that true justice is impartial, and that no man can be judge in his own cause.

Human dignity: a dignity that inspires pride, is rooted in self-reliance and provides the satisfaction of being a useful and respected member of the community.

Concern for the disadvantaged and dispossessed: but a concern that neither panders nor patronizes.

The right to participate in public decisions: which carries with it the duty to abide by those decisions when reached, recognizing that no one can have his own way all the time.

Human fulfillment: in the sense not of unlimited license, but of maximum opportunity.

The right to grow, to reach upward, to be all that we can become, in a system that rewards enterprise, encourages innovation and honors excellence.

In essence, these all are aspects of freedom. They inhere in the concept of freedom; they aim at extending freedom; they celebrate the uses of freedom. They are not new. But they are as timeless and as timely as the human spirit because they are rooted in the human spirit.

Our basic values concern not only what we seek but how we seek it.

Freedom is a condition; it also is a process. And the process is essential to the freedom itself.

We have a Constitution that sets certain limits on what government can do but that allows wide discretion within those limits. We have a system of divided powers, of checks and balances, of periodic elections, all of which are designed to insure that the majority has a chance to work its will—but not to override the rights of the minority or to infringe the rights of the individual.

What this adds up to is a democratic process, carefully constructed and stringently guarded. It is not perfect. No system could be. But it has served the nation well—and nearly two centuries of growth and change testify to its strength and adaptability.

They testify, also, to the fact that avenues of peaceful change do exist. Those who can make a persuasive case for changes they want can achieve them through this orderly process.

To challenge a particular policy is one thing; to challenge the government's right to set it is another—for this denies the process of freedom.

Lately, however, a great many people have become impatient with the democratic process. Some of the more extreme even argue, with curious logic, that there is no majority, because the majority has no right to hold opinions that they disagree with.

Scorning persuasion, they prefer coercion. Awarding themselves what they call a higher morality, they try to bully authorities into yielding to their "demands."

On college campuses, they draw support from faculty members who should know better; in the larger community, they find the usual apologists ready to excuse any tactic in the name of "progress."

It should be self-evident that this sort of self-righteous moral arrogance has no place in a free community. It denies the most fundamental of all the values we hold: respect for the rights of others. This principle of mutual respect is the keystone of the entire structure of ordered liberty that makes freedom possible.

The student who invades an administration building, roughs up the dean, rifles the files and issues "non-negotiable demands" may have some of his demands met by a permissive university administration. But the greater his "victory" the more he will have undermined the security of his own rights.

In a free society, the rights of none are secure unless the rights of all are respected. It is precisely the structure of law and custom that he has chosen to violate—the process of freedom—by which the rights of all are protected.

We have long considered our colleges and universities citadels of freedom, where the rule of reason prevails. Now both the process of freedom and the rule of reason are under attack. At the same time, our colleges are under pressure to collapse their educational standards in the misguided belief that this would promote "opportunity."

Instead of seeking to raise lagging students up to meet the college standards, the cry now is to lower the standards to meet the students. This is the old, familiar, self-indulgent cry for the easy way. It debases the integrity of the educational process.

There is no easy way to excellence, no short-cut to the truth, no magic wand that can produce a trained and disciplined mind without the hard discipline of learning. To yield to these demands would weaken the institution; more importantly, it would cheat the student of what he comes to a college for: his education.

No group, as a group, should be more zealous defenders of the integrity of academic standards and the rule of reason in academic life than the faculties of our great institutions. If they simply follow the loudest voices, parrot the latest slogan, yield to unreasonable demands, they will have won not the respect but the contempt of their students.

Students have a right to guidance, to leadership, to direction; they have a right to expect their teachers to listen, and to be reasonable, but also to stand for something—and most especially, to stand for the rule of reason against the rule of force.

Our colleges have their weaknesses. Some have become too impersonal, or too ingrown, and curricula have lagged. But with all its faults, the fact remains that the American system of higher education is the best in this whole imperfect world—and it provides, in the United States today, a better education for more students of all economic levels than ever before, anywhere, in the history of the world.

This is no small achievement.

Often, the worst mischief is done by the name of the best cause. In our zeal for instant reform, we should be careful not to destroy our educational standards, and our educational system along with them; and not to undermine the process of freedom, on which all else rests.

The process of freedom will be less threatened in America, however, if we pay more heed to one of the great cries of the young today. I speak now of their demand for honesty: intellectual honesty, personal honesty, public honesty.

Much of what seems to be revolt is really little more than this: an attempt to strip away sham and pretense, to puncture illusion, to get down to the basic nub of truth.

We should welcome this. We have seen too many patterns of deception:

In political life, impossible promises.

In advertising, extravagant claims.

In business, shady deals.

In personal life, we all have witnessed deceits that ranged from the "little white lie" to moral hypocrisy; from cheating on income taxes to bilking insurance companies.

In public life, we have seen reputations destroyed by smear, and gimmicks paraded as panaceas. We have heard shrill voices of hate, shouting lies, and sly voices of malice, twisting facts.

Even in intellectual life, we too often have seen logical gymnastics performed to justify a pet theory, and refusal to accept facts that fail to support it.

Absolute honesty would be ungenerous. Courtesy compels us to welcome the unwanted visitor; kindness leads us to compliment the homely girl on how pretty she looks. But in our public discussions, we sorely need a kind of honesty that has too often been lacking; the honesty of straight talk; a doing away with hyperbole; a careful concern with the gradations of truth, and a frank recognition of the limits of our knowledge about the problems we have to deal with.

We have long demanded financial integrity in public life; we now need the most rigorous kind of intellectual integrity in public debate.

Unless we can find a way to speak plainly, truly, unself-consciously, about the facts of public life, we may find that our grip on the forces of history is too loose to control our own destiny.

The honesty of straight talk leads us to the conclusion that some of our recent social experiments have worked, and some have failed, and that most have achieved something—but less than their advance billing promised.

This same honesty is concerned not with assigning blame, but with discovering what lessons can be drawn from that experience in order to design better programs next time. Perhaps the goals were unattainable; perhaps the means were inadequate; perhaps the program was based on an unrealistic assessment of human nature.

We can learn these lessons only to the extent that we can be candid with one another. We face enormously complex choices. In approaching these, confrontation is no substitute for consultation; passionate concern gets us nowhere without dispassionate analysis. More fundamentally, our structure of faith depends on faith, and faith depends on truth.

The values we cherish are sustained by a fabric of mutual self-restraint, woven of ordinary civil decency, respect for the rights of others, respect for the laws of the community, and respect for the democratic process of orderly change.

The purpose of these restraints is not to protect an "establishment," but to establish the protection of liberty; not to prevent change, but to insure that change reflects the public will and respects the rights of all.

This process is our most precious resource as a nation. But it depends on public acceptance, public understanding and public faith.

Whether our values are maintained depends ultimately not on the Goverment, but on the people.

A nation can be only as great as its people want it to be.

A nation can be only as free as its people insist that it be.

A nation's laws are only as strong as its people's will to see them enforced.

A nation's freedoms are only as secure as its people's determination to see them maintained.

A nation's values are only as lasting as the ability of each generation to pass them on to the next.

We often have a tendency to turn away from the familiar because it is familiar, and to seek the new because it is new.

To those intoxicated with the romance of violent revolution, the continuing revolution of democracy may seem unexciting. But no system has ever liberated the spirits of so many so fully. Nothing has ever "turned on" man's energies, his imagination, his unfettered creativity, the way the ideal of freedom has.

Some see America's vast wealth and protest that this has made us "materialistic." But we should not be apologetic about our abundance. We should not fall into the easy trap of confusing the production of things with the worship of things. We produce abundantly; but our values turn not on what we have, but on what we believe.

We believe in liberty, and decency, and the process of freedom. On these beliefs we rest our pride as a nation; in these beliefs, we rest our hopes for the future; and by our fidelity to the process of freedom, we can assure to ourselves and our posterity the blessings of freedom.

PART **I**

THE
EDUCATIONAL
ROLE
OF THE
UNIVERSITY

Before the liberal university was struck by the unrest of the 1960s, its basic principles and ideals were clear and almost universally accepted. It was assumed that as an institution the university was neutral and could not take positions on religious or political issues. It served all interests in society equally and was open to views of all kinds, no matter how heretical. The standards for admitting students and faculty into the scholarly community were objective, the same for all regardless of economic or racial background. Although the university was constrained not to take positions on the issues of the day, the individual scholar was free to write whatever he chose without fear of dismissal, reprimand, or other pressures. At the same time, however, it was expected that he would not abuse his position to propagandize his students and would therefore exercise self-restraint in the classroom.

Such was the liberal vision that had prevailed for half a century. But institutional neutrality, pluralism, objectivity, academic freedom, professional responsibility—all these fundamental articles of academic liberalism came into question with the advent of the student revolt. Claims of neutrality were seen as a smokescreen for active support of the government and the status quo. The "multiversity," allegedly serving all interests, was found to be serving corporate interests alone. Instead of an open, pluralistic academy, critics saw a repressive, bureaucratic institution that fragmented knowledge and channeled students into uncreative niches in the social structure. Objective standards were a cover for elitism. Academic freedom was an illusion that obscured the power exercised by the government and foundations over the direction of research and the content of education. Professional responsibility, another ideological device, required the faculty to accept their role in the system regardless of the ideas they held.

CHAPTER 1

Institutional Neutrality:
Is the University Value Free?

The challenge to the liberal conception of the university brought into question its most basic distinctions. A new generation of radical students and teachers could discern no clear lines separating the university from society, thought from action, disinterest from bias. To believe that the university could be detached from its surroundings, the radical critics said, was to ignore its subservience to the interests of the powerful and the wealthy. To divorce thought from action was to ask that men not take their thoughts seriously enough to act on them. To claim disinterest was itself a bias that enabled academics to avoid dealing with questions of ethics and values. To speak of a commitment to human learning and to be silent on human problems was criminally irrelevant. In the ideals of liberalism, radicals discerned only myths, dodges, prescriptions for hypocrisy, rationalizations for privilege.

The left was not alone in questioning the doctrines of the liberal university. Often the right found fault with its philosophy too, agreeing that institutional neutrality was a myth, even an undesirable ideal, and that the university should not be closely linked with the state and other outside interests. But the right and left agreed only in their criticism of liberalism, not in the direction they hoped the universities would take in changing. The right saw neutrality as a disguise for subversive activities and insisted that the universities not be neutral but "pro-American." Traditionalists saw the intrusion of government into the academy as a poisoning of the realm of pure thought and wanted the university to withdraw from society. The left, on the other hand, sought to make the university an adversary of the system, or at least its conscience and reformer.

The first set of documents that follows here deals with the question of institutional neutrality. A statement by a faculty committee at the University of Wisconsin sets forth the classic position that the university must remain neutral on political issues. The president of Brandeis University, Morris Abram, gives a modified defense of the same position, admitting that complete neutrality is not practicable, but insisting that it is still a worthwhile ideal. Robert Paul Wolff argues that neutrality is a logical impossibility and does not regard it as a goal worth retaining. But instead of recommending that universities drop the pretense, Wolff suggests that even if universities are not neutral, they had better pretend to be for the sake of the left. The myth, he says, is the left's only protection from a conservative society.

Agreeing with Wolff's analysis of neutrality, but not in sympathy with his political advice, is the New University Conference, a nation-wide association of radical graduate students and faculty members. The group contends that institutional neutrality is a veil for partnership with the oppressive forces that rule America, and urges that universities become creative, humane, and radical bases for transforming the society.

Two positions on the right have been put forth concerning the question of neutrality. Traditional anticommunists like Douglas Peterson hold that universities are not neutral since they harbor subversives. To make the schools pro-American, Peterson calls for a "faculty and student house cleaning" and the enactment of a mandatory code of ethical and civic behavior. Others on the right, laissez-faire libertarians like David Friedman, maintain that the university, as currently structured, is caught in a hopeless contradiction, required both to take positions on truth and to remain neutral. The only way out of the dilemma, according to the advocate of the free market, is to abolish the university's corporate structure and substitute a medieval university in which students would pay teachers directly for their services. Since there would be no institutional framework, the problem of institutional neutrality would vanish.

From the report of the Ad Hoc Committee on Mode of Response to Obstruction, Interview Policy, and Related Matters, University of Wisconsin, Madison campus, March 13, 1968. This section taken from the "Majority Statement" signed by Gary L. Baran, Haskell Fain, Andrew H. Good, Roland Liebert, Hugh T. Richards, Wendy K. Rifkin, Norman B. Ryder, and Joel Samoff.

The Logic of Neutrality

The present official posture of the university with respect to the war, and all other public issues not directly affecting the institution, is neutrality. It is maintained that the university should be an arena within which ideas are received, examined and evaluated, but never subjected to final collective endorsement or rejection. The prime responsibility of the institution is to protect the ideas and opinions of its individual members from external pressures toward conformity with one or another kind of orthodoxy.

Many are now insisting that the university has a moral obligation to bear witness, by word and deed, on such questions of fundamental social importance as American involvement in Vietnam, and protest as a corporate structure against the violation of values which the university should especially cherish. The guilt of many for tolerating sickness in the body politic cannot be gainsaid, and especially the guilt of those who are sheltered within institutions dedicated to the protection of freedom of thought. Yet this undeniable responsibility must remain a matter for the consciences of individual members of the academic community. The burdens of explicit institutional commitment are for other organizations to bear, not because of academic indifference to this grave and urgent controversy, but because a university, by becoming a political actor, would threaten its reason for being.

Were the university to decide to take a stand, many critical questions would arise. What person or group is entitled to speak for the institution as a whole? By what procedure can a position on any issue be determined? How would the minority be bound by that decision? What argument would prevent the institution from moving from words to deed, expelling those who disagree with the decision, applying loyalty tests as criteria for admission or employment, and banning from the campus all speakers for the opposition? By such departures from academic ideals, the university might find itself transformed into something resembling the medieval church, with the self-appointed charge of proclaiming dogma and rooting out doctrinal error. No longer would it be able, nor indeed would it be disposed, to protect the heretic and the dissenter. In brief, the price for departure from institutional neutrality may well be abandonment of the unique and indispensable role of the university in a democratic society.

From an address by President Morris B. Abram, Brandeis University, at the annual meeting of the College Entrance Examination Board, October 27, 1969.

Neutrality as an Ideal

Let us take an issue which the radicals raise in such strident terms—the issue of the university as a neutral institution. Here I wish to enter a public confession of error.

I said last September in my inaugural address: The university is a neutral forum. It is a neutral place. I was rather colorful about it. I said, the purpose of the university is to hold a soapbox steady so that faculty and outside speakers and occasionally administrators could mount it and have their say, but that the university was neutral. I have learned a lot in this last year. I have learned a lot from faculties, from students, and from administrators. I have learned a lot by trying to examine the issues and the evidence—as a lawyer should. The university is not a neutral place. The university cannot be a neutral place. It is committed to something. It is committed first of all to education. It is also committed to gradual ameliorative change and reform, and it takes an optimistic view of society, not a cynical view that could lead to revolution.

A university may be the habitation of revolutionary men and women, and so long as their overt conduct does not destroy or impinge upon the rights of others, the university should be a hospitable place to them. However, the university cannot be committed to revolution. It cannot be neutral about that. Nor is the university ever neutral, even about what it teaches, because everything the university as a corporate organism does, it does through men. I have tried too many cases before too many juries and seen too many judges not to know that man cannot be an objective calculating machine. Everything we know and everything we believe derives from a lifetime of experiences strained and filtered through our personalities from birth.

But this does not mean that the university has no obligation to try to be neutral. The institution in our society which has that obligation in a very advanced form is the court, but I know of no judge who is really, truly neutral. That doesn't mean the judicial system should be brought down or should be changed into the Nazi or Soviet system. The judge takes an oath to try to be neutral, and if you read the opinion of a Holmes or a Brandeis or a Stone or a Hughes, you will see how these men strived and struggled to be neutral. And so must the university.

However, I would reject out of hand any attempt by the radical students or the misinformed and misguided students, radicals or otherwise, to say that because the university cannot possibly be completely neutral that it ought to be bent and tilted towards this form of ideology. That is the road to death and to doom, and would mean the end of the university as we know it.

From an article in Change *magazine by Professor Robert Paul Wolff, Department of Philosophy, Columbia University, September-October 1969.*

The Myth of Value Neutrality

In the dialectic of charge, response and confrontation which dominates the campus these days, one of the most familiar disputes revolves about the role of the university as supporter or opponent of government policy. Characteristically, the interchange proceeds something like this:

1. The university is engaged in a variety of extra-educational activities, such as contract research, the scheduling of job interviews, transmission of class standing to draft boards, and so forth. These activities accumulate haphazardly without deliberate university control and in the absence of a coherent policy.

2. Radical students and faculty focus attention upon some few of the extra-educational activities as evidences of the university's positive support for a controversial and evil government policy. Transmission of class standing to draft boards supports the Vietnam war. Acceptance of contract research on counterinsurgency

supports the reactionary imperialism of the United States abroad. The university's real estate dealings discriminate against the poor and the black in the surrounding community.

3. The university defends its activities on the grounds that it takes no position with regard to social or political issues. It leaves its faculty free to teach what it likes and to do research as it chooses. It opens its doors to speakers of all persuasions and recruiters for virtually any enterprise which is not illegal. Individuals within the university may engage in whatever political activities they like, but for the university as an institution to take an official political stand would be in violation of its fundamental principles of value neutrality and academic freedom.

4. The radicals reply that the university *is* endorsing positions and policies by its actions, but that it is endorsing the *wrong* positions and the *wrong* policies. What is needed is an about-face, so that the university will throw its considerable prestige and power into the fight against a reactionary establishment.

This debate, in all the many forms it takes from university to university, revolves about one of the oldest tenets of the liberal tradition—the myth of the value-neutral institution. Just as the state, in classical liberal economic theory, is expected to stand clear of the competitive battles waged between firm and firm or capital and labor, merely maintaining the freedom and order of the marketplace of commodities, so the university is expected to stand clear of the intellectual battles waged between doctrine and doctrine, dogma and dogma, in the marketplace of ideas. Its sole function is to regulate the contest, ensuring a place in the debate to every position and every party. The university administration is charged with the responsibility of protecting those within the academy from the repeated assaults by outside critics, while at the same time guaranteeing that absolute freedom of debate reigns within. From this freedom in the marketplace of ideas, it is confidently believed, the greatest possible advance in truth and wisdom will flow.

As a prescription for institutional behavior, the doctrine of value neutrality suffers from the worst disability which can afflict a norm: what it prescribes is not wrong; it is impossible. A large university in contemporary America simply cannot adopt a value-neutral stance, either externally or internally, no matter how hard it tries. This observation is scarcely original with me; indeed, I should have thought it was a commonplace of social analysis. Nevertheless, it is often and willfully forgotten.

A large university, in respect of its employees, faculty, students, land holding, endowment and other material and human resources, is in many ways comparable to a large corporation. Columbia University, for example, is one of the largest property owners in the city of New York; the University of California must surely be one of the major employers in the state; and cities like Ann Arbor, Cambridge and Princeton have somewhat the air of company towns. Now one of the first truths enunciated in introductory ethics courses is that the failure to do something is as much an act the doing of it. It is perfectly reasonable to hold a man responsible for *not* paying his taxes, for *not* exercising due care and caution in driving, for *not* helping a fellow man in need. In public life, when a man who has power refrains from using it, we all agree that he has *acted politically*. Omissions are frequently even more significant politically than commissions in American politics, for those in positions of decision usually rule by default rather than by consent. Hence, acquiescence in governmental acts, under the guise of impartiality, actually strengthens the established forces and makes successful opposition all the harder.

For example, let us suppose that a university cooperates with the Selective Service System, motivated in part by a simple desire to be helpful to legitimate government agencies and interested students, and in part by the conviction that deliberate refusal to cooperate would constitute an institutional opposition to the draft which would violate the principle of political neutrality. Obviously, the university strengthens the draft system, positively by its cooperation and negatively by its failure to take the deliberate step of opposition which was open to it. To be sure, public refusal would have a greater political effect against, than quiet cooperation would have for, the government. Hence, there must be better reasons for opposition than there are for cooperation. But the reasons need not be overwhelming or apocalyptic, and, in any event, the action, positive or negative, is a *political* act based on *political* considerations. No major institution can remain politically innocent in an open society.

When pressed with such obvious arguments, administrators frequently retreat to the claim that they merely follow the law. Dow Chemical is permitted to recruit because it and its activities are legal. No moral or political judgment is superimposed on the accepted law of the land.

Now we live in a society which pursues policies by enacting laws. Hence, mere obedience to law is at the same time support for established policy. Suppose, to take a case which is presumably no longer possible, that a school in a state which legally forbids marriages between whites and blacks refuses to hire a white scholar on the grounds that he is married to a black woman. It thereby lends its great institutional weight to the enforcement of an evil social policy, even though it does so merely by obeying the law. There is no difference between this hypothetical case and the case of defense research or cooperation with the draft, except of course that all good white liberal professors and administrators are opposed to the wicked segregation in the South, while many of the same people feel quite comfortable with America's foreign policy or with their own university's behavior in the surrounding neighborhood.

When we turn to the internal organization of the university, we find the same unavoidable evaluative bias. Whatever one thinks of the radical complaint that American capitalism prepares young men for the rigors of the corporate world by the lockstep character of education, it is obvious that an institution imposes some set of values on its students merely by requiring that they maintain a passing grade-average, attend classes regularly, take examinations on time and leave after completing an appropriate assortment of courses. To be sure, the vehicle for the imposition of values is the *form* rather than the *content* of the educational process, but the effect is imposition nonetheless.*

An analogous bias is built into the free marketplace of ideas, which usually pretends to be neutral among competing dogmas and doctrines. By permitting all voices to be heard, the university systematically undermines all those doctrines which claim exclusive possession of the truth. For some strange reason, American intellectuals cannot perceive that their own commitment to free debate is also a substantive political act, no more neutral than the prohibition of dissent in religiously or politically authoritarian nations.

---

* Let me say that I *approve* by and large of the values thus imposed. I am personally very strict with regard to lateness of papers and the like. But I recognize that I must *justify* such requirements with an argument and not claim to be neutral on the issues involved.

Finally, every university expresses a number of positive value commitments through the character of its faculty, of its library, even through the buildings it chooses to build. Astronomy departments ignore astrology, psychiatry departments ignore dianetics, philosophy departments ignore dialectical materialism. Universities build laboratories for experimental research, thereby committing themselves to the importance of the scientific enterprise; libraries devote scarce resources to the accumulation of rare and ancient manuscripts; whole faculties are organized to teach and study social welfare, veterinary science, law or business. Each of these institutional decisions embodies an evaluation which can easily become the focus of a political dispute.

The conclusion is obvious. No institution can remain politically neutral either in its interaction with society or in the conduct and organization of its internal affairs. To pretend otherwise is merely to throw up a smokescreen; it is a way of rationalizing the value commitments already made, by attempting to remove them from the area of legitimate debate. Students for a Democratic Society speak of the need to *politicize* the campus. Moderate professors and students oppose this *politicization,* which they protest would alter the character of the university for the worse. But the truth is that every campus is now politicized, necessarily and unavoidably. The radicals do not wish to inflict politics on a realm which once was happily apolitical. They only wish to force an awareness of the already political character of the university, as a first step toward changing the policies which the university embodies or pursues.

On the basis of this analysis, it might appear that the university should drop the mask of impartiality, openly acknowledge the political biases implied by its policies and educational practices, and confront the problem of deciding how its political orientation should be determined. That would, indeed, be the honest and consistent course to follow. To be sure, any system of majority rule or collegial decision would still leave members of a dissident minority unhappy at being associated with an institution whose avowed policies differed from their own; but that must inevitably be true in any case, and at least the policy would be openly and fairly arrived at.

However, the honest and consistent course is not always the best; and I am persuaded that in the United States at the present time, such a course would have reactionary rather than progressive consequences. There are two reasons why radicals would be ill-advised to expose the incoherence and hypocrisy of the doctrine of institutional neutrality. In the first place, faculties and student bodies tend, by and large, to be conservative in their leanings; and once the university is forced to bring its policies out into the open, the majority is liable to move the direction of those policies even farther to the right. Students are always surprised to discover the melancholy facts of faculty-student conservatism. Since the liberals and radicals on the campus make most of the noise and grab most of the headlines, it is easy to be fooled into thinking that the campus is a hotbed of radical conviction barely contained by a manipulative and repressive administration. Inevitably, the day of disillusion arrives when a faculty vote or student referendum reveals the radicals to be in a distinct minority.

It would be tactically unwise, therefore, to push to an open vote such matters as university acceptance of defense research or the policy of open recruiting. But this is hardly the greatest danger which the politicization of the university invites. Far worse is the ever-present threat of pressure, censorship and witch-hunting by conservative forces in society at large. The universities at present are sanctuaries for social critics who would find it very hard to gain a living elsewhere in society. Who but a university these days would hire Herbert Marcuse, Eugene Genovese or Barrington Moore, Jr.? Where else are anarchists, socialists and followers of other unpopular persuasions accorded titles, honors and the absolute security of academic tenure? Let the university once declare that it is a political actor, and its faculty will be investigated, its charter revoked, and its tax-exempt status forthwith removed. How majestic and unassailable is the university president who protects his dissident faculty with an appeal to the sanctity of academic freedom.

It is a bitter pill for the radicals to swallow, but the fact is that they benefit more than any other segment of the university community from the fiction of institutional neutrality. For the present, therefore, I would strongly urge both students and professors to hide behind the slogans "lehrfreiheit" and "lernfreiheit," and give up the attempt to politicize the campus. If this advice is too cautious to satisfy their revolutionary longings, they may look on the universities as those protected base camps which, Mao Tse-tung tells us, are the foundation of a successful protracted guerrilla campaign.

From official statements of the New University Conference, which describes itself as "a national organization of radicals who work in, around, and in spite of institutions of higher education, who are committed to struggle politically to create a new, American form of socialism and to replace an educational and social system that is an instrument of class, sexual and racial oppression with one that belongs to the people." The first statement, an excerpt from "The Student Rebellion" was issued in February 1969, and the second, "A Declaration of Beliefs," was issued in 1968.

Official Neutrality: A Veil

We in the New University Conference share the basic goals and commitments of the student movement. We share with student activists the aim of constructing a grass-roots movement in this country that can have real effect in stopping American efforts to dominate other peoples, that can win a fundamental reordering of priorities in this country so that genuine equality can become a realistic hope, that can disrupt the drift toward technologically-based authoritarianism and a garrison state, that can find new modes of political and social organization which will permit our vast resources to be shared for the benefit of all men and provide the basis for personal liberation.

We have hoped that the university could be a center of work toward these ends. That hope, however, seems increasingly illusory. We have all come to realize that through the veil of "official neutrality" and protestations of innocence, the universities—including the "great centers of learning"—are partners with the most pernicious forces in our society.

Our experience at the university has taught us that higher education exists primarily to serve the white middle class, and only marginally to serve minority groups and working-class youth. Though covering itself with the cloak of democratic rhetoric, the university rejects democratic governance within its community in both theory and practice. The trend toward the fragmented and impersonal multiversity, existing on the largesse of the corporations and the permanent war economy, is not merely a product of social complexity. Rather, it is the institutionalization of the narrow interests of the most privileged minority of the faculty and administrators. These men serve their own interests and careers by gaining control of huge budgets, which sometimes turn them into corporate servants at yet another branch office, sometimes make their laboratories government outposts, and too often leave the whole institution financially dependent on military expenditures. With boards of trustees composed of the wealthy elite, whose interests are so often identified with the university's, or with some abstract rationale for more living space, urban universities disrupt and "develop" their surrounding communities quite without regard for the wishes of, or the human cost to, the residents of these neighborhoods.

• • • • • • •

War overseas and injustice at home are among the defining characteristics of American society and no institution is free of their stain. This is not less true of the university itself. Increasingly, the giant institutions of this society—government, the military, corporations and foundations—call upon the university to supply the experts and the expertise of social manipulation and international coercion, and increasingly the university is flattered to comply.

But if the university as an institution has come to collaborate so intimately with the more vicious tendencies in American life, this is certainly not true of a large part of the university's community. The resistance movement to the war in Viet Nam, the struggle for Black liberation and the radical community organizing projects, for example, have been encouraged, led, filled-out and supported by faculty, graduate students and other intellectuals in overwhelming numbers.

The frustrations and difficulties of those struggles have increasingly taught us that it is not enough to be radical downtown or in Washington. Our radicalism must extend to the campus and to the classroom, to our teaching, our studies and our writing.

We reject the view that the university is or can be isolated from the larger society. The demands of domestic technology and international intervention have already changed the university from an enclave for humane scholars into one of the dominant institutions of America's aggressive society. The technology and the techniques which seek to pacify ghetto militants, student activists and Asian revolutionaries have already become a major export of the American university. The professor-technicians, whose moral and political commitments lie outside the university, have already become a dominant force on campus and their prestige and their priorities are already a central part of the university's value system, expressed in everything from university appropriations to the undergraduate curriculum.

We reject the view that it is the business of the university to export experts and expertise for purposes of aggressive and manipulative suppression, just as we reject the view that the university is the natural collaborator only of those who already wield power in American society.

We are committed to the struggle for a democratic university, one within which we may freely express the radical content of our lives and one which will be the antagonist and not the ally of pacifiers, domestic and international.

We believe in a university which enfranchises all those who participate in its community: faculty, students, graduate students, administrative and maintenance personnel. We reject any value system which monopolizes university decision-making in the hands of the wealthy, the highly-placed and the over-prestiged.

We believe in a university which does not hesitate to incorporate radical subject matter and radical opinion into its curriculum, which does not hide an implicit counterrevolutionary morality beneath the banner of dispassionate objectivity. We reject the view that the university preserves its integrity merely by passing on the commonplace opinions of the now dominant groups and forces in American life.

We believe in a university which welcomes graduate students as colleagues and their work as an addition to the intellectual life of the time. We reject the view that graduate students are fit only for arid scholastic exercises and under-paid teaching assistantships.

We believe in a university in which scientific research redounds to the benefit and enlightenment of mankind, one in which scientists are free of the fear that their work will find application in the bureaucracies of expansion, coercion and killing. We believe in a university whose social scientists reject alliance with power and devote not only their thoughts but also their professional activities to the liberation struggles being waged here and abroad.

We believe in a university which prepares professionals, not one which simply trains professional employees. We believe in a university which does not sacrifice everything to the needs of its institutional clients and calls the result "excellence." We reject the view that some universities train management, and all the rest labor, as we reject the view that teaching is a form of second-class citizenship.

We believe in a university which is not an enclave of humanity for a privileged few, but is instead a base from which humane values and actions emanate to transform the university itself and also the larger world beyond.

Finally, we believe in a university which plays a creative and exemplary role in American society. We believe in a university which exports radical graduates, radical opinion and the radical example of its internal democracy. We believe in a university which is the common resource of all those who struggle to purge American society of its impulse to war and oppression.

From an essay by Douglas Peterson, a student at the University of Minnesota, reprinted in The New Guard, *journal of Young Americans for Freedom, in March 1968.*

The American Cause and the American University

THE MYTH OF THE NEUTRAL UNIVERSITY

Much of the blame for the continuing existence of revolutionary thought and action on the university campus can be attributed to the view that the university is "neutral territory." The "neutral territory" idea is the same concept which has turned European, Near Eastern, Far Eastern, and South American universities into safe havens for subversives and revolutionaries, and which is now well along toward doing the same thing to American campuses. Witness the almost universal hue and cry that arises in the academic world whenever law enforcement officials or legislative investigating committees attempt to deal with unlawful or subversive activities on a university campus. . . .

"Neutral territory" thinking, aided by deliberate Communist agitation and nurtured in the darkness of general ignorance concerning the true nature of the problem, has encouraged the development of the American university into a dangerous breeding ground for revolutionary thought and action. Nor is the danger of the university problem restricted to the campus itself. Carried off the campus by undergraduate and faculty activists and filtered into society through graduates and university research programs, the revolutionary ideas flowering on the campus have become a threat to the entire fabric of American society. Not only are increasing numbers of campus rebels showing up in the ranks of off-campus demonstrations, but more and more supercharged, socialist university graduates are moving into influential positions in all levels of government, industry, labor, and even the military. The non-socialist citizens of the United States are facing the horrible specter of revolutionary ideologists on the university campus, and throughout the structure of American society, cooperating in an all-out effort to remove the American Republic from its foundational principle of liberty made orderly under law.

In spite of all the claims made that the contemporary American university is "neutral territory" dedicated to the pursuit of scientific knowledge in all areas of human endeavor, it is readily apparent that neutrality on the American campus is little more than myth. On the contrary, the American university, acting in the name of neutrality, has actually become a major source of very non-neutral, anti-American thought and action. Instead of dedicating itself solely to the objective pursuit of scientific knowledge, the American university has become the main "think tank" for efforts to radically alter the social, economic, and political structure of the United States.

NEEDED: A TRULY AMERICAN UNIVERSITY

To begin with, no institution, based upon the philosophical presuppositions of its founders and directors, can achieve total neutrality. But not only is total neutrality unachievable, it is also undesirable, especially if the university in question is tax-supported. When citizens of the United States have a portion of their income confiscated for purposes of educating other citizens of the United States, they should at least be offered the minimal assurance that their tax dollars will be used to train loyal citizens and not revolutionaries. *Furthermore, since government does not usually fix philosophical orientation for private colleges and universities,* this article deals primarily with tax-supported institutions.

It would appear that the minimum requirements for a university to be truly American are that the university must be pro-

American in principle: all faculty and administration personnel must be required to affirm their loyalty to the United States Constitution. The goal of such a university must be the training of capable, loyal American citizens, as well as those foreign students who are willing to submit to the rules and regulations of the university. Faculty, administrators, and students who actively participate in or support subversive activities must be dismissed without delay. On the one hand, there must be safeguards built into the university structure for protecting the university, and society outside the university, from revolutionary anarchy, but on the other hand, *there must be means of protecting students and faculty from academic totalitarianism and censorship.* . . .

University regents and trustees must be influenced by direct pressure through newspaper articles, radio and television editorials, scholarly research papers, and mass distribution of literature to arouse public interest, and by indirect pressure brought by influencing government figures, who appoint the regents or handle university appropriations.

Once the public is aware of the real nature of the university problem and prepared to expect direct action on the situation, and once the university trustees and regents sense enough public pressure to cause them to take action, the practical efforts to clean up and reshape the American university can begin.

The first step would be the removal and replacement of incompetent, cowardly, and disloyal university administrators. Removal could be achieved by outright dismissal, where gross violations or negligence is involved, or by refusal to renew contracts in the case of less sensational records.

After competent and loyal administrators are installed, the process of straightening out the faculties and student bodies can begin. Those students and faculty members with long records of serious subversive, immoral, or disruptive activity should be removed swiftly. All other faculty and students must then be put on notice that university regulations are meant to be strictly enforced, and that unlawful and subversive activities will not be tolerated.

Following hard on the heels of faculty and student house cleaning, must be the enacting of a basic code of ethics, moral, and civic behavior, which all members of the university community must be required to obey as long as they are under the jurisdiction of the university. This code and its enforcement should be based upon the essential constitutional principles of justice, order, and liberty under law, and should be conformable to at least the generally accepted mores of American society at large, if not to an even higher view of moral and social conduct. . . .

A smart-aleck university student spouting his revolutionary idiocies from a campus soapbox may seem little more than ludicrous and disgusting. But when the same student, bejeweled with a bachelor's, master's, or doctor's degree, moves into the State Department, the Congress, or even the Presidency, he and all those like him become a deadly menace to freedom—only then it's too late to do anything about them.

Article by David Friedman, a student, Harvard College, in The New Guard, *Summer 1968.*

The Impossibility of a University

The corporate university contains an implicit contradiction. It cannot take positions on truth. It must take positions on truth. The second necessity makes the left-wing demand for a "responsible university" emotionally appealing; the first makes not merely the acceptance of that demand but its very consideration by the university something fundamentally subversive of the university's proper ends.

The university cannot take positions on truth because, if it does, the efforts of its members will be diverted from the search for truth to the attempt to control the decision-making process. How inconsistent these objectives are is clear in as simple an example as the hiring of new faculty members. If the university must take a public position on a question that is an important matter of controversy within some department, if the university must come out for or against the tax surcharge, or for or against the Quark model of elementary particles, then those members of the department who are on one side of the controversy must, in order to be sure that the university comes out in favor of truth, not error, try to keep the other side from acquiring additional votes, and try even harder to keep it from acquiring additional persuasive voices.

To hire an incompetent supporter of the opposing position would be undesirable; to hire a competent supporter, who might persuade enough faculty members to reverse the university's stand, would be intolerable. Departments in a university that reaches corporate decisions on important matters will thus tend to become groups of true believers, closed to all who do not share the proper orthodoxy. They so forfeit one of the principal tools in the pursuit of truth—intellectual conflict.

Even without this cause, departments have some tendency to become uniform, since academicians, like others, tend to underestimate the competence of those who disagree with them. But this is an error of judgment, not the intentional imposition of an orthodoxy, and it is counteracted by the presence of objective standards of scholarship, and by the recognition that diversity is desirable.

The reasons why the university must take positions on truth are more obvious. A modern university is a huge corporation, with expenditures of tens of millions of dollars, and an endowment of hundreds of millions. It must act, and to act it must decide what is true. What conditions lead to high crime rates in areas around the university—should it protect its members by hiring university police or should it spend its energies on neighborhood relations or community organizing? What effect will certain fiscal policies have on the stock market, and thus the university's endowment—should the university support them?

These issues are important to the university, and these are issues of professional controversy within the academic community. In some areas, such as politics, the university may proclaim its neutrality, but neutrality, as the Left quite properly says, is also a position. If one believes that the election of Eugene McCarthy, or of Ronald Reagan, would be a national tragedy, and so a tragedy for the university and its community in particular, how can one justify allowing the university, with its vast resources of wealth and influence, to remain neutral?

In practice, the best solution possible within the present structure of the university has not been the neutrality of the university but the ignorance or impotence of the university community. So long as students and faculty do not know that the university is bribing politicians, or investing in countries with dictatorial regimes, or whatever, or so long as they have no way of controlling the university's actions, those actions will not hinder the university in its proper function, the pursuit of truth, however much good or damage they may do in the outside world. Once the community becomes conscious that the university does, or even that it can, take actions having some serious effect on the outside world, and that the members of the community can effect those actions, the game is up.

Can this be avoided? Not, I think, within the structure of our present corporate universities. The university community, primarily the faculty, has ultimate control in most of the better universities, and this is probably desirable; a university run from the outside, by a government or by a self-perpetuating board of trustees, has problems that are different but no less serious. The university can pretend to make no decisions, or pretend that decisions are all made by the administrators, ignoring the faculty's effective power, for a time. But the reality will eventually be pointed out, by foolish men who wish to make the university "moral" or by clever men who wish to destroy it.

The only ultimate solution is to abolish the corporate university and have its functions served by institutions controlled in an essentially economic rather than political manner. If the university is replaced by a market place, where individual members of the university community, or small organizations within that community, freely contract with each other in their mutual interest, the difficulties I have discussed vanish. Market places do not take positions.

CHAPTER 2

Education and Society:
What Functions Should
the University Serve?

To Clark Kerr and other liberal spokesmen, the modern American university represents a unique triumph of pluralist society, combining service to all sectors of the public and dedication to the advancement of human knowledge. The "multiversity" is a city "of infinite variety," offering a "vast range of choices" to students and a variety of roles to the faculty. The student's freedom to learn and the professor's freedom to do as he pleases are both "triumphant." According to Kerr, the multiversity has "few peers in the preservation and dissemination and examination of the eternal truths; no living peers in the search for new knowledge, and no peers in all history among institutions of higher learning in serving so many of the segments of an advancing civilization."

Kerr's analysis of the university as a "knowledge factory" is the starting point for the radical critique of the university. Carl Davidson, a leader of Students for a Democratic Society (SDS), links student discontent and the rise of demands for student power to the bureaucratic and fragmented character of the multiversity.

The need of corporate capitalism to create a "new working class" of technicians and experts, Davidson says, produces "isolation, manipulation and alienation" in the university. But the manipulators have overlooked one thing: "men are not made of clay." Davidson concludes: "What we are witnessing and participating in is an important historical phenomenon; the revolt of the trainees of the new working class against the alienated and oppressive conditions of production and consumption within corporate capitalism."

Following the Davidson pamphlet, a short excerpt from the radical booklet "How Harvard rules" describes the university's functions as central to "the social system of technological warfare-welfare capitalism." The university performs direct services for business and the military through research and training, and indirectly serves them by weaving "a democratic veil which enshrouds a concentrated, highly organized and totally undemocratic system of wealth and power."

The ideological functions of the university are the principal subject of Richard Lichtman's essay "University: mask for privilege?" Lichtman contends that if the university performs all the functions society imposes on it, as Kerr's analysis implies, it will eventually come to perform a most essential function for society —the legitimation of its established structure. He tries to show that this is precisely the import of much contemporary academic work. Lichtman calls upon the university, and intellectuals in general, to rebel, and break their bonds of subservience to imperial America.

Regimentation and inauthenticity are the themes of the declaration by the Radical Action Cooperative, "Life, not survival—a manifesto." This short-lived anarchist group describes the university as a "production line of servant-technicians" turning men into robots and subordinating human spontaneity and experience to efficiency, status, and artificial values. Denouncing the "cretinism" of the university and society, the manifesto issues a call to rebellion: "The choice between being a cynic and being a revolutionary is the choice between impotence and sexuality."

Criticism of Clark Kerr's view of the university as a "knowledge factory" and "service station" has come from persons outside the radical left. These criticisms are of two kinds.

One is that by the traditional humanist, a position well represented here by one of its foremost spokesmen in the United

States, Jacques Barzun. Barzun describes himself and Robert Hutchins as the "only two radicals in the whole country" on educational matters. Like many on the left, Barzun disapproves of the university's role as a service station. But Barzun's remedy is to return to the concept of the traditional university dedicated to learning and study and set apart from society. He denies any validity to student demands for a relevant curriculum or for participation in decision-making, and says that the grievances are on the side of universities, not students. "What are the misdeeds and tyrannies of the universities?" Barzun asks. "Where has any list of them appeared?"

Governor Ronald Reagan of California represents the view of conservative political leaders. While viewing student unrest as the product of a minority of radicals, he agrees that this minority can find a response in a larger group upset by the "knowledge factory" and the "assembly line." He charges the universities, particularly those run by liberals like Clark Kerr, with having no regard for the "individuality, aspirations and dreams" of most students. As a solution, he calls for a policy to reestablish the primacy of teaching over research.

From the book by Clark Kerr, President of the University of California, entitled The Uses of the University, *1963.*

The Uses of the University

The multiversity is an inconsistent institution. It is not one community but several—the community of the undergraduate and the community of the graduate; the community of the humanist, the community of the social scientist, and the community of the scientist; the communities of the professional schools; the community of all the nonacademic personnel; the community of the administrators. Its edges are fuzzy—it reaches out to alumni, legislators, farmers, businessmen, who are all related to one or more of these internal communities. As an institution, it looks far into the past and far into the future, and is often at odds with the present. It serves society almost slavishly—a society it also criticizes, sometimes unmercifully. Devoted to equality of opportunity, it is itself a class society. A community, like the medieval communities of masters and students, should have common interests; in the multiversity, they are quite varied, even conflicting. A community should have a soul, a single animating principle; the multiversity has several—some of them quite good, although there is much debate on which souls really deserve salvation. . . .

The "Idea of a University" was a village with its priests. The "Idea of a Modern University" was a town—a one-industry town —with its intellectual oligarchy. "The Idea of a Multiversity" is a city of infinite variety. Some get lost in the city; some rise to the top within it; most fashion their lives within one of its many subcultures. There is less sense of community than in the village but also less sense of confinement. There is less sense of purpose than within the town but there are more ways to excel. There are also more refuges of anonymity—both for the creative person and the drifter. As against the village and the town, the "city" is more like the totality of civilization as it has evolved and more an integral part of it; and movement to and from the surrounding society has been greatly accelerated. As in a city, there are many separate endeavors under a single rule of law.

The students in the "city" are older, more likely to be married, more vocationally oriented, more drawn from all classes and races than the students in the village; and they find themselves in a most intensely competitive atmosphere. They identify less with the total community and more with its subgroups. Burton R. Clark and Martin Trow have a particularly interesting typology of these subcultures: the "collegiate" of the fraternities and sororities and the athletes and activities majors; the "academic" of the serious students; the "vocational" of the students seeking training for specific jobs; and the "nonconformist" of the political activists, the aggressive intellectuals, and the bohemians. These subcultures are not mutually exclusive, and some of the fascinating pageantry of the multiversity is found in their interaction one on another.

The multiversity is a confusing place for the student. He has problems of establishing his identity and sense of security within it. But it offers him a vast range of choices, enough literally to stagger the mind. In this range of choices he encounters the opportunities and the dilemmas of freedom. The casualty rate is high. The walking wounded are many. *Lernfreiheit*—the freedom of the student to pick and choose, to stay or to move on—is triumphant.

Life has changed also for the faculty member. The multiversity is in the main stream of events. To the teacher and the researcher have been added the consultant and the administrator. Teaching is less central than it once was for most faculty members; research has become more important. This has given rise to what has been called the "non-teacher"—"the higher a man's standing, the less he has to do with students"—and to a threefold class structure of what used to be "the faculty": those who only do research, those who only teach (and they are largely in an auxiliary role), and those who still do some of both. In one university I know, the proportions at the Ph.D. level or its equivalent are roughly one researcher to two teachers to four who do both.

Consulting work and other sources of additional income have given rise to what is called the "affluent professor," a category that does include some but by no means all of the faculty. Additionally, many faculty members, with their research assistants and teaching assistants, their departments and institutes, have become administrators. A professor's life has become, it is said, "a rat race of business and activity, managing contracts and projects, guiding teams and assistants, bossing crews of technicians, making numerous trips, sitting on committees for government agencies, and engaging in other distractions necessary to keep the whole frenetic business from collapse."

The intellectual world has been fractionalized as interests have become much more diverse; and there are fewer common topics of conversation at the faculty clubs. Faculty government has become more cumbersome, more the avocation of active minorities; and there are real questions whether it can work effectively on a large scale, whether it can agree on more than preservation of the status quo. Faculty members are less members of the particular university and more colleagues within their national academic discipline groups.

But there are many compensations. "The American professoriate" is no longer, as Flexner once called it, "a proletariat." Salaries and status have risen considerably. The faculty member is more a fully participating member of society, rather than a creature on the periphery; some are at the very center of national and world events. Research opportunities have been enormously increased. The faculty member within the big mechanism and with all his opportunities has a new sense of independence from the domination of the administration or his colleagues; much administration has been effectively decentralized to the level of the individual professor. In particular, he has a choice of roles and mixtures of roles to suit his taste as never before. He need not leave the Groves for the Acropolis unless he wishes; but he can, if he wishes. He may even become, as some have, essentially a professional man with his home office and basic retainer on the campus of the multiversity but with his clients scattered from coast to coast. He can also even remain the professor of old, as many do. There are several patterns of life from which to choose. So the professor too has greater freedom. *Lehrfreiheit,* in the old German sense of the freedom of the professor to do as he pleases, also is triumphant.

What is the justification of the modern American multiversity? History is one answer. Consistency with the surrounding society is another. Beyond that, it has few peers in the preservation and dissemination and examination of the eternal truths; no living peers in the search for new knowledge; and no peers in all history among institutions of higher learning in serving so many of the segments of an advancing civilization. Inconsistent internally as an institution, it is consistently productive. Torn by change, it has the stability of freedom. Though it has not a single soul to call its own, its members pay their devotions to truth.

The multiversity in America is perhaps best seen at work, adapting and growing, as it responded to the massive impact of federal programs beginning with World War II. A vast transformation has taken place without a revolution, for a time almost without notice being taken. The multiversity has demonstrated how adaptive it can be to new opportunities for creativity; how responsive to money; how eagerly it can play a new and useful role; how fast it can change while pretending that nothing has happened at all; how fast it can neglect some of its ancient virtues. What are the current realities of the federal grant university? . . .

The American university is currently undergoing its second great transformation. The first occurred during roughly the last quarter of the nineteenth century, when the land grant movement and German intellectualism were together bringing extraordinary change. The current transformation will cover roughly the quarter century after World War II. The university is being called upon to educate previously unimagined numbers of students; to respond to the expanding claims of national service; to merge its activities with industry as never before; to adapt to and rechannel new intellectual currents. By the end of this period, there will be a truly American university, an institution unique in world history, an institution not looking to other models but serving, itself, as a model for universities in other parts of the globe. This is not said in boast. It is simply that the imperatives that have molded the American university are at work around the world. . . .

The knowledge industry. Basic to this transformation is the growth of the "knowledge industry," which is coming to permeate government and business and to draw into it more and more people raised to higher and higher levels of skill. The production, distribution, and consumption of "knowledge" in all its forms is said to account for 29 percent of gross national product, according to Fritz Machlup's calculations; and "knowledge production" is growing at about twice the rate of the rest of the economy. Knowledge has certainly never in history been so central to the conduct of an entire society. What the railroads did for the second half of the last century and the automobile for the first half of this century may be done for the second half of this century by the knowledge industry: that is, to serve as the focal point for national growth. And the university is at the center of the knowledge process. . . .

Spatially the modern university often reflects its history, with the library and the humanities and social sciences at the center of the campus, extending out to the professional schools and scientific laboratories, and surrounded by industry, interspersed with residence halls, apartments, and boarding houses. An almost ideal location for a modern university is to be sandwiched between a middle-class district on its way to becoming a slum and an ultramodern industrial park—so that the students may live in the one and the faculty consult in the other. M.I.T. finds itself happily ensconced between the decaying sections of Cambridge and Technology Square.

Universities have become "bait" to be dangled in front of industry, with drawing power greater than low taxes or cheap labor. Route 128 around Boston and the great developing industrial complexes in the San Francisco Bay Area and Southern California reflect the universities in these areas. The Gilpatric report for the Department of Defense explained that 41 percent of defense contracts for research in the fiscal year 1961 were concentrated in California, 12 percent in New York, and 6 percent in Massachusetts, for a total of nearly 60 percent, in part because these were also "centers of learning." Sterling Forest outside New York City seeks to attract industry by location next to a new university campus. In California, new industrial laboratories were located next to two new university campuses before the first building was built on either of these campuses.

Sometimes industry will reach into a university laboratory to extract the newest ideas almost before they are born. Instead of waiting outside the gates, agents are working the corridors. They also work the placement offices. And the university, in turn, reaches into industry, as through the Stanford Research Institute. . . .

There are those who fear the further involvement of the university in the life of society. They fear that the university will lose its objectivity and its freedom. But society is more desirous of objectivity and more tolerant of freedom than it used to be. The university can be further ahead of the times and further behind the times, further to the left of the public and further to the right of the public—and still keep its equilibrium—than was ever the case before, although problems in this regard are not yet entirely unknown. There are those who fear that the university will be drawn too far from basic to applied research and from applied research to application itself. But the lines dividing these never have been entirely clear and much new knowledge has been generated at the borders of basic and applied research, and even of applied knowledge and its application.

Growth and shifting emphases and involvement in society all take money; and which universities get it in the largest quantities will help determine which of them excel a decade or two hence. Will federal support be spent according to merit or according to political power? Will private donors continue to do as well as they recently have for those universities that have done well already? Will the states find new sources of revenue or will their expenditures be held under a lid of no new taxes? The answers to these questions will help predict the standings on the next rating scale of universities.

However this turns out, the scene of American higher education will continue to be marked by great variety, and this is one of its great strengths. The large and the small, the private and the public, the general and the specialized all add their share to overall excellence. The total system is extraordinarily flexible, decentralized, competitive—and productive. The new can be tried, the old tested with considerable skill and alacrity. Pluralism in higher education matches the pluralistic American society. The multiversity, in particular, is the child of middle-class pluralism; it relates to so much of the variety of the surrounding society and is thus so varied internally. . . .

Intellect has also become an instrument of national purpose, a component part of the "military-industrial complex." Our Western City of Intellect finds its counterpart or counterparts in the East. In the war of the ideological worlds, a great deal depends on the use of this instrument. Knowledge is durable. It is also transferable. Knowledge costs a great deal to produce, less to reproduce. Thus it only pays to produce knowledge if through production it can be put into use better and faster. The Communist City of Intellect has been a planned community. It grows only in certain directions and in certain ways. This allows concentration of effort but limits growth and recognition except in restricted segments of the intellectual world. This City flourishes in science and in military might but lags in the humanities and the social sciences. Whole areas that would be covered by a really modern City of Intellect are largely unpopulated.

The two Cities of Intellect are not only sources of weapons— they also form a potential bridge between their two societies. Knowledge is universal. Its creators generally prefer freedom. To the extent the Eastern City of Intellect grows and makes contact with the Western, it almost inevitably changes its own society. Here a certain type of society really may carry the "seeds of its own destruction." It either competes and changes, or it loses some of its over-all power of competition. . . .

From a pamphlet by Carl Davidson, a leader of SDS, 1967.

The Multiversity: Crucible of the New Working Class

The Present Malaise of Education

"Happiness is Student Power" was the most catching slogan emblazoned on the many banners and picket signs during the

Berkeley Student Strike in December 1966. But, as most college administrators know only too well, Berkeley and its rebellious students are not an isolated phenomenon among the vast variety of American campuses. Far from being an exception, Berkeley has become the paradigm case of the educational malaise in the United States; and, in the last few years, that malaise has been transformed into a movement. Indeed a spectre is haunting our universities—the spectre of a radical and militant nationally coordinated movement for *student power*. . . .

Obviously the cry for "power" in and of itself is a vacuous demand. Student power is not so much something we are fighting *for*, as it is something we must have in order to gain specific objectives. Then what are the objectives? What is our program? There is much variety in the dispute on these questions. But there is one thing that seems clear. However the specific forms of our immediate demands and programs may vary, the long-range goal and the daily drive that motivates and directs us is our intense longing for our liberation. In short, what the student power movement is about is *freedom*.

But aren't students free? Isn't America a democracy, even if it is a little manipulative? To answer those kinds of questions and many others that are more serious, it is important to look more closely at and come to an understanding of the malaise motivating our movement.

What do American students think of the educational institutions in which they live an important part of their lives? The most significant fact is that most of them don't think about them. Such young men and women made up that apathetic majority we called the "silent generation" in the 1950s. While the last few years has shown a marked and dramatic growth of a new radicalism, we should not forget that the apathetic and the cynical among the student population are still in the majority. But this need not be discouraging. In fact, we should view that apparent apathy among the majority of students with a certain qualified optimism.

What makes people apathetic? My feeling is that apathy is the *unconscious* recognition students make of the fact that they are *powerless*. Despite all the machinations and rhetoric used by hotshot student *politicos* within administration-sponsored student governments, people's experience tells them that nothing changes. Furthermore, if and when change does occur, students fully recognize that they were powerless to effect those changes in one way or another. If this is in fact the case, then why shouldn't students be apathetic? The administration rules, despite the façade of student governments, of dorm councils, and of student judicials. And when *they* give us ex-officio seats on *their* academic committees, the result among most students is that deeper, more hardened kind of apathy—cynicism.

The apathetic students are correct *as far as they go*. They are powerless. The forms given us for our self-government are of the Mickey Mouse, sand-box variety. I would only be pessimistic if a majority of students really accepted the illusion that those institutions had meaning in their lives, or that they could significantly affect those institutions. But the opposite is the case. The apathy reflects the reality of their powerlessness. When that reality confronts the lie of the official rhetoric, the contradiction is driven home—and the apathetic become the cynical. What that contradiction—that daily living with a lie—all adds up to is a *dynamic* tension and alienation. And that, fellow organizers, is the necessary subjective condition for any revolution.

It is important to understand that students are alienated from much more than the social and extracurricular aspect of their education. In fact, their deepest alienation is directed at the educational process itself. The excerpts that follow are from a letter written to the *New York Times* by a young woman student:

> I came to this school not thinking I could even keep up with the work. I was wrong. I can keep up. I can even come out on top. My daily schedule's rough. I get up at 6.30. . . . After dinner I work until midnight or 12.30. In the beginning, the first few weeks or so, I'm fine. Then I begin to wonder just what this is all about: am I educating myself? I have that one answered . . . I'm educating myself the way *they* want. So I convince myself the real reason I'm doing all this is to prepare myself; meantime I'm wasting those years of preparation. I'm not learning what I want to learn . . . I don't care about the feudal system. I want to know about life. I want to think and read. When? . . . My life is a whirlpool. I'm caught up in it, but I'm not conscious of it. I'm what *you* call living, but somehow I can't find life. . . . So maybe I got an A . . . but when I get it back I find that A means nothing. It's a letter *you* use to keep me going . . . I wonder what I'm doing

here. I feel phony; I don't belong. . . . You wonder about juvenile delinquents. If I ever become one, I'll tell why it will be so. I feel cramped. I feel like I'm in a coffin and can't move or breathe. . . . My life is worth nothing. It's enclosed in a few buildings on one campus; it goes no further. I've got to bust.

Tell the truth. Every American student knows that's the way it is. Even our administrators recognize what is going on. In 1963, a year or so *before* the first Berkeley insurrection, Clark Kerr prophesied, "the undergraduate students are restless. Recent changes in the American university have done them little good. . . . There is an incipient revolt." Kerr is not only concerned about the students. He also casts a worried glance at the faculty. "Knowledge is now in so many bits and pieces and administration so distant that faculty members are increasingly figures in a 'lonely crowd', intellectually and institutionally." The academic division of labor and depersonalization among the faculty is more than apparent to the students. Incoming freshmen scratch their heads, trying to understand any possible relevance of many of the courses in the catalog, some of which they are required to take. Also, some of the best belly-laughs are had by reading the titles of master's and doctoral theses, like one granted Ed.D. at Michigan State University: "An Evaluation of Thirteen Brands of Football Helmets on the Basis of Certain Impact Measures." What's worse, even if a course seems as though it might be relevant to our lives, like Psychology or Political Science, we are soon told by our professor that what we'll learn only has to do with the laboratory behavior of rats, and that "political science" has nothing to do with day-to-day politics. A student from Brandeis sums it up nicely:

> By the time we graduate, we have been painstakingly trained in separating facts from their meaning. . . . We wonder that our classes, with few exceptions, seem irrelevant to our lives. No wonder they're so boring. Boredom is the necessary condition of any education which teaches us to manipulate the facts and suppress their meaning.

Irrelevancy, meaninglessness, boredom, and fragmentation are the kinds of attributes that are becoming more and more applicable to mass education in America. We are becoming a people required to know more and more about less and less. This is true not only for our students, but also for our teachers; not only in our universities, but also in our secondary and primary schools— private as well as public.

What should education be about in America? The official rhetoric seems to offer an answer: education should be the process of developing the free, autonomous, creative and responsible *individual*—the "citizen" in the best sense of that word. Furthermore, higher education ought to encourage and enable the individual to turn his personal concerns into social issues, open to rational consideration and solution. C. Wright Mills put it clearly: "The aim of the college, for the individual student, is to eliminate the need in his life for the college; the task is to help him become a self-educating man. For only that will set him free."

But what is the reality of American education? Contrary to our commitment to individualism, we find that the day-to-day practice of our schools is authoritarian, conformist, and almost entirely status oriented. We find the usual relationship between teacher and student to be a disciplined form of dominance and subordination. We are told of the egalitarianism inherent in our school system, where the classroom becomes the melting-pot for the classless society of America's "people's capitalism," where everyone has the opportunity to climb to the top. Again, the opposite is the case. Our schools are more racially segregated now (1967) than ever before. There is a clear class bias contained both within and among our public schools—not even considering the clear class nature of our private schools and colleges. Within the secondary schools, students are quickly channeled—usually according to the class background of their parents—into vocational, commercial, or academic preparatory programs. . . .

From individual freedom to national service, from egalitarianism to class and racial hierarchical ossification, from self-reliance to institutional dependence—we have come to see education as the mechanistic process of homogeneous, uncritical absorption of "data" and development of job skills. But it is something more than that. The socialization and acculturation that goes on within American educational institutions is becoming increasingly central in the attempts to mold and shape American youth. This is mainly the result of the declining influence and, in some cases, the collapse of other traditional socializing institutions such as the church and the family. The schools, at all levels, end up with the job of maintaining, modifying, and transmitting the dominant themes of the national culture. . . .

It seems clear that bourgeois education in the US is in its historically most irrational and decadent state. Primary, secondary, and university systems are fusing together, thoroughly rationalizing and dehumanizing their internal order, and placing themselves in the service of the state, industry, and the military. Kerr is quite clear about this when he speaks of the "multiversity" making a common-law marriage with the federal government. John Hannah, president of Michigan State, was even clearer in a speech given in September 1961: "Our colleges and universities must be regarded as bastions of our defense, as essential to preservation of our country and our way of life as super-sonic bombers, nuclear-powered submarines and intercontinental ballistic missiles." The fact that none of the three weapons systems Hannah mentioned could have been designed, constructed, or operated without college-educated men proves that this is not just Fourth of July rhetoric. Hannah gives us an even better look at his idea of education in an article entitled "The School's Responsibility in National Defense," where he comments:

> I believe the primary and secondary schools can make education serve the individual and national interest by preparing youngsters for military service and life under conditions of stress as well as preparing them for college, or for a job or profession. . . . I would not even shrink from putting the word "indoctrination" to the kind of education I have in mind. If we do not hesitate to indoctrinate our children with a love of truth, a love of home, and a love of God, then I see no justification for balking at teaching them love of country and love of what this country means.

Hannah's comment about "life under conditions of stress" is related to a remark made by Eric A. Walker, president of Pennsylvania State University, a few years ago. There had been a series of student suicides and attempted suicides within a quite short period of time. Many students and faculty members started grumbling about the newly instituted "term" system—a kind of "speed-up"—relating the stress and strain of the new system to the student suicides. Dr Walker's response to this unrest was to comment on how the increased pressure on the students was a good thing, since it enabled them to "have their nervous break-downs early," before they graduated and had jobs and families when having a nervous breakdown would cause them more difficulties.

Despite the crass attitudes of so many of our educators, or the dehumanization of the form and content of our educational institutions, it would be a mistake to think the problems are only within the educational system. While it is true that education has been stripped of any meaning it once had, and Dr. Conant is reduced to defining education as "what goes on in schools and colleges," our system of schools and colleges is far from a point of collapse. In fact, it is thriving. The "knowledge industry," as Kerr calls it, accounts for 30 per cent of the Gross National Product; and it is expanding at twice the rate of any sector of the economy. Schoolteachers make up the largest single occupational group of the labor force—some three million workers. Twenty-five years ago, the government and industry were hardly interested in education. But in 1960, the aggregate national outlay, public and private, amounted to $23,100,000,000. As Kerr says, "the university has become a prime instrument of national purpose. This is new. This is the essence of the transformation now engulfing our universities." In short, our educational institutions are becoming appendages to, and transformed by, US corporate capitalism.

Education is not being done away with in favor of something called training. Rather, education is being transformed from a quasi aristocratic classicism and petty-bourgeois romanticism into something quite new. These changes are apparent in ways other than the quantitative statistics given above. For example, we can examine the social sciences and the humanities. The social and psychological "reality" that we are given to study is "objectified" to the point of sterility. The real world, we are to understand, is "value free" and pragmatically bears little or no relation to the actual life-activity of men, classes and nations. In one sense, we are separated from life. In another, we are being conditioned for life in a lifeless, stagnant, and sterile society.

For another example, there is more than a semantic connection between the academic division of labor and specialization we are all aware of, and the corresponding division of labor that has gone on in large-scale industry. But it is important to understand what that connection is. It does *not* follow that because technology becomes diversified and specialized, then academic knowledge and skills must follow suit. André Gorz makes the relevant comment:

> It is completely untrue that modern technology demands specialization: quite the reverse. It demands a basic 'polyvalent' education, comprising not a fragmentary, pre-digested and specialized knowledge, but an invitation—or, put more precisely, a faculty of self-initiation—into methods of scientifico-technological research and discovery.

If it is not the new technological production that deems necessary the kind of isolated specialization we know so well, then what is responsible? Gorz spells it out again: "Capitalism actually needs shattered and atomized men" in order to maintain its system of centralized, bureaucratized and militarized hierarchies, so as "to perpetuate its domination over men, not only as workers, but also as consumers and citizens."

From this perspective, we can begin to understand that the educational malaise we as students and teachers have felt so personally and intensely is no aberration, but firmly rooted in the American political economy. In fact, the Organized System which Paul Goodman calls "compulsory mis-education" may miseducate us, but it certainly serves the masters of that system, the US ruling class, quite well. As Edgar Z. Friedenberg wrote: "Educational evils are attributed to *defective* schools. In fact, they are as likely to be the work of *effective* schools that are being directed toward evil ends by the society that supports and controls them" . . .

I think we can conclude that the American educational system is a coherent, well-organized, and—to the extent that the rulers are still ruling—effective mechanism. However, it has turned our humanitarian values into their opposites and, at the same time, given us the potential to understand and critically evaluate both ourselves and the system itself. To that extent the system is fraught with internal contradictions. Furthermore, the events comprising the student revolt in the last few years demonstrate the likelihood that those contradictions will continue to manifest themselves in an open and protracted struggle. As Kerr predicted, we are a source of danger and incipient revolt. And the fact that Kerr was fired and the police used in the face of that revolt only goes to prove that those contradictions are irreconcilable within the structure of corporate capitalism. . . . The central problem of

radically transforming the educational system is that of the transformation of the teaching and the learning body—the faculty and
students. And this transformation, while it *begins* with the demands of the students' and teachers' work situation, cannot take
place unless it occurs *within* and is organically connected *to* the
practice of a mass radical *political* movement.

The Political Economy of the Multiversity

THE KNOWLEDGE FACTORY

What sense does it make to refer to the university as a factory?
Is it just a good analogy? Or is there more to it than that? According to Kerr, "The university and segments of industry are becoming more and more alike." He also informs us that "The university is being called upon to . . . merge its activities with industry
as never before." Furthermore, in terms of control, the merger
that Kerr speaks of seems to have been completed. According to
a study by H. P. Beck,

> Altogether the evidence of major university-business con-
> nections at high levels seems overwhelming. The numerous
> high positions of power in industry, commerce, and finance
> held by at least two-thirds of the governing boards of these
> 30 leading universities would appear to give a decisive major-
> ity more than ample grounds for identifying their personal
> interests with those of business.

Indeed, the boards of regents or trustees of almost every college
and university in the country read off like corporation directories.

But it is not ample proof to call a university a factory merely
because it is controlled by the same people who control industry.
We must look deeper. Let us look at a relatively recent development within the US political economy—the "innovation industry." This aspect of corporate capitalism, usually referred to as "R
and D," Research and Development, has become a major industry. Since 1940 it has grown twenty-seven times over; and it now
accounts for approximately 5 per cent of the over-all federal
budget. What is important for us to see is that 20 per cent of the
work and production of the innovation industry is done directly

within the university. In fact, it is this phenomenon that, since the Second World War, has been transforming the academic landscape into what we now call the "multiversity." Entirely new areas of work have been created—research assistants and technicians, industrial consultants, research promoters, contracting officers, and research project managers.

While research and development can be seen only as an adjunct to the real business of the university—teaching—the position it occupies is much more strategic.

> The men who teach in America's graduate schools determine for the rest of us not only what is true and what is false, but in a large measure what is 'done' and 'not done'. Since the graduate schools are usually a generation ahead of whatever segment of society they lead, their influence at any particular moment always looks modest. Over the years, however, they are perhaps the single most important source of innovation in society.*

And those innovations are important in more ways than we might think. According to Mills, "Research for bureaucratic ends serves to make authority more effective and more efficient by providing information of use to authoritative planners." In the end the multiversity becomes the vanguard of the *status quo,* providing the know-how to gently usher in the New Order of 1984. The clearest manifestation of this trend can be seen in the sciences. Mills concludes: "Science—historically started in the universities, and connected rather informally with private industry—has now become officially established in, for, and by the military order."

So far, we have only seen the connection between the universities and the factories of industry in a secondary sense. It is true that there are parallels between the form and content of the educational system and large-scale industry. It is true that the same people determine the decision-making parameters of both systems. It is true that the non-teaching intellectual work—the innovation industry—produces a commodity directly consumed by industry. All of this is still not sufficient evidence to call our schools

* Christopher Jencs, "The Future of American Education," *The Radical Papers,* p. 271.

"factories," except in an analogous sense. Before we can draw that conclusion, we must look at the *primary* function of our educational system—the work of teaching and learning. . . .

The colleges and universities have gone beyond their traditional task of socialization and acculturation. They are deeply involved in the production of a crucial and marketable commodity —labor power. Again Gorz comments, "the work of learning (and teaching), of extending and transforming professional skills, is implicitly recognized as socially necessary and productive work, through which the individual transforms himself according to the needs of society (and industry)." It is this aspect of the university that is most crucial for the political economy. The production of an increase in socially useful and necessary labor power is the new historic function of our educational institutions that enables us to name them, quite accurately, knowledge factories. In this process of historical change, liberal education has been transformed into its opposite and what we are witnessing is the advent of training and indoctrination. The core of the university with its frills removed has become the crucible for the production, formation, and socialization of the new working class.

What does the interior of the new knowledge factory look like? Where are the workshops? Specifically, these are to be found in the classrooms, the faculty offices, the study rooms in the libraries and homes, the psychological counseling offices and clinics, the conference rooms, the research laboratories, and the administrative staff offices. What kind of machinery can we find in these mental sweatshops? What kind of apparatus have our rulers constructed in the name of our enlightenment? The machinery of knowledge-production pervades the university. And, despite its invisibility, it is no less real or tangible. The productive apparatus consists of grades, exams, assigned books, papers, and reports, all the curriculum and scheduling requirements, non-academic *in loco parentis* regulations, scientific equipment and resources, the mechanics of grants and endowments, disciplinary procedures, campus and civil police, and all the repressive and sublimative psychological techniques of fear and punishment. Most, if not all, of this machinery and the purposes it is used for are beyond the control of the students and faculty who work with it. All government, all control, all the parameters of decision-making have fallen into the hands of the administrative representatives of the ruling class. At best, hand-picked "representatives" of student and faculty "opinion" are prearranged. For example, female students are permitted to determine how strict or "liberal" their dorm hours might be; but the underlying assumption of whether they should have curfews at all is beyond question. Or, while some (but not all) college professors are free to teach *what* they please, they are not "free to decide *how* to teach—whether in large numbers or small, in departmentalized courses or others, one day a week or five."

In the past the work of teaching and learning was a two-way process with the Socratic dialectic as its purest form. However, with the advent of the corporate state and its corresponding appropriation of the cultural apparatus, education has become increasingly one-dimensional. Teaching is reduced to an uncritical distribution of pre-established skills, techniques and "data," while learning is transformed into the passive consumption of the same. In its broadest sense, culture—that which is man-made—is turned into its opposite—anticulture—the creature of expanding production. Education, meaning "to educe," to draw out from, has become something that the state *gives* to people. Finally, teacher and students, both dehumanized distributors and consumers of the knowledge commodity become commodities themselves—something to be bought and sold in the university placement office.

But it is not enough for the knowledge factory to produce skilled labor power in the form of a *raw material*. The commodity must be socially useful as well. When describing the multiversity's machinery Clark Kerr tells us that academic processes and requirements are "part of the process of freezing the structure of the occupational pyramid and assuring that *the well-behaved do advance even if the geniuses do not*" (emphasis mine). Our rough edges must be worn off, our spirit broken, our hopes mundane, and our manners subservient and docile. And if we won't pacify and repress ourselves with all the mechanisms they have constructed for our self-flagellation, the police will be called.

Like any good training program, the knowledge factory accurately reproduces all the conditions and relations of production in the factories of advanced corporate capitalism—isolation, manipulation, and alienation. First, the teaching and learning workers of the knowledge factory are alienated from each other, isolated and divided among themselves by grades, class ranks, and the status levels of the bureaucratic hierarchy. Secondly, they are alienated from the product of their work, the content and purpose of which have been determined and used by someone other than themselves. Finally, they are alienated in the activity of education itself. What should be the active creation and re-creation of culture is nothing more than forced and coercive consumption and distribution of data and technique. Throughout the educational apparatus, the bureaucratic mentality prevails. History and ideology have come to an end. Science, the humanities, even philosophy have become value-free. Politics are reduced to advertising and sales campaigns. Finally government and self-determination become matters of administration and domination.

THE MEANING OF THE STUDENT REVOLT

Our manipulators have overlooked one fundamental factor; there is one facet of human history to which the bureaucratic *Weltanschauung* is blind. Men are not made of clay. Despite all the official pronouncements asserting the end of this or that, the wellsprings of human freedom still run deep. All the attempts to teach ignorance in the place of knowledge have come to naught. The student revolt is an historic event. Someone (the Berkeley students?) let the cat out of the bag. The emperor has no clothes.

Our rulers are aware of this. The bureaucrats of corporate capitalism must cut back and control the quality of and content of "liberal" education. They know only too well that a widespread culture rising out of critical thought might challenge, during a crisis, the existing relations of production and domination. The CIA control of the National Student Association and other "cultural" organizations prove this only too well.

But the corporate ruling class is not primarily interested in containing and pacifying us *as intellectuals.* Their real concern with us lies in our role as the highly skilled members of the new working class. As Gorz points out, "skilled workers . . . possess *in their own right* . . . the labor power they lend." Their skills are an attribute of *themselves* and not just the material means of production. Gorz continues:

> The problem of big management is to harmonize two contradictory necessities: the necessity of developing human capabilities, imposed by modern processes of production and the political necessity of insuring that this kind of development does not bring in its wake any augmentation of the in-

dependence of the individual, provoking him to challenge the present division of social labor and distribution of power.

From this analysis, we can understand the student revolt in its most strategic and crucial sense. What we are witnessing and participating in is an important historical phenomenon: the revolt of the trainees of the new working class against the alienated and oppressive conditions of production and consumption within corporate capitalism. These are the conditions of life and activity that lie beneath the apathy, frustration, and rebellion on America's campuses. André Gorz predicted a few years back: "It is in education that industrial capitalism will provoke revolts which it attempts to avoid in its factories."

Nevertheless, the "student power" movement is still vague and undefined. Its possibilities are hopeful as well as dangerous. On the one hand, student power can develop into an elitist corporate monster, mainly concerned with developing better techniques of "co-managing" the bureaucratic apparatus of advanced industrial society. On the other hand, a student power movement might successfully develop a revolutionary class consciousness among the future new working class, who would organize on their jobs and among the traditional working class around the issues of participatory democracy and worker control. The character of the future movement will depend to a great extent on the kind of strategy and tactics we use in the present. The struggle will be protracted, that is certain. There is no certain or predetermined victory. We should not forget that 1984 is possible. And not many years away. But we have several years of experience behind us from which we can learn a great deal.

From How Harvard Rules, *a critique of Harvard University, compiled by the Africa Research Group, a movement research organization based in Cambridge, Mass., and* The Old Mole, *a radical newspaper, in 1969.*

The Rulers and The Ruled

Harvard University is an ivory tower: an ivory tower atop a castle which is part of a kingdom which, in turn, directs a far-reaching empire. What was long ago clear to the business and political directors of "American Civ." is today clear to everybody else:

American universities—including their historic and elite quintessence, Harvard—are no ethereal communities of scholars. The proverbial absent-minded professors, the archive rats, the bohemians, and the assorted academic odd-balls who are still found on numerous campuses are only the sad but noble remnants of an utterly shattered classical bourgeois ideal of *Universitas*. Today, far from being cut off from the "real world outside," American universities are absolutely central components of the social system of technological warfare-welfare capitalism. The functions, goals, structure, and organization of the universities are directly and indirectly determined by the needs and perspectives of that social system.

Thus it is not really surprising to find that the members of universities' ruling bodies are simultaneously corporation and bank directors, state functionaries, and military chiefs. Nor is it surprising that universities not only tend, increasingly, to *look* like, but actually are key centers of business and military activity. Nor, further, is it particularly amazing that daily life in nearly all universities is bureaucratized, fragmented, mechanized, and mechanical; and that it reproduces itself in the new directors, service personnel, and consumers it "educates."

To be certain, American universities, particularly Harvard, do not contain the systematic and coordinated terror and regimentation of military barracks, concentration camps, or industrial factories. Universities are, most of them, "liberal institutions." This is true in the sense that they are part of the theory and practice of liberal corporate capitalism whose contemporary historical role began with the Open Door policy in Asia at the turn of the century and Wilson's make-the-world-safe-for-democracy intervention against social revolution in Russia and Eastern Europe. It is also true in the sense that universities do indeed function as forums of intellectual debate, dissent, and critical thinking. To equate this latter set of facts with "the University," however, is to confuse a part with the whole—the whole which students are educated to be blind to. For *one* of the central functions of the forum-dialogue-criticism aspect of the university is to weave a democratic veil which enshrouds a concentrated, highly organized, and totally undemocratic system of wealth and power. From the point of view of the university as a structure of power and control, debate, dissent, and criticism are healthy and productive only so long as they leave the power structure untouched. This is a system of dual power in which one side has no power. It is the truth of the phrase: "the market place of ideas," in which ideas and men of ideas are transformed into commodities.

Article by Richard Lichtman, Assistant Professor of Philosophy, University of California, Berkeley, in Center Magazine, *January 1968.*

The University: Mask for Privilege?

Nothing can better illustrate the collapse of reason as an independent, critical agent in our society than a comparison of the remarks of two observers, separated by one hundred years, on the nature of a university education. In the middle of the nineteenth century one of its astutest critics noted:

> The proper function of a University in national education is tolerably well understood. At least there is a tolerably general agreement about what a University is not.
>
> It is not a place of professional education. Universities are not intended to teach the knowledge required to fit men for some special mode of gaining their livelihood. Their object is not to make skillful lawyers, or physicians, or engineers, but capable and cultivated human beings. It is very right that there should be public facilities for the study of professions . . . But these things are no part of what every generation owes to the next, as that on which its civilization and worth will principally depend. They are needed only by a comparative few . . . and even those few do not require them until after their education . . . has been completed . . . Men are men before they are lawyers, or physicians, or merchants, or manufacturers; and if you will make them capable and sensible men, they will make themselves capable and sensible lawyers or physicians.
>
> What professional men should carry away with them from a University, is not professional knowledge, but that which should direct the use of their professional knowledge, and bring the light of general culture to illuminate the technicalities of a special pursuit . . . And doubtless . . . the crown and consummation of a liberal education . . . [is that the

pupil be taught] to methodize his knowledge; to look at every separate part of it in its relation to the other parts, and to the whole . . . observing how all knowledge is connected, how we ascend to one branch by means of another, how the higher modifies the lower and the lower helps us to understand the higher . . . combining the partial glimpses which he has obtained of the field of human knowledge at different points, into a general map . . . of the entire region.

This view has given way in our time to a very different conception:

The University . . . once was an integrated community . . . It had a single purpose . . . The conversation was in common.

This community chose to destroy itself. It became larger. It became heterogeneous. It came to talk in many tongues . . . With the rise of science over the past century, more and bigger laboratories have been required . . . The pressure of population, the explosion of books, the scientific revolution . . . all press for size beyond the limits of the face-to-face and mouth-to-ear community.

Knowledge has expanded and expanded, from theology and philosophy and law and medicine and accounting to the whole range of humanities, the social sciences and the sciences and the professions. More knowledge has resulted from and led to more and more research on a larger and larger scale. Research has led to service for government and industry and agriculture . . . all of this is natural. None of it can be reversed . . . Small intellectual communities can exist and serve a purpose, but they run against the logic of their times.

The campus has evolved consistently with society. It has been pulled outward to society and pulled to pieces internally. The campus consistent with society has served as a good introduction to society—to bigness, to specialization, to diffusion of interests.

The welfare-state university, or multi-university, developed particularly in the United States to provide something for nearly everybody—for farmers, for the minor and newer professions, for the general citizen who wanted to satisfy his curiosity . . . It made the welfare of society in nearly all its aspects a part of its concern . . . the University has served many masters in many ways.

The University and segments of industry are becoming more and more alike. As the University becomes tied to the world of work, the professor—at least in the natural and some of the social sciences—takes on the characteristics of an entrepreneur . . . The two worlds are merging physically . . . [The University is] a mechanism held together by administrative rules and powered by money.

The first of these comments is from John Stuart Mill; the second, from Clark Kerr, until recently President of the University of California.

I have quoted them at length because they illuminate one of the great transitions of the modern age—the decline of autonomous, rational criticism, and the rise of what Professor Herbert Marcuse entitled "one-dimensional man."

They represent the early and terminal stages in the development of centralized, bureaucratic economic power—extended now to such a point that it is able to absorb what was once proclaimed to be a transcendent center of analysis and judgment.

We need not romanticize Mill's age, nor pretend that the university students of whom he spoke acted in radical concert to revise the foundations of their time. They were, in their own way, as readily absorbed into the hierarchy of domestic civil service and foreign imperialism as students of our own society are absorbed into comparable institutions. Of crucial significance is that the very ideal of autonomy has been denied and that those who speak for higher education in this country come increasingly to derive their definition of purpose from the existing agencies of established power.

The pronouncements of Mill and Clark Kerr differ in several significant ways. The first stresses coherence, the second fragmentation; the first is exclusionary, the second is ready to incorporate any interest that society urges upon it; the first distinguishes between higher and lower knowledge, while the second distributes its emphasis in accordance with available financial support. Of greatest importance, perhaps, is that the older view regards itself as bound by intrinsic canons of culture, while the current conception accommodates and molds itself to prevailing trends.

The first view holds to an ideal of transcendence while the second is grossly imminent in its time. For contemporary doctrine, the ancient tension between what the world is and what it might become has all but vanished. The current perspective is an apologia, a celebration, an ideological consecration of this most lovely of all possible worlds—in short, a consenting academy.

This conclusion follows directly from Mr. Kerr's own analysis, for if the University performs all the functions that society imposes upon it, it will in due course most ably fulfill the predominant function every social system requires for its very existence—the justification of its established structure of power and privilege, the masking or idealization of its deficiencies, and the discrediting of dissent.

The history of all previous societies reveals to us a group of men whose primary function was to legitimate established authority. Our own time is only notable for the special urgency it imposes on the task. There are various domestic and international reasons for this development.

The first concerns the growing complexity of our technological order and its encompassing social organizations. The requirements of intelligence become more exact and the skills needed for managerial and bureaucratic roles more demanding. Accompanying these economic developments is the parallel transformation of the society from one concerned primarily with the manipulation of material things to one concerned with the manipulation of individuals. The role of physical labor declines and the role of intellectual skills and personal services is augmented in a growing white-collar stratum.

There is a change in emphasis in the industrial system from force to persuasion, a growth of public relations, managerial counseling, and mass advertising; in short, an extensive shift from production to consumption and from overt authority to covert ideological inducement.

Second, the development of a mass society tied less to specific locations and cultural traditions than to the common mass media for the formation of their life styles produces a populace eager to be formed and potentially dangerous to the status quo if it is not adequately standardized.

Again, the growing education level and sophistication of some sectors of the population make it necessary to mollify the possible dissent of those who might discover flaws in the social facade.

But, paradoxically, the development of education facilitates this enterprise, for there are some deceptions which only a semi-educated man could be expected to believe or sacrifice his life for.

But the most important internal need for ideology grows from the slowly developing awareness of the discrepancy between what this social system has the power to provide its members and what it actually makes available to them. Technological resources are adequate to provide a very high level of material welfare to the entire population if the control over these facilities can be made to pass progressively from the hands of a self-authenticating business autocracy to the authority of the people as a whole.

Venerable arguments for the necessity of social injustice, class privilege, physical and cultural deprivation, and the dehumanization of labor are being corroded by the potentialities of abundance. Those who hold power in this system, then, are forced to construct elaborate theories to justify persisting misery. Here, the aid of the University can prove extremely valuable.

But there are two additional motives for illusion which derive from the international position of the United States today. Both stem from the fact of America's predominant economic power and expansiveness in the world, from its dominance over foreign economies on a global scale, and from the need generated by its productive system for subservient foreign nations to act as the suppliers of its resources and the outlets for its dislocations.

The two challenges come from the Soviet Union and China on the one hand, and from the underdeveloped third of the world on the other. The first are threats because they reject capitalistic values and compete with us in the world for economic power. The second set of nations is even more disquieting, however, for they are seeking their self-liberation at the precise moment at which the United States has emerged unmistakably as the world's dominant imperialist power. But we are not prepared to grant them control of their own industrial development, and our counter-effort is an attempt to destroy their movement toward economic autonomy through financial pressure when possible, and military intervention when necessary.

The national attempt at defense against these threats to the United States world hegemony produced the hysteria of the last twenty years of rabid anti-communism and cold-war containment—the euphemism for America's self-righteousness in domination. Intellectuals have played a significant role in producing the obfuscations of the time, and the educational system has been one of the leading contributors to the pathology of awareness.

Vigorous rebellion or revolution may fail to occur for two very different reasons: either because men are so equal to each other in their social relations that it is unnecessary, or because, while radically unequal, they perceive no way of altering their situation. But the development of technology in this country is making it progressively clearer to the impoverished in this country and to the underdeveloped countries that the suffering and injustice they are forced to undergo is not inevitable. Therefore, the more technology develops, and the more its benefits are expropriated by the privileged of the world, the greater becomes the need of the dominant class to cloak its injustice and to pretend that its actions are in the common interest or beyond the powers of men to change.

The growing division between what the world is and what it might become is the primary force behind the intensification of ancient ideological functions.

The consequence of these various internal and external pressures is that the United States is urgently compelled to disarm radical dissent and insure the performance of roles necessary to continued international hostility.

Those in power recognize the importance of domestic consensus to achieve these ends. The educational views of men like Mr. Kerr, which stress the need for molding reason to the pattern of contemporary power, appear conveniently to facilitate economic and military service and the soothing of discontent.

A University patterned after Mill's ideal could not possibly perform this task, but the contemporary University performs it masterfully. Approximately 75 per cent of the research budget of the University derives from Federal contracts, and, as Mr. Kerr notes: "Expenditures have been largely restricted to the physical and bio-medical sciences, and to engineering, with only 3 per cent for the social sciences and hardly any support for the humanities."

This distribution is defended on the grounds that it represents the national interest and the flow of money after "the most exciting new ideas." What we are being offered here is a new version of the invisible hand in which Gresham's Law is inverted to the effect that good money always drives out bad money and produces just that balance which promotes the public good.

The Federal funding of the University is only one of the media through which the pattern of society is impressed on higher education, but it exemplifies the defects transmitted through all the available media. The most crucial of these corruptions is the destruction of the internal community of the University and its replacement by a series of fragmented and isolated departmental structures without common speech, common imagination, or common purpose.

Mill's conception of a university as a place in which the student was taught to "methodize his knowledge; to look at every separate part of it in its relation to the other parts, and to the whole," is not only all but nonexistent in the current academic world, it is increasingly difficult for a growing number of educators to understand. Mr. James A. Perkins, President of Cornell, for example, has suggested that the conflict between research and scholarship might be reconciled by simply abandoning liberal education and beginning the process of specialization at matriculation. (*The University in Transition.* Princeton University Press: 1966.)

The causes of the diffusion of the University need be noted solely for the light they throw on the nature of the disintegration involved. The reason most intrinsic to the University is the fact that knowledge has been growing at a very rapid rate, making it continually more difficult for any one thinker to grasp the whole domain. But this in itself would not produce the fragmentation which occurs (since it is not the case that everything known must be taught by a university) except for the presence of other factors.

First, there is a tendency to refinement in specialized roles which seems to occur in all advanced technological societies. Next, there are the distinctly American elaborations of this theme. One derives from the anti-intellectualism of our life with its distrust of achievement for its own sake and consequent insistence that thought subserve specific ends and redeem itself through the practical results of concrete actions. To this must be added the sense of many intellectuals that if they cannot alter the shape of massive, unresponsive social power they can at least derive some satisfaction by serving it.

In this mood reason gives up the claim to direct social change. It settles instead for the immediate rewards of technical manipulation and becomes an efficient means to ends beyond its power or judgment.

The tendency is strengthened by a widespread assumption that in America the good life has already been achieved in a system of democratic, corporate pluralism. The quest of the ages having been completed, there is nothing more for reason to do but maintain the current structure and make the necessary minor corrections. This tendency is supported by the loose, casual patterning of American life, the laissez-faire climate of American political and economic history, and the general conviction that the pursuit of private, local ends will miraculously produce a public good.

It is not that public life is devoid of integration and rational planning. Industrial firms plan to the limits of their ability, and the foresight of some oligopolies and international cartels is undoubtedly extensive. But these plans are made and the activities coordinated for the sake of individual corporate ends, not for the sake of the polity as a whole. Nothing displays such technical intelligence and ingenuity as an automated factory and produces such irrational dislocation in the lives of men who are unemployed through this human achievement. The sense of the whole system is of rationality defeating its own humane requirements.

As Mr. Kerr has led us to expect, this pattern of sporadic rationality in conflict with its own potential achievement is found within the structure of the University. There, education is defined mechanically as the piling up of specific skills and bits of information, as a mound is constructed out of the piling up of individual grains of sand. The student is never required to state the relevance of one area of understanding for another, nor relate their distinctive methodologies and insights in coherent, synthetic connection. It is assumed that the summation of individually correct answers will produce something more than fragmented understanding.

The center of this disruptive environment is the individual department, where men competing for recognition establish small empires under a mutual security agreement that insures each the safety of his own domain. This safety is further enhanced against the forays of others by increasingly narrowing the limits of one's investigation until the subject is so esoteric that each individual can rightly claim to be the only living authority in the field.

Such a systematic fragmenting of knowledge cannot be corrected by the simple insertion into the curriculum of a few interdisciplinary courses. If the teachers of these courses have to win departmental approval, they are likely to come under the wrath of specialists who rightly see in the man of vision a threat to their insular success. Furthermore, as the current system prevails, the continued existence of comprehensive teachers is more and more problematical.

The immediate result is that the University is more and more populated by scholar-researchers who more closely resemble idiot-savants than men of wisdom; students find it more and more difficult to gain some comprehensive vision of themselves as world-historical beings.

In the social sciences it is very close to the truth to maintain that any problem which appears open to solution within a specific discipline is either misunderstood or of secondary importance. But the most important, over-all effect of this continued division of incommunicable skill is its ideological consequence—the tendency to stifle social consciousness and the need for radical social change.

A large social vision need not be radical, but a fragmented vision cannot be radical. The piecemeal, technical thinker can see a small advantage here and a corresponding defect there. His vision is additive; he sums up the merits and defects of a system and makes his judgment in the face of the total balance. What he lacks is dialectical understanding, the capacity to see how a specific social defect is rooted in a large structural pattern—for example, how the abuses revealed in the drug industry stem from the irresponsible power and social avarice of corporate liberalism as a system, and indicate the hopelessness of conventional attempts at regulation. Or the technical thinker sees a particular social benefit, such as the increase in average working class wages and gross national product, but he lacks any capacity to place this fact in the context of fixed maldistribution of income, or in the larger system of exploitative relations which America bears to the underdeveloped nations of the world.

That ideology is generally an inversion of reality is borne out by the current educational situation, for the University is in the process of intellectual dissolution at that precise moment of history in which the development of centralized, burcaucratic corporate power has been dominating progressively larger areas of national and international life and drawing the world's economy and destiny into an increasingly seamless whole.

The period of American domination over the world economy

coincides with the period in which global concepts have been increasingly abandoned by large numbers of social scientists, whose range of interest has contracted; in specific areas of inquiry the problems they confront are of very limited relevance to the emerging world reality.

This confinement of understanding disrupts the foundations of intellectual life. The man of reason is being dismembered before our eyes. In his place appear pairs of adversaries—the teacher stands against the researching scholar, the man of thought against the man of action, the neutral analyst against the man of passionate commitment.

In the University the teacher retreats before the onslaught of the research technologists and knowledge diffusers. Every university maintains a house Negro or two—a professor whose advancement has been based predominantly upon his power as a teacher and who is dragged out on ceremonial occasions to silence the critic. But for every such anachronism there are one hundred practitioners of the conventions who have scrambled to respectability over a mass of journals and anthologies. The teacher who embodies a vision, whose life manifests in its own activity the content of his teaching art, is vanishing from sight.

What the current generation of students discovers immediately in those who profess to teach them is an almost impassable chasm between the nature of their intellectual pronouncements and the content of their lives. This is one of the grounds of the charge of irrelevance in education and one of the main reasons for student disaffection. Nor is it a defect that can be remedied without transforming the University, and that would in turn require the radical reconstruction of the society in which the University exists.

As William Arrowsmith has commented,

> At present the universities are as uncongenial to teaching as the Mojave Desert to a clutch of Druid priests. If you want to restore a Druid priesthood, you cannot do it by offering prizes for Druid-of-the-year. If you want Druids, you must grow forests. There is no other way of setting about it.

If it is in fact true that the University has become a service adjunct to prevailing social powers it should not be surprising that so much of its activity is taken up in the intense cultivation of disinterested intelligence. There is a clue to this process in one of the works of the German aesthetician Wilhelm Worringer. In his book, *Abstraction and Empathy* (International Universities Press: 1963), he identifies naturalism with a feeling of confidence in the external world, and particularly the organic, living world. The experience of naturalistic art is held to depend on the subject's identification with organic forms as exemplified in his own existence. Abstract art, on the contrary, is traced to a feeling of anguish and confusion in face of the complexity and instability of living beings; it is viewed as an attempt to flee this realm of dissolution for the sanctity of abstract order.

A great deal of contemporary research appears to be similarly motivated. If it is not immediately useful to established power it tends to withdraw and place between itself and the anxieties and responsibilities of the world what Bullough called "aesthetic distance" and what W. H. Auden referred to as "lecturing on Navigation while the ship is going down."

The University can accommodate itself to national power in one of two ways—overtly or covertly, through subservience or indifference, through the performance of assigned tasks, or the distraction and trivialization of potentially critical thought.

For subservience we can do no better than the introduction to Seymour Martin Lipset's *Political Man* (Doubleday: 1959). We discover there a number of astounding things: "that the United States [is] a nation in which leftist values predominate"; that "the values of liberty and equality become institutionalized within America to a greater extent than in other nations"; that "the values of socialism and Americanism are similar"; that, economic systems apart, Herbert Hoover, Andrew Carnegie, and John D. Rockefeller "advocated the same set of social relations among men" as Marx, Engels, and Lenin; that democratic regimes are characterized by an underlying desire to avoid war.

The key to this innovative reconstruction of history is provided in the last chapter of the volume, wherein we are informed that

> . . . the fundamental political problems of the industrial revolution have been solved: the workers have achieved industrial and political citizenship; the conservatives have accepted the welfare state; and the democratic left has recognized that an increase in over-all state power carries with it more dangers to freedom than solutions for economic problems.

How good it must be to see the world as sociologists see it—devoid of economic exploitation, of Iran, Guatemala, the Dominican Republic, and Vietnam; devoid of poverty, injustice, and brutalized technology. History may yet record these sweet reflections less as a hymn to quietude than as the last muffled cry of the ostrich as its mouth fills up with sand. . . .

The fragmented intellect lives in comparative safety and quiet in the security of its own conceptual enclave. Here, it sets barriers against reason and the world. One social scientist tells us:

> . . . science achieves its unparalleled powers by the continuous breakdown of its problem into smaller units and refinements of methods made possible by this division. On the other hand, so deeply entrenched is the humanistic supposition that "to see a man at all one must see him whole" that not even the continuous work on the dikes of their separate disciplines by academicians can keep social thought flowing in its prescribed channels without continuous leakage into and from others. (Don Martindale, *Functionalism in the Social Sciences.* American Academy of Political and Social Sciences: 1960.)

One can almost feel the shudder along the author's pen as he notes the "leakage" which tends to confuse the comfortable precision of his categories. Nor are we surprised when he proceeds to inform us that the social sciences must analyze their "problems dispassionately in a value-neutral manner," and that the aim of "turning these disciplines into genuine sciences"—that is, of breaking them down into smaller conceptual units—"is only possible through dredging operations to remove moral commitments that block the development of scientific objectivity." In these few lines, fragmentation, neutralism, the assimilation of the social to the physical sciences, and the confinement of thought to disinterested contemplation, the entire mythos of contemporary social science is concentrated and made apparent.

The connection among these factors is no mere accident. There are some perceptive comments on this matter in E. P. Thompson's *The Making of the English Working Class* (Pantheon: 1964). At one point the author comments on the contemporary discussion among historians on what has come to be known as "the standards of living controversy." He maintains:

The objection to the reigning academic orthodoxy is not to empirical studies, per se, but to the fragmentation of our comprehension of the full historical process. First, the empiricist segregates certain events from this process and examines them in isolation. Since the conditions which gave rise to these events are assumed, they appear not only as explicable in their own terms but as inevitable . . . But there is a second stage, where the empiricist may put these fragmentary studies back together from a multiplicity of interlocking inevitabilities, a piecemeal processional . . . we arrive at a post facto [sic] determinism. The dimension of human agency is lost.

We have come across the language of inevitability before. It was Mr. Kerr who informed us that the "community of scholars disappeared gradually and inevitably over the centuries . . . [that the University] must adapt sufficiently to its culture if it is to survive. All of this is natural. None of it can be reversed." One is inclined to reply that the inevitability of history could only have proceeded through the choice of human beings like Mr. Kerr and others who played a significant role in forming education in our time. In Mr. Kerr's analysis, however, human agency is made to dissolve, and a new rational man appears who is simply the vessel of necessity.

The crux of this conception is Mr. Kerr's judgment that the process is *natural,* a view which assimilates human history to the processes of nature and the physical sciences, in which the observer contemplates the behavior of material which possesses no responsibility for the direction of its process.

No reading of the future could have prescribed to American educators the choice they should have made for the American University—this choice was dependent upon the values, principles, and limited wisdom they brought to their understanding of history. What we are really being told in these fragments is that the American educator chose to capitulate to one of the tendencies of his time, that he agreed to relinquish his rational autonomy, and that, having made this specific decision, he is now incapable of regarding himself as anything more than the medium through which the course of the future blindly passes. But this logic unmasks the myth of neutrality, for the choice of passivity, the commitment to subservience, produced the observer's sense that he is the mere conductor of an irreversible process.

The same loss of rational autonomy and moral responsibility which underlies the division between thought and action is the source, too, of the dichotomies of fact and value, means and ends.

The prevailing credo of contemporary social inquiry limits reason to an analysis of those means which will lead most efficiently to given ends; reason is strictly precluded from passing judgment on the ends themselves. The value of the exercise is said to lie in the accumulation of stores of neutral knowledge, useful for whatever ends we intend to employ them.

The significance of this position is that it places reason and technological expertise at the disposal of prevailing power. The thinker who has abdicated responsibility for the purpose of his life by placing control over his actions in powers beyond his authority has made himself a hostage to the times. Having relinquished his claim to normative reason, he is without mooring in the world. The tides of current times, degenerate as they may be, will sweep the uncommitted in their course.

We are witness to the spectacle of men of small imagination, limited in comprehension to diminishing areas of inquiry, lacking the capacity to note the import of their activity for the more pervasive aspects of human enterprise, subservient to an establishment that does not hesitate to use them for the most inhuman and obnoxious ends—men of technical reason, as skilled at killing as at healing, progressively unconcerned with the distinction, and unaware that value resides anywhere but in technique itself. So, crippled reason pays obeisance to power and the faculty in man most apt to nurture life becomes the instrument of violence and death.

The consequence of fragmentation and of a division in the life of reason is the destruction of human autonomy. The University is thickly populated by cynical or silent men. In response to the compartmentalization of intelligence, pseudo-syntheses appear—unified visions of social man, built on the crudest model of physics or animal psychology. A widespread behaviorism appears in social thought, grounded in a methodology derived third-hand from a defunct philosophy. Quality, uniqueness, creativity, and the moral dimension of existence fall before a reductive insistence upon measurement, qualification, and restrictive processes of infinitely tedious and irrelevant observation. The view of man which emerges is ahistorical, atomistic, mechanical, disjunctive, and, again, ostensibly neutral.

We are instructed by an advocate of scientific method in sociology:

> Scientific knowledge operates . . . as a sort of mental hygiene in the fields where it is applied . . . the advancement of the social sciences would probably deprive us in large measure of the luxury of indignation in which we now indulge ourselves as regards social events . . . Such indignation ministers to deep-seated, jungle-fed sentiments of justice, virtue, and a general feeling of the fitness of things, as compared with what a scientific diagnosis of the situation evokes. (George A. Lundberg, *Can Science Save Us?* Longmans, Green: 1947.)

Justice, then, according to this account, is merely a vestige of primitive existence, to be dispensed with by mature, scientific awareness. We ought not to be surprised, then, when the author develops the logical conclusion of his analysis in the following suggestion:

> If social scientists possessed an equally demonstrably relevant body of knowledge [as physical scientists] . . . that knowledge would be equally above the reach of political upheaval. The services of real social scientists would be as indispensable to Fascists as to Communists and Democrats, just as are the services of physicists and physicians.

This is merely the rationale of intellectual subservience carried to fruition. If the militarized, economic bureaucracy that defines established power in this country has no need for culture, if neutral technology is what it wants, the handmaiden of power but compliant as to ends, what shall we expect the "service-station" University to become but the internalized, refined, and rationalized conception of this barbarism?

If the humanities present man with an embodied vision of his full potentialities, they are of no use to power, and they will decline. Thought and action define each other; men of technical reason and great power brutalize the world, confirming by that fact those views which contract humanity to its prevailing business and which send men forth into the world again with more restricted versions of themselves. The dehumanization of man is reflected in the dehumanization of the study of man; its categories contract and dissolve.

We come at last to the scholarship of civility: devoid of passion, lacking love or outrage, irrelevant to the agency of man. "The advancement of learning at the expense of man," Nietzsche wrote, "is the most pernicious thing in the world."

Exactly what is the moral obligation of the University as a corporate body? It is no use telling us now, as we were told recently by Richard Hofstadter, that while individual members of the University may voice conviction, the University as a public institution is bound to strict neutrality. Mr. Kerr has demolished that argument for all time. It is no less neutral to oppose society than to support it, to refuse a place to military service than to credit it.

Neutrality is only conceivable with isolation. Nothing in the public realm can fail, at specific points, to aid or undermine established power. Man's existence is only possible through action, which requires the selection of choices and the foreclosure of others. One cannot, in all instances, avoid choice; the only hope is to choose responsibly, in light of the largest understanding and the most humane commitment.

As the University is rooted in the world, it must, at given moments, choose a public course. The liberal contention that the University should refrain from criticism is an expression of "preferential neutralism," a transparently hypocritical device for the maintenance of continued service.

Of course, it is not the corporate function of the University to speak to every public issue, nor even to the vast majority of prevailing social concerns. The fundamental purpose of the University does not encompass any specific policy in regard to most contemporary matters. In its public pronouncement and corporate activity, the University should refrain from endorsing particular views in the overwhelming number of cases. But when the University's support is solicited by established agencies of power, it must decide if the services requested of it violate its defining purpose, and reject them if they do. And so, it is also obligated to protest when society has undertaken to violate, in regard either to the University itself or to humanity at large, values that the University is specifically charged to honor.

To discover the public function of a University one must begin with its internal imperative—the gathering of a community of scholars in devotion to disinterested knowledge. Such, at least, is the traditional wisdom. But it is not adequate to our time.

John Stuart Mill wrote for an age in which the distinction between pure and applied research was largely valid. The man of science could pursue his theory in the general expectation that it would not be employed to endanger mankind. Today the distinction between pure and applied science is disappearing with the growth of a state power so imperious and technologically competent that it can transform the most esoteric knowledge into techniques of terror.

Science has itself contributed to the creation of that state machinery which now makes the enterprise of science hazardous. It has done so because it has lacked responsibility for its growth. It is too late now to fall back on the platitudes of academic freedom; no biochemist can be sure that in pursuing the structure of an enzyme he is not perfecting a lethal form of warfare. This government will have to be disarmed before the clear and present danger now subverting thought can be dissolved. Until men of knowledge act to change the world, they cannot claim the unrestricted right to understand it.

But what is the obligation of those members of the University whose knowledge cannot be technologized? To answer this question we must answer another. What is the true nature of the University?

The University is the institutionalized embodiment of the life of the dialogue; that is, of communal inquiry. Dialogue is rooted in the fact that men are imperfect and perfectible. Comprehensive knowledge is not given to man in an instant. It is the elaboration of history. Nor is it given to any single man; it is the cooperative achievement of a human community. Dialogue cannot be perfected unless it is free, and the basis of rational freedom is the self-determination of imperfect reason by its own ideal. It is freeing because it liberates intelligence from matter that is extraneous or destructive of its inherent purpose—knowledge.

A mind in pursuit of knowledge is one in which the various facets of awareness are active, cumulative, and mutually relevant, wherein observation, inference, imagination, and evaluative judgment inform each other in a cumulative achievement. It is a process which depends upon creativity—the capacity to construct new alternatives. To this end the University cultivates the arts, whose function is not merely to act as a critical interpreter of experience, but to manifest to us, through concrete works, those ideal possibilities of existence of which we were previously unaware. Whatever the differences between art and discursive reason, they share a common enterprise: they cultivate the human spirit, which is the capacity of man to transcend his present context for the sake of a more comprehensive, articulate, and worthy vision of himself. That vision, in all its forms, is culture, which it is the obligation of the University to honor and protect.

The peculiar alienation of the intellectual leads him to pursue culture as an abstract end. He becomes blind to the simple fact that there is no knowledge independent of the "knowings" of individual men, nor any realm of art or science separate from the creations of actual, concrete human beings. What the University is meant to house and celebrate is not a detached domain of lifeless categories, but the spiritual existence of man, in which those categories live and take their meaning.

What is the obligation of the University in a world in which one nation is reducing the people of another to the most primitive functions of its existence; when the very rudiments of civilization are being extinguished and the orders of life upon which reason grows are being destroyed by systematic violence? In such circumstances it is the obligation of the University to rebel against the violation of man and align itself in public witness with humanity.

Today, the University is required to condemn the government of the United States for its barbaric crusade against the life and spirit of the people of Vietnam. A university that will not speak for man, whatever tasks it continues to perform, has ceased to be a human enterprise.

The University can deny its times because, like any human agency, it is not wholly absorbed in its social context. It has a special capacity to transcend its social constraints because it embodies a tradition of intellectual diversity and articulate criticism and because, of all human functions, thought is the most difficult to curtail. But while the University is uniquely promising, it is also uniquely threatened by the pressures of ideology to which we have already referred. The University is in constant tension between its ideal critical capacity and the powers of secular service that delimit its hope. Therefore, while the protest movement is centered in the University, the activity of protest is not central to the University.

It is possible to act to change the world because we are not totally imminent in it; but it is necessary for us to change the world because we do not very much transcend it. Here is the point of truth in the conception of the multiversity. The sheer understanding that society is corrupt does not place one outside corruption. For we do not experience social existence at a distance, we ingest it. The act by which the University affirms its humanity and denies American barbarism does not constitute the cure of the University.

It may be, as Hegel has noted, that the hand that inflicts the wound is the hand that cures it. But it does so only through an anguished labor. One cannot throw off all he has been made in the density of the social world with a simple shrug of the understanding. Plato knew this truth two thousand years ago. We are still bound by it. The University has been molded by current powers and we have been formed and malformed in our turn. The alienation of society has become our apathy and fragmentation; its anti-intellectualism and glorification of technology, our play at neutralism in an inversion of ends and means; its crude devotion to wealth and power, our imbalance and intellectual prostitution.

To reconstitute one's self is for a man to remake the world in which he is defined. To know what we might become is not a simple act of the intellect; it requires that we engage in such committed action as can destroy the deforming boundaries of our lives. So, action and thought require each other, inform each other, and complete each other. The obligation imposed on the intellectual, as it is imposed on any one man, is not merely to speak against the world but to refashion it.

It is not a violation of the purpose of a university that some part of its activity serve society; but the University must determine through its own critical agency that the society it is to serve is a place in which the spirit of man may be nurtured and advanced.

The University is at this moment an ideological institution, a mask for systematic dominance and privilege. But as Marx noted: "The call for men to abandon their illusions about their condition is a call for men to abandon a condition which requires illusion." A free and human community of scholars can only flourish when the multitudinous communities of the exploited, the wretched, and the brutalized peoples of the earth have broken the bonds of their subservience and established themselves as men of full stature. To participate in the projection and the making of that world is the responsibility of the intellectual.

Paper by the Radical Action Cooperative, a group at Teachers College, Columbia University, July 28, 1968.

Life, Not Survival—A Manifesto

The Disaster

The University

The University functions as a production line of servant-technicians to operate our inhuman, economic-oriented system. Like other commodity businesses, Teachers College is client-oriented rather than being a community of scholars. It treats people (students, faculty, employees, and neighbors alike) as objects serving this system of inhuman values. Students are the raw material, which, treated as objects, turn into robots. The criterion of efficiency demands homogenization, the elimination of all differences between individuals. Human lives and joyful experience are at best only second in priority.

Education in this sense is conditioning, where the grades are the bell associated with the pellets rewarding conformity. We have been conditioned to seek "good grades" as if they were a genuinely satisfying reward. We wind up postponing any real fulfillment indefinitely: from high school to college, to an advance degree, to a good-paying job, to a suburban home, sexy Madison Avenue wife, kids, car, boat, etc. Once you've gotten there, what you find is an imitation giving no satisfaction at all, just as the Society in front of us is an imitation. Just taste an ice-milk popsicle, or a bottle of coke, or a piece of "Wonder" bread. . . .

The Irrational Commodity System

The logical results of our commodity system are irrational. Almost everything is inauthentic. The question is never, "Is this a good, useful, satisfaction- and joy-producing product?", but rather, "Does it sell?". The fantastic absurdity of this system is revealed in its necessity to create artificial needs. It was not sufficient merely to stuff the consumer full of real products, for he became so gorged as to threaten no longer to consume. So the system had to create needs for unreal products: milk-less milk shakes, fat-less fat (or imitation margarine), etc. Further artificial commodities help alienate us from ourselves: cosmetics, deodorants, etc. Modern man consumes himself out of existence. His face is something to put make-up on (as in the expression, "Put your face on"), his body is to put clothes on, his feet to put shoes on; otherwise, there are no face, body, and feet. His body as a whole is no more than a vehicle for commodities.

The University Concluded

We've seen that the University serves the purposes of the production and consumption commodity system rather than the realization of the individual's life. Instead of offering a unitary outlook on reality, the University imposes a partial and fractionated perception of reality expressed through its innumerable artificially separated disciplines. Thus, the communication of "knowledge" is reduced to "education" that is, to an ever-increasing conditioning. Similarly, culture becomes a sales agent for commodities; life becomes a commodity in itself. Culture defines the norms of prestige, status, and other artificial satisfactions; having been inculcated with culture, we buy what it tells us to buy. The end of this system of education is nothing more than performance, while creativity is not recognized and is often penalized for being dysfunctional to high rates of performance.

The World at Large

The cretinism of the University is the same as that which permeates a world where we, Blacks and Whites together, starve in the midst of affluence. This starvation is both physical, emotional, and spiritual (the distinction is analytic; concretely they are interdependent). We work at obsolete and boring jobs and are manipulated by the carrot and the stick. The carrot is the meaningless monetary reward which is incapable of buying anything worthwhile; the stick is the fear of the Bowery, the Draft and death. Because he recognizes the existence of both the carrot and the stick, the Conservative has a logically consistent argument. The Liberal, in contrast, denies the existence of the stick, for his professed humanism makes it impossible to accept the pain of another human's suffering. His blindness renders him incapable of coming up with truly workable solutions to problems. He has an unfounded faith in gradualism and continues to support a system which murders Kennedys, Martin Luther Kings, thousands in Vietnam, and more thousands in the streets of our cities. The material and psychological misery is disguised by the empty labels of "Peace," "Freedom," and "Democracy." Furthermore, the response of this monster system to the attempts of rational men to change it is to repress that change in the name of "Law and Order."

Driven by the System's efficiency syndrome, in the name of economics, the Eichmanns of this system, the McNamaras and the McLuhans, perpetuate in their inhuman-scientific way the unidimensionality of this world.

Daily Death

What this all boils down to in our daily lives is subjection, dependence, pursuit of artificial desires, alienated choices, and stultified existence. The grand result is raising the "Standard of Boredom," expressed in the ultimate absurdity "THINK MONEY." If you think of this phrase only as an absurdity, then you become a revolutionary to replace the entire system, for you have nothing to lose. The choice between being a cynic and being a revolutionary is the choice between impotence and sexuality, for all humans, males and females alike.

A New Society—Our Aspiration

Driven to the brink of suicide, the individual and the society as a whole have no other choice than to radically change perspectives. In doing so, we transcend deterministic economic history and begin to create history ourselves. We create a nutrient biological and psychological environment, one that promotes the development of every individual's creativity. We respect every individual because we believe in his creative potential, not because of his superficial appearance (black, white, red, or yellow) or by happenstance of birth (rich or poor). We seek to build cooperative interaction between individuals in society as opposed to the individualistic, competitive American model. We seek to avoid independent specialization—specialization as an end in itself divorced from other areas of human concern. We seek to develop into whole men and women, integrating the intellectual, emotional, and physical sides of our beings. We seek to replace anxiety, guilt, and shame as the driving mechanisms of modern men with security, self-trust, and joy. We prefer to let men work from the presupposition of security rather than of insecurity.

We recognize the ultimate purpose of life as the realization of the creative potential of every individual, as opposed to an existence torn to the shreds of schizophrenia in role-playing, work, family life, leisure, etc.

From a statement by Jacques Barzun, University Professor, Columbia University, at congressional hearings on campus unrest conducted by the House of Representatives, Special Subcommittee on Education of the Committee on Education and Labor, May 9, 1969.

The Danger of "Public Service"

I think the American university has made a record as possibly the freest institution ever conceived, and its record for 75 years is something to be proud of.

But it is generally unknown to the American public, even to those who have been through it. They don't know how it works. Maybe that is a tribute to how well it did work. At any rate, the chairman referred to the last book I wrote, called "The American University," in which I undertook, because of my sense of the public's ignorance of a university, to show how it works, what the elements are that come together and how they mesh and produce the results that they have produced.

If I may summarize the description, it is simply this: In order to maintain the proper conditions for science and scholarship in the American university, all legitimate freedoms were protected. Faculty tenure protected the scholars from the trustees, from the administration, and from one another.

The students had wide freedoms, too. They had easy and informal access to their teachers, they had a wide choice of programs, they were saved at every turn from wasting time through changes of mind because they could transfer most of their credits from one program to another, and, moreover, they had the right to publish newspapers untouched, and even to be rude and insulting in them.

They had many opportunities to criticize the program and their own teachers to their advisors, to the dean, and they could hear outside opinions ad lib. Their clubs could invite anybody, and almost everybody got a hearing sometime, somewhere on a campus.

The administration of this institution served, and did not command. It was a buffer between the trustees and the faculties. It interpreted each to the other, and interpreted both to the alumni.

The administration worked very largely with faculty advice and consultation. There are many committees that faculties complain of. The trustees tended to withhold their hand from administration, and certainly altogether from academic matters. The image of the trustees dominating, demanding, and ordering is a complete myth.

And we should note on the question of prestige the success of great cases of support for academic freedom by presidents against alumni feeling and against trustee dismay, beginning with Lowell of Harvard in 1916, which led to his statement of what academic freedom is, a statement just as good today as it was then, right down to President Brewster of Yale, who defended Staughton Lynd when the alumni were up in arms.

The record of the administrations in supporting freedom on the campus is notable. The American university, in a word, was governed by influence, and not power. Nobody had power in the university, not even the president.

Its acts internally did not spring from any decision-making, as the cliché now supposes, but from deference to the common interest. Everybody deferred to something else for the purpose of common academic life. The purposes were rationality and civility, all of which was shattered when the first bull horn was heard on the campus.

Now, how did the deterioration take place? It was very rapid and very surprising to everybody. I think in the first place the university was partly responsible. It indulged a mistaken desire to enlarge its role through what it called public service, as if it had not performed public service before.

This new role was inevitable in time of war, but it continued after 1945, and turned the university into a sort of catch-all institution for doing whatever anybody thought was worth doing that wasn't done somewhere else.

Government, industry, the foundations, particularly the big ones, and private donors all had schemes for the university to carry out.

This was a logical result of seeing the great value of knowledge and expertise, but it was mistaken in the belief that the good results could be engineered, something which in my book I call "preposterism."

That is, putting before what comes as a natural result later.

We see that certain things are good when they occur naturally. We say, "Why can't we do them on purpose from the start?"

That seems to me a vitiating attempt.

Results were very unexpected. With their good intentions, faculty members became globetrotters and project directors, and that resulted in the universities true service being damaged, and moreover obscured it in the eyes of the public, which didn't know much about universities anyway.

Under the new and multiplying "services," teaching was neglected, and a sort of buzzing activity replaced quiet thought.

On the other hand, the result of these new activities out in the world brought forth the normal criticism that the public has a right to level at any of its service centers.

So, the university became a common target, an object of complaint, pressure, abuse, and further demand. By its very nature, it couldn't fight back. It has no press of its own, it has no party behind it. It is vulnerable, and it fell.

So, we ask, what is the true idea of the university, how does it best serve society?

My answer is very simple. It is radical. In fact, I might say that in university matters, there are perhaps only two radicals in the whole country, Mr. Robert Hutchins and myself. We got to the root of what a university was ever set up for, and we say it was to learn and to teach.

Students learn, teachers teach, and learn some more. The idea of the university in one word, is "study." There is no limit to what can be studied at the university, provided that the subject is capable of being reduced to principles, which then form the basis of training.

The university produces trained minds, and they, of course, can go out and apply concretely and usefully to all sorts of problems, current problems, what they have learned from a broad and deep survey of reality.

So, for example, if there are rational solutions to urban and minority problems, those solutions will rise from a study of this kind, and I am convinced that the roundabout way is the shortest path.

Solutions aren't likely to come by asking universities to improvise action centers in the middle of slums, staffed by scholars and scientists who are not equipped to do the work, regardless of how much foundation money is behind them.

The desire to do something at once, without forethought, is the very opposite of the idea of a university. But it is the yielding to this impatient desire for the last 25 years that has weakened the fabric of the universities and laid the ground for their present destruction.

To cite just one factor in this situation, the phenomenon of constantly growing administration at the center of the university has been crippling. There are only a certain number of things that can be done in any one institution, and stuffing it and bulging it with other things of a different kind only leads to a general sense of confusion and frustration.

One might note in passing that asking the universities through their personnel to serve immediate purposes, current difficulties, is the exact parallel of the students demand for relevance, by which they merely mean, most of them, topicality.

Now, what about the student demands, are they justified, or unjustified?

I think the demands that they do not make, or that they make only in passing, are the justified ones.

They are entitled to better teaching than they have had, a stronger grip on their minds and their emotions by the tasks set before them. They have a right to feel from the administration and the faculties that they are the center of attention for the whole institution, and they have the right to experience demands of a certain kind, to be gripped by the work that they do.

The other demands, the demand for student power, or even for participation, whatever that may mean, seems to me rooted in a tangle of misconceptions and impracticalities.

To mention only one. If a student were in fact capable of framing a curriculum, then I think he should be given a diploma, and not a voice, because he would know everything necessary for earning that diploma.

Moreover, there is a real impossibility in this notion of representation. I have discussed this with students on several occasions very quietly and not in any spirit of refutation, and after 2 hours or so, they all come to the conclusion that each student can only represent himself, that there is no device or organization by which they can elect someone who they are sure will say on every important subject what they themselves feel.

In other words, there is a kind of fallacy in transporting the excellent democratic system from where it belongs, in our political structure, into the university.

Moreover, the adversary position, which the whole restructuring of universities implies is one that is destructive of good work. All the legalisms that follow are very bad. If everybody's energy is devoted to finding out whether section 19 has been actually carried out or not, they are not doing the work of the university. They are engaged in litigation, or political life, or whatever you want to call it, but not university work.

I think among the student demand for participation there is something that has been concealed hitherto, but very noticeable if one is attentive, a demand for relaxing standards. They don't want grading, they don't want foreign language requirements, they don't want required courses. They want to set up courses on subjects that they have thought of, and with instructors that they have chosen.

This is educational escape, even though they may not think of it as such. They may think of it in other terms.

Again, of course, as we, I think, all agree, the demands that the students make are vitiated by the way they make them. For example, how can anything to do with curriculum or the composition of the faculty be dealt with by physical obstruction and destruction? How can they be worked out or agreed upon in the short time that students suppose that they can be? "Within 2 weeks we must have a new program of this kind or that kind."

The method of the ultimatum or sit-in seems to me to lead to nothing but disaster. No curriculum has been improved by all the violence and anguish that have occurred, and the very term "nonnegotiable," which they use, defines the protestors as what they are in fact, people who want to gain their ends by intimidation and blackmail, and anyone who thinks that can lead to a better university or better student life doesn't know what a university is.

We must remember that the Western World had student-governed universities for about 300 years. If one reads the annals of the University of Bologna or Paris between 1200 and 1500, one sees it was a continuous shambles, with students no better satisfied, but fighting each other, terrorizing the faculty, and spending their time in elections, taking oaths, and paying fines, because that was the structure, the supposed system by which it worked.

They got to the point, for example, where the student rector, the head of the university, was elected for 1 month, and of course, his gang tried to have things go their way during that month. Then they had to have a means of getting the rector out of office, because he wanted to stay there, and finally they had to pass a rule under the pressure of the Church, the Papal Legate of Paris, that the rector must be at least 19 years old.

Now, if we want to go back to that, all right, but the kind of university work we have been accustomed to will not come out of that institution.

Now, they have other demands for changing the world via the university, and those demands are equally unreal, it seems to me. The university has no power to change the city or the State or the country, except through study, through new discoveries, through the slow work of minds actually coping with the actuality.

That requires peace and quiet. It can't be done with guerrilla warfare outside the window.

Now, the lack of imagination that is implied by this sort of demand is enormous. Students who are in the rebel groups apparently think that whole masses of people, a university of 15,000, 20,000, 25,000 people, can operate the way they do in their small tribal system, so to speak. Even in their own small groups they split and divide and abuse each other, so it is not likely that the world is going to be reformed through their aid.

Youthful idealism seems to me no excuse for that lack of imagination which totally ignores what the conditions of real accomplishment are, and what they are always going to be.

The world's evil is very resistant, and indignation of any kind is a very cheap emotion. Anybody can have it.

Finally, there are those who plan revolution and think that they are beginning the overthrow of the whole system by toppling colleges and universities. I think those, if one could for a moment adopt their view, are going about it the wrong way, in an irrelevant fashion and in an irrelevant place.

They can bring about, if they are determined and we let them, the shutdown of every college and university in the land, but that will still leave them facing the troops on the streets and the hillsides. That is where revolutions are fought out. We have enough examples of that in our own time. The University of Tokyo was terrorized until it shut down, but it led to nothing except the elimination of a seat of learning.

At this point, we ask "What are the remedies to the peculiar American situation which would avoid such results?"

They are certainly not as clear as the diagnosis, and some of those that suggest themselves aren't very pleasant to think of and to take.

But first, one thing has to be clear. Everyone must be sure in his own mind that he wants to save the colleges and universities. If a person does not, the simplest thing is to let them go on the way they have been for the last 3 years, and it is obvious that if people make no move to say what they care for, they have no right to complain when it is torn to pieces in front of their eyes.

Now, if a rescue operation is to be undertaken, it must aim at restoring the characteristic atmosphere and way of life of the university, which is discussion, civility, decent behavior.

It isn't true that campus disruption is a lawful parallel to political action, as many people, including a former Solicitor General of the United States, seem to believe. It is not like labor disputes, and it certainly is not like political activity, which the Solicitor General mentioned, such as contributing to party funds, lobbying, and holding cocktail parties.

Very far from it. The analogy doesn't apply. The relationships are utterly different, and even the methods are different.

Nor is it true that the tyrannical misdeeds of the universities justify any amount of vandalism, as it were, by a sort of delayed retaliation.

Far from being a sanctuary for violence, the university demands a higher standard of behavior than, let's say, a political rally, and, incidentally, what are the misdeeds and tyrannies of the universities? Where has any list of them appeared?

The promiscuous name calling and the imputation that the universities abet social abuses don't, to me, fulfill the specification of a list of grievances. The grievances, rather, are on the side of the universities and colleges: work disrupted, property defaced, libraries damaged, scholars manhandled and their research papers burned, the thought and speech of everyone in the university contaminated and debased.

These are offenses that can't be condoned as a lark or accepted as a legal form of self-expression, and the American universities won't recover from these blows for a long time. Indeed, decades perhaps if they are to last that long, they will have to make use of strong means. Even if, as the Declaration of Independence says in another troubled time, it entails "organizing powers in such form as to them shall seem most likely to affect their safety and happiness."

We now have student despotism as bad as that of George the Third, and under those conditions, as the Declaration goes on, "it is their right, it is their duty, to throw off such governance and to provide new guards for their future security."

I quote the Declaration of Independence because I believe in independent universities.

From a speech by Governor Ronald Reagan of California, delivered before the Commonwealth Club in San Francisco, June 13, 1969.

The Knowledge Factory: A Source of Student Rebellion

Is there a revolutionary movement involving a tiny minority of faculty and students finding concealment and shelter in the disappointment and resentment of an entire college generation that finds itself being fed into a knowledge factory with no regard for their individuality, aspirations or their dreams?

The answer is an obvious "yes," and the challenge to us is to establish contact with these frustrated young people and join in finding answers before they fall to the mob by default.

At this moment in California, the danger of this happening is very real. And why not?

When Chancellor Heyns was meeting with law enforcement

officials and joining in their request for police and National Guard protection, other chancellors in our system were endorsing protests and hunger strikes. Faculty groups were passing resolutions deploring police tactics without so much as making a phone call to learn the facts.

I am firmly convinced these represent a minority, but they are activists. The majority of faculty are scholars too busy with their own research and writing to engage in such extra-curricular activities. Are they also too busy to teach?

Young men and women go to college to find themselves as individuals. They see the names of distinguished scholars in the catalogue and sign for courses with the belief they will learn and grow and be stimulated by contact with these men. But all too often they are herded into classes taught by teaching assistants hardly older than themselves. The feeling comes that they are nameless, faceless numbers on an assembly line—green cap at one end and cap, gown and automated diploma at the other. They want someone to know they are there—they aren't even missed and recorded as absent when they aren't there.

The symptoms of rising rebellion have been evident for some time. They no longer bother to vote in student elections. So that other tiny group with its revolutionary purpose elects the student body officers and editors who proceed to speak in the name of the university. This generation—better informed, more aware—deserves much more.

First, those who administer and teach must make it plain they will not be coerced by threats of force. They must spell out in advance those kinds of misconduct they will not tolerate and that there will be *no* negotiation with any who threaten violence. But this is only for that revolutionary minority—the university can dispose of the threat they represent in a week if it will take a stand.

The greater problem has to do with those others, and it begins with establishing communication. Their legitimate grievances must be understood and solutions must be forthcoming. "Publish or perish" as a university policy must be secondary to teaching. Research, a vital and essential part of the process, must not be the standard by which the university rates itself. Its function is to teach and its record must be established on the quality of graduates it offers to the world—not on the collecting of scholarly names in its catalogue.

The few subversives on our campuses will be a problem much easier to handle if the members of that so-called "great silent majority" have inner convictions, beliefs and confidence in our society and in us as adults.

PART II

THE
UNIVERSITY
AS A
FIRM

In the course of fulfilling its primary function of education, the American university has become a large-scale complex organization with numerous employees and a sizeable capital endowment invested in land and securities. While this has been true for at least a half century, it is only in the last few years that students and faculty have come to feel that the university's business activities were their business.

Many have decided that the operations of the university as a firm are based on certain objectionable assumptions, which are more than technical matters and which should be subject to open debate and change. In particular, radicals have argued that the liberal university operates on the same basic principles as other capitalist firms and, indeed, is often particularly exploitative because of the special legal privileges it enjoys as a non-profit corporation. For example, universities have in many states not been subject to labor legislation guaranteeing workers the right to organize unions.

The right of maintenance, cafeteria, library, secretarial and other low-paid university employees to unionize was one of the first issues to arise. Students often took the lead in pressing standard labor-organizing rights on reluctant university administrations. Once launched, however, professional trade-union organizers usually took over the reins of such movements. In recent years, the question of unionization has become intertwined with the racism issue, at least for urban universities, since a large proportion of low-paid university personnel come from minority groups. Though historically important, the controversy over unionization in the university did not really raise any new questions about American society. We do not include material on this debate as it is essentially a variant of the classic debate about the right to unionize that took place in the U.S. in previous decades.*

The trade union issue involves the internal organization of the university as a firm. It is the university's external operations, however, that have recently come under the most intense fire. Questions have arisen about the ties of the university to American business, particularly, the disposition of endowment capital. Controversies have also centered on the role the university plays in its immediate neighborhood—"the community." These two issues—investment policy and community relations—are treated separately below.

* See, however, Volume II, pp. 222–26 and 296–99 for discussion of a "campus worker-student alliance." Other issues related to campus workers besides unionization were raised by SDS beginning in 1969. See also pp. 393–97 of this volume, on women employees.

CHAPTER 3

Investments and Corporate Ties:
The Case of Princeton

Universities and profit-making corporations are linked in a variety of ways. The directors of America's leading concerns serve on boards of trustees. Faculty members in many fields work as consultants for business organizations. Often research done in universities produces technological discoveries that corporations turn to profit. Talent, of course, is one of the university's principal products used by business.

But of the links between universities and corporations, the one that has stirred the most controversy has been the allocation of university investments. Since no group has yet insisted that a university not invest its money anywhere, the issue typically centers on where it is preferable to invest.

The investment issue was clearly focused at Princeton University. On April 15, 1968, representatives of five student organizations—including Black students, Africans, SDS, and a group interested in southern African problems—asked the trustees to divest the university of all investments supporting the white-dominated regimes in southern Africa. The trustees responded with the ancient dictum that business operations should not reflect political preferences.

Continued pressure by students led to the establishment of a faculty-student committee that issued three reports with separate opinions. One, the so-called Malkiel report, endorsed by all the faculty and administration representatives, was prudent in tone and recommended that, insofar as it was right to take moral considerations into account, there were more effective ways of doing so than those suggested by the protesting students. The dissent by William Scott and Carl Spight on behalf of Black student organizations stressed the "common cause" of all Black people, rejected the pragmatic objections to action as fallacious and spurious, and insisted that Princeton take "genuine steps to disengage itself" from apartheid and racism.* When the faculty adopted the Malkiel report on January 20, 1969, they amended it to take into account some of the student criticism. They asked "that Princeton not hold any securities in companies which do a primary amount of their economic activity in South Africa." In the end, the university's president announced that the trustees would accept this compromise position.

The issue of the university's corporate role may not end here, either at Princeton or elsewhere. Criteria for determining the morality of business investments are notoriously difficult to agree upon. Also, it has recently been suggested that the university not only invest selectively, but use its investments to change the policies of corporations. For example, when consumer spokesman Ralph Nader and others ran candidates for the board of directors of General Motors against the incumbents in 1970, students at various universities demanded that their institutions support Nader with their shares of GM stock. At Brown University the trustees agreed to the demand.

In addition, students have requested that the university conscientiously use not only its investment power, but its purchasing power as well. The protracted strike of General Electric workers in the fall of 1969 led to demands for university boycotts of GE products.

* The third report, not reprinted here, was written by another student, a member of SDS.

From a letter to the trustees of Princeton University from a group of student leaders, April 15, 1968.

To the Trustees

Gentlemen:

In light of the continuing revelation of the extent to which all we Americans participate in structures of institutionalized injustice and racism, and as part of our general attempt to examine the relationship of various persons and institutions in New Jersey to the problem of social injustice in southern Africa, we have had occasion to look at the location of the investment of the monies and endowments of Princeton University.

As you may realize, ca. $100 million of your funds are invested in American companies which are operating in the Republic of South Africa. This figure does not include either your funds in companies with indirect investments in southern Africa through British and European corporations or the gifts and bequests to the University which derive from profits in the southern African economies.

Because the University has sought over the years to profess a tradition of service to humanity and to values above the narrow confines of short-term economic self-interest, we feel it is not unreasonable to ask you to reconsider this current policy of investment in those American financial institutions which undergird one of the most rigid systems of racial injustice in the world. Furthermore, some other American institutions already have pioneered this re-thinking of investment policy and have begun selectively to sanction and reward American companies to encourage those which choose to serve value above narrow immediate profit considerations.

Specifically, we feel that the following steps can be taken by the Trustees of the University in response to a morally intolerable situation in which we all presently participate:

1) Resolve that no *future* monies, endowments, or investments of the University will be invested in banks, companies, and other financial institutions which presently participate in the South African, Rhodesian, Angolan, and Mozambique economies.

2) Resolve to begin the process of reinvestment of present allocations of stock, bonds, and other investments, taking funds from

such economic organizations and reinvesting those funds in organizations which choose not to become involved in the southern African area.

3) Refuse to accept monies, bequests, and endowments which come to the University primarily from the profits made in southern Africa.

We realize that, over the years, there have been many arguments about the most effective means of change in southern Africa. On the basis of this past ambiguity, American individuals and institutions have continued to enjoy the rich (almost exorbitant) profits extracted from southern Africa under the protection of the repressive governments there. We now believe that there exists clear evidence that continued U.S. investment in southern Africa does *not* encourage change in those systems of political, economic, and racial injustice. Rather, our continued investment in and support of the southern African countries is serving to strengthen the powers of coercion and repression by the white, minority regimes. Furthermore, from such positions of strength these minority regimes are able to plot strife and disruption in the independent black and multi-racial states of Africa and to flaunt the resolutions of the United Nations. . . .

We shall be happy to meet at the April meeting with the Finance Committee of the Trustees or with the Trustees as a whole to discuss further with you this opportunity for the University to give expression to these basic humanitarian values. We feel such an action on your part at this time would be a very fitting tribute to Dr. Martin Luther King, Jr., and to the other fallen civil rights workers in this land and in southern Africa.

Sincerely yours,

William Scott, Co-Chairman
New Jersey Comm. on Southern Africa (NJCOSA)

Robert Blockum
Committee for Black Awareness

David Wiley, Co-Chairman
New Jersey Comm. on Southern Africa (NJCOSA)

Muhammed Diop
Pan-African Students Association

Rod Hamilton
Association of Black Collegians

Fred Bogardus
Students for a Democratic Society

Reply to the letter of the student leaders from the Board of Trustees, Princeton University, April 19, 1968.

The Trustees Respond

Gentlemen:

The Finance Committee of the Board of Trustees has considered your petition. We are sensitive to and respect the grave concerns you express. The policy of apartheid is contrary to the principles for which this university stands. Nevertheless, I must report that we cannot agree with the course which you urge on us.

Throughout its history, Princeton University has found that the best contribution it can make toward solutions for the many social, political and economic problems which confront our society and the world has been by providing free, open, and vigorous programs of instruction and research. It would be unwise in our judgment for a university to attempt to use its invested funds as a "club" to influence the political and social views of a country.

In the selection of a particular company or industry for investment, many factors are taken into consideration. If the management of a company clearly pursued a general policy of racism and injustice in its national or worldwide operations, undoubtedly we would consider this reason not to invest in its securities. However, to condemn a particular company because some small part of its total activities may seem to run counter to a particular social or political tenet, is usually to oversimplify a large and complex set of issues.

For example, are the long-run interests of black people everywhere best served by our not retaining a small amount of the stock of a company which does business in South Africa but which, on balance, has a highly progressive philosophy of management and race relations? In the light of the Kerner Commission Report, could it be argued that we should divest ourselves of American investments, including U.S. Government Bonds? Or consider the current policy of our country of encouraging trade and investment in Eastern Europe and other communist countries. Should we set ourselves against this policy in the handling of Princeton's investments?

We think not. Rather, we consider it is much better to attack problems of racism, injustice, poverty, political and religious oppression positively, by doing what we can to support and sustain the free and impartial pursuit of knowledge and ideas, as we have in the past. In the final analysis, it seems to us, this is why our society holds so much hope in our educational institutions, and why these institutions, in turn, hold such an awesome responsibility for the future.

I and other of the Trustees shall be glad to discuss these issues more fully. I have asked the Financial Vice-President, Mr. Mestres, to try to arrange with you a time and place for such a meeting.

Sincerely,

Harold H. Helm
Chairman, Committee on Finance
The Board of Trustees

Editorial in The Daily Princetonian, *student newspaper, Princeton University, April 19, 1968.*

March on Apartheid

If a university cannot uphold human values and maintain high standards of human decency in all facets of its affairs, what institution in American society will? It is bad enough that a myriad of American corporations have to pour $100 million into apartheid-ridden southern Africa, but does Princeton University have to own an interest in them? This university can find other means to get a fair return on its endowment which do not lend support—symbolic and material support—to economies whose political and social institutions are so repressively racist. Whether at home or abroad, Americans should not sacrifice standards for profit.

The Trustees' committee on finance has no more important business to consider this weekend than the cleansing of its investment portfolio. This community should demonstrate to the committee that it wants decent human values upheld by marching today.

Letter to the Committee on Finance, Board of Trustees, Princeton University, from a group of Black student leaders.

Why Blacks Are Concerned

Dear Mr. Helm:

We wish to thank you for the prompt reply to our letter regarding the University's investments and the invitation to a meeting with several members of the Board of Trustees. It was encouraging to see that the University was addressing itself immediately to this matter of grave concern. From the nature of some of the comments contained in your response, however, it was quite apparent that we (the black signatories of the petition) had failed to make clear the position which the Negro community has assumed on the southern Africa issue. We, therefore, feel it imperative to clarify our basic attitudes regarding this matter.

It should be understood that American blacks, particularly students, are deeply concerned about the plight of the people of southern Africa and consider the struggle there and in America as a mutual one. Having shared a common heritage, common color, and a common enemy, we are increasingly coming to regard ourselves as one people. Consequently, American Negroes feel that their future is inextricably bound up with that of the African people.

It is quite obvious to us that no individual black can be free from the degradation of racial discrimination until every black person is free of it. We fully agree with Dr. Ralph Bunche's assertion that there can be no emancipation and no escape for the individual American Negro until the entire group is emancipated; that there can be no dignity for one without dignity for all; that no Negro can ever walk down any American street with full security and serenity until all Negroes can do so throughout the world.

This point is vividly impressed upon us when we see that at the same time the South African government denies all rights to that country's black citizens, it also prohibits visits by American Negroes of all professions to South Africa; prevents American blacks from serving in what constitutes the United States' largest African diplomatic mission; refuses to accept black Americans at the NASA tracking stations in South Africa; and bars American Negroes from working in South Africa with American businesses operating there. Thus it is obviously apparent that just as the rights of black people in South Africa are denied by Apartheid, our rights as American citizens are also curtailed by the same system.

Therefore, as long as white Americans participate, to any degree, in the exploitation and degradation of black Africans, we have no choice but to view their statements of liberalism regarding human rights in America as pure hypocrisy. In the same vein, we are compelled to take a similar position toward Princeton University in light of its involvement in Apartheid. It hurts us, as black students, to know that the buildings and facilities that we use here were provided through the oppression, forced labor, and murder of our black brothers. Our suspicion of the University can only begin to change when the University has taken genuine steps to disengage itself from all programs which contribute to the denial of human rights and liberties.

We trust that Princeton has the moral fortitude and commitment to do so.

Sincerely yours,

William Scott
Co-Chairman, New Jersey
Committee on Southern
Africa

Homer U. Ashby, Jr.
Association of Black
Collegians

Robert Blockum
Committee on Black
Awareness.

From the report of the Ad Hoc Committee on Princeton's Investments in Companies Operating in Southern Africa (known as The Malkiel Report), January 15, 1969. The report was signed only by the faculty members thereof.

The Malkiel Report

What Constitutes Investment in Southern Africa?

Before the Committee could turn to the question of whether Princeton should sell any of its holdings, it had to examine criteria for determining whether the University is involved in apartheid. It was difficult to set criteria, for it is not easy to define precisely which companies appreciably contribute to the economies of southern Africa. We should note at the outset, however, that

Princeton owns no stocks or bonds of companies that have more than a peripheral interest or investment in the region or that directly support the governments involved.*

Several criteria for involvement were considered, and two polar cases should be mentioned.

One possible criterion defined a company as "substantially supporting the governments in power" only if it is domiciled in southern Africa, if its major operations are in southern Africa, or if it lends money directly to the governments involved. Such companies offer the most significant support to the economies of southern Africa or directly aid the governments in power. Ownership of stock in these companies could reasonably be construed as supporting immoral governments. Were this criterion accepted, it would turn out that Princeton is involved not at all, for as noted above, the University holds no securities of companies in this category.

A second criterion, which was suggested by one of the Committee members, represents the opposite pole: Under this criterion, any company that profits at all—directly or indirectly—from the economies of southern Africa should be considered as helping to support racist regimes. Thus, any company that either operates directly in southern Africa, has a subsidiary or affiliate in southern Africa, or that trades with southern Africa, either directly or by making intermediate products that are then sold to the southern African economies, would be considered to be a company that profits from racial injustice and that contributes to the system of oppression.

By this second criterion it is probably true that almost every company in Princeton's portfolio is contaminated. Nor is it clear that replacements could be found, since it is almost impossible to find a company that is not involved to some extent with the economies of southern Africa, directly or indirectly, through trade. . . .

Needless to say, there are many intermediate criteria that might

* While firm evidence is neither publicly available nor accessible to our Committee, we have estimated that the involvement in southern Africa of the companies whose stock is owned by Princeton represents an insignificant part of the companies' total sales and profits. On average, we believe that operations in southern Africa contribute less than one percent to total sales and profits for those companies listed in the Scott proposal.

be selected. The one our Committee considered most carefully was the criterion suggested by Messrs. Scott et al. in their April 15 petition to the Trustees. In this petition, a list of companies was submitted which had been selected by the following criterion: Companies were included only if they had affiliates or subsidiaries operating in southern Africa. . . . These holdings amount to $127 million, approximately one third of Princeton's total holdings of common stocks. It was argued that these were the companies most directly involved in southern Africa and also most visible to the oppressed black population. Consequently, these companies were symbols of support of these economies by United States corporations. Because the original petition concerned these companies, we utilized this criterion in judging the extent of Princeton's involvement in the economies of southern Africa and in estimating the possible advantages and disadvantages of withdrawing its investments from these companies. In further discussion we shall call the shares of these firms the "designated" shares.

We should note, however, that the signers of this document were not satisfied with this criterion. The basic problem is that the extent of a corporation's involvement in southern Africa cannot be judged simply by the existence of an affiliate or a subsidiary that operates therein. For example, some companies may do a great deal of trading with countries in southern Africa without having either a sales subsidiary or an affiliate, and thus would be exempt from criticism. . . .

Arguments Advanced for Selling the Designated Shares

The first argument advanced for selling the designated shares is one that was emphasized by the student members of our Committee and one that in our opinion represents the most important advantage to be gained from disengagement. This advantage is the effect such an act would have on black people all over the world. We were convinced that by such an action Princeton University could make more credible to black people its determination to continue working toward the abolition of racial discrimination, even when it resulted in a considerable sacrifice by the University. While it was argued that Princeton's hiring and admissions policies represented clear evidence of its concern for racial equality, it was forcefully argued that it would be virtually impossible to demonstrate to black people that the maintenance of Princeton's investment holdings did not indicate a disregard for racial justice. To blacks all over the world, southern Africa is a symbol of the domination of blacks by whites. The particular companies chosen for disinvestment do have one common characteristic: Since they have subsidiaries or affiliates operating in southern Africa, they do give the appearance of United States corporations supporting racist regimes. Disengagement would certainly be one way to show that Princeton University means what it says about racism.

A second argument for selling the designated shares was connected with the moral issue alluded to earlier: It was argued that holding stocks and bonds in any company operating in southern Africa is immoral. Therefore, it was argued, disengagement would help bring the investment policies of the University closer to the values and goals it self-consciously seeks as an institution.

There are several reasons, however, why we did not consider this second argument sufficient to justify Princeton's selling of the designated shares. In the first place, as noted above in the discussion of criteria for defining involvement in southern Africa, we are not convinced it is reasonable to consider these $127 million of Princeton's investments as actually supporting racist regimes in southern Africa, nor as substantially profiting from the exploitation of black workers. The involvement of these companies in the economies of the region and the extent to which they profit from this involvement is extremely small. Secondly, other companies in Princeton's portfolio may contribute through trade at least as much to the economies of southern Africa as those companies on the designated list. Finally, as we emphasized in our earlier discussion of criteria of involvement, it is simply not possible to cleanse the University's portfolio of all investments that may directly or indirectly contribute to or profit from the racist policies of the governments of southern Africa.

One further point should be made concerning the morality of selling shares of the designated companies: Many of the designated companies pursue notably progressive policies in their domestic operations or in their business relationships in other parts of Africa. An example is that of the Xerox Company, which has been a leader in providing job training to disadvantaged workers and financial and other aid to ghetto businesses. In conjunction with a local community action organization, FIGHT,

Xerox recently made a substantial contribution toward setting up ghetto businesses in Rochester. In many other ways Xerox has also exercised its corporate responsibility for social progress. We were, thus, troubled that Xerox would be on the designated list when that company has for a long period of time been a leader in the fight for equal opportunities for all citizens in the United States.

The Committee studied carefully a third argument that is most frequently claimed for the policy of selling the designated shares —namely, that such sales would help contribute to the abolition of apartheid and racism in southern Africa. We could find no evidence that this argument is valid. Indeed, we find no reason to believe that Princeton's disengagement would have any effect on the South African economy. We came to this conclusion on the basis of the following arguments:

First, it should be emphasized that Princeton's holdings of the shares of each company operating in southern Africa represent an insignificant fraction of the total number of shares of that company outstanding. . . . Thus, the sales of our holdings would be most unlikely to have any permanent influence on the market prices of the shares. Our shares would simply be transferred to other buyers. True, if many educational and charitable institutions followed suit, the market prices of these shares might fall. But such a snowball effect is unlikely. Indeed, several educational institutions have already considered the question of selling such shares and have decided to leave their holdings intact. And even if other institutions did sell, the testimony before our committee indicated that corporate policies would be unaffected.

Even in the unlikely event that U.S. corporations did want to disengage from a country such as South Africa, evidence received by the Committee indicated that willing buyers exist for any properties U.S. interests would want to sell. Buyers from Japan, West Germany, and several other European nations would purchase any U.S. assets offered for sale and would willingly increase their annual flow of investment funds to South Africa in response to any diminution of new U.S. investments. In addition, the South African government itself would not view as an unfavorable development an opportunity to buy such assets itself; to employ the growing accumulation of savings in South Africa to increase domestic ownership of the economy's manufacturing facilities.

Thus, we can see no way in which Princeton's actions could by themselves lead to any effect on the South African economy, nor do we believe that Princeton's actions could precipitate a series of events that would have any appreciable effect on the economy or the viability of the government. Consequently, we concluded that selling the designated shares would not contribute to the goal of helping to combat apartheid and racism in South Africa.

The Disadvantages of Withdrawing Investments from the Designated Companies

A. *Financial Costs*

The Committee conducted a careful investigation of the financial costs likely to be associated with a withdrawal of the funds invested in the designated shares. . . . Here we simply state the major conclusions of our analysis:

1. The designated securities have provided higher returns than nondesignated securities. . . .

2. There are significant transactions costs involved in changing the composition of the portfolio. . . .

3. Adoption of the April 15, 1968 proposal to the Trustees could severely impair the University's fund-raising ability. . . .

B. *Other Disadvantages*

In addition to the financial costs to the University described in the preceding section, we analyzed several other disadvantages that could be of even greater importance to the University. The two most important of these are described below:

We believe that selling our investments in the designated shares would, in effect, formally establish a policy of using moral criteria in selecting our investment portfolio. While no one would defend a practice of investing in companies whose profits result from patently immoral activities, the very clear danger is that selling the designated shares would lead to demands that the University discriminate on political and social grounds as well in making its investments. Such a policy could have many undesirable effects on the University.

First, such a policy would commit the investment managers to a continuing series of decisions on the possible moral-political-social effects of all investments. Since most investments involve businesses with a wide variety of associations, the investment managers would be obligated to investigate and make judgments about the moral-political-social effects of all these associations. We doubted that it was always possible to obtain the necessary information, and we concluded that such responsibility would severely hinder investment management.

The problem is that once the precedent had been established, a case could be made for avoiding investment in virtually any company. Indeed, some members of the University community have freely admitted that once this action was taken on South African investments, the next step might well be to turn the attack on munitions makers, companies with "unfair" labor practices, companies dealing with discriminatory unions, companies with investments in Portugal, etc. Reference was also made to the likelihood of conservative pressures that we avoid investment in companies that do business with communist countries. The dangers involved seem very clear. It is hard to imagine a company completely free of connections that might be considered objectionable on moral, political, or social grounds by some part of the University community.

We also questioned whether it would be prudent to use the University's investment portfolio as a vehicle to promote this institution's general policy against racism. As was mentioned above, selling our shares would have no effect on the actions of the corporations whose shares were sold nor on the economies of southern Africa, while the financial costs would be so heavy as to severely limit the University's effectiveness. Moreover, if we were to use our economic power to try to influence corporate or government policy, we would invite retaliatory strategies on the part of corporations or the government. That is, the University might well be subjected to increasingly severe outside pressures, in the face of which it would have difficulty retaining its responsibility to provide an environment in which ideas can be freely expressed and developed. No university can afford thus to jeopardize its basic mission and its effectiveness as a home for intellectual freedom.

Conclusion Regarding the Sale of the Designated Shares

The weight of the argument developed above leads us to recommend that the University not sell the designated shares. The issue is not one of institutional purity, for we have seen that selling the proposed $127 million of investments would not cleanse the portfolio of all morally questionable investments.* Indeed, sale of these securities would be, for us, settling for an appearance of moral concern while sacrificing its reality. Nor could the sales be justified on the grounds of institutional effectiveness, for available evidence indicates that there would be no effect on the South African economy if the University divested itself of these security holdings. Selling our shares would not bring closer the day of emancipation for black people in South Africa. On the other hand, the effects on the University's financial position could be extremely deleterious and many important and beneficial University programs could be endangered. Moreover, the ability of the University to perform its basic mission and to sustain a unique environment as a home of intellectual freedom might be endangered by such action.

We do *not*, however, wish to minimize the importance of symbolic moves on the part of an institution such as Princeton University. We were convinced that the action of selling the designated shares would be one way of making credible to black people all over the world our professed concern to work toward the abolition of racism. We therefore sought other means that might do the cause of racial justice more good in the long run and Princeton less harm.

We concluded that if we are seriously interested in improving conditions for the black man in southern Africa, we can be at least as effective by using the corporate connections we have than by disengagement. Indeed, pressing our views through all available channels, consistently and repeatedly may be a more realistic and ultimately perhaps even a more effective solution in the long run. We have no illusion that such actions alone will end apartheid and racism and we recognize that our effectiveness will be limited at best. But there are several actions we can take as a university that can take advantage of our unique strengths as an educational institution. In the next section we turn to the specific proposals recommended.

---

* Moreover, it might be argued that to be completely "pure," Princeton should also dispose of its large holdings of IBM and Xerox machines that support its educational programs and administrative facilities.

Recommendations

A. *Expressions of Our Views to Those Corporations Whose Stock We Hold*

Despite our recommendation not to sell the designated shares held in Princeton's portfolio, we as individuals feel strongly that, as members of the stockholding community, we have a high-priority obligation to speak out forcefully against corporate practices we consider immoral. Specifically, these are the views we share:

1. We are concerned about the involvement of U.S. corporations with foreign countries, such as those in southern Africa, that enforce policies of racial injustice. We want to express our belief that U.S. corporations should not associate with these governments.

2. We are particularly concerned about U.S. corporations and financial institutions that directly aid the South African government. Particularly, we abhor the practices of several U.S. banks in granting South Africa a substantial line of credit, which helped bolster the shaky government after the Sharpsville massacre of 1960.

3. From testimony taken during our deliberations, we have reason to believe that the labor practices of many U.S. corporations operating production facilities in South Africa are little different from, and in some cases may even be less progressive than, those of South-African-owned corporations. . . .

Several methods of expressing the above views are possible. The University as a stockholder might itself make such representations to the companies whose shares it holds, though this might raise some of the dangers discussed [earlier under the heading B. *Other Disadvantages*]. A less direct method would be to have such representations made by the members of the Committee (if possible together with some of Princeton's Trustees) acting as individuals. In either case, we believe Princeton's action would be far more effective if it were joined by other universities, as the stockholdings of several universities might represent a sizeable block of the outstanding shares. . . .

B. *Programs to Aid the Black People of Southern Africa and to In-fluence Long-Run Change in Race Relations*

As stressed earlier in this report, there is deep concern in the Princeton University community about racism in southern Africa as well as race relations in other parts of the world. In teaching, research, and other activities, faculty members and students may be able to make positive contributions to improvement of race relations, and they also may be able to strengthen the forces in opposition to apartheid. The initiative for action, however, must come from concerned faculty members and students who are willing to devote time and energy to development of programs in this area. We see it as the role of the University to encourage, and support financially, programs sponsored by faculty and students who have honest and strong commitments to work in this field. This approach would not be intended to be primarily propagandistic or symbolic and it would not be likely to induce immediate change in southern Africa. Yet the contribution of the University community might help establish the fundamental conditions of change in the long run.

There are several possible areas of activity which concerned members of the University might explore. A few of these are suggested below. The first three offer possibilities for immediate action; the other three are probably more appropriate for longer-range consideration.

1. Programs for expanding the study of race relations in Princeton's course offerings. . . .

2. Sponsorship of conferences and research on apartheid and racism. . . .

3. Exchange programs involving African leaders, scholars, and students. . . .

4. Establishing an institutional relationship with the University of Botswana, Lesotho, and Swaziland. . . .

5. Collaboration with other African institutions. . . .

6. Programs for the education of refugees from southern Africa . . .

Leon Gordenker
Frederick Harbison
Burton G. Malkiel, Chairman
Ricardo A. Mestres
John E. Schrecker

Excerpts from the dissent, on behalf of Black Princeton student organizations, prepared by William R. Scott and Carl Spight, January 1, 1969. They acknowledge drawing upon the arguments advanced by the American Committee on Africa and the University Christian Movement.

A Dissent from the Malkiel Report

. . . In summary, it was the opinion of the student representatives that:

1) Any trade and investment strengthens the system of Apartheid and represents complicity.
2) Prospects for peaceful change through the liberalization of white attitudes is extremely bleak.
3) Any material support, no matter how limited, of the present government of South Africa is deplorable.
4) Complete disengagement from South Africa is practically an impossibility. However, we are convinced that in this, as in many other instances, limited action is not without moral, symbolic, and political significance.
5) Despite the financial losses which might occur, U.S. institutions should disengage from support of and identification with the status quo in South Africa.

The representatives from the faculty and administration arrived at a variety of closely related opinions none of which agreed with the student position that Princeton should withdraw its investments from corporations operating in South Africa. Their decision was based, apparently, on two criteria:

1) the substantial financial loss which the withdrawal of funds would involve, and
2) the supposed ineffectiveness such a policy would have on changing the situation in South Africa.

It was their unanimous decision, nevertheless, that Princeton should engage in providing educational assistance to students in southern Africa, particularly through the auspices of the University of Botswana, Lesotho, and Swaziland. Hoping to get a general consensus on at least one point, Chairman Malkiel asked the student representatives if they were willing to support this proposal along with the rest of the committee.

At the final session on November 11, the black students presented a statement in which they declared that they could not "accept either in part or in whole the position arrived at by the committee's representatives from the administration and faculty.

. . . Our decision is based upon the fact that no real validity was given to our insight and understanding of the South African situation derived from our experiences as black people. . . . When the black members of the committee arrived at a position fundamentally different from that of the other members, but based upon an examination of the same evidence, their process of reasoning was interpreted as being non-objective and irrational. . . . The position which was ultimately decided upon by the committee was the product of an analytical process founded *solely* upon the frame of reference of white America. For all intents and purposes, the black referent was totally ignored." The SDS representative also refused to support any aspect of the "Malkiel" position. Consequently, an even split between the students on one hand and the faculty and administration on the other resulted, necessitating separate reports from the students.

As black people, we recognize our common cause with that of black people all over the world who have been systematically victimized by racism, oppression, and colonialism. Our experience informs us that our struggle for human rights is a group cause and consequently our effort must be a group effort. To ignore and thereby tacitly accept South African racism in exchange for either American corporate tokenism, complicity in economic exploitation, or assimilation into the Princeton status quo, we cannot do.

Our own history in America has clearly illustrated for us the full and tragic human dimensions of treating people as objects, as chattel, to be manipulated at will. We cannot accept as relevant an argument giving primacy to economic considerations, a concern for materialism, at the expense of human (i.e. moral) considerations. We refuse to limit our concerns to such narrow confines.

Experience has shown us that arguments based on the premise that symbolic gestures are "empty" proceeds from a frame of reference which again gives primacy to the status quo. Indeed, were not the first "sit-ins" in the South symbolic gestures?

It has been our experience far too often that arguments for "efficacy" and "feasibility" are embedded in a frame of reference which ignores and excludes a viewpoint and subsequent set of priorities rooted in the black experience. Our inputs into the operational equations for action have been and are systematically minimized and manipulated to optimize gains irrelevant to the black frame of reference. A clear example of this was the reaction of the Malkiel Committee to the inputs of its four black members.

Our experience, therefore, dictates that in regard to the question of Princeton's investments we demand that the validity of our insight and understanding of the South African situation derived from our experiences as black people be recognized, and any future dialogue regarding this matter deal with the *implementation* of the following proposals:

1) Resolve that no *future* monies, endowments, or investments of the University will be invested in banks, companies, and other financial institutions which presently participate in the South African, Rhodesian, Angolan, and Mozambique economies.

2) Resolve to begin the process of reinvestment of present allocations of stock, bonds, and other investments, taking funds from such economic organizations and reinvesting those funds in organizations which choose not to become involved in the southern African area.

3) Refuse to accept monies, bequests, and endowments which come to the University primarily from the profits made in southern Africa.

4) Cease to grant admission and scholarships to white South Africans as long as their government refuses to:
   i) admit virtually all black Americans to that country
   ii) grant transit visas to an ever increasing number of American citizens wishing to visit the independent nations of Lesotho and Swaziland
   iii) grant passports to virtually all black South Africans seeking to pursue studies (particularly in the scientific and technological fields) in the United States and elsewhere.

By adopting the above-mentioned proposals, Princeton University will have taken genuine steps to disengage itself systematically from the support of Apartheid and, in fact, racism in general. We trust that Princeton has the moral fortitude, commitment, and foresight to do so. In conclusion, it should be stated that as long as white Americans participate, to any degree, in the exploitation of black people in Africa, we have no choice but to view their professions of liberalism regarding human rights in America as pure hypocrisy.

Letter from Professor Burton G. Malkiel to President Robert Goheen of Princeton University, January 15, 1969.

Amendment to the Report

Dear President Goheen:

Since the time that the report of the faculty and administration members of the Ad Hoc Committee on Princeton's Investments in Companies Operating in Southern Africa was filed, an additional piece of information has come to our attention:

The First National Bank of Chicago, whose shares are currently held in Princeton's portfolio, is a member of the consortium of banks that has granted a revolving credit of 40 million dollars to South Africa. We were unaware of this fact when the report was written, since this bank had not been listed among the consortium banks in the information that was available to our Committee.

It is necessary now to append the following statements to our report:

1. We consider this bank to be "supporting an immoral government" by the criterion listed . . . and our Committee believes a genuine moral issue is raised by Princeton holding these shares.

2. Our Committee did not decide what action should be taken if Princeton did hold shares in companies directly supporting racist governments, since we believed no such shares were held in our endowment portfolio. Nevertheless, we believe the logic of our report dictates that we give serious consideration to

   a. attempting to influence the First National Bank of Chicago to disassociate itself from this consortium; and

   b. in the event that the First National Bank of Chicago does not agree to disassociate itself, selling the shares.

Letter from President Robert Goheen to the university community, March 4, 1969.

Princeton's New Policy

On my own behalf and on behalf of the Executive Committee of the Board of Trustees, I want at this time to make the following statement concerning the University's investments in companies which do business in South Africa. . . . In matters of this kind, one has always to balance a wide range of legitimate moral obligations and concerns, none of which can be satisfied completely and some of which will be in conflict. With the specific matters at issue, having considered the various proposals, having had the benefit of the recommendations of both the Faculty and the Undergraduate Assembly, and having deliberated on the various aspects of the issue for more than a year, we have concluded:

(a) That, as a matter of policy, the University will not hold securities in companies which do a *primary* amount of their economic activity in South Africa.

(b) That, divestment of securities of companies on the so-called "designated list"—all of which (as for example, Xerox, IBM, or Johnson & Johnson) do a very small volume of their business in South Africa—cannot be accepted for two major reasons. First, for reasons stated in the Malkiel report, such a policy offers no substantial prospect of affecting the system of *apartheid* in South Africa, while many of these same companies pursue notably progressive policies both domestically and in other parts of Africa. Second, the proposed policy of divestment (entailing an estimated loss each year of some $3.5 million in University income, not to mention very substantial transaction costs) would greatly weaken Princeton's capacity to carry on and extend its current programs of teaching, research, and student aid. Under these circumstances, for us deliberately to reduce the University's ability to pursue its mission as an educational institution would be to fail to honor critical obligations—those relevant to Princeton's future effectiveness as well as those of immediate moment.

(c) That, while we understand the arguments for refusing to accept monies and bequests which may derive from profits made primarily in South Africa, we do not believe that so broad and absolute restriction can be accepted by the University on either moral or other grounds. In point of fact, it is often exceedingly difficult to determine the ultimate source of gifts or bequests; for example, shares of stock given to the University may have been purchased recently by the donor with funds derived from totally different activities. No less importantly, while there are circumstances in which one can imagine the acceptance of a gift as seeming to confer approval of the activities which produced it, in most circumstances there need be no such implication at all—and especially so if the University takes pains to avoid such an interpretation.

[Now], let me clarify the University's recent action with respect to the stock of the First National Bank of Chicago, about which there has been considerable misunderstanding. The Malkiel committee had recommended certain actions with reference to this bank because of its membership in a consortium granting credit to the Government of South Africa. In endorsing the Malkiel report on January 20th, the Faculty supported this recommendation. But even before that vote had been taken, action had been initiated by the Trustees to sell the University's holdings in bank stocks. That action had been undertaken primarily on investment grounds—in the effort to find securities better suited to the University's total investment program. The important fact now is that the University does not hold this stock. I can also say flatly that Princeton has no plans to purchase stocks of banks offering direct support to the Government of South Africa.

CHAPTER 4

The Surrounding Community:
What Is the Role
of the University?

Universities, especially urban universities, are often surrounded by economically declining areas that are the target of "urban renewal" programs. The universities have been growing at a rapid pace in the last twenty years and have needed more and more urban land; they have been "expanding." To do so, they have used their resources and their access to governmental assistance to purchase surrounding units, often housing units, and demolish them, replacing them with new university complexes. In the process, the universities have often been ruthless to the urban poor, and needlessly destructive.

Many universities viewed urban renewal as a great opportunity to do social good through eugenics while simultaneously offering to faculty and students a laboratory for applied research. Clark Kerr in *The Uses of the University* saw this ecological phenomenon as providing the university with "an almost ideal location . . . so that students may live in the [middle-class district on its way to becoming a slum] and the faculty consult in the [ultramodern industrial park]"—these being the two immediate environments he expected to find for the urban university.

The Morningside Gym episode at Columbia can only be understood in the context of that university's long history of expansion on Morningside Heights in New York City. Protest had been intermittent over the years, largely coming from some of the local residents and from some student groups. In December of 1967, the Faculty Civil Rights Group issued a report critical of university expansion. The report got little notice and was ignored by the administration.

Meanwhile, for over ten years a controversial project had been in gestation—construction of a new university gymnasium on public park land adjoining the university. The gym became the great symbolic issue of Columbia's expansion, although—or perhaps even because—Columbia made some concessions to community sentiment by including in its plans a small section of the gymnasium for the community (with a separate entrance). In February 1968, ground was broken, despite community protests and 26 arrests. Two months later came the Columbia rebellion. The Black students occupied a university building in protest, demanding that Columbia end construction of the gym. Radical white students also made "Gym Crow" a central issue of the strike, as is indicated by the excerpt from the Strike Coordinating Committee's pamphlet, "Why we strike."

The administration of President Grayson Kirk was not convinced by resistance to the plans. As late as June of 1968, Kirk was still defending the gymnasium project, although by that time the Trustees had temporarily suspended construction. Kirk still asserted the benevolence of the project and warned that, if the site were abandoned, "the neighborhood boys would be the sufferers." Kirk resigned in August 1968 to be succeeded by Andrew W. Cordier as Acting President. On February 27, 1969, Cordier announced that the gym in the park was forever abandoned, precisely because of community opposition.

The university's relationship with the surrounding community was debated on other campuses. One poignant example comes from Detroit where the Wayne State University newspaper, *The South End*, called attention to the university's policy toward neighborhood children, and the ways in which the university discriminated against them in favor of the middle-class children of the professors.

The People's Park episode was a different issue in that Berkeley is not a metropolis but a college town. Here, in many ways, the students themselves *are* the community, or a large part of it. If at Columbia the university wanted to use park land for a gymnasium, at Berkeley the students and others wanted to use university land, slated to be a playing field, and turn it into a public park.

We start with an anonymous proclamation by supporters of People's Park, followed by an official justification of the administration's position by Chancellor Roger Heyns. Critiques came from many sides. Most centered around questions of life style and repression. Brent Tempest, Sports Editor of *The Daily Californian*, was against "fences," all fences. A pamphlet that the Radical Student Union reprinted in their crisis journal *Outcry* challenged the very basis of private property, reminding everyone that the land was originally stolen from the American Indians. A letter by lecturer and poetess Denise Levertov asked the faculty to rise in defense of "human values." The Third World Liberation Front hailed the campaign for People's Park as part of the struggle of all "oppressed people." A bitter editorial in the *Daily Californian* sugg that the same attitude of the administration which led it to fence off the park also led it to use repressive measures against protesters (one man had been killed by police, gas had been sprayed on a crowd from a police helicopter). In the wake of the controversy, Mario Savio offered an interpretation of the significance of People's Park. For him, it involved "seizing the means of leisure," a first step in the social revolution of the "postindustrial generation." The immediate outcome of the People's Park campaign, six months later, is depicted briefly by a newspaper report in the *San Francisco Chronicle*.

Columbia—The Morningside Gym

Leaflet from Black Students in Hamilton Hall, Columbia University, issued during a sit-in, April 24, 1968.

Our Demands

Black community students have barricaded themselves in Hamilton Hall of Columbia University. They have wide Harlem support and support from white students. Black students have barricaded themselves in to dramatize Columbia University's attempt to control the Harlem community and therefore hinder Black self-determination.

More specifically, Columbia University reveals itself as a white racist institution that encroaches upon the Harlem community through ownership of the Harlem Hospital, Morningside Heights area, buildings in Delano Village, and usage of a public park as a gym site. In addition to this, Columbia University has raped the minds of Black people through the so-called sociological surveys. Finally, Columbia has ties with the Institute for Defense Analysis, which deals in counter-insurgency activities both inside America —i.e., mace and police "riot control" tactics—and abroad wherever there is a people's liberation struggle.

Our four demands are as follows. The university must:

1. end all construction on Columbia's gym in Harlem's Morningside Heights.
2. drop all charges against all persons arrested in demonstrations against the gym.
3. sever all faculty, staff and university ties with the Institute for Defense Analysis.
4. [give] total amnesty for the students involved in present demonstrations.

From a pamphlet of the Columbia Strike Coordinating Committee, Why We Strike, *Columbia University, May 1968.*

"Gym Crow"

In 1959 Columbia University began planning an athletic facility for student and community use to be built in Morningside Park. Columbia pursued the appropriate legal steps to acquire a lease for a site in the park in the state legislature and the city's Board of Estimate. In 1961 Columbia secured a fifty year lease to a two acre gym site with only minor resistance from local political leaders or institutions. Columbia's rent was set at a nominal $3,000 a year.

Between 1961 and 1966 (when Columbia was trying to raise money for construction) members of the community began unfolding details of the enterprise and a small but persistent community opposition began pushing the university to reopen discussion of the gymnasium question. It was pointed out that only 11% (later increased to about 15%) of the facility would be open to community youngsters. Since Morningside Park serves the crowded West Harlem area, the university was vulnerable (regardless of whatever good intentions its administrators had) to the charge of building a segregated gym. What is more, the lending arrangement which Columbia had requested forbid that the large undergraduate gym ever be available for use by any other party but Columbia. This meant that the large gym would be unavailable for local youngsters even during the summer.

Later the opposition found more to be concerned about. Although university officials were quick to say that it would cost more than $1.5 million to build the community portion, trustee Harold McGuire, chairman of the gym fund, admitted that it would cost *at least* $1.7 million to buy a site of private land that large in the Morningside Heights area. Adding to this the cost of razing such a site in a residential area and the settlements, court costs, and ill feeling generated by removal of local residents, the university clearly had a lot to gain by building in the park.

In the mid-fifties the city had granted Columbia exclusive use during most of the school year of a large athletic field adjacent to the gym site (the only one in Morningside Park) for use by their R.O.T.C., Phys. ed. classes, intramural athletics, and track team. With the new indoor gym Columbia would have a centralized athletic complex for the first time in many years.

It was later revealed to those who looked carefully at the lease, that Columbia, which had claimed to be responsible for financing the ongoing operation of the community gym, was only going to pay for heat and lights. And the plans themselves showed that community portion was on a basement floor, with a separate backdoor entrance.

In the beginning of 1966 criticism started to mount. Commissioner of Parks Hoving called the entire arrangement irregular. He objected that the public (in this case an oppressed segment of the population) was being given a sop instead of a respectable portion. He also contended that though the park site selected was in need of landscaping, it was potentially one of the most beautiful in the city. All three of West Harlem's elected officials took active stands against the gym (the old ones had retired or been defeated). The Department of Parks itself and a number of interested taxpayers tried to find legal grounds for rescinding the lease. But by mid-1966 it was clear that Columbia was on solid legal footing and only the public concern of her own officials could change the location or design of the new gym.

In the face of mounting opposition the university decided to add a small swimming pool to the community gym. (The large gym would have an olympic size pool.) The measure was taken without consultation with Harlem representatives. Columbia still remained sole user of 85% of a segregated building.

The first two weeks of construction in February, 1968 were greeted with three demonstrations in which Columbia had to arrest 26 students and community residents so that construction could proceed. Despite warnings from students and community groups that further construction would precipitate a racial confrontation between Harlem blacks and the university, Columbia insisted that Harlem would see that the gym "would be a good thing for them" after it was in operation.

Columbia trustees have been criminally imperceptive in their refusal to consider moving or changing the segregated character of the gym. Although public opinion called for a reopening of the gymnasium issue university administrators preferred to hide behind legal arrangements that were foisted upon an unorganized constituency. The action of the trustees and administration shows them to be oblivious to all the race questions that have been raised in our cities in this decade.

We have demanded the end of construction.

The trustees have so far agreed only to a temporary halt in order to consult. With whom they do not say. We continue to strike to stop the C. U. gym.

Finally, we call attention to the crass insensitivity which Columbia has directed to the community in this matter, and in tenant eviction and harassment in the other areas of their expansion.

From "A Message to Alumni, Parents, and Other Friends of Columbia," by Grayson Kirk, President of Columbia University, June 1, 1968.

What Is the Gymnasium Problem?

I find it difficult to write calmly to our alumni and friends about the gymnasium. The whole project has been so distorted by its opponents that reason and objectivity no longer seem to apply to a plan that was devised as a benefit to the community as well as to the University.

The idea of the gymnasium in Morningside Park grew naturally out of our success with the Columbia-Community playing field which has existed in the park since 1957. When the playing field proposal for the southern end of the park first was launched, the park land in question was garbage-littered and virtually unused by anyone. On the basis of a permit from the Parks Department, Columbia spent $250,000 to reclaim the land, transform it into an athletic field, and to construct a small field house. The plan was that Columbia would use the field for our students during school days and would staff at University expense an athletic program for neighborhood teen-age boys during week-ends and on a full-time community use basis during the summer months. The program has been so outstandingly successful that more than 2,500 youngsters, divided into a hundred teams, now use the field each year. Were it not for this program—Columbia directed and Columbia financed—these boys would be on the streets of Harlem and not on the playing field during the hot summer months.

The plan for a joint-use gymnasium, adjacent to this field, was developed by the Parks Commissioner and myself, with the help of many University associates. In brief, we all agreed that the rocky escarpment in the park along Morningside Drive could be utilized to build a combination University-Community gymnasium that would be of benefit to both parties and would not in any significant way occupy usable park land. It was agreed by all that the building should be in reality two buildings, one superimposed on the other. Since most of the community users would not come from Morningside Heights, it was decided that the lower floors, with a ground-floor entrance opening to the East, would be set aside for the Community, while the upper floors, opening on to Morningside Drive, would be devoted to the needs of Columbia undergraduates.

Columbia agreed to find the funds to finance the entire building cost and to staff the athletic programs in the community gymnasium at its own expense. We drew plans to put into the community gymnasium all the floor-space and athletic facilities which the Parks Department indicated it wished to have available.

We went into this program hesitantly because we recognized the legal and political hurdles that would have to be overcome before such a project could be carried out. One by one these steps were taken, and they were taken with full publicity. The project was approved successively by the Mayor, the Board of Estimate, the City Council, the Municipal Art Commission, two successive Parks Commissioners, both houses of the State Legislature and the Governor. Open public hearings were held by the Board of Estimate before its approval was given.

When all these City and State officials and bodies had officially approved the proposal, a lease for the necessary land (2.1 acres) was signed and we began to draw our final plans and to try to raise the necessary funds for what we knew would be a costly building and program. To date, we have raised $5,900,000* of the $11,500,000 needed for construction.

The third Parks Commissioner, Mr. Hoving, unlike his two predecessors, was not sympathetic to the plan and he used his official position to encourage neighborhood groups to try to block its execution. Also, some citizens on the Heights, who had no interest in the gymnasium project *per se* but who were opposed to the physical expansion of the University on the Heights, seized upon the project as a means of causing trouble generally for Columbia.

After many meetings with City officials and neighborhood leaders, the University voluntarily proposed, and the Board of Estimate approved, an amendment to the lease to authorize the University at its own expense to add a swimming pool to the community facilities. The cost of this pool, plus costs of supervision, meant that the University was making a total contribution to the community of nearly $3,000,000 to provide a facility nowhere else available for the teen-age boys of the community.

Much has been made of the fact that only 16 percent of the total floor-space of the combined building will be in the community gymnasium, but I must reiterate that we placed in that part of the building exactly what the Parks Department desired. Far from being a "land grab" by the University, it is a sincere and costly attempt to give to the community a badly-needed facility whereby during the winter as well as summer months neighborhood boys will be engaged in healthful athletic competition under trained supervision and all at Columbia's cost.

If the present opposition should prevail, and if the University

---

* $3,591,000 actually received, balance in pledges.

permanently abandons the project and builds its gymnasium else-where on the Heights, the neighborhood boys will be the sufferers. Columbia will have a gymnasium in some other location, though it will lose several million dollars in the shift, but the teen-age boys of the neighborhood then will have none.

From a news article in the Columbia Daily Spectator, *student newspaper, Columbia University, October 7, 1969 (after the gym plan was dropped).*

Aftermath

Spokesman for both Columbia and the New York City Parks Department yesterday disclaimed responsibility for filling in the excavation in Morningside Park where Columbia's new gymnasium was to have been built. . . .

Wayne State

From an editorial by William Bunge in The South End, *the official student newspaper of Wayne State University, February 11, 1969.*

Wayne-in-Exile

To the Children of Fascistic, Jewish, Arabian, Communistic, Black, Poor, Administrative, Rich and all Other Parents.
    The pool around Helen DeRoy Auditorium is perfect for children's wading. One summer day not so long ago a group of neighborhood children found this delight and started splashing about in it. They did so until the campus guards spotted them and they were removed in no uncertain fashion. Why do the big athletic field, the swimming pool, the tennis courts, the basketball courts have so few children?
    If a map of children were made of Detroit, Wayne is teeming with kids and only the greatest vigilance by the campus police holds back the flood. Nor is Wayne different from other city-located, suburban-commuter schools in this regard. At Marygrove College Mr. Fitzgerald chases children with their bicycles off the campus. He has a little motor scooter and in cases of "hot pur-

suit" roars off campus and up the neighborhood alleys after them. Marygrove used to welcome the children of the neighborhood. They used to be able to cut through the campus, ride bikes in the parking lot, use the nursery school tot lot. But no more. They have been driven into exile and onto the crowded streets.

At the University of Detroit the campus police have been witnessed literally throwing rocks at children bicycling around their campus fountain. Last spring the baseball team, with two priests as defending witnesses, literally threw young boys over the campus fence on their faces when they found the neighborhood kids playing the great American pastime on their turf.

How many children of faculty members have been transported in from the distant suburbs to the campus to see where daddy works? "Somehow" suburban children are made to feel at home on campuses, while poor city children are conditioned into feeling they do not belong.

Of course, the conscious or subconscious anti-children policy of the campus has a "logic." "If we let these Black kids onto campus they will know how to burn us down when they grow up. But if we keep driving them off they will not notice that we are here and we will not attract lightning." Wayne, as a suburban school, organically reacts against everything that lives in Detroit. It can accept suburban-minded Negroes but not inner-city oriented Blacks. It can accept everything from "out there." But it can accept nothing, city Blacks, city Jews, hippies, city artists, nothing, not even the children, from Detroit. . . .

This driving off of the children, of their figurative as well as literal presence, is the deepest wound the campus imposes on Detroit. We tear down the children's homes for more free campus expansion. We tear down their tender pride with the hounding of our instructed campus police. This must be reversed.

Let the neighborhood children play on the grass, for God's sake. Let children splash in the wading pool. Let them be under foot at athletic events. Let the Athletic Department turn part of their attention and facilities, especially in the summer, over to the tots across Trumbull.

Let the campus have a Children's Week, or at least a Children's Day, in which the faculty "stoops" to lecture to the school children so that these children will know that Wayne is "their school" when they are all grown up and ready to go to college.

Berkeley—The People's Park

An anonymous proclamation by supporters of People's Park, early May 1969.

Proclamation

When the sane people don't do it, when all the good middle class people don't do it, then the madmen have to do it, and the madmen say that we're going to have freedom or we're going to have chaos; we're going to be part of the total destruction of America or we're going to be part of the liberation of America.

—Eldridge Cleaver

A new Berkeley is being planted in People's Park. Creating the Park has been the most spontaneous and positive event in the emerging showdown between the Industrial-University Machine and our Revolutionary Culture. We have struggled for Rights, for Space, and now we struggle for Land. We need the Park to live and grow, and eventually we need all of Berkeley.

The Machine cannot "contain" us because we're stealing everybody's children. They cannot suck us dry and wear us out because we nourish ourselves by working together every day. They cannot stand having us on the Avenue, near the University, they cannot stand our Life resisting their Expansion of Commerce. They want us to give up trying to live, they want us out of town, they want us dead. If they can get away with it, they will seize the land, arrest us by the hundreds, use gas on the Avenue like it was DDT.

We become stronger every day. Our continued planting in the park, backed by a united front of community support, might win for us. But if this strategy fails, we are not left only with the romantic finale of "going down with the park." We can let them know the consequences before they send the bulldozers.

WE TAKE A SOLEMN OATH to wage a war of retaliation against the University if it BEGINS to move against the Park. We are prepared to defend ourselves and the Park if other methods fail. If the University attempts to seize $1.3 million dollars worth of land now claimed by the people, we will destroy $5 million dollars worth of University property. We will not strike until the University proves by concrete deeds—such as the sending of surveyors or posting trespass notices—that it intends to take away our Park. But we will strike before they rip off the Park with their goddamn bulldozers.

If we fight the same way we work—together in teams, with determination—we will win. Get together with the people you've worked with, and take an oath like ours. Figure out how to save the Park and save yourselves: from cameras, clubs, gas and anything they throw at us.

NO SURVEYORS
NO FENCES AGAINST THE PEOPLE
NO BULLDOZERS
BE MASTERS OF SILENCE, MASTERS OF THE NIGHT
WITH SHOVELS AND GUNS
POWER TO THE PEOPLE AND THEIR PARK
By MADMEN

Statement by Chancellor Roger Heyns, University of California, Berkeley, The Daily Californian, May 14, 1969.

The Administration Position

We have been presented a park we hadn't planned or even asked for. But, strange as it may seem, no one seems to be happy about it. The people who have been working on the park are anxious about the future of this gift. The residents in the area are unhappy about the crowds, the behavior, and the noise. The City officials are worried about the crime and control problems it presents. Some of the citizens of the state are angry at what they conceive to be the seizure of University property. It can be surmised that some others are unhappy because this was not the intended use of the land purchased with a precious million dollars. The intramural people feel that long needed additional playing fields are in jeopardy. Most people are worried about a confrontation, although some people are afraid there might not be one. As for me, I feel the burden of these worries and several more I haven't mentioned.

The strategists are having a field day, however. "The University is inflexible." "The University is vacillating." "The University never takes time to hear what people have to say." "The University should have moved in immediately!" "We've got the perfect issue: The people versus the heartless University, creativity versus bureaucracy." And on and on.

At this point I hope everyone will reread the statement issued by the Office of Public Information on April 30, 1969. It made clear that the land was designated for University use in 1956; that the Regents voted to acquire it in June 1967, for the purpose of intramural and recreational play fields, an important campus need. The statement went on to make three points: (1) The University was going ahead with its plan to use the land for recreational purposes. (2) We were willing to discuss the design of the field, and possible uses of the area by the community. (3) We were willing to discuss the possibility of alternative sites on which the University, the City and the community might join to create a park-like facility.

Since that time we have met with many people and heard lots of opinions. On May 8, I asked the Chancellor's Advisory Committee on Housing and the Environment to assist in further modification of the plan. We had agreed that it was to return with a procedure for planning which would permit broad consultation. I asked this committee to develop an alternative design to the original one discussed for the use of the area in question. I urged that it discuss ideas and proposals from students and from the community. I also asked that the chairman work with the Office of Architects and Engineers, whose knowledge of the site and whose planning up to this point will be useful. We estimated that it would take about three weeks to arrive at a design. I indicated that after the design was developed, I would consult with the City to have it evaluated from its viewpoint and I would be responsible for the final decision. I indicated that although the need for playing fields was important and had to be met, the plan might well be modified to accommodate the interest of other University recreational needs and purposes. I stated the following limits on a modified final design:

1. The functions of the field must be related to University needs, particularly student needs for recreational space.

2. The area must remain under the control of the University, with respect to planning and eventual use.

3. The field must not present police or other control problems.

4. It must not be used for the gathering of large crowds for meeting purposes.

In order for the plan to be effective, it was necessary that all further development of the area be stopped.

Unfortunately, this plan could not be carried out. The individuals working on the land have refused to organize a responsible committee with which the University could consult and also refused to stop further activity in the field. It is now clear that no one can speak for the anonymous developers, and no one can control the growing safety, health and liability problems in the area.

So what happens next? First, we will have to put up a fence to reestablish the conveniently forgotten fact that the field is indeed the University's, and to exclude unauthorized persons from the site. That's a hard way to make a point, but that's the way it has to be. I hope that this will make some of the people mentioned in paragraph one relax. The fence will also give us time to plan and to consult. Regretfully, this is the only way the entire site can be surveyed, soil tested, and planned for development. We tried, as I said, to get this time some other way and failed—hence the fence.

Then we will start work on the field itself. The Office of Architects and Engineers has proposed a design which is consistent with the needs stated when The Regents (at our request) moved to acquire the land. The design of the entire area isn't completed, but the western area will consist of a playing field for softball, touch football and soccer. The northeast area can then be developed as an outdoor recreational area to include greenery and play equipment for the children of married students. This plan would save the large redwood (a value learned from previous University experience) and would permit the development, on the eastern part, of other recreational use such as volleyball and basketball.

We will start with the western section and its use, i.e., the playing fields. We will not remove the projects developed spontaneously until we see how many of them can be incorporated into the design. (Of course, people who doubt our intentions may be permitted to come in and remove their contributions. More about this later.) This should make some others in paragraph one happy, or if not happy at least cautiously optimistic.

Now, on the advice of counsel, I must issue the following stern warning:

"The University is now prepared to proceed with site development. This property (Bowditch, Haste and Dwight) belongs to

The Regents of the University of California and will not be available to unauthorized persons. Any equipment or other property on these premises not belonging to the University and not removed promptly may be deemed to be abandoned. Moreover, persons on these premises without authority from the University shall be subject to the laws prohibiting trespass."

A final comment. By this time most of us should be quite sophisticated about these situations. There is no serious shortage of people who would like nothing better than to have us all in a turmoil all summer. There are some people who will try to get us to lose our cool. We will honestly try to accommodate most of the objectives that the people who have been working on the park had in mind. But we are also interested in the people for whom the park is a problem. Above all, we are interested in the many thousands of students who will be attending this University in the years to come.

Article by Brent Tempest, sports editor of The Daily Californian, *student newspaper, Berkeley, May 16, 1969*

No Fence, No Fun

When I was a kid I used to hate cyclone fences—it seemed then that everytime I tried to get into a ball game or trip into the forest there was always one of those damn chain-link fences between me and my destination.

If the goal of my travels was especially delicious (girl scout camp or a junk yard with polliwog colonies in old oil drums), then there was usually barbed-wire rimming the top.

The chain-link part of the fence was usually negotiable—by squeezing the toes of your tennis shoes in the little gaps between chain-links, you could wriggle your way to the top.

You feel especially precarious clinging there with the fence swaying and your fingers all white and cold, gripping chain mesh. Barbed wire at the top was usually at a 45-degree angle to the fence and made you feel extremely naked and vulnerable clinging there.

After several years of negotiating cyclone fences as a kid, I began to associate the fencing off of anything with the importance of that which was being fenced. I soon avoided going places that were not fenced in—pragmatic American reasoning: "whatever isn't fenced in is probably not worth seeing."

In the past year I've been continually reminded of my childhood maxim—no fence, no fun. During the Jazz Festival I came face-to-face with one of the better planned fences I've ever seen. . . .

People's Park is fenced in. People's Park is fenced in. People's Park is fenced in—cyclone fence, constructed by America's cyclone fence mafia in one night. It's natural: take something as creative and restful as a park and you have to fence it in—or else no one would think it was worthwhile.

But the problem is that it is not going to remain a park—it's destined, at least in part, to be cemented and made into basketball and volleyball courts. Very sporting.

Do you remember pictures of the East German soldiers playing volleyball behind the Berlin Wall—very sporting.

* * * * *

Walking across campus on his way to the library a friend of mine picked up a shotgun shell that had been emptied at running students—on the bottom of the shell it said: "For quail." Very sporting.

My friend asked the policeman if he'd seen any good coveys. The policeman said: "What?" My friend asked him why he was on campus—the policeman smirked and replied: "I'm here—can you dig it?", really, a policeman: "Can you dig it?"—really!

Everything was very sporting—quail hunts, volleyball courts, soccer fields, and rock throwing.

Everybody was being very sporting except the people who called the police in early in the morning and fenced the park off in record time to avoid conflict . . . that is an action akin to winning a football game by forfeit.

They should have at least waited for the other team to show up —it was natural for the other team to be upset—they came late and decided to construct their own playing field (from Bancroft to Parker) and they forced the other team to play.

* * * * *

Ronald Reagan—an old sportsman (he rode the lead horse in the Rose Bowl parade)—tipped his glasses forward and said: "The police found stakes, bamboo poles, rocks and bricks on the property. Someone must have had in mind some kind of disturbance."

Dear Ronald, not all houses are made of ticky-tacky, some are made of stakes, bamboo poles, rocks and bricks. It would be pretty silly of us to plan a disturbance and come armed with sticks and stones against the cyclone fence, mafia's guns and gas.

But watch out Ronald—someday we may prepare for a disturbance and when we do we'll bring guns. Very sporting.

Anonymous leaflet reprinted in Outcry #2 (*Radical Student Union*), *University of California, Berkeley, May 24, 1969. Lightly imprinted on the leaflet was the figure of an American Indian.*

Who Owns the Park?

Someday a petty official will appear with a piece of paper, called a land title, which states that the University of California owns the land of the People's Park. Where did that piece of paper come from? What is it worth?

A long time ago the Costanoan Indians lived in the area now called Berkeley. They had no concept of land ownership. They believed that the land was under the care and guardianship of the people who used it and lived on it.

Catholic missionaries took the land away from the Indians. No agreements were made. No papers were signed. They ripped it off in the name of God.

The Mexican Government took the land away from the Church. The Mexican Government had guns and an army. God's word was not as strong.

The Mexican Government wanted to pretend that it was not the army that guaranteed them the land. They drew up some papers which said they legally owned it. No Indians signed those papers.

The Americans were not fooled by the papers. They had a stronger army than the Mexicans. They beat them in a war and took the land. Then they wrote some papers of their own and forced the Mexicans to sign them.

The American Government sold the land to some white settlers. The Government gave the settlers a piece of paper called a land title in exchange for some money. All this time there were still some Indians around who claimed the land. The American army killed most of them.

The piece of paper saying who owned the land was passed around among rich white men. Sometimes the white men were interested in taking care of the land. Usually they were just interested in making money. Finally some very rich men, who run the University of California, bought the land.

Immediately these men destroyed the houses that had been built on the land. The land went the way of so much other land in America—it became a parking lot.

We are building a park on the land. We will take care of it and guard it, in the spirit of the Costanoan Indians. When the University comes with its land title we will tell them: "Your land title is covered with blood. We won't touch it. Your people ripped off the land from the Indians a long time ago. If you want it back now, you will have to fight for it again."

Open letter to fellow faculty members by Denise Levertov, Department of English, Berkeley, in The Daily Californian, *May 16, 1969.*

Human Values and People's Park

Yesterday with some young poets (students) I was at People's Park shoveling up garbage into a truck and taking it away to the city dump. Around us others were digging, planting flowers, enjoying the sun and good fellowship, playing with children, peacefully rapping. The Park was a little island of Peace and hope in a world made filthy and hopeless by war and injustice.

Early this morning my husband and I were awakened by the familiar, ominous sound of a police helicopter zooming back and forth over the streets of Berkeley. By 7:30 A.M., when we got to the Park, the bulldozers were already destroying the happy place human beings had begun to construct for each other, and a different kind of garbage—the concrete around the bases of fence posts—was being poured into it, in place of what we had removed the day before.

A university is supposed to teach, among other things, the Humanities. Are you, brothers and sisters who teach, going to let this inhumane thing happen, in your name—our name—the name of the University of which we, the Faculty, are a part—without a squeak? Do we believe in humane values, in constructive, creative life, or don't we? Or does the average professor—as many of the kids believe, or at least suspect—consider Property as sacred, and people and their needs and aspirations as dispensable?

Those whose first consideration is to save their own skins, preserve their status in the existing system, maintain their own property interests, will some day—soon—find that they too are victims of the new McCarthyism. Recent developments in the area of Hiring and Firing are more than straws in the wind. Wake up. Remember your own humanity. You are people, not teaching machines. Join with other people in outraged resistance to the smashing of human endeavors. A Faculty Strike might help. We might not restore the Park to the People, but we might at least give some sign that all those books, all those poems, all that philosophy, all that body of civilized knowledge we are paid to transmit MEANS something, means something to US; that we believe in the "values" we are supposed to convey.

From an editorial in The Daily Californian, *University of California, Berkeley, May 19, 1969.*

And There Are No Parks Outside the Gates of Eden

History is full of parallels.

The Russians were in Czechoslovakia; the Guard is in Berkeley. Columbia was going to build a gym and moved against blacks; Berkeley builds a playing field against the people. To protest a stadium at UCLA students held a football game in the administration building. Saturday the men of Barrington blocked off the street in front of their co-op and played soccer.

We have taken over the streets, closed the stores, and are busy recruiting the National Guard. We have our playing fields. The University has our park, but cannot keep it.

How long can the University allow its students to be wantonly shot down in the streets without an outcry? How long can any human being stay silent in the face of the death terror which walks among us? . . .

People's Parks are a new idea that a Field Station could study. Pittsburgh has one, and there will be more. The University has an opportunity now to put itself on the side of the future.

The University was warned months ago there was a crime problem where the park is now, and asked to fence the area. Instead, it has contributed to our soaring crime rate, contributed to hospital overloads, to alienation and anomie.

But even though there have been beatings and gas and shootings, the spirit of the people grows. Now two parks have been started in Berkeley, and a garden to grow food for the poor. The spirit grows, despite repression. In the face of adversity, man's will to survive increases. . . .

Eric Hoffer, a member of the President's Commission on Violence, speaking at a U.S. Senate hearing last week, said we need "Chancellors of universities and mayors of cities who will get up in the morning and spit on their hands and say, 'Who am I going to kill today?' "

He should have added "congressmen" and "governors." We seem to have the rest already.

Letter to the People of People's Park from the Third World Liberation Front (TWLF) Steering Committee, published in The Daily Californian, *Berkeley, May 23, 1969.*

Their Foe Is Ours

To The People of People's Park:

It is in the spirit of brotherhood that we write to you. You have shown through courageous and consistent action that you, like us, are frustrated, tired of and disgusted with the forces that conspire against us all.

We have learned in the past that you do not judge a person by what he says, or what he thinks, but by what he does. You have fought. You have been hurt. The REAL TEST IS YET TO COME. WILL YOU COME BACK? We do not suggest that you come again, unorganized, naive, and with only your moral indignation. COME BACK ORGANIZED, PREPARED TO GIVE AS WELL AS RECEIVE—COME BACK A MILLION.

And to Brother Rector, because in his death he gained a brotherhood with all oppressed people, we express our sympathies to his memory and family. AND TO YOU—ORGANIZE.

TO PEOPLE OF COLOR ON THIS CAMPUS. IT IS ALL TOO CLEAR THAT THOSE WHO TAKE A PARK AWAY ARE OF THE SAME FAMILY THAT BRUTALIZE OUR

COMMUNITIES, TERRORIZE OUR WOMEN, AND DE-
STROY THE ESSENCE OF FREEDOM ITSELF. JOIN IN
THIS STRUGGLE, WE MUST SEE THAT THEIR FOE IS
OURS.
POWER TO THE PEOPLE
POWER TO THE PEOPLE OF COLOR
POWER TO THE PEOPLE OF JUSTICE
T.W.L.F. Steering Committee

*Speech given by Mario Savio, leader of Free Speech Movement in 1964, at
Berkeley, June 1969.*

People's Park

Why are we all here? Some of the good brothers and sisters
started building a park on land they'd ripped off and though it
was far better for people to have a park there, than want a park,
everyone from the governor down to John DeBonis had apoplexy.
They even murdered one of our people. We are here because
some of our people sensed in the air that we'd all had vacation
enough; that sitting on our butts smoking dope—good as it was—
wasn't getting us any closer to the Aquarian Age. So, ready or
not, it was time to proclaim the social revolution by seizing the
means of leisure.

What are we? We are the first post-industrial generation. A generation that misses the social revolution our parents failed to
make like Adam and Eve missed the Garden of Eden. Thanks to
John Maynard Keynes and defense spending, capitalism, obscene, gory capitalism, managed somehow to stumble right on
through the period of industrialization; and for some of us anyway has even made it over into this era of post-industrial economy.

We are the first generation with time on its hands. Try to remember back to the distant fifties. The 1950's—the period which
functions in our mythology much as the Dark Ages did to the
men of the Enlightenment. In the dark 50's one of the things
which used to worry what they called social commentators was
this: Whatever would the people of future ages of automation do
with so much free time? Quite a problem. Why, people might go
quite mad with the boredom. Now that American capitalism had

solved all the major problems and was fast going away with much of the worthwhile work. And they would always follow the defense spending, and historical accident, and some supercamp camp director like Clark Kerr or Daniel Bell to figure out things for all the poor alienated people to do.

Well, the future is here right now. We are those very same poor souls. So what do we do with all of our free time? As I see it, the greatest hope implicit is that in our leisure time—so to speak—we will make a social revolution.

How so? The last hope of the ruling class was that they could buy us off by selling us enough of our own records that maybe we might even provide a market against the unlikely threat of nuclear disarmament. Well, it hasn't worked quite that way. They make money with our records, but the music turns out to be awfully subversive. Then in People's Park we started using their property. Making the worst fear of the ruling class—a black alliance. As long as the young blacks could expect us to help them only as a guilty accomplice—only to help them do their thing—help free them—before long they would have very good reason to distrust us. You can't trust an ally who is doing you a favor—you can only trust a comrade who is in it for himself.

This is the great strategic hope implicit in People's Park and the most important reason why the establishment should fear us.

We in the post-industrial sector cannot be bought off, because to do our thing we must challenge on as fundamental a level as our black brothers and sisters—the property relations of this society. It is thus a deeply revolutionary cry which was raised by People's Park and post-industrial capitalism seized the means of leisure. But there is a great question also raised by People's Park, a dark brooding question; evidently we must now all live through a great historical collision between us and the old men and the old way. They didn't just let the people have the park—instead they put up a stiff fight—and for the present they may even have won.

When enough new men come up fast enough to make the difference between liberation and disaster what do we do to maximize the effects of our still small numbers? How can we, indeed can we, prevent the old order from doing its very worst even as it gasps its last? For if anything about People's Park and the occupation of Berkeley is at all clear it is this: the former ruling class must turn over to us, the new men, the means of leisure, including the means of production, to be run democratically by all for the benefit of all. First, if they can they would fight to the social death, which is fascist.

What is fascist? This is one definition; I don't mean to pre-empt those people who are more interested in history and economics. I think fascism is a kind of social psychosis. The men of the old order lead dismal, life-denying, mere existences. A shared social neurosis on which each can play his private variation. These tired men and women spend most of their lives in unconscious conspiracy with one another to expect fictitious fantastical satisfaction from real psychological and biological means.

The old society is universally hierarchical—almost all the people have social betters or forces of one sort or the other. And one of the fantastical satisfactions of the old masked men, except for being bossed and kicked around all the time, is that somewhere there is someone less well off, someone socially inferior. This authoritarian hierarchical structure is present not only in society as a whole but also in the character of every man and woman. As in Plato's *Republic,* "Justice, writ large in the state, is writ small in each man's soul." Every day the fascist in every man fights to suppress the rebel. The inner subordination has a very simple social function. To discourage rebellion.

It all fits together nicely. It is closed upon itself so that it can't see itself and can't talk to itself. And every man who helps to preserve the status quo by fighting to suppress social insurgency is awarded a bonus in fictitious satisfactions.

Pity the pigs. The danger of fascism is great, as it is now, when this latent, largely unconscious but pervasive, authoritarianism threatens to become the overt scene of social life. This can happen if a significant minority at the bottom discover the way to see out of the otherwise closed box and then ask for real satisfaction instead of fiction. This throws the whole precarious system into great danger since everyone higher up must then face the utter emptiness of years of pretend life. The temptations of men of all social classes to hold ranks against these insurgents may then be overwhelming even though all this fantasy really only benefits the upper classes. For every man is infected deep in his soul by this authoritarianism.

In America, two substantial groups have found windows by which to see out of this hierarchy. First, the black and evermore other non-anglo minorities at the bottom of the ladder who never achieved significant status anyway. And second, we post-industrial whites whom technological evolution has now taken quite beyond the division of labor itself and therefore beyond the relevance of the whole hierarchy. But for most Americans the hierarchy status is still the standard of personal worth. We niggers, white and black, are challenging that standard; we are spitting on it, we are trampling it. In the great rush to suppress our rebellion the old men of the old order may in significant numbers cross over the lines from daily and controlled neurosis to psychotic madness. That is what fascism could mean in the United States.

We of the first post-industrial generation are natural communists. For us, property is not a thing to keep men apart and at war, but rather a medium by which men can come together to play, like People's Park, and learn the importance of communal fellowship and cooperation.

The future is ours, as a matter of course and thanks to the park and the hard if uncomprehending labor of our parents. We were born to build a cooperative commonwealth upon the wreckage of this class-ridden barbarism. Only one thing can go wrong—there might not be a future. The immediate task before us is preservation; is the prevention, or failing that, the defeat of fascism. How this is to be accomplished, if it is to be accomplished, is something that we will have to learn together in the coming months and years. We should all hope, but we can't expect, that all of us here today will live to see the full true worth of our own proper age when we can take up the means of leisure without preparing to battle the police.

Report by William Moore in the San Francisco Chronicle, *January 1, 1970 on the outcome of the People's Park controversy.*

Aftermath

The first paying customer skidded into the new commercial parking lot on the former People's Park yesterday—to the accompaniment of spraying gravel and howls of derision from several dozen protesters.

At 10:32 A.M., Joseph Bishop, a balding laundry operator, drove his brown automobile through the picket-encircled Haste Street entrance, thereby becoming the first person to break the boycott that has kept the 130-space lot empty since it opened Tuesday morning.

Bishop hopped out, briskly walked over to the central parking meter, and plunked 50 cents into the slot.

"I needed a place to park," he growled to reporters. "I'm not a crusader. I've just put up with a lot of junk over the years."

He stomped off amid a flurry of picket-inspired references to his ancestry.

Within an hour, three more cars rolled in, and by noon, the man who leased the lot from the University of California—Frank Chaves, vice president of the Parking Company of America—was positively beaming.

"Wonderful, just wonderful," he said, as he stood happily next to stall number 15. Nearby, more than a dozen Berkeley policemen sauntered about.

Then, at 12:13 P.M., a black luxury model purred through the south gate to the fenced-in lot. The driver, a distinguished-looking gentleman, stopped alongside the meter and deposited 50 cents.

"We're the silent majority," said his attractive middle-aged wife. "Our patience has reached its limits."

Dan Siegel, the former student body president at the campus, emerged from the swelling crowd of protesters and tried to persuade the couple to reconsider.

"Why aren't you people gainfully employed?" the driver asked Siegel.

A policeman arrived and asked the couple if they were being intimidated.

"Not really," said the husband, "just bothered."

With that they drove off to a deafening roar of epithets from pickets.

By the end of the day, about a dozen cars had parked, most of them inexpensive models in the planned obsolescence tradition of Detroit.

And as two photographers—one of them an underground newsman, the other a plainclothes policeman—stood nearby, snapping pictures of each other, Chaves announced the day's receipts to the press: $6.50.

PART III

THE UNIVERSITY, THE GOVERNMENT, AND THE WAR

Almost everyone agrees that the conflict on American university campuses would not have taken the same form nor had the same intensity—some say would never have occurred at all—were it not for the Vietnam war. Questioning American involvement in Vietnam has led many to question the basic morality of American foreign policy. From that point, many have gone on to a fundamental critique of the whole American social system.

It was in the academy, among professors and students, that this intense questioning first began and took root. Its first manifestation took the form of the educational enterprise, the teach-ins that originated at the University of Michigan and spread throughout the country. But with time, the form and objects of protest became more varied, as radicals challenged almost every aspect of the university's connection with the U.S. government, especially those linked to prosecution of the war in Vietnam.

CHAPTER 5

The Rise of Defiance

Open defiance took root in 1966–67.* One widely-circulated statement of opposition was "A Call to Resist Illegitimate Authority," issued in the fall of 1967 and signed initially by over 100 American intellectuals, including many college professors. It focused on the draft, offering to lend support to "those who undertake resistance to this war." Specifically this was intended to give moral support to the then growing number of college students who were burning their draft cards and refusing induction. If in 1967 this was the position of a minority whose views were thought to be extreme, by April 1969, over 250 student body presidents and college newspaper editors joined in a statement, encouraged by the National Students Association, in which they "publicly and collectively" refused induction and supported others who did the same. About the same time, Resist (the organization which grew out of the first call) issued "A New Call to Resist Illegitimate

* A narrative of early campus anti-war activity from the radical viewpoint may be found in Carl Davidson, "Toward institutional resistance," Volume II, Chapter 6, pp. 129–38.

Authority," going beyond opposition to the war to opposition to "the institutions that support and maintain it," such as schools and universities.

The next logical step was taken in September 1969 when the Columbia University Senate (composed of faculty, students, administrators, and others) voted 51-25-3 to express opposition to the war, endorse the October Moratorium for Peace, and even to call for "immediate withdrawal" from Vietnam. This was probably the first such resolution by an official university body. A few days later, the Harvard Faculty of Arts and Sciences passed a similar statement of views against the war. Following President Nixon's decision to send troops into Cambodia in late April 1970, such statements were adopted at dozens of universities. They became almost routine rather than extraordinary. The spring 1970 student strike—the first coordinated campus-based action aimed at national policy—represented a climax of student anti-war activity, with at one point approximately 500 colleges and universities on strike or shut down by their administrations.

Statement signed initially by over 100 intellectuals, issued by Resist, *1967.*

A Call to Resist
Illegitimate Authority

To the young men of America, to the whole of the American people, and to all men of good will everywhere:

1. An ever growing number of young American men are finding that the American war in Vietnam so outrages their deepest moral and religious sense that they cannot contribute to it in any way. We share their moral outrage.

2. We further believe that the war is unconstitutional and illegal. Congress has not declared a war as required by the Constitution. Moreover, under the Constitution, treaties signed by the President and ratified by the Senate have the same force as the Constitution itself. The Charter of the United Nations is such a treaty. The Charter specifically obligates the United States to refrain from force or the threat of force in international relations. It requires member states to exhaust every peaceful means of set-

tling disputes and to submit disputes which cannot be settled peacefully to the Security Council. The United States has systematically violated all of these Charter provisions for thirteen years.

3. Moreover, this war violates international agreements, treaties and principles of law which the United States Government has solemnly endorsed. The combat role of the United States troops in Vietnam violates the Geneva Accords of 1954 which our government pledged to support but has since subverted. The destruction of rice, crops and livestock; the burning and bulldozing of entire villages consisting exclusively of civilian structures; the interning of civilian non-combatants in concentration camps; the summary executions of civilians in captured villages who could not produce satisfactory evidence of their loyalties or did not wish to be removed to concentration camps; the slaughter of peasants who dared to stand up in their fields and shake their fists at American helicopters;—these are all actions of the kind which the United States and the other victorious powers of World War II declared to be crimes against humanity for which individuals were to be held personally responsible even when acting under the orders of their governments and for which Germans were sentenced at Nuremberg to long prison terms and death. The prohibition of such acts as war crimes was incorporated in treaty law by the Geneva Conventions of 1949, ratified by the United States. These are commitments to other countries and to Mankind, and they would claim our allegiance even if Congress should declare war.

4. We also believe it is an unconstitutional denial of religious liberty and equal protection of the laws to withhold draft exemption from men whose religious or profound philosophical beliefs are opposed to what in the Western religious tradition have been long known as unjust wars.

5. Therefore, we believe on all these grounds that every free man has a legal right and a moral duty to exert every effort to end this war, to avoid collusion with it, and to encourage others to do the same. Young men in the armed forces or theatened with the draft face the most excruciating choices. For them various forms of resistance risk separation from their families and their country, destruction of their careers, loss of their freedom and loss of their lives. Each must choose the course of resistance dictated by his conscience and circumstances. Among those already in the armed

forces some are refusing to obey specific illegal and immoral orders, some are attempting to educate their fellow servicemen on the murderous and barbarous nature of the war, some are absenting themselves without official leave. Among those not in the armed forces some are applying for status as conscientious objectors to American aggression in Vietnam, some are refusing to be inducted. Among both groups some are resisting openly and paying a heavy penalty, some are organizing more resistance within the United States and some have sought sanctuary in other countries.

6. We believe that each of these forms of resistance against illegitimate authority is courageous and justified. Many of us believe that open resistance to the war and the draft is the course of action most likely to strengthen the moral resolve with which all of us can oppose the war and most likely to bring an end to the war.

7. We will continue to lend our support to those who undertake resistance to this war. We will raise funds to organize draft resistance unions, to supply legal defense and bail, to support families and otherwise aid resistance to the war in whatever ways may seem appropriate.

8. We firmly believe that our statement is the sort of speech that under the First Amendment must be free, and that the actions we will undertake are as legal as is the war resistance of the young men themselves. In any case, we feel that we cannot shrink from fulfilling our responsibilities to the youth whom many of us teach, to the country whose freedom we cherish, and to the ancient traditions of religion and philosophy which we strive to preserve in this generation.

9. We call upon all men of good will to join us in this confrontation with immoral authority. Especially we call upon the universities to fulfill their mission of enlightenment and religious organizations to honor their heritage of brotherhood. **Now is the time to resist.**

Statement of over 250 student body presidents and college newspaper editors, distributed by U.S. National Students Association, April 25, 1969.

Vietnam and the Draft

Students have, for a long time, made known their desire for a peaceful settlement. The present negotiations, however, are not an end in themselves, but rather, the means to a complete cease-fire and American extrication. And until that cease-fire is reached, or until the Selective Service System is constructively altered, young men who oppose this war will continue to face the momentous decision of how to respond to the draft.

In December of 1966, our predecessors as student body presidents and editors, in a letter to President Johnson, warned that "a great many of those faced with the prospect of military duty find it hard to square performance of the duty with concepts of personal integrity and conscience."

Many of the draft age have raised this issue. In the spring of 1967, over 1000 seminarians wrote to Secretary of Defense McNamara suggesting the recognition of conscientious objection to particular wars as a way of "easing the coming confrontation between the demands of law and those whose conscience will not permit them to fight in Vietnam." In June of 1967, our predecessors submitted, along with a second letter to the President, a petition signed by over 10,000 draft-eligible students from nine campuses, calling for alternative service for those who cannot fight in Vietnam. There have been many other similar attempts to influence Congress and the Administration. Nonetheless, despite all our efforts, the Selective Service System has remained impervious to constructive change. Presently, thousands of fellow students face the probability of immediate induction into the armed forces.

Most of us have worked in electoral politics and through other channels to change the course of America's foreign policy and to remove the inequities of the draft system. We will continue to work in these ways, but the possible results of these efforts will come too late for those whose deferments will soon expire. We must make an agonizing choice: to accept induction into the armed forces, which we feel would be irresponsible to ourselves, our country, and our fellow man; or to refuse induction, which is contrary to our respect for law and involves injury to our personal lives and careers.

Left without a third alternative, we will act according to our conscience. Along with thousands of our fellow students, we campus leaders cannot participate in a war which we believe to be immoral and unjust. Although this, for each of us, is an intensely personal decision, we publicly and collectively express our intention to refuse induction and to aid and support those who decide to refuse. We will not serve in the military as long as the war in Vietnam continues.

From a second statement issued by Resist, *1969.*

A New Call to Resist Illegitimate Authority

Opponents of the Vietnam War have worked to end it in many ways, some through conventional politics, some by supporting draft resistance or attacking university complicity in militarism. Others have carried resistance further, destroying draft files and developing opposition within the armed forces.

We believe that resistance to many forms of illegitimate authority is necessary to bring health to this country and make it a constructive force instead of a terror in the politics of nations.

Therefore, we support those who resist by

- refusing to register for the draft or submit to induction
- impeding the operations of draft boards and induction centers
- expressing anti-war views while in the armed forces, or refusing to obey illegal or immoral orders, or absenting themselves without leave
- conducting rent and workers' strikes, boycotts, and similar direct actions aimed at ending exploitation in the fields, in factories, in housing
- organizing against harassment by police, by the FBI, by the courts, and by Congress
- organizing sit-ins, strikes, and any principled actions at schools and universities, to end racist practices and direct complicity with militarism. . . .

Two years ago, the first Call to Resist Illegitimate Authority focused on the war and the draft. **But we cannot oppose the war without opposing the institutions that support and maintain it.** Imperialism, militarism, economic exploitation, undemocratic power, racism: though the words may seem stale, they describe the exercise of illegitimate authority in the United States today. Again, we call upon all to join us in the struggle against illegitimate authority. **Now is the time to resist.**

Resolution of the Columbia University Senate, September 26, 1969.

Resolution on Vietnam

Resolved, The University Senate expresses its opposition to the war in Vietnam. While as individuals we differ in detail, this body agrees that the most reasonable plan for peace is the immediate withdrawal of all U.S. troops. We join in a united and continuous national effort to bring our troops home.

Therefore, be it resolved that the Columbia University Senate authorizes students, faculty, and staff who wish to participate in and/or observe the October 15 Moratorium for Peace be permitted to do so without penalty or prejudice. This authorization will make possible the widest participation in the educational and memorial programs being planned.

CHAPTER 6

The Draft

The draft, of course, was the aspect of government policy that hit closest to home for students. Draft-card burning became the tactic of the committed relatively early in the opposition to the Vietnam War. When deferments for graduate students were eliminated and later when occupational deferments were reduced, many hitherto apolitical students began to think about the war.

The draft impinged directly on the university as an educational institution in several ways. For one thing, the Selective Service intended that it do so. On July 1, 1965, the Selective Service System included in its Orientation Kit a memorandum on "channeling," indicating that the draft was being used as a way of guiding occupational choice and hence university careers. It was only in 1967 that the memorandum came to light outside the Selective Service bureaucracy. When it did, it was taken up by student protesters as proof of what they had been saying about the way the American system worked and the university's direct involvement in it. A clear statement of this critique was issued by the Columbia University chapter of the Resistance, an organization of those refusing induction.

There was another mode of impingement that bothered the faculty even more than channeling. Draft deferments were based, in part, on class rank. This meant that each time a professor assigned a student a grade, he was also assigning a position on a scale of likelihood to be drafted—and thus performing a service needed to carry on the war. In effect, he was helping the Selective Service decide which men it would take.

In May 1966, a group of 142 professors at universities in the Chicago area drew up a statement opposing the use of class rank by the Selective Service as an intrusion into the educational process. The professors added that they did not wish to give "an intrinsically arbitrary decision a cover of pseudo-objectivity." At Columbia, where the issue was also raised, a faculty committee at first recommended that class ranks not be withheld from the government, but their views were subsequently rejected by the Faculty as a whole, and the University Council. Columbia's Trustees, however, fearful of the political implications of refusing the Selective Service information on class standing, decided to abolish the computing of class rank altogether, as a progressive educational measure. Thus the final action could not be construed as a protest against the war.

A third way in which the draft affected universities arose out of student protest itself. On October 24, 1967, General Lewis B. Hershey, the Director of Selective Service, sent a letter and memorandum to local draft boards declaring that all draft-card burners should be considered "delinquent" and immediately inducted. The general later added that students who obstructed campus military recruiters would also be reclassified, and indeed some were. These rulings caused an uproar, with many charging that the Selective Service had no right to impose penalties on civilian protesters. This view, later upheld by the courts, was reflected in an appeal from the Ivy League college presidents to President Lyndon B. Johnson to overrule General Hershey. The Selective Service director was eventually forced to back down on the issue.

Memorandum from National Headquarters, Selective Service System, July 1, 1965.

Channeling

One of the major products of the Selective Service classification process is the channeling of manpower into many endeavors, occupations, and activities that are in the national interest. This function is a counterpart and amplification of the System's responsibility to deliver manpower to the armed forces in such a manner as to reduce to a minimum any adverse effect upon the national health, safety, interest, and progress. By identifying and applying this process intelligently, the System is able not only to minimize any adverse effect but to exert an effect beneficial to the national health, safety, and interest.

The line dividing the primary function of armed forces manpower procurement from the process of channeling manpower into civilian support is often finely drawn. The process of channeling by not taking men from certain activities who are otherwise liable for service, or by giving deferment to qualified men in certain occupations, is actual procurement by inducement of manpower for civilian activities which are manifestly in the national interest.

While the best known purpose of Selective Service is to procure manpower for the armed forces, a variety of related processes take place outside delivery of manpower to the active armed forces. Many of these may be put under the heading of "channeling manpower." Many young men would not have pursued a higher education if there had not been a program of student deferment. Many young scientists, engineers, tool and die makers, and other possessors of scarce skills would not remain in their jobs in the defense effort if it were not for a program of occupational deferments. Even though the salary of a teacher has historically been meager, many young men remain in that job, seeking the reward of a deferment. The process of channeling manpower by deferment is entitled to much credit for the large number of graduate students in technical fields and for the fact that there is not a greater shortage of teachers, engineers, and other scientists working in activities which are essential to the national interest.

More than ten years ago, it became evident that something additional had to be done to permit and encourage development of young scientists and trained people in all fields. A million and a half registrants are now deferred as students. One reason the Nation is not in shorter supply of engineers today is that they were among the students deferred by Selective Service in previous years. Similarly, Selective Service student deferments reduced what otherwise would have developed into more serious shortages in teaching, medicine, dentistry, and every field requiring advanced study. The System has also induced needed people to remain in these professions and in industry engaged in defense activities or in the support of national health, safety, or interest.

The opportunity to enhance the national well being by inducing more registrants to participate in fields which relate directly to the national interest came about as a consequence, soon after the close of the Korean episode, of the knowledge within the System that there was enough registrant personnel to allow stringent deferment practices employed during war time to be relaxed or tightened as the situation might require. Circumstances had become favorable to induce registrants, by the attraction of deferment, to matriculate in schools and pursue subjects in which there was beginning to be a national shortage of personnel. These were particularly in the engineering, scientific, and teaching professions.

This was coupled with a growing public recognition that the complexities of future wars would diminish further the distinction between what constitutes military service in uniform and a comparable contribution to the national interest out of uniform. Wars have always been conducted in various ways but appreciation of this fact and its relationship to preparation for war has never been so sharp in the public mind as it is now becoming. The meaning of the word "service", with its former restricted application to the armed forces, is certain to become widened much more in the future. This brings with it the ever increasing problem of how to control effectively the service of individuals who are not in the armed forces.

In the Selective Service System the term "deferment" has been used millions of times to describe the method and means used to attract to the kind of service considered to be most important, the individuals who were not compelled to do it. The club of induction has been used to drive out of areas considered to be less important to the areas of greater importance in which deferments were given, the individuals who did not or could not participate in activities which were considered essential to the defense of the Nation. The Selective Service System anticipates further evolution in this area. It is promoting the process by the granting of deferments in liberal numbers where the national need clearly would benefit.

Soon after Sputnik I was launched it became popular to reappraise critically our educational, scientific, and technicological inventory. Many deplored our shortage of scientific and technical personnel, inadequacies of our schools, and shortage of teachers. Since any analysis having any connection with manpower and its relation to the Nation's survival vitally involves the Selective Service System, it is well to point out that for quite some time the System had been following a policy of deferring instructors who were engaged in the teaching of mathematics and physical and biological sciences. It is appropriate also to recall the System's previously invoked practice of deferring students to prepare themselves for work in some essential activity and the established program of deferring engineers, scientists, and other critically skilled persons who were working in essential fields.

The Congress, in enacting the Universal Military Training and Service legislation declared that adequate provisions for national security required maximum effort in the fields of scientific research and development, and the fullest possible utilization of the Nation's technicological, scientific, and other critical manpower resources. To give effect to this philosophy, the classifying boards of the Selective Service System defer registrants determined by them to be necessary in the national health, safety, or interest. This is accomplished on the basis of evidence of record in each individual case. No group deferments are permitted. Deferments are granted, however, in a realistic atmosphere so that the fullest effect of channeling will be felt, rather than be terminated by military service at too early a time.

Registrants and their employers are encouraged and required to make available to the classifying authorities detailed evidence as to the occupations and activities in which the registrants are engaged. It is not necessary for any registrant to specifically request deferment, but his selective service file must contain sufficient current evidence on which can be based a proper determination as to whether he should remain where he is or be made available for service. Since occupational deferments are granted for no more than one year at a time, a process of periodically receiving current information and repeated review assures that every deferred registrant continues to contribute to the overall national good. This reminds him of the basis for his deferment. The skills as well as the activities are periodically reevaluated. A critical skill that is not employed in an essential activity does not qualify for deferment.

Patriotism is defined as "devotion to the welfare of one's country." It has been interpreted to mean many different things. Men have always been exhorted to do their duty. But what that duty is depends upon a variety of variables, most important being the nature of the threat to national welfare and the capacity and opportunity of the individual. Take, for example, the boy who saved the Netherlands by plugging the dike with his finger.

At the time of the American Revolution the patriot was the so-called "embattled farmer" who joined General Washington to fight the British. The concept that patriotism is best exemplified by service in uniform has always been under some degree of challenge, but never to the extent that it is today. In today's complicated warfare when the man in uniform may be suffering far less than the civilians at home, patriotism must be interpreted far more broadly than ever before.

This is not a new thought, but it has had new emphasis since the development of nuclear and rocket warfare. Educators, scientists, engineers, and their professional organizations, during the last ten years particularly, have been convincing the American public that for the mentally qualified man there is a special order of patriotism other than service in uniform—that for the man having the capacity, dedicated service as a civilian in such fields, as engineering, the sciences, and teaching constitute the ultimate in their expression of patriotism. A large segment of the American public has been convinced that this is true.

It is in this atmosphere that the young man registers at age 18 and pressure begins to force his choice. He does not have the inhibitions that a philosophy of universal service in uniform would engender. The door is open for him as a student to qualify if capable in a skill badly needed by his nation. He has many choices and he is prodded to make a decision.

The psychological effect of this circumstantial climate depends upon the individual, his sense of good citizenship, his love of country and its way of life. He can obtain a sense of well being and satisfaction that he is doing as a civilian what will help his country most. This process encourages him to put forth his best effort and removes to some degree the stigma that has been attached to being out of uniform.

In the less patriotic and more selfish individual it engenders a sense of fear, uncertainty, and dissatisfaction which motivates him, nevertheless, in the same direction. He complains of the uncertainty which he must endure; he would like to be able to do as he pleases; he would appreciate a certain future with no prospect of military service or civilian contribution, but he complies with the needs of the national health, safety, or interest—or is denied deferment.

Throughout his career as a student, the pressure—the threat of loss of deferment—continues. It continues with equal intensity after graduation. His local board requires periodic reports to find out what he is up to. He is impelled to pursue his skill rather than embark upon some less important enterprise and is encouraged to apply his skill in an essential activity in the national interest. The loss of deferred status is the consequence for the individual who has acquired the skill and either does not use it or uses it in a nonessential activity.

The psychology of granting wide choice under pressure to take action is the American or indirect way of achieving what is done by direction in foreign countries where choice is not permitted. Here, choice is limited but not denied, and it is fundamental that an individual generally applies himself better to something he has decided to do rather than something he has been told to do.

The effects of channeling are manifested among student physicians. They are deferred to complete their education through school and internship. This permits them to serve in the armed forces in their skills rather than in an unskilled capacity as enlisted men.

The device of pressurized guidance, or channeling, is employed on Standby Reservists of which more than 2½ million have been referred by all services for availability determinations. The appeal to the Reservist who knows he is subject to recall to active duty unless he is determined to be unavailable is virtually identical to that extended to other registrants.

The psychological impact of being rejected for service in uniform is severe. The earlier this occurs in a young man's life, the sooner the beneficial effects of pressured motivation by the Selective Service System are lost. He is labeled unwanted. His patriotism is not desired. Once the label of "rejectee" is upon him all efforts at guidance by persuasion are futile. If he attempts to enlist at 17 or 18 and is rejected, then he receives virtually none of the impulsion the System is capable of giving him. If he makes no effort to enlist and as a result is not rejected until delivered for examination by the Selective Service System at about age 23, he has felt some of the pressure but thereafter is a free agent.

This contributed to establishment of a new classification of I-Y (registrant qualified for military service only in time of war or national emergency). That classification reminds the registrant of his ultimate qualification to serve and preserves some of the benefit of what we call channeling. Without it or any other similar method of categorizing men in degrees of acceptability, men rejected for military service would be left with the understanding that they are unfit to defend their country, even in war time.

An unprejudiced choice between alternative routes in civilian skills can be offered only by an agency which is not a user of manpower and is, therefore, not a competitor. In the absence of such an agency, bright young men would be importuned with bounties and pirated like potential college football players until eventually a system of arbitration would have to be established.

From the individual's viewpoint, he is standing in a room which has been made uncomfortably warm. Several doors are open, but they all lead to various forms of recognized, patriotic service to the Nation. Some accept the alternatives gladly—some with reluctance. The consequence is approximately the same.

The so-called Doctor Draft was set up during the Korean episode to insure sufficient physicians, dentists, and veterinarians in the armed forces as officers. The objective of that law was to exert sufficient pressure to furnish an incentive for application for commission. However, the indirect effect was to induce many physicians, dentists, and veterinarians to specialize in areas of medical personnel shortages and to seek outlets for their skills in areas of greatest demand and national need rather than of greatest financial return.

Selective Service processes do not compel people by edict as in foreign systems to enter pursuits having to do with essentiality and progress. They go because they know that by going they will be deferred.

The application of direct methods to effect the policy of every man doing his duty in support of national interest involves considerably more capacity than the current use of indirection as a method of allocation of personnel. The problem, however, of what is every man's duty when each individual case is approached is not simple. The question of whether he can do one duty better than another is a problem of considerable proportions and the complications of logistics in attempting to control parts of an operation without controlling all of it (in other words, to control allocation of personnel without controlling where people eat, where they live, and how they are to be transported) adds to the administrative difficulties of direct administration. The organization necessary to make the decisions, even poor decisions, would, of necessity, extract a large segment of population from productive work. If the members of the organization are conceived to be reasonably qualified to exercise judgment and control over skilled personnel, the impact of their withdrawal from war production work would be severe. The number of decisions would extend into billions.

A quarter billion classification actions were needed in World War II for the comparatively limited function of the Selective Service System at that time. Deciding what people should do, rather than letting them do something of national importance of their own choosing, introduces many problems that are at least partially avoided when indirect methods, the kind currently invoked by the Selective Service System, are used.

Delivery of manpower for induction, the process of providing a few thousand men with transportation to a reception center, is not much of an administrative or financial challenge. It is in dealing with the other millions of registrants that the System is heavily occupied, developing more effective human beings in the national interest. If there is to be any survival after disaster, it will take people, and not machines, to restore the Nation.

Article in The Resistance, *Columbia University, June 1, 1968.*

University Complicity
with War and the Draft

In resisting the draft, large numbers of students have come to realize the ulterior functions of conscription. In the words of the Selective Service's infamous memo "On Manpower Channelling": "Delivery of manpower for induction, the process of providing a few thousand men with transportation to a reception center, is not much of an administrative or financial challenge. It is in dealing with the other millions of registrants that the System is heavily occupied, developing more effective human beings in the national interest."

In other words, the draft is not designed to service the military so much as to funnel the entire younger generation into other, less obvious, directions and occupations. The process of registration, classification, periodic examination, and final induction or deferment conditions them to the authoritarian rule over the people by the state.

At age 18, when men first register for the draft, they face six years of intense uncertainty regarding their future. Those who can afford it go on from high school to college and are deferred. Those who cannot afford or qualify for higher education either are induced to enlist or left to hold some low-paying job until employers are satisfied that they have fulfilled their service or are over-age. In this way, 40% of all enlistees are seduced into terminating their personal anxiety about the future by "getting it over with" or are tempted to sign up for an "education" and on-the-job training in uniform.

Meanwhile, college graduates find themselves once again confronted with uncertainty and the prospect of induction. Most of them manage to find employment with corporations whose contribution to society have been deemed "in the national interest," and for this they receive 2-A deferments.

With the expectation that they would not have to serve on the front lines, other students volunteer for Officers' Candidates School. Until recently, most could continue in graduate school and idle until age 26. Almost none contemplated resistance because of their fear of isolation in jail or the future prospect of professional ostracism, rending null and void their $10,000 worth of study and means of livelihood. Thus, even the learned, who have had the luxury to study Socrates, Jefferson, Thoreau and Gandhi, and thus who should know better, silently acquiesce or are routinely bribed into complicity.

As the affluent agonize, the poor, promised a better life in the services, exercise "choice, not chance" and shoulder the burden of the war. With college-trained second lieutenants, they comprise most of the combat casualties. In bitterness, the lower classes defensively support the war in understandable reaction to affluent students who deride the war and the GI's, who fight it behind their deferments and exemptions.

That the uneducated die abroad in the interests of the military-industrial complex at home which the educated administer is now widely conceded by most students. The incestuous relationship between the universities and the defense complex and the role of higher education in serving as the biggest social "channel" of all are just beginning to be understood and analysed.

As early as World War I, American universities had abdicated their traditional function as centers of learning. As the American Left was systematically repressed, the universities bowed to the chauvinistic demands of the government and fired numerous professors who opposed US involvement in European imperial affairs. In many schools, such as Columbia University, students who resisted conscription were expelled or denied readmission.

Though conscription for the war ended with the Treaty of Versailles, the universities cooperated with the military during the twenties and thirties, serving as the chief medium of imposing militaristic values on young people. Hundreds of colleges and high schools during these decades instituted compulsory ROTC for all male students. In 1927, at the University of Michigan alone 100 students were dismissed during the academic year for refusing to participate in drill.

Only comparatively recently have some schools liberalized ROTC requirements and made enrollment voluntary. Others, of course, still require it.

During World War II, the influence of the military over education expanded in the way of research and development of weaponry, medicine, and communications in conjunction with university faculty and campus laboratory facilities. The atomic bomb, for instance, was developed secretly at the U. of Chicago and napalm at Harvard.

During the Cold War, universities consolidated their multi-million dollar partnership with the Pentagon and State Department. Literally thousands of students have studied and faculty taught on government funds over the last 20 years, particularly in the area of devising programs to pacify the Third World.

With the end of the Second World War, the US military faced an uphill battle to convince Congress to retain conscription . . .

In return for supporting the principle of conscription and helping to administer the functioning of the draft, universities suddenly benefited from the influx of thousands of youths anxious to flee the draft.

The Selective Service managed to create a climate of hysteria among the middle-class youth community by periodically manufacturing a "manpower crisis" in the same way that the Pentagon and its representatives in Congress simultaneously concocted a "missile gap" during the 1950's in order to finance the arms industry. The invention of "the manpower pool" constituted the greatest contribution to universal philosophical categories since the introduction of the "international Communist conspiracy" into the rhetoric of the Cold War.

In maintaining this gigantic fraud, the Selective Service, with the support of the Association of American Colleges and the American Council of Education, initiated in the early 1950's a series of testing examinations to sustain the level of fearful anxiety on campus. Purportedly these exams were designed to meet the "critical" shortage of voluntary enlistments by drafting idling or poorer students. In fact, the Selective Service never had any intention of drafting students because the alleged shortage did not exist. During the much-publicized tests of 1966–67, for instance, students were led to believe that unless they scored 70 or better they could be inducted and sent to Vietnam. Consequently millions of students, many of whom opposed the war, rushed to take these exams. Yet none of those who scored below the norm (about 10% in Northern schools and 40% in Southern ones), except a few civil rights workers and anti-war activists, were ever drafted as a result.

The tests, in truth, served primarily to placate Congressional and public advocates of a volunteer army who hoped to see the draft die a natural death when the Selective Service Act expired in 1967. Rather than closing ranks and fighting conscription collectively, students competed among themselves to place high in class rank. Some professors of liberal leaning even vowed to give all A's to their students, lest a C+ rather than a B− send someone off to the war and haunt their conscience.

The complicity of higher education in waging the war in Vietnam extends further than teaming up with the government to co-opt potential draft resistance, and is well documented. In the early 1950's, Michigan State contracted to train the secret police force of Pres. Diem. The U. of Penn. undertook classified research in chemical and bacteriological warfare. Columbia University put out the welcome mat for the Institute of Defense Analysis. A complete list would include almost every college and university in the nation.

In return for their cooperation, the universities received millions of dollars directly in the form of research grants in non-defense, as well of course as defense fields, and millions indirectly for dormitory and classroom construction.

The composition of the board of trustees of any major school best illustrates the collusion between academia, the military, and industry. Of the 14 members of the Board of Overseers at Harvard, for example, 10 are bankers (with major investments in South African apartheid), 2 are industrialists (including the director of the United Fruit Co.) and 2 are government officials (including the former deputy director of the CIA).

It is this type of men, whose activities comprise a Who's Who of international exploitation, who literally own the universities, as more indirectly they control the legislature, the executive, and the judicial branches of government. On the basis of precedent and power, they arrogate to themselves the "right" to pass on university curricula, fire teachers, impose restrictive moral codes on students, permit military and corporate recruiters on campus, and "reserve" the authority to dismiss students without any recourse who challenge the system. Normally, they prefer to operate through liberal administrators, but when they fail, as in the case of Pres. Kirk at Columbia, they enter the picture directly.

As their roles indicate, the major purpose of higher education in America today is to service the domestic and international empire which they own. The universities tolerate radical tendencies within the liberal arts fields, at times offering them comfortable niches, so long as students and teachers do not try to translate their learning into practice. In this respect, they act exactly like the Selective Service which countenances conscientious objection to war but not war-makers. Both systems reward intelligent administrators and technicians who work within the system silently, or at most work to change it in the spirit of reform. Further, like the government and business, universities express righteous indignation at right-wing causes like that of Joe McCarthy, the Birchers, or Sen. Goldwater who would carry out their identical policies with embarrassing candor and awkwardness.

Around the nation, young people are increasingly rebelling against the perversion of knowledge, skill and power by their elders. If they had their choice, millions would never enter college in the first place, and certainly never go on to grad school. The college board exams and the Selective Service testing examinations—which are both administered by the Educational Testing

Service—symbolize the impersonal regimentation which they experience in every aspect of their lives.

But America is not free. Many young people are still deceived into enlisting in school or the armed forces to avoid the draft—an institution created precisely for these purposes. Rather than allow themselves to be channelled into the dehumanizing institutions that currently exist, our generation is taking control of its destiny and creating an alternative, free society.

Statement circulated by a group of professors in the Chicago area, entitled an "Educators' Statement of Principle on Selective Service," May 1966.

Education and the Draft

There are some profound incompatibilities between the aims of education and the aims of warfare. Among the various costs of the war in Vietnam is a corrosive effect on education. This corrosive effect on education would be decreased if the Selective Service Administration would *cease systematically involving colleges and universities in its operations.*

It has been announced that draft boards are being advised to decide draft status of students on class rank as determined by grades. The Selective Service Administration also intends to use a general aptitude test of the kind which was used during the Korean War. The test presumably handles the objection that the significance of class rank varies among colleges.

When deferment is tied to performance in class an atmosphere is generated which seriously interferes with the educational process. Those who taught during the Korean War can well remember such things as the students' panic when a book on reserve was not immediately available, the dampening of free exploratory discussion, the increased tendency of students to take excessive notes and memorize them instead of attempting to critically evaluate material presented to them, and the excessive concern with grades manifested, for example, in anxious bickering over examinations and how they were graded. This is to say nothing of the effect on the professors who know that their grades were relevant to draft status decisions.

Educators have often pointed out the negative effects of excessive emphasis on grades. Requests by draft boards for grade information only exacerbates these negative effects. Experimentation with alternatives to grading, which may result in better education is handicapped by the necessity of supplying grades to the Selective Service Administration.

There are no ultimately just criteria by which to decide who shall and who shall not be conscripted. The interest of the Selective Service Administration in making these decisions less arbitrary is laudable and understandable. These decisions are difficult. However, the professor should not be made a party to these decisions since it interferes with the performance of his duties. Furthermore, the seeming precision of rank in class cannot overcome the intrinsically arbitrary character of the decision. It is important that we do not lend to an intrinsically arbitrary decision a cover of pseudo-objectivity when, in the course of so doing, we impede the educational enterprise of all college and university students.

For the sake of the national welfare there should be as radical a separation of the activities of the Selective Service Administration from the educational enterprise as possible. Even in such things as the administration of tests, it would be better if this be done without call upon the colleges and universities, that the two enterprises not be confounded. It is hard to believe that rank in class really predicts the contribution to the national welfare that a student will eventually make. It is, however, easier to see how interference by the Selective Service Administration in the educational enterprise has a negative effect.

From the report of the Faculty Committee on the Draft, the Faculty of Columbia College, April 14, 1966.

Against Withholding Class Rank

We are aware that it is the prospective use of class rank in granting deferments that poses the greatest difficulty for many members of the faculty. Although it is reasonable to suppose that if some students are to be deferred, then it is the best students who ought to be deferred, we are not entirely confident that rank in class accomplishes this end. Given the disparity in quality among the many educational institutions in the country, it appears that the use of class rank contains its own inequities. (The selective service test may mitigate this somewhat.) Further, we are aware that reliance on class rank may introduce a disruptive element into education. One member of the committee maintains, moreover, that the institutional integrity of colleges and universities is impaired by such procedures.

Notwithstanding these considerations, the committee maintains that *no* change ought to be introduced at the present time in the current Columbia policy on students' records. Under this policy a student's rank in class will be supplied to his draft board on his request (and only on his request). This does not necessarily represent an endorsement by us of the use of class rank by selective service boards. Two of us believe that a student's request to have such information supplied cannot be rejected. A student is morally, and perhaps also legally, entitled to have access to this part of his record for any legitimate use. (The decision of the Law School to refuse to supply rank in class to prospective employers we regard as distinguishable from the case we are considering.) Secondly, we would argue that if it is morally repugnant that the giving of a low grade may put a student into the army, then it is also repugnant to refuse a student his class rank, since this might put him into the army as well. Thirdly, if the use of class rank by draft boards introduces a disruptive element into the educational process, then we ought also recognize that any refusal to supply class rank may have the same effect, as the consequence of an increase in students' anxieties. Finally, the members of this committee agree in rejecting any proposal to abandon, at this time, the computing of class rank. If this is a debatable educational practice, we think it ought to be debated in "a cool hour." And given the new selective service procedure, it may be a gross injustice to our students to abandon this computation now. . . .

Resolution of the Trustees of Columbia University, April 3, 1967.

Class Standing Discontinued

WHEREAS, the University Council has advised the Trustees of its recommendation that, for pedagogical reasons, the policy contained in the following resolution be accepted by the Trustees:
"RESOLVED, That the Faculty of Columbia College re-

spectfully requests of the University administration that class standing calculations for undergraduate students not be reported to Selective Service Boards," and

WHEREAS, although the Trustees are loath to modify recommendations of the University Council on matters of educational policy, they are nevertheless obliged to consider broader implications of such decisions in the determination of University policy; and

WHEREAS, the Trustees are convinced that the adoption of the policy advised by the University Council might be regarded by many persons as an intrusion by the University, as a corporate body, into the political arena, an intrusion which the Trustees regard as unwise and which they have assiduously sought to avoid; and

WHEREAS, as long as the University maintains class standings, in the opinion of the Trustees the University may not properly refuse to furnish them to students upon their request; and

WHEREAS, the Trustees have been informed by the University administration that from a practical standpoint no hardship would be imposed upon individual students by the discontinuance of the maintenance of class standings for any purpose by the University;

NOW, THEREFORE, the Trustees do hereby

RESOLVE, that it shall be the stated policy of the University to discontinue as of this date the maintenance of all class standings by the University.

CHAPTER 7

Government-Sponsored Research

The most critical link between universities and the government has been through federally-funded research. Controversy has centered principally on projects sponsored by the military and the Central Intelligence Agency. Military research projects became common during the Second World War, continued with increasingly generous financing during the Cold War, and finally came under attack during the Vietnam War. In most cases, the universities contracted with the government for specific projects to be done by faculty members, research assistants and graduate students. In a few cases, the ties were fully institutional. For example, the Institute for Defense Analyses—a military research consortium that became a major issue in 1968—was formally comprised of twelve member universities, including Chicago, Columbia, and Princeton.

The objections to military research were made on a variety of grounds, both liberal and radical. Where universities were institutionally involved in military research, as with the Institute for Defense Analyses, liberals often argued that such a role was inconsistent with the ideal of institutional neutrality. Liberals also objected to the existence of classified research projects on campus, maintaining that they were incompatible with the ideal of free and open inquiry. A third objection made by liberals to military research projects was that they compromised the independence of the university community. For example, Senator Fulbright argued that "Pentagon-sponsored field reasearch in counter-insurgency" was not "an appropriate activity for social scientists who ought to be acting as independent and critical commentators on their government's policies."

These issues were occasionally raised by radicals, but they did not constitute the crux of the radical critique. The radicals argued that military research was in itself wrong—not because the university should be neutral, or because all research should be open, or because the university should be free of government influence. Their emphasis was that the resources of the university community should be brought to bear on socially constructive research. They opposed military research as support for the Vietnam War and American counter-insurgency throughout the Third World.

Those who defended military research, classified and otherwise, contended the key issue was academic freedom, the freedom of each individual professor and student to do whatever kind of research he chose. Some, like the physicist Edward Teller, warned that if universities refused to do military work, the United States would soon be effectively "disarmed."

The documents in this section follow an historical sequence. In "The military research network—America's fourth armed service," radical investigator Michael Klare describes the historical development of military research at American universities after World War II. Klare analyzes how research has been organized under the Defense Department and how various research organizations are linked with corporations and the military through interlocking directorates. He suggests that it may do no good for radicals to demand that universities sever ties with military research organizations since they can easily be reconstituted as nonprofit research corporations.

It was this realization which led students at Stanford to demand that the Stanford Research Institute (SRI), owned by the university, not be severed or sold, but reconverted "from war research to peace research." *

In the first document from Stanford, a faculty committee defends the existence of some classified research on campus. Due to

* For text of student demands, see Appendix, Volume II.

"nationalistic strife," the faculty report states, the university cannot realize its goal of free dissemination of scholarly research. To place limits on research would be to limit academic freedom.

Two radical pamphlets attack military research at Stanford. After describing some work done by SRI, the radicals suggest that the same facilities could be used to study ways to eliminate poverty, decentralize government, or reduce environmental pollution. They oppose severance or sale of SRI because war research would continue undisturbed. "We must ultimately answer to the Vietnamese people," they conclude.

A research engineer, writing to Stanford's president, contends that the radicals are interfering with individual rights by seeking an end to military research, recruiting and training.

Despite such objections, the university decided to ban most classified research. In its new policy statement, the Academic Council declared that the principle of openness in research "is one of overriding importance." Nevertheless, Stanford did not yield on the research institute. Ties were severed and a separate board of trustees formed.

Two politicians, both in the Democratic Party, had very different reactions to the controversy over military research. J. William Fulbright declared that universities have neglected their public trust as independent institutions "and have gone dangerously far toward becoming servants of the state." Hubert Humphrey, on the other hand, testifying before a House committee, warned universities that they would suffer more than the government by refusing military research. He suggested it would not be "very smart" for them to reject grants.

The controversy at the Massachusetts Institute of Technology in the fall of 1969 presents the issue of government-sponsored research in a more advanced stage. MIT had already banned classified research and accepted the premise that more research on domestic social problems was needed. The attack was now purely based on the radical critique. In "Why smash MIT?" the radicals described seven major military research projects at MIT and claimed that the promise of reconversion was false. In a reply to the radicals, MIT President Howard Johnson insisted that the university was not concerned with weapons research and that it had "made an immense contribution to the quality of life of this nation." He said MIT would try to "move some of the technological capacity of our two off-campus laboratories to the problems of domestic and civil life."

From The University-Military Complex, *published by the North American Congress on Latin America (Box 57, Cathedral Station, N.Y., N.Y. 10025), March 1969. This section was written by Michael Klare.*

The Military Research Network—America's Fourth Armed Service

"Our colleges and universities must be regarded as bastions of our defense, as essential to the preservation of our country and our way of life as supersonic bombers, nuclear-powered submarines, and intercontinental ballistic missiles."
—John A. Hannah, President of Michigan State University (now Director of AID) at a Parents' Convocation in 1961.

The Military Unification Plan, drafted in 1947 by Clark Clifford, established the present composition of the U.S. Military Establishment: it separated the Air Force from the Army and established three military departments—Army, Navy and Air Force—which were made subordinate to the centralized command structure of the Department of Defense. The Plan identified three services, but a fourth, as crucial to the national defense as the others, was not given formal recognition. This service is the network of university laboratories and non-profit research institutes that constitute the University-Military Complex. Without the support of this Fourth Service, the United States would not have produced the atomic bomb, would not have acquired the intercontinental ballistic missile, and would not have developed a counterinsurgency strategy for intervention in Vietnam.

Until the present century, new weapons were developed by hit-or-miss experimentation, or through the continuous refinement of existing devices. It is only [during] the past three decades that instrumentalities of warfare have emerged from organized scientific investigations, in which the talents of many researchers are pooled in the quest for novel military systems. The Manhattan Project of World War II was the prototype of such efforts—at its peak thousands of scientists were engaged in the various subtasks of the project without being aware of the final objective of their work. Subsequent ventures have required a comparable investment of manpower and resources, and there is every indication that this pattern of cooperative research will continue in the future. For this reason the Defense Establishment has found it necessary to establish a group of research organizations, each capable of conducting large-scale "R&D" (research and development) activities in some field of interest to the military. Since the only reservoir of trained scientific manpower available for such work is the university campus, it was thus inevitable that the Pentagon should call upon the universities to collaborate in the foundation of a military research network.

This network was initially organized, on a temporary basis, during the Second World War when many universities set up makeshift laboratories for weapons research. During the course of the War, many of these laboratories grew into sizeable installations, employing thousands of scientists and technicians. Working at such facilities, university scientists were responsible for many of the technological advances brought about under pressure of war, including the atomic bomb, the proximity fuze, and modern radar. These efforts were coordinated by the National Defense Research Committee, the first body of civilians to have an important policy function in the area of military research.

While most of the wartime university research was limited to the physical sciences, other disciplines—including the social and medical sciences—were also active. The biologists expanded our arsenal of chemical and biological weapons; the anthropologists prepared manuals on the primitive societies whose islands and jungles we invaded, and the social scientists were active in the fields of intelligence, psychological warfare and military government. In an unusually frank statement, the former Vice President of Columbia University, Lawrence H. Chamberlain, recalled that during the War, "at the same time that university science departments were co-opted for purposes of war, the knowledge and skills of the social sciences and to a lesser extent the humanities departments were also conscripted for military service."

The World War II university laboratories had been organized on the premise of expediency, and were not intended to outlast the War. As victory approached, however, many of the participating scientists sought to prevent the dissolution of these installments. The reasons for this are not difficult to determine: for the first time in American history, scientists and academicians had come to enjoy positions of considerable prestige and influence in Washington and at the Pentagon. Experiments that were prohibitive in cost before the war now had abundant government financing. Moreover, the establishment of large research organizations had freed many professors from the restraints of conventional academic procedure and permitted them to pursue their experiments without being accountable to their colleagues in tradition-minded university departments. For some scientists—more interested in the application of their research to the "real world" of industry and national security than to the advancement of higher education—this development was most welcome. In describing this phenomenon, Dr. Chamberlain noted that "the need for applying a blend of disciplines and skills to the problems of little-known areas—for purposes of warfare, governmental administration and diplomacy—precipitated the establishment of new research and instructional patterns because the conventional departmental structures were simply not adequate to meet the demands of the job." These new patterns, developed as a wartime expedient, would now become a permanent feature of campus life.

The unique characteristics of university warfare laboratories—the concentration of scientific personnel under conditions of relative autonomy from regular university functions (i.e., teaching)—also proved to be of advantage to the military. With the dawn of the Cold War, the Pentagon found itself with the task of "containing communism" on a front that stretched from Berlin to Seoul. As the former colonial powers of Europe became disengaged from their possessions in Africa and Asia, the U.S. theater of operations expanded to incorporate the defense of the new states on behalf of the "Free World." In many instances this meant shoring them up from the threat of "internal disequilibrium," i.e., from movements for national liberation. These enormous tasks required an unprecedented expansion of the U.S. military establishment and of its ability to engage in unconventional warfare and counterinsurgency. As a result, the Pentagon found it prudent to re-establish the network of university research organizations to cope with the many problems engendered by its new role of policeman to the world.

The Cold War also provided a new impetus on the part of the

universities to engage in defense work. Participation in military research not only provided the reward of being part of the "stirring events of the time," but also, in the feverish days of Cold War hysteria, constituted a demonstration of one's loyalty. Thus when in 1967 a special faculty committee was established at Princeton to determine the University's corporate relationship with the Institute for Defense Analyses (IDA), the strongest argument voiced in favor of continued affiliation was that such a tie "symbolizes a choice by the University to integrate itself into the life of the nation, to relate itself to the pressing problems of contemporary society, and to acknowledge its obligations to the defense of the society of which it is a part." (When the august professors spoke of "the pressing problems of contemporary society," they did not mean the alleviation of oppressive ghetto conditions.)

For this combination of reasons, scores of semi-autonomous military research organizations were created by American universities in the postwar period. Most of these institutions engage in research on military "hardware"—the equipment and weaponry of conventional warfare. Increasingly, however, these installations are developing programs in military "software"—i.e. research in systems analysis, war-gaming and human factors engineering. Systems analysis, and the related technique of operations research, represents one of the most important postwar contributions of the university research network to military science. Through these techniques, complex phenomena are reduced to their component subsystems, each of which is then examined individually. Using computer simulation methods, the subsystems are brought to their most efficient operation (the process of "systems optimization"), and then the total system is reassembled to perform at optimum output ("systems integration"). This methodology has been used to evaluate everything from missile propulsion systems to battlefield tactical doctrine. "Human factors engineering" represents the application of systems analysis to the problem of getting optimum performance out of human beings (or, as the military likes to put it, out of man/man and man/machine systems). Several of the organizations listed below are engaged almost exclusively in software research; most of the others apply software systems to their studies of military hardware.

War Research Is Good Business

As military appropriations soared, ambitious researchers—many of them associated with the Defense Department as consultants—were able to secure substantial research contracts from the government. Most of these contracts went to the autonomous research organizations like Michigan's Willow Run Laboratory and the Cornell Aeronautical Laboratory which could satisfy the Pentagon's strict security requirements. Today some of these organizations enjoy the budget and facilities of a good-sized college. The University of California, for instance, operates the Lawrence Radiation Laboratory and the Los Alamos Scientific Laboratory— installations which have a combined staff of 11,850 scientists, technicians and administrators, and an annual operating budget, in 1966, of $265 million (an amount that exceeds the total endowment of all but a handful of the larger universities). Many scientists associated with these research organizations have been able to further augment their income by setting up defense-oriented "spin-off" industries which market the products developed in university laboratories.

In fact, as one penetrates deeply into the university research network, the distinction between academic and non-academic functions disappears altogether. The trustee or administrator of a university research institute is more than likely the executive of a spin-off industry located in the nearby industrial park, and at the same time a consultant to the Pentagon bureau which administers contracts in his field of research. The independent "think-tanks" like RAND and IDA often act as the middlemen in this consortium. Through such an arrangement, the government can buy top scientific talent while by-passing low civil service talents and avoiding accountability to Congress. Defense industry corporations, whose executives often dominate the boards of trustees of the research institutes and think-tanks, gain access to classified information and have the opportunity to "evaluate objectively" the projects they are trying to sell to the government. The universities, in return for their participation in the consortium, receive large research contracts and lucrative consulting fees for their professors. Examples of this arrangement can be found on every large, research-oriented campus. Stanford, with its wholly-owned subsidiary, the Stanford Research Institute (annual volume of research: $60 million) and adjacent Stanford Industrial Park, could provide dozens of examples, as could MIT, Michigan and Johns Hopkins. The "arrangement" is not, however, unique to these schools. The Director of Columbia's Electronics Research Laboratory (ERL), Lawrence O'Neill, was at one time a professor and associate dean at the Columbia School of Engineering, a consultant to the Department of Defense and the Institute for Defense Analyses, and owner of Federal Scientific Corporation, a company set up to profit from research initiated at ERL. O'Neill now heads the Riverside Research Institute, an organization established last year to replace ERL and expand its Pentagon-financed operations.

The spirit of cooperation that characterizes the components of the U.S. military research network is not surprising when one discovers that more often than not the universities themselves are governed by men representing the corporations that stand to profit most from the university's research activities. An examination of the trustees of almost any college or university will produce at least one or two gentlemen associated with a major defense contractor, and in some cases the number will be much higher. Returning to the example of Columbia, one would find a total of five trustees with important positions in defense industries. Trustee William A. M. Burden, for instance, is a director of Lockheed Aircraft (the third-highest U.S. defense contractor) and also chairman of the Institute for Defense Analyses. Burden is also a director of the Farfield Foundation, used by the CIA to channel over $1 million to the Congress for Cultural Freedom, a key instrument of intellectual cold-warism.

America's Fourth Armed Service, the university research network, is not represented at the Cabinet level with its own Secretary. This Service, nevertheless, has its representatives at the highest levels of policy formulation. The Pentagon's Advanced Research Projects Agency (ARPA), an elite organization responsible to the Director of Defense Research and Organization, maintains very close ties with the university warfare laboratories, many of which hold contracts from ARPA. Each of the other three Armed Services have a scientific advisory board composed of scientists and professors; the Secretary of Defense has his own advisory commission, the Defense Science Board (DSB). The present chairman of DSB, Robert L. Sproull, is Vice President and Provost of the University of Rochester and a former director of ARPA. Complementing these bodies is the President's Science Advisory Committee, which represents the Fourth Service in the White House.

Most of the relationships which link together the components of the university-military complex are informal, or go on behind the doors of closed meetings of the board of trustees. Nevertheless, over the years, many of the university research organizations have acquired a special relationship with the Department of Defense as Federal Contract Research Centers (FCRC's) or Department of Defense Information and Analysis Centers (DoDIAC's). These facilities are operated under ongoing Pentagon contracts which oblige the universities to maintain continuous research activities in a particular field of interest to the military. American University's Center for Research in Social Systems, for example, is the FCRC responsible for research on counterinsurgency, while Penn State's Ordnance Research Lab is the FCRC engaged in research on torpedo design. All of the research organizations listed below [omitted here] have some on-going relationship with the Department of Defense—either as an FCRC or DoDIAC—or under contract with one of the other three military services.

In the past two years, campus opposition to Vietnam-related warfare research has compelled a number of universities to reexamine their ties with the Pentagon; as a result defense laboratories at Columbia and Cornell Universities have been removed from university control and re-organized as autonomous non-profit research organizations on the model of the RAND Corporation. Sometimes described as "universities without students," the non-profit research institutes maintain a campus-like environment and informal working conditions in order to recruit academic scientists who would otherwise shun Pentagon work. By hiring university scientists as consultants and part-time researchers, by serving as a conduit for military research contracts, and by providing a "neutral" setting for meetings of professors and generals, the "non-profits" constitute a crucial link between the Pentagon and the universities. Thus even the changes at Cornell and Columbia will not fundamentally alter the composition of the military research network: the cohesion of the University-Military Complex, after all, depends not so much on formal arrangements as on its ability to funnel information to the Pentagon and money back to the campus—a process which continues unabated.

Stanford and Classified Research

From a report by the faculty Committee on Research Policy to the Academic Council, Stanford University, September 1, 1967.

University Policy Regarding Classified Research

Principles in Contention: The Underlying Dilemma

The basic objective of the university is to select and to nourish scholars of the highest quality and to facilitate investigation and teaching by them in all areas of knowledge. From this purpose flow two principles: first, that the scholar must be free to select his area of inquiry and second, that he must be free to disseminate his findings without constraint from within or without the university community. In a world where nationalistic strife constitutes a major element of the environment, a university cannot achieve full realization of these fundamental principles.

Such a range of scholarly freedom does not exist anywhere in the world today, and its attainment is beyond the powers of any single university. Application of new knowledge can often be pressed into the service of a nation or group of nations; hence, for reasons that are as understandable as they are regrettable, the United States and other nations have reserved the power by law to control the dissemination of certain types of knowledge. The exercise of that power is not limited to knowledge generated under government contracts or grants, classified or unclassified at their inception: the fruits of research having no prior government sponsorship are subject to controls on dissemination.

As a practical matter the efficient exercise of control on dissemination is facilitated by the fact that large portions of the new knowledge being generated in certain fields, particularly but not exclusively in the area of applied physical science, is the fruit of government funds. Research in this area is often enormously expensive and is heavily dependent upon governmental subsidy whether its situs is in industry or educational institutions.

Given the inescapable reality that much of the current investigation in these areas is subject in some degree to governmental control, the range of choice open to the university is obviously limited: it may choose to participate or not to participate in this investigation. To participate it must accept certain constraints. To decline achieves a freedom that is largely illusory: the particular university avoids the constraints, but it does not succeed in freeing the area of investigation or those scholars who choose to participate in it.

The choice then is to accept certain limitations on dissemination, subordinating one basic principle of the university, or to deny to many scholars in the university the opportunity to carry on effective investigation in their chosen fields of inquiry, thus subordinating a different principle. As a practical matter, the second choice will, in some proportion of cases, have the consequence of driving a group of scholars from the university to institutions which have struck the balance differently.

We believe that here, as is often true when important principles contend, the wisest choice is not uniformly to subordinate either principle to the other. A more particularistic approach is possible. Depending on the characteristics of the research project proposed and of the restraints that attend it, primacy can be given now to one, now to the other of these objectives with the aim of maximizing, in the aggregate of instances, attainment of the basic academic objective. That is the approach the Committee has tried to implement during the past year, and it is the course the Committee recommends for the future.

General Rules

This is not to say no generalizations are possible. The Academic Council adopted certain general rules in the resolution that established this Committee; our inquiries have persuaded us that they are sound, and we recommend their preservation. They are, in substance, the following:

a) No research on a thesis or dissertation should be undertaken if, at the time the topic is set, there is any substantial possibility that it will lead to a classified thesis or dissertation.

b) No classified thesis or dissertation should be accepted as the basis for a degree unless, in the judgment of the Committee on the Graduate Division, the imposition of classification could not reasonably have been foreseen until the work was so far advanced that modification of the thesis topic would have resulted in substantial inequity to the student.

c) Scholarly activities not accessible for scrutiny by the entire Advisory Board should not be considered in connection with appointments, reappointments or promotions.

d) The University should enter no contract and accept no grant that involves the collection of social or behavioral data in a foreign country and requires the security clearance of any person involved in the project.

In addition to the foregoing rules, the Committee's inquiries have persuaded it of the wisdom of adopting one more general prohibition. It is the following:

e) The University should enter no contract and accept no grant to carry out research under circumstances that restrain the freedom of the University to disclose (1) the existence of the contract or grant or (2) the general nature of the inquiry to be conducted or (3) the identity of the outside contracting or granting entity; Provided, that clause (3) shall not apply either (a) to anonymous gifts or grants that do not call for the performance of specified lines of inquiry, or (b) to research grants or contracts from individuals or non-governmental entities who request anonymity out of a justifiable motivation to protect individual privacy. . . .

From a pamphlet produced by the Stanford chapter of SDS, early 1969.

Stanford, the Trustees, and Southeast Asia

Prior to four years ago, it was not customary for people living in the Stanford-Palo Alto region to question (or research) the kind of products that this region is producing—their social benefits or their social harm. Electronic aids to warfare in World War Two seemed quite legitimate—the US was fighting Nazi fascism then. War research and weapons made for the Korean War seemed justified by the "threat of communism." It was only with the Vietnam War that very many Americans were goaded into doubting their government's use of public resources, such as men (soldiers), academic resources (weapons and counterinsurgency), and taxes (subsidies to build defense industry).

During antiwar protests in 1965–1966, people belonging to the Stanford Committee for Peace in Vietnam did extensive research on the role of West Coast industries in the Vietnam War. They found that the men who direct the major "defense" industries and serve on government advisory boards are the same men who are legally entrusted to run Stanford. They found many professors doing chemical and biological warfare studies, or doing classified research.

The political principle that radicals four years ago expressed has become increasingly accepted by the student and faculty communities of the university. "We are responsible to challenge inhuman practices of our community; the right to life and self-determination of the Vietnamese (or Thai) people is greater than the individual's right to do anything he wishes in the academic community of Stanford. The social institutions of America which cause suffering must be changed, no matter how sacred and innocent they seem to be on the surface."

Though more people understand and sympathize with the radical position now, their actions to date have not been effective enough to stop *one* war contract, *one* bomb's production, *one* new weapon research-development process. The only changes have been liberalization of university course and living regulations and a certain amount of changed political attitudes among students.

All of which are simply more privileges that we ought to have had as rights in the first place.

None of which bring us any closer to changing the destructive effects Stanford has on the peoples of the world outside (and to a less extensive degree inside) Stanford.

From a pamphlet produced by the Stanford Research Institute Coalition, a student protest group, early 1969.

From War Research to Peace Research

Toward a New Research Orientation

Stanford and SRI have all of the resources necessary to enable them to make significant contributions to the solutions of today's crucial social problems. The facilities and brainpower available are first-rate. A major shift in priorities away from war-related research would allow Stanford and SRI to become important centers of social progress.

A great deal more research could be done on living conditions in the domestic colonies, and on programs to eliminate the poverty and misery that afflicts a large segment of our population. Research into possibilities for governmental decentralization and the setting up of cooperative stores and enterprises would go a long way toward enabling inner city dwellers to play major roles in making the decisions that vitally affect their lives. To date, the most significant research in this whole area done at SRI has been on the use of firearms in ghetto revolts.

Much research needs to be done in the field of environmental studies. Investigations need to be conducted into imbalances in the ecology, especially man-made ones, that will affect the health and prosperity of future generations. There is plenty of work to be done on such topics as soil conservation and pollution controls. SRI's work on air pollution, however, has actually hindered the development of effective smog control.

SRI's Environmental Research Department is headed by Elmer Robinson, a meteorologist who is also chairman of the Bay Area Air Pollution Control District, an organization originally designed to control smog in the Bay Area. The most important contract undertaken recently by this department was a massive, world-wide study sponsored by the American Petroleum Institute. A report on this project entitled "Where Does It All Go?" (the smog, that is) was printed in the December, 1968 issue of the *SRI Journal*. This report is noteworthy for its lack of emphasis on industrial pollution. Automobiles, power plants, and home furnaces are mentioned as sources of smog, but big industry and especially the huge oil refineries are largely ignored. The report talks in some detail about natural sources of air pollution. "Even oceans and vegetation generate air pollutants . . . in large amounts." The report notes that the main source of hydrocarbons, the major components of smog, are such natural entities as swamps and trees. The great clouds of smoke billowing over the Standard Oil Refinery in Richmond don't seem to count for much.

The report claims that industrially-produced air pollution accounts for just five per cent of the total. As in other instances, the use of statistics is misleading here, for in the United States, seventy per cent of the population is concentrated in the major cities, on one per cent of the land. This is where the bulk of the industrially-produced smog is also concentrated. Naturally-produced smog over swamps, oceans, and mountains is of relatively little importance. It would seem that the report's conclusion that the significance of industrial pollution is slight serves the needs of the giant oil companies who financed this study and not the needs of the people who have to live in and breathe the polluted air. While some good work on air pollution has been done, most of it serves to rationalize the destructive and dangerous practices of the major smog producers, many of whose directors sit on SRI's board.

Were SRI to be creatively used to tackle social problems, valuable research could be done in the area of air pollution, and in other fields such as population control and food production. A reorientation of international research might result in the utilization of SRI's resources to devise meaningful land reform programs and models of property ownership and capital accumulation appropriate to the particular problems of development now being faced by the emerging nations. Granted that funds are not readily available for such work at present. But the first step toward the realization of this goal must be to end Stanford and SRI's involvement in CBW, counterinsurgency, and other war-related research. Only then will Stanford and SRI researchers be free to do positive and socially useful work.

The Academic Freedom Argument

Many members of the university community defend war research done today at American universities and affiliated research institutes with an academic-individual freedom argument. The individual scientist's right to do the research of his choosing is the primary value here. It must be admitted that there is a moral tension in restricting the freedom of an individual in order to guarantee the freedom of others. Yet this argument has a hollow and uncomfortable ring to it when the right of a Stanford or SRI scientist to do chemical-biological warfare or counterinsurgency research is placed against the fundamental right of several million Vietnamese, Thais, and Peruvians both to determine their own destinies and to life itself.

Fundamental to any definition of democracy is the principle that decisions must be made either directly or by elected representatives of the people to be affected by these decisions. Today, American government officials and corporate leaders are making life-and-death decisions for the people all over the world. Stanford and SRI scientists who work directly to make American economic and military domination in the Third World possible must bear a large part of the responsibility for the increasingly visible, inhuman results.

Some members of the university community emphasize to dissenters that they are understating the extent of academic freedom and disinterested inquiry in the university. This is in part a hangover from the McCarthy principle. But now the demands of the government and foundation marketplace increasingly circumscribe academic freedom to do research on important ecological and socio-economic problems.

Some scientists working on applied, or mission-oriented, research disclaim any responsibility for the uses to which their work is put. In some cases, they deny any knowledge of the effects of their work. Any project that is intrinsically interesting from a narrowly scientific point of view is fair game for them to tackle. And while beneficial civilian applications that sometime spin off Defense Department-funded projects are frequently cited, it should be clear that the Pentagon is supporting applied research precisely because it is of military value. Any applied research in the military field at Stanford (STL) and SRI should be scrutinized very closely. If the research is classified, we must oppose it until we know what results it may have on other human beings.

DoD-funded basic research that is not of immediate military value is a much more difficult problem to resolve. Many scientists say that they prefer not to do their basic research under military contracts but have no choice, since the Defense Department is the only institution with the resources to finance research in their particular areas of specialization.

The only short and medium-term solution is for all scientists to organize themselves in order to control the uses to which their work is being put by other institutions. . . . [They] should also push collectively to take the funding and administration of their projects out of the hands of the Defense Department. This would not only begin to dam up the direct channeling of research to the Pentagon, but would also serve to reduce the power of our $80 million military establishment and its rubber-stamping Congressional committees.

In the long run, not until all research, both basic and applied, is used to advance the welfare of society instead of to produce better weapons will the concept of academic freedom regain its true meaning.

Classified Research:
Stanford and SRI

The only way for members of the Stanford-Midpeninsula community to resolve the academic-freedom-social responsibility question fully is to examine questionable research contracts and trace the effects of the research on Americans and people of the Third World.

Yet a substantial part of Stanford and SRI's military work is classified, so that the community cannot make decisions on the basis of the actual *content* of the research. Classification undermines the basic democratic decision-making process. But more importantly, classified research often is found in areas where the basic right of other countries to self-determination should not depend on any decision-making process, be it secret or open, at Stanford.

According to the Institute's officers, SRI has "143 projects valued at approximately $85 million in which the research reports and some of the documents may be classified. Included with the 143 projects are 57 (valued at approximately $44 million) in which the contract documents and most of the research results are classified." If SRI's references to "public responsibility" are to be more than public-relations rhetoric, it must be willing to open these contracts to community review.

At the Stanford Electronics Labs, there is over $2.2 million in classified military work. Typically, "security clearance is necessary because classified background data is received from the sponsor and a part of the research results applicable to problems of the sponsor may be classified." The bulk of the classified work is contained in four contracts worth $1.2 million in the Systems Techniques Laboratory. Three other classified contracts (one of these is part of an STL contract) are found in the Radioscience and Systems Theory Labs. This classified work is described in the Counterinsurgency and ABM sections above. [omitted here—Ed.]

University scientists often attempt to justify contracts requiring security clearances since they feel they must keep up with "the state of the art." The issuance of classified research reports to the Defense Department is completely unjustifiable. A newly studentized faculty committee has been reviewing all classified contracts at Stanford, yet has accepted these 6 classified contracts at Stanford. It may now be appropriate for the Stanford community to review the University Committee on Classified Research's work.

In conclusion, demands for immediate declassification should clearly be part of any movement opposed to CBW, military counterinsurgency research, economic development or investment studies done alongside counterinsurgency operations, ABM and electronic warfare work, and other war-related research.

Controlling SRI: Oppose Severance or Sale

The first response of many people in the university community to the problems posed by SRI's war research has been "Sell it. Not only do we feel uneasy about the moral implications of SRI's work, but the Institute's work is second-rate. The university should have nothing to do with SRI."

Sale of SRI would leave Stanford without legal responsibility for the Institute's work, yet would not remove the university's moral responsibility for creating SRI, for accepting SRI's research over the years, and for allowing SRI to continue this research. Stanford would be purifying itself at the expense of Vietnamese, Thais, and Peruvians who don't care what Stanford's legal relationship is to the CBW and counterinsurgency research which helps destroy their families and crops.

It has been suggested that Stanford sell SRI under a restrictive covenant, a covenant which would bar certain types of research done at the Institute. There is no clear precedent for this solution. The difficulty of defining areas of objectionable research precisely enough to stymie SRI lawyers establishes major risks in this approach. But equally important is the simple fact that severance will reduce the "mental visibility" of SRI and the whole Midpeninsula defense complex to the Stanford community. SRI, the Industrial Park, and the Stanford Electronics Labs will remain where they are for some time to come. The important question is whether the members of the Stanford-Midpeninsula community treat their opposition to Stanford and SRI's war research as a one-shot issue or as a first step toward reorienting the Midpeninsula research and industrial apparatus toward socially constructive work.

If SRI is brought under closer control by the university, closer, more certain surveillance will result than through the courts. The possibility of modifying guidelines over the years will be left open. Stanford students and faculty will have to confront much more directly their moral and social responsibility to stop war research at its local roots. And very importantly, Stanford resources might be able to cushion socially constructive work at SRI from the batterings of the government marketplace. SRI would remain a research institution, but might slowly turn into a center for research into crucial social problems.

Obviously, Stanford administrators will not be happy with the added burden of SRI work, and some Stanford faculty will not want to grant any of their prestige and privileges to "second-rate researchers." Yet the silence of the Stanford community has facilitated SRI's growth, and the university will have to accept the inconvenience that normally follows moral responsibility in the United States today.

From all available indications, the trustees of Stanford University will not want to bring SRI under closer control by a morally-concerned university community. They will certainly not be happy with setting up moral and political controls over SRI or the Systems Techniques Lab's research. They would prefer to retain the informally close relationships that exist between Stanford and SRI now (53 faculty consult at SRI), but if they begin to feel community pressure mounting, it is likely that the trustees will decide to sell SRI. Another possibility is that they will set up a board of trustees for SRI under a new non-profit charter. This would legally constitute giving SRI away, the height of moral and fiscal irresponsibility.

But most likely, the trustees will simply try to stall this spring in the face of a growing political storm. As a possible model, we have the example of the Cornell handling of the Cornell Aeronautical Lab (CAL), like SRI, a wholly-owned subsidiary of its parent university. The trustees set up a committee in summer 1967 to look into CAL's relationship with Cornell, approved severance at its January 1968 meeting, and finally accepted a letter of intent to buy from EDP Technology, a computer software company, in June 1968.

At its April 8 meeting in San Francisco, the Stanford trustees will most likely set up a trustee committee to study the SRI Committee's report. The trustees committee would report back to the next scheduled trustees meeting in the middle of May, and it would not be surprising if the trustees did not make their final decision until their June meeting. Palo Alto would be quiet then.

Our best bet to head off possible trustee stalling early this spring is to ask the trustees at their April 8 meeting in San Francisco to hold a special decision-making meeting on campus in middle to late April. A two-week discussion period of the SRI Committee report (to be released April 12) would afford the University-Midpeninsula community and the trustees enough time to make their decisions. After hundreds of years of foreign intervention and twenty years of U.S. interference with their lives, the Vietnamese are expecting a decision from us.

Parts or hopefully all of this special meeting would be open to the community. But members of the community themselves must decide whether to accept the trustees' decision on SRI and Stanford's war research. And we must ultimately answer to the Vietnamese people.

Letter from Dr. Bill B. May, research engineer at the Stanford Electronics Laboratories, addressed to President Kenneth Pitzer of Stanford, April 15, 1969.

The Issue Is Academic Freedom

As a staff member of the Systems Techniques Laboratory, I feel that it is my duty to inform you of my impressions of the general nature of the conflict presently engulfing the University. Though most of my comments are directly related to the affairs surrounding the occupation of the Applied Electronics Building, I believe that these comments have significance to the University community as a whole. Thus, I would hope that as much thought and reasoning would be applied to these comments as is presently being devoted to the demands of the dissidents.

Though the problems are far from being simple, I believe that a statement of the general nature of the conflict can be made in fairly simple terms. Namely, the central question is: who has the power to control the activities within the University; or, in other words, does anyone have the *right* to individual freedom within the University?

Individual freedom has been defined as the right to control one's actions, providing these actions do not interfere with the rights of others. Within the University today, I can see a most definite erosion of the right of individual freedom. To name some examples, the ROTC Department and its students exist without interfering (by any reasonable definition) with the rights of others, yet the attempt is being made to eliminate ROTC by members of the community who take no part in the activities of ROTC.

Earlier, the CIA interviewed on campus. Interviews with students were purely optional and did not interfere with the rights of any member of the community. Yet, the attempt (which was largely successful) was made to eliminate this activity at the expense of the *rights* of those students who chose to interview this organization.

And now, a segment of the University community has chosen to eliminate research which has no relation to this segment and which does not interfere (in any logical way) with the rights of this segment.

What will be the targets in the future? Already, businessmen (GSB) are looked upon with disfavor; physical education, particularly varsity competition, does not aid in solving the social problems of the world and furthermore is open to far more academic criticism than ROTC. Most of the engineering and physical science research (unclassified or not) directly benefits the Department of Defense, not always due to support by DOD, but mainly because DOD is the main user of advanced technology. Liberal arts departments can be criticized for only educating future professors of liberal arts (i.e., a closed society), rather than solving problems of society. It can be asked whether the enormous

SLAC * expenditures benefit the ghettos, or solve problems of pollution. It is clear that no segment of the University is immune from criticism, and thereby a target for elimination by another segment of the community.

The point that I hope to get across is the ridiculous character of a university which is controlled by power groups whether they be student dissidents who find that they can achieve their goals by forcing the administration to choose between an easy course of amputation or the much more difficult course of standing behind certain principles, or whether these power groups are engineers vs. liberal arts professors in a democratic Academic Senate. With regard to the latter, a democracy does not necessarily protect the rights of a minority. Rather, the rights are protected by a set of principles—a Bill of Rights—which states the basic freedoms for the members of the community.

One of these freedoms has received a great deal of publicity of late—namely, academic freedom. Though it is an intimately familiar term to the university community, I doubt that the university community would agree on a definition. To many people, academic freedom means the latitude to teach a course in the way he sees fit, to others it means the right to hold whatever political doctrine he sees fit (e.g., certain professors on the faculty of various political stripes) and to us in the Systems Techniques Laboratory it meant (in happier times) the right to perform research on subjects of interest which are appropriate in our minds to a university program, a contention confirmed by the regular scrutiny of a duly constituted committee of the Academic Senate. *There no longer is any set of ground rules, there is no Bill of Rights, there is no Academic Freedom.* All that remains is a power struggle.

As a partial solution to the conflicts within the University, I strongly propose that a Bill of Rights be written for the Stanford community—students, staff, and faculty—and that this Bill of Rights include Academic Freedom together with a definition which is satisfactory to the community as a whole. The foundation for these Rights should be the free expression of views and the individual control of one's actions to the extent that they do not interfere with the rights of others. Furthermore, these Rights should be basic to the community, and actions by governing bodies (ASSU,† Academic Senate, administration, etc.) should not be in conflict with these Rights.

* Stanford Linear Accelerator Center.
† Associated Students of Stanford University.

I urge you to consider my assessment of the difficulties presently facing the University and to determine the feasibility and desirability of my proposal for alleviating some of these difficulties.

Policy statement of the Senate of the Academic Council, Stanford University, April 24, 1969.

Stanford's New Policy

Based upon recommendations from the Academic Council Committee on Research Policy, the Senate, on April 24, 1969, adopted New Research Policy Guidelines on Secrecy in Research as follows:

Resolved:

1. That the principle of openness in research—the principle of freedom of access by all interested persons to the underlying data, to the processes, and to the final results of research—is one of overriding importance. Accordingly it is the decision of the Senate that that principle be implemented to the fullest extent practicable, and that no program of research that requires secrecy (as hereafter defined) be conducted at Stanford University, subject to the exceptions set forth in Paragraph 4 of this Resolution.

2. That a research program shall be regarded as requiring secrecy (a) if any part of the sponsoring or granting documents that establish the project is not freely publishable, or (b) if there is a reasonable basis for expectation that any documents to be generated in the course of the research project will be subjected by an outside sponsor to restrictions on publication for a period in excess of that reasonably required for the sponsor to ascertain whether information he is entitled to have treated as confidential would be disclosed by publication, or (c) if access will be required in the course of the project to confidential data so centrally related to the research that a member of the research group who was not privy to the confidential data would be unable to participate fully in all of the intellectually significant portions of the project.

3. That the rules adopted by the Academic Council on September 29, 1967, are hereby amended and, as amended are reaffirmed:

a. No research on a thesis or dissertation should be undertaken if, at the time the topic is set, there is any substantial possibility that it will lead to a secret thesis or dissertation.

b. No secret thesis or dissertation should be accepted as the basis for a degree unless in the judgment of the Committee on the Graduate Division, the imposition of secrecy could not reasonably have been foreseen until the work was so far advanced that modification of the thesis topic would have resulted in substantial inequity to the student.

c. Scholarly activities not accessible for scrutiny by the entire Advisory Board should not be considered in connection with appointments, reappointments or promotions.

d. The University should enter no contract and accept no grant to carry out research if the grant or contract restrains the freedom of the University to disclose (1) the existence of the contract or grant or (2) the general nature of the inquiry to be conducted or (3) the identity of the outside contracting or granting entity, or (4) the research results; provided, that clause (3) shall not apply either (a) to anonymous gifts or grants that do not call for the performance of specified lines of inquiry, or (b) to research grants or contracts from individuals or non-governmental entities who request anonymity out of a justifiable motivation to protect individual privacy.

4. That a program of research, appropriate to the University on other grounds, shall not be regarded as unacceptable by reason of secrecy merely because one or more of the following circumstances exist:

a. In a program of research involving the examination, through interview techniques or otherwise, of a living human being, reasonable provision may be made to protect the rights of that individual to privacy.

b. In a program of research the purposes of which would be significantly advanced by access to information generated elsewhere which had been subjected to security classification, provision may be made for security clearance and for access to that information on the part of one or several of the participating investigators provided that the classified information is peripheral to the research program in the following sense:

the relationship between the classified data and the overall research endeavor must be sufficiently remote so that (1) a member of the research group who did not hold a security clearance would nevertheless be able to participate fully in all of the intellectually significant portions of the project; and (2) there is no substantial basis for an expectation that any part of the final results of the research, or any but a trivial part of the research processes, will be subject to restriction on publication more enduring than those described in Paragraph 2.

c. In a program of research sponsored by an outside entity, provision may be made for a short delay in the publication of research results, the period of delay never to exceed one year, if (1) the sponsor has a *bona fide* intention to apply for a patent covering applications of the research in a country whose laws establish either (a) a "race-to-file" patent system, or (b) that patentability would be destroyed by publication earlier than as provided in the sponsorship arrangement; and (2) the delay provided for does not exceed that reasonably required to accomplish the sponsor's patenting objective in that country.

d. If, in a program of research, an outside person or entity has made available to the investigator confidential information, provision may be made to preserve confidentiality and for a short delay in the publication of research results during which time the information source may examine the proposed publication in order to assure that the investigator has not disclosed, intentionally or unintentionally, any portion of the confidential information supplied; provided that any such provision for delay must contain assurances from the information source that he will conduct his review as expeditiously as possible, that he will not attempt to thwart publication for any reason except to protect confidential information previously supplied, and that he will indicate with specificity any sentence or sentences which he contends constitute such a disclosure.

e. If, in a program of research, private papers, documents, diaries or analogous materials have been provided to the investigator, provision may be made to preserve the confidentiality of those materials for the purpose of protecting the individual privacy of the author, or of the addressee, or of the immediate family of either the author or the addressee.

5. This policy shall be reviewed at least annually by the Committee on Research Policy in one of its meetings. This meeting and others primarily devoted to considering a revision of research policy shall be announced publicly through the University calendar and other suitable means.

Views from Washington

From a speech by Senator J. William Fulbright at Denison University, April 18, 1969.

Militarism and American Democracy

A university in the classic sense is an idealistic rather than a "pragmatic" institution, primarily committed to moral rather than expedient purposes, to the pursuit of truth and meaning rather than the sale of goods and services. In recognition of this special status, universities are generously supported by tax exemptions and both public and private contributions. The university in turn has a responsibility to protect its status as an "idealistic" institution, not to the point of remoteness or irrelevance to the problems of society, but by maintaining a sufficient degree of detachment from political authorities to make certain that it does not become a "pragmatic" institution, a paid producer of goods and services, a hireling of the state.

It is difficult to say exactly where the line should be drawn in practical application but the general principle seems clear: a university maintains its integrity only insofar as its preponderant resources are committed to the education of its students and the disinterested pursuit of knowledge—not only that knowledge which contributes to the solution of technical and social problems but the whole range of nonutilitarian scholarship which contributes to man's understanding of himself. Other activities—including the performance of specific services to the state—are appropriate only insofar as they are subordinate in scale and compatible in character with the university's primary responsibilities.

To a far greater extent than its European counterparts the American university has always had a penchant, in Alfred North Whitehead's phrase, for "mating itself with action," and this has contributed both to the welfare of the country and the vitality of the university. But, coupled with an unprecedented need for funds in the years since World War II, the penchant for action has also turned out to be a serious weakness of our universities. Tempted by lucrative government contracts, many universities—especially the big and famous ones—have become neglectful of their paramount responsibilities and have gone dangerously far toward becoming servants of the state. Because the major source by far of government contract funds is the military establishment, the universities have been drawn primarily into military, or militarily useful, research in the physical and social sciences, becoming in the process card-carrying members of the military-industrial complex.

The government by and large has been well-satisfied with the contributions of academic experts—although my Committee has come across more than a few instances in which it seemed to us that the government had been defrauded. And, in the irreverent words of a report written by two professors from Michigan State for the United States Advisory Commission on International Educational and Cultural Affairs, the government's delight "has been matched by squeals of joy in the academy." The attractions, say the two professors, are profit, prestige, and "opportunities to orbit deans around the world." *

Even more irreverently, Dean Don K. Price of the Kennedy School of Government at Harvard offered a limerick apropos of the universities' response to government blandishments:

> "There was a young lady from Kent,
> Who said that she knew what it meant,
> When men took her to dine
> Gave her cocktails and wine
> She knew what it meant—but she went."

---

* Walter Adams and Adrian Jaffe, *Government, The Universities, and International Affairs: A Crisis in Identity,* Special Report Prepared for the U.S. Advisory Commission on International Educational and Cultural Affairs, 90th Cong., 1st Sess., House Doc. No. 120 (Washington: U.S. Government Printing Office, 1967), p. 10.

What it has meant is the wholesale neglect of students by prominent faculty members, the wholesale neglect of unsalable forms of scholarship, the distortion of curriculum and research toward merchantable activities, and the taking into camp of leading academics by the military-industrial complex. No one of course requires this of the universities; it comes about not as a result of direct federal control but simply from the influence purchased by lavish government funds. Lacking a use for philosophy and poetry, the Defense Department and the Central Intelligence Agency offer no funds for these disciplines; the government is a patron only of the more lethal arts.

The University of California at Berkeley, according to a student publication, receives almost 90 percent of its research grants in the physical sciences and almost 70 percent of its research grants in the social sciences from the federal government. Berkeley, as you know, is also one of the centers of student rebellion. I think there is a relationship. I also think there is a relationship between student dissent and the fact that the Naval Biological Laboratory administered by Berkeley's School of Public Health is engaged in research for the Navy in biological warfare. With the participation of faculty members of the School of Public Health, research is conducted in the field of "aerobiology," which has to do with the transmission of communicable diseases.

Research in chemical and biological warfare is not one of those activities that can be regarded as appropriate to an "idealistic" institution. Nor is Pentagon-sponsored field research in counterinsurgency an appropriate activity for social scientists who ought to be acting as independent and critical commentators on their government's policies. Far from being victims of anti-intellectualism as some of these scholars complain when their activities are criticized, they themselves are perpetrating a virulent form of anti-intellectualism. They do so by contributing to the corruption of their universities, the militarization of American society, and that persistent degradation of values which goes by the polite name of "credibility gap."

From testimony by Vice President Hubert H. Humphrey before the Panel on Science and Technology of the House Committee on Science and Astronautics, January 24, 1968.

A Word to Our University Friends

This permits me to say a word to some of our university friends here. I know many times I read in the press there is a little rebellion on some campuses about government research projects, projects in universities. I don't know whether I ought to say this or not, but I'm a rather free-wheeling man. I feel if you don't want the money, there is another place for it. I sort of feel that if the university wants to exclude itself from the life of the nation, then it will most likely find itself living a rather barren life . . .

I hope that our Universities and our Government can work together. I hope that there will not be a breach because if there is it will not be the Government that suffers, because the Government can set up its own laboratories.

I don't think that is very smart. I think that the Government ought to work with the private sector. . . . But if a nation is denied that then it has to have some way to protect itself. . . .

Massachusetts Institute of Technology

Article in the Cambridge radical student publication, The Old Mole, *November 7–21, 1969.*

Why Smash MIT?

MIT isn't a center for scientific and social research to serve humanity. It's a part of the U.S. war machine. Into MIT flow over $100 million a year in Pentagon research and development funds, making it the 10th largest Defense Department R&D contractor in the country. MIT's purpose is to provide research, consulting services, and trained personnel for the U.S. government and the major corporations—research, services, and personnel which enable them to maintain their control over the people of the world. NAC's (November Action Coalition's) campaign was directed against MIT as an institution, against its central purpose. It focused, however, on seven specific projects which are illustrative of the worst kinds of projects the Institute carries out for imperialism. Last week's actions are part of a continuing campaign to end these seven projects:

MIRV & Helicopter

MIRV (Multiple Independently-targeted Re-entry Vehicles) and the *Helicopter Stabilization Project:* These projects are being done at the Instrumentation Laboratories, which are considered capable of the most sophisticated and reliable guidance work of any lab in the country. The MIRV is designed to give the U.S. a first-strike capability: the capability of launching a nuclear attack without being destroyed in return. Each MIRV missile contains many warheads each of which can be aimed at a different target. While MIRV gives U.S. imperialism fantastic world-wide power, the helicopter stabilization project is designed specifically for counter-insurgency operations like Vietnam. Its goal is an all-weather guidance and stabilization system for helicopters, which would alleviate many of the present difficulties in establishing accurate aim from rapid-fire machine-guns in helicopters in Vietnam, especially in bad weather.

ABM & MTI

ABM (Anti-Ballistic Missile) and *MTI* (Moving Target Indicator): These projects are being done at the Lincoln Laboratories, established in 1951 "for the purpose of creating effective solutions to urgent national defense problems" (MIT *President's Report 1968*). ABM, like the MIRV, is intended to give the U.S. a first-strike capability. And, as Senator Richard Russell has said, "The first country to deploy an effective ABM system . . . is going to control this world militarily." The MTI is a radar system that allows guerrillas moving through dense foliage to be detected three miles away by a helicopter traveling up to 200 miles per hour, in all weather, day or night. Test models are already in use in Vietnam.

Com-Com

Com-Com Project and *International Communism Project:* Both of these projects are being done at MIT's Center for International Studies. The CIS was established in the early 1950's to deal with some of the "social science problems" in the implementation of U.S. foreign policy. It was funded by the CIA from its inception until 1966, when Director Max Millikan announced that "for practical and not moral reasons" ties were officially cut. Millikan came to the Center after a two-year stint as assistant director of the CIA.

The Com-Com Project is directed by Ithiel de Sola Pool. Pool is a political "scientist" who has spent much time in Vietnam in the past few years as part of the DoD's Chieu Hoi program (a program to induce Viet Cong defection). Com-Com is a program of technical and communications research in psychological warfare.

The International Communism Project was originally funded by the CIA (now by the Ford Foundation) to provide analysis of intelligence information about radical and revolutionary movements throughout the world on the basis of public documents. (At least one of CIS's two *Old Mole* subscriptions must go here.) The U.S. intelligence apparatus would like an independent check and analysis of this information done outside the government, which the project has provided.

Project CAM (or, the Cambridge Project): This project, conceived by Pool, former ARPA (Advanced Research Projects Agency of the DoD) official J.C.R. Licklider, and ARPA official Bob Taylor, will receive $7.69 million from the DoD over the next five years. It is intended to develop general theory which will help solve those DoD and U.S. Government problems which are considered "behavioral-science problems." It will use existing data collections of such things as interviews with NLF defectors and peasant attitudes. As Pool has stated, "[Some students] are under the impression that the Project will deal with counter-insurgency problems and peasant attitudes. These topics of research are nothing new. They have been going on all the time in various sectors of the community. These areas would be strengthened by the project . . ."

Phony Conversion

In reaction to the demands that those seven projects be stopped and the planned November Actions around them, MIT President Howard Johnson and other members of the administration have attempted to make it seem as if the Lincoln and Instrumentation Labs are going to be "converted." They replaced the I-Labs director, C. Stark Draper (the guided missile expert) with Charles L. Miller, who is supposed to be interested in "urban problems." They announced a new research policy at the two Labs.

However, their "new" research policy turns out to be very much like the old one. The labs will continue to do everything short of the final development of weapons systems. Thus, according to the "new" criteria, the ABM, MTI, and the helicopter stabilization projects were all acceptable and even the initial research into MIRV would be permitted.

In either case, administrators have said that *all* projects will continue until completion. In addition, a memorandum from Miller to Johnson which was made public by the NAC on Oct. 28 showed that funds for any sort of "conversion" are not forthcoming. Miller himself referred to "conversion" (always in quotes in his memo) as a "misleading illusion."

From a statement made by President Howard W. Johnson of MIT to a special faculty meeting, November 3, 1969.

The Real Issues at MIT

Of all the institutions in our society, the university is most nearly defenseless.

It has to be. The university exists so that there may be somewhere a place for the courageous and direct confrontation of ideas. The free flow of ideas cannot take place in an atmosphere of physical confrontation; an open mind cannot long exist in the face of force or threat.

It does not matter where force may come from—from the Legislature, from the police, from the alumni, from outsiders, or, indeed, from the administrators. Once force crosses the threshold, the university is diminished.

It is clear to me that here at M.I.T. we cannot ourselves and with only our own resources deal with force or the threat of force. We are vulnerable; we were created vulnerable; and we will remain so as long as we are free.

Universities today are grappling with unresolved issues. These issues are their life blood. We have such issues: student discontent with the current educational process; the relation of the university to society, consequences of scientific and technological progress; the balance between study and action, just to mention a few.

Particularly, for a great institute of technology, we have the hard questions of how our capabilities relate to the defense of the nation. We struggle these days with that issue in its most emotional form, at a time when this country is fighting a war in which few of our students and faculty believe.

Our 8,000 students and 1,000 faculty work, study, teach and do research that has no direct connection to military weapons. Quite the opposite. M.I.T., since its founding, has made an immense contribution to the quality of life of this nation.

It is our policy now to exclude secret research from the campus. No classified theses are being prepared. And we are currently engaged in a test of the proposition of whether we can move some of the technological capacity of our two off-campus laboratories to the problems of domestic and civil life.

The faculty supports this test. It did so by a vote of several hundred to a few just 10 days ago. More importantly, the faculty will, I hope, participate actively in this effort. This is going to be a much tougher job than recreating the many academic laboratories after World War II.

In the area of education, we have created a commission of faculty and students to look searchingly at everything that M.I.T. does—all the way from how we teach and learn to how we govern ourselves. Called the M.I.T. Commission, this group is charged to see that what we do in the 1970's is responsive to the times and to human needs.

Those are some of the real issues within the institute. The faculty, all of us, must try to understand them, to propose effective policies and press forward toward resolving these issues.

CHAPTER 8

Recruiting on Campus:
Can Some Recruiters
Be Banned?

Every academic year, especially between January and April, representatives from corporations and government agencies make visits to college campuses to recruit graduates to work for them. University placement offices provide the recruiters with office space and telephones, schedule their appointments with students, and often distribute notices on campus to publicize their visits. This system of recruiting began in the 1920s, and, because it was generally considered a service to students, universities did not until recently feel called upon to justify the practice.

But with the Vietnam War, campus recruiting became a major issue. Throughout the country students demonstrated against—and often blocked—visits by recruiters for the armed services, the CIA, and war-related corporations, such as Dow Chemical. Radicals charged that the universities supported the war by opening their campuses to military recruiters and providing them with facilities. Generally the universities responded that they accepted recruiting representatives from all legal organizations and that to refuse facilities to some recruiters would be to violate the principle of "institutional neutrality." Supporters of recruiting argued that if military recruiters were banned, the rights of those students who wanted to meet them would be violated. (For this position, see the letter by Bill B. May in the preceding chapter, pages 231–34.)

The American Civil Liberties Union presents the viewpoint of those who opposed selective exclusion of recruiters. The Union maintained that universities might welcome *all* recruiters or ban *all* recruiters, but it was not legitimate to pick and choose.

One of the most influential essays against war-related recruiting was Howard Zinn's "Dow shall not kill." Zinn, a history professor at Boston University, denied that civil liberties were in question. No one was trying to restrict the freedom of speech of Dow representatives, he said; it was their freedom of action which radicals wanted to curb. As we pass laws against "murder, rape, arson," so may we restrict Dow Chemical from recruiting for napalm production. In the absence of appropriate governmental legislation, Zinn wrote, protesters may justifiably resort to civil disobedience since "fundamental rights, like life, health, liberty" are at stake and the "legal channels for redressing the grievances are inadequate."

Henry Steele Commager, the Amherst historian, took a similar position, arguing as Senator Fulbright did on the issue of military research, that the university was "under no obligation whatsoever to make its facilities available to what is not educational." He insisted that the university has always been engaged in the process of making moral distinctions, and that it certainly could do so on the recruiting question. Indeed, Commager emphasized, it must do so on the Vietnam War, or stand accused of moral delinquency.

Statement by American Civil Liberties Union, February 19, 1968.

Corporation and Government Recruiters on the College Campus

Many American colleges and universities are currently confronting a major controversy with respect to the use of campus facilities by corporations and government agencies for discussion with students concerning career recruitment. In some instances, the disruption caused by demonstrations against the presence of particular recruiters on college grounds has led institutions to rescind temporarily their invitations to controversial recruiters and to re-examine their traditional policy of extending invitations to accredited agencies on a non-discriminatory basis.

The complexity of the problem is reflected in the differences of opinion within the academic community concerning the university's role with relation to recruitment. The American Civil Liberties Union has given careful attention to the many aspects of this controversy in an effort to understand and determine where the civil liberties and academic freedom issues lie. We offer the following conclusions.

On-campus career recruitment is essentially a service to students and not central to the educational purposes of the university. Therefore, college and university officials may decide, as a matter of institutional policy, to refuse the use of their facilities to all recruiting agents of any category without infringing on the basic precepts of academic freedom or civil liberties.

On the other hand, if the established policy of the institution permits outside recruitment, it is incumbent on the administration, in the interests of academic freedom, to assure that facilities are made available, in accordance with established policies and procedures, and without discrimination, to the representatives of any commercial firm or government agency, including the military, invited to the campus for that purpose by any authorized administrative, faculty or student group. The same rules and regulations that normally govern the appearance of outside invited persons on campus should prevail.

The Union believes that any decision to exclude some recruiters, arising primarily from a political controversy, poses questions of civil liberties interest. Whether based on the imposition of an ideological test, concern for the physical safety of its students, disruption of the orderly processes of the institution, or protection of students from the threat of reprisal by draft reclassification, the barring of accredited outside agencies strikes against the concept of the open university and the right of students to hear all points of view. Moreover, selective exclusions that deny students access to particular recruiters are discriminatory in their application and suggest a possible infringement of the spirit of the equal protection clause of the Constitution.

For these reasons, it is our judgment that no issues of civil liberties are raised if an educational institution decides as a matter of policy to admit *all* accredited recruiting agents to the campus or to admit *none,* but a decision to admit some and exclude others would be discriminatory and an incursion into the basic principles of academic freedom.

We also believe that free speech and academic freedom require that protests on campus relating to recruitment by any segment of the academic community should also be fully protected. This includes all forms of legitimate protest such as speeches, peaceful demonstrations, picketing, rallies, etc. However, demonstrators who are moved by conscience or the intensity of their convictions to use means of protest which result in depriving others of the opportunity to speak or be heard, physically obstruct movement or disrupt the educational or institutional process cannot expect support on civil liberties grounds and must be prepared to accept the consequences of their action. We assume that regardless of the manner in which protest is expressed, procedures of due process will be strictly observed by the college and university where infractions are charged.

A collateral issue to on-campus recruitment is raised by the use, in some instances, of outside police to quell disturbances on university grounds. Traditionally, universities have been self-governing institutions which have settled their internal dissensions and difficulties through the art of discussion and persuasion and, only when unavoidable, by the use of campus authority and discipline. We believe that outside police should not be summoned to a campus to deal with internal problems unless all other techniques have clearly failed and then only on the basis of rules made in advance with the participation, consultation, and preferably, concurrence of representatives of students and faculty who have been selected in a truly representative fashion.

Article by Professor Howard Zinn, Department of History, Boston University, that originally appeared in Boston University News *in 1967; reprinted as a leaflet on many campuses.*

Dow Shalt Not Kill

Many faculty members and students, being passionate opponents of American violence in Vietnam, and also insistent civil libertarians, are troubled by the recent demonstrations against Dow Chemical. No dilemma exists where the action is merely protest— by picketing, leafleting, speaking—against Dow, napalm, and the war. That is plain exercise of speech, press, and assembly. But physical interposition, where Dow recruiters are blocked from carrying on their recruiting, opens puzzling questions. As one concerned both with civil liberties and the war, I would like to think aloud for a while, in print, and try to reach some conclusions.

First, it seems to me that the "civil liberties" of Dow Chemical are not in question. "Civil liberties" encompass various forms of freedom of expression, as well as certain procedural guarantees against arbitrary police or judicial action, and are fairly well covered by the first, eighth and fourteenth Amendments. No one is abrogating Dow's right to express its views; indeed, the recent demonstrators in this area invited the Dow representative to state his case publicly, and gave him a platform for this purpose. If Dow wanted to set up a table, or hold a meeting, to declare its views, any interference would be a violation of civil liberties.

However, the actions of an individual or group which (unlike even the most malicious or slanderous speech) have immediate and irremediable effects on the lives and liberties of others, must sometimes be restricted for the health and safety of the public. Thus, we pass laws against murder, rape, arson. Thus, we regulate the sale and manufacture of harmful products. We even restrict the restaurant owner's freedom to choose his customers by racial standards.

To put it more broadly: the whole body of criminal and social legislation is designed to restrict some people's freedom of action (not their civil liberties) in order to safeguard the health and happiness of others. Therefore, a *law* which prevented Dow Chemical Company from recruiting people who might be engaged in the manufacture, sale, or promotion of a substance to be dropped on men, women, and children in order to burn them to death would be easily as justifiable as the Meat Inspection Act of 1906. It would (unlike a law interfering with talk for or against such a substance) no more be an infringement of civil liberties than a law barring the indiscriminate sale of deadly poisons at the corner grocery.

The doctrine that the "civil liberties" of corporations are violated by regulatory laws was predominant in this country during the age of "the Robber Barons," and was constitutionally sanctioned for about fifty years, until 1938. Then, a sharply-worded opinion by Justice Black (*Connecticut General Life Insurance Co. v. Johnson*) declared that corporations should no longer be considered "persons" to be protected by the due process clause of the 14th Amendment. It soon became established in constitutional law that the regulation of business was *not* a deprivation of a civil liberty, that what is known as "substantive due process" would apply only to cases where real persons were being deprived of their rights of free expression. Today, it is well-established constitutionally that the U.S. government could make illegal the manufacture of napalm, and charge any persons recruiting for a napalm-manufacturing company with conspiring to violate the law.

But: there is no such law. Indeed, the government itself has ordered the napalm manufactured by Dow, and is using it to burn and kill Vietnamese peasants. Should private citizens (students, faculty—in this instance) act themselves, by physical interposition, against Dow Chemical's business activities? To do so would be to "take the law into your own hands." That is exactly what civil disobedience is: the temporary taking of the law into one's own hands, in order to declare what the law should be. It is a declaration that there is an incongruence between the law and humane values, and that sometimes this can only be publicized by breaking the law.

Civil disobedience can take two forms: violating a law which is obnoxious; or symbolically enacting a law which is urgently needed. When Negroes sat-in at lunch counters, they were engaging in both forms: they violated state laws on segregation and trespassing; they were also symbolically enacting a public accommodations law even before it was written into the Civil Rights Act of 1964.

Most of us, I assume, would support civil disobedience under *some* circumstances: we would commend those who defied the Fugitive Slave Act by harboring a Negro slave, and those who symbolically enacted emancipation by trying to prevent soldiers in Boston from returning Anthony Burns to his master. Otherwise—to declare that the law in *all* circumstances is to be obeyed —is to suppress the very spirit of democracy, to surrender individual conscience to an omnipotent state. Thus the issue becomes:

under what circumstances is civil disobedience justified, and is the Dow Chemical situation one of those circumstances?

It seems to me there are two essential conditions for the right to civil disobedience. One is that the human value at stake must involve fundamental rights, like life, health, liberty. There is no real cause, for instance, to disobey a traffic light because it is inconveniently long. But human slavery, or racism, or war—these are overwhelmingly important. Thus, the argument "What if everyone disobeyed the law every time it displeased them" falls before the observable fact that those who engage in civil disobedience are almost always law-abiding citizens who on certain very important issues deliberately, openly, temporarily violate the law to communicate a vital message to their fellow citizens.

What of Dow Chemical and napalm? Four American physicians, in a report "Medical Problems of South Vietnam," have written: "Napalm is a highly sticky inflammable jelly which clings to anything it touches and burns with such heat that all oxygen in the area is exhausted within moments. Death is either by roasting or by suffocation. Napalm wounds are often fatal (estimates are 90%).

"Those who survive face a living death. The victims are frequently children. Napalm is dropped daily on the villages, the forests, the people of Vietnam by American bombers; the saturation bombing of that tiny country is one of the cruelest acts perpetrated by any nation in modern history; it ranks with the destruction of Lidice by the Germans, the crushing of the Hungarian rebellion by the Russians, the recent mass slaughter in Indonesia." Dr. Richard E. Perry, an American physician, wrote in *Redbook* magazine in January, 1967, on his return from Vietnam: "I have been an orthopedic surgeon for a good number of years, with rather a wide range of medical experience. But nothing could have prepared me for my encounters with Vietnamese women and children burned by napalm. It was shocking and sickening, even for a physician, to see and smell the blackened flesh."

We are not, then, dealing with trivialities, but with monstrous deeds. This fact somehow becomes lost in the bland, reasoned talk of businessmen and university officials, who speak as if Dow were just another business firm, recruiting for some innocuous purpose, making radios or toothpaste.

The root issue, it should be clear, is not simply napalm; it is the Vietnam war as a whole, in which a far-off country is being systematically destroyed, and its population decimated, by the greatest military power on earth. The war itself is the object of the civil disobedience; the use of napalm is one particularly bestial tactic in this war.

This brings us to the second condition for civil disobedience: the inadequacy of legal channels for redressing the grievance. This is manifestly true in the case of the Vietnam war, which is being waged completely outside the American constitutional process, by the President and a handful of advisors. Congress is troubled, but follows sheeplike what the White House decrees. The Supreme Court, by tradition, leaves foreign policy questions to the "political" branches of government (the President and Congress) but recently one of its more conservative members, Justice Potter Stewart, said that perhaps the Court should review the constitutionality of the war. This, after 100,000 American casualties!

Citizens have taken to the auditoriums and to the streets precisely because they have no other way to protest; yet both President and Vice President declare with the brazenness of petty dictators that no civic outcry will change their policy. If ever there was an issue which called for civil disobedience, it is this runaway war.

Then why do we become uneasy when students interfere with Dow Chemical? Occasionally, we read of housewives blocking off a busy intersection because children have been killed there as a result of the lack of traffic lights. These housewives thereby interfere with the freedom of automobiles and of pedestrians, in order to temporarily regulate, or even disrupt, traffic, on behalf of the lives of children—hoping this will lead to the permanent regulation of traffic by government. (Those are not the automobiles that killed the child, anymore than this Dow Chemical representative, or the student he is recruiting, is actually dropping the napalm bomb.)

Why do we so easily sympathize with actions like that, where perhaps one child was killed, and not with actions against Dow Chemical, where countless children have been victims? Is it possible that we subconsciously distinguish between the identifiable children down the street (who move us), and the faceless children of that remote Asian land (who do not)? Is it possible also that the well-dressed, harassed representative of Dow Chemical is more human, therefore more an object of sympathy, to the well-dressed, harassed officials of the University (and to us), than the burning, bleeding, blurred faces of the Vietnamese?

There is a common argument which says: but where will these student actions lead? If we justify one act of civil disobedience, must we not justify them all? Does the KKK then have the right to disobey the Civil Rights Acts? Where does it stop? That argument withers away, however, once we recognize the distinction between free speech, where absolute toleration is a social good, and free action, where the existence of values other than free speech demands that we choose right over wrong and respond accordingly. We should remember that the social utility of free speech is in giving us the informational base from which we can then make social choices in action. To limit free speech is to distort our capacity to make such choices. To refrain from making choices is to say that beyond the issue of free speech we have no substantive values which we will express in action. If we do not discriminate in the actions we support or oppose, we cannot rectify the terrible injustices of the present world.

Whether the issue of the Vietnam war is more effectively presented by protest and demonstration (that is, the exercise of speech, press, assembly) rather than by civil disobedience, is a question of tactics, and varies with each specific situation. Different student groups (at Harvard and M.I.T. for instance) have used one or another against Dow recruitment, and each tactic has its own advantages. I tend to favor the protest tactic as keeping the central issue of the war clearer. But if students or faculty engaged in civil disobedience, I would consider that morally defensible.

So much for student-faculty action—but what of the University Administration? The University acceptance of Dow Chemical recruiting as just another business transaction is especially disheartening, because it is the University which tells students repeatedly on ceremonial occasions that it hopes students will be more than fact-absorbing automatons, that they will choose humane values, and stand up for them courageously.

For the University to sponsor Dow Chemical activities as a protective civil liberty means that the University (despite its course in Constitutional Law) still accepts the 19th century definition of substantive due process as defending corporations against regulation, that (despite a library with books on civil liberties) the University still does not understand what civil liberties are, that (despite its entrance requirement of literacy) the University has not read in the newspapers of the terrible damage our napalm bombs have done to innocent people.

The fact that there is only an indirect connection between Dow recruiting BU students, and napalm dropped on Vietnamese villages, does not vitiate the moral issue. It is precisely the nature of modern mass murder that it is not visibly direct like individual murder, but takes on a corporate character, where every participant has limited liability. The total effect, however, is a thousand times more pernicious, than that of the individual entrepreneur of violence. If the world is destroyed, it will be a white-collar crime, done in a businesslike way, by large numbers of individuals involved in a chain of actions, each one having a touch of innocence.

Sometimes the University speaks of the "right of recruitment." There is no absolute right of recruitment, however, because (beyond the package of civil liberties connected with free expression and procedural guarantees, which are the closest we can get to "absolute" right) all rights are relative. I doubt that BU would open its offices to the Ku Klux Klan for recruiting, or that it would apply an absolute right of private enterprise to peddlers selling poisonous food on campus. When the University of Pennsylvania announced it would end its germ-warfare research project, it was saying that there is no absolute right to do research on anything, for any purpose.

The existence of University "security" men (once known as campus police) testifies that all actions on campus are not equally tolerable. The University makes moral choices all the time. If it can regulate the movement of men into women's dormitories (in a firm stand for chastity or perhaps some other value equally dear) then why cannot it regulate the coming and going of corporations into the University, where the value is life, and the issue is suffering?

And if students are willing to take the risks of civil disobedience, to declare themselves for the dying people of Vietnam, cannot the University take a milder step, but one which makes the same declaration—and cancel the invitation to Dow Chemical? Why cannot the University—so much more secure—show a measure of social commitment, a bit of moral courage? Should not the University, which speaks so often about students having "values," declare some of its own? It is written on no tablets handed down from heaven that the officials of a University may not express themselves on public issues. It is time (if not now, when? asks the Old Testament) for the University to forsake the neutrality of the IBM machines, and join the human race.

Article by Professor Henry Steele Commager, Department of History, Amherst College, in The New Republic, *February 24, 1968.*

The University as Employment Agency

From Harvard Yard to Madison and Berkeley, students are taking into their own hands and hearts, what university administrators have failed to take into their hands or their minds: the problem of the obligation of the university to private corporations and to government. Students are protesting and, where protests are ineffective, demonstrating against the practice of lending the facilities of the university to recruitment of students by corporations and the military. Sometimes their protest takes the form of forcibly banning recruiters from university facilities, thus exposing them to the wrath of deans and presidents who, unwilling to face the central issue of on-campus recruitment, embrace with enthusiasm the marginal issue of bad manners.

For the explosion of this controversy on campus, the university authorities have only themselves to blame for not formulating any policy which could stand the test of logical scrutiny. Most of them are still sullenly taking refuge in precedent, or involving irrelevant arguments of "freedom of information." Student demonstrations against recruitment are, then, a monument to the absence of foresight and of imagination in university administrators, and an excess of imagination in students. All who are concerned with the academic enterprise will agree that an excess of imagination and of moral passion in the young is to be preferred to the absence of either in their elders.

The basic principle which should govern the relations of the university to recruiters is that which should govern all other activities of the academy. The university is not an employment agency; it is not an adjunct of corporations; it is not an instrument of government. Wherever feasible the university should make available its facilities to legitimate educational enterprises.

It is under no obligation whatsoever to make its facilities available to what is not educational.

Guided by this simple principle the university can deal with the awkward problem of recruiting with reasonable consistency and fairness. There are and will be exceptions and borderline cases—as Supreme Court opinions testify daily—exceptions and borderline cases in the interpretation of the Constitution and the Bill of Rights. So far, however, none of these borderline cases has caused any difficulties. Students have not protested against recruitment by the Peace Corps, or Head Start, or the United Nations, and it is unlikely that they will. The organizations whose recruiting has precipitated the crisis throughout the academic world are not borderline cases. By no stretch of the imagination can it be alleged that Dow Chemical Company, the Marines or the CIA are educational enterprises, or that they contribute to the educational enterprise. Dow Chemical is a business corporation; its business is to make money, and it recruits students at universities because that is one of the ways it hopes to make money. No university is under any obligation whatever to help Dow Chemical make money. The Marines and the Navy, admirable as they no doubt are, are not educational enterprises. Their business is to fight. The university is an interested party in this enterprise, just as it is an interested party in tax collecting or in the maintenance of law and order, but it is under no more obligation to lend its facilities to the Marines and the Navy than it is to lend them to the Department of the Treasury or the Department of Justice.

But, it is asserted, every student has a right to hear what these, and other, organizations have to say. So they have, and a university which sought to deny them this right would be derelict in its duty to its students, and to its own character. The argument is, however, wholly irrelevant to the situation which confronts us. Every student has a right to a great many things that the university is not obliged to provide. He has a right to read all newspapers, all magazines and all books, but the university is not obliged to provide him with all newspapers, magazines and books. It subscribes to *The New York Times* and *Foreign Affairs*, not to *Playboy*. Any student who wants to read that can buy it at the local newsstand, but anyone who argued that the principle of free access to information required the university library to subscribe to all publications would be regarded as bereft of his senses. So any student who wants to hear what Dow Chemical or the CIA wants to say could, without serious inconvenience, visit them off-campus. Dow Chemical, like all corporations, can rent space in local office buildings just as it buys space in local newspapers. The Marines and the CIA can use the local post office to conduct interviews. Except at a very few colleges, so remote from civilization that there are neither stores nor offices nor post offices available, no student (and no recruiter) will be seriously inconvenienced if universities adopt the common-sense rule of confining the use of their facilities to purposes incontrovertibly educational.

Balanced against what is merely ingrained habit, or, at the most, inconvenience to a few students of walking a few blocks to an office building or post office, are two considerations of importance. First is the principle (if it rises to the dignity of that), that the college should not throw open its facilities indiscriminately to all comers—business, religious, fraternal, political, military—for if it did, it would find those facilities swamped. It must and in fact it does, even now, discriminate. Even those who defend most ardently the "right" of students to interview Dow Chemical are not prepared to provide facilities for the Rotary, the Lions and the Kiwanis, the Elks and the Masons and the Woodmen of the World, the Baptists, the Mormons and the Jehovah's Witnesses, and so on *ad infinitum.* The only sound basis for discrimination is educational. The second principle is more fundamental. When the university is called upon to weigh the conflicting claims of those who plead habit or convenience, against those who plead deep moral convictions—moral convictions which are shared by a large segment of our society and are therefore neither eccentric nor perverse—it should not hesitate to tip the balance on the side of moral convictions. Certainly it is unworthy of the academy to drift—or to allow itself to be maneuvered into—a position where out of stubbornness, out of thoughtlessness, out of inertia, it flouts the legitimate moral sentiments of its students and its faculty. To argue that some students may entertain moral convictions about seeing recruiters on-campus rather than off-campus is frivolous, for it ascribes moral significance to what is a mere matter of personal convenience.

Some institutions, prepared to concede that they are not under any obligation to provide facilities for recruiting to private corporations, do insist, or at least assert, that they have some kind of moral obligation to cooperate with government, especially at a time of crisis and war. Therefore, they add, even though government has ample facilities already available to it in federal, state and local government buildings, the university should stand ready to lend its premises to government recruiters. This is a plausible argument when used selectively, but not persuasive when applied indiscriminately.

Time and again in the past, the university has acknowledged an obligation to cooperate with state and national government—and keep in mind that what we are considering here is not any legal obligation to obey the law, but a voluntary cooperation which is beyond the obligation of the law. Does it follow from past and current practice, that the university has an obligation to cooperate with every branch, every department, every bureau of government for any and all purposes?

Such a conclusion is untenable, and universities have already rejected it. Few universities are prepared to make available to snooping committees of legislatures, or even to the FBI, the names of members of all student organizations. Many have refused to provide draft boards with records of student grades. No self-respecting university now would cooperate with un-American activities committees, state or national, in investigating professors. Nor are universities under obligation to lend their facilities indiscriminately to the enforcement of laws. The laws of Massachusetts (and until recently of Connecticut) made use of contraceptives by anyone, single or married, a misdemeanor; it is scarcely conceivable that any university in that state, public or private, would entertain a request from state law enforcement agencies to help discover and bring to justice members of faculty or student body who violate these laws. Nor do universities yield, generally, to the plea of convenience. If students want information on taxes, they expect to go to the local tax authorities, or perhaps to a bank; if they want information on voting they go to the town hall; if they want to take out a driver's license, they go to the local police. The universities are not expected to provide these services for the students, or even to provide the facilities where these particular government agencies can give out "information."

Even when it comes to carrying on scientific research, which is clearly educational in character, universities do not casually or indiscriminately make available their offices and laboratories or libraries, but select what is valuable to *them,* and then draw up contracts which carefully safeguard the right of the university to supervise the research, protect scholars and avoid secrecy, and which provide, too, for compensation for the use of academic facilities.

Does the university then have the right—the moral right, for the legal is clearly beyond dispute—to decide with which governmental activities it will cooperate? Does it have the right to say Yes to the Peace Corps, but No to the Marines; Yes to the Smithsonian Institution, but No to the CIA?

Let us consider—because it is the most controversial of them all—the obligation of the university to the CIA.

The readiness of the university to lend its facilities, and its good name, to the CIA is the most notorious example of the fix in which it finds itself when it blindly follows the principle of the Open Door to all government agencies. For the CIA is, by definition, subversive of the academy. Its business is subversion at home as well as abroad, and by giving it a free hand and ample money, the Congress has endorsed this function. It has, by its own admission, subverted universities, scholars, student organizations, research, publications, even churches and philanthropic institutions. Its whole character is at war with what the university stands for. It loves secrecy, but the university flourishes only in the light. It takes refuge in anonymity, but the university must know the credentials of those to whom it gives its confidence. It is chauvinistic, but the university is by its nature cosmopolitan and international. It works not to find and certainly not to proclaim truth, but the major purpose of the university is to extend the frontiers of truth.

Clearly the university is under no obligation to collaborate with the CIA simply because it is a government agency. This conclusion has not only the sanction of centuries of the history of universities; it has legal sanction as well. For to the argument that the university should not look beyond the official credentials of an agency of the government—an argument advanced with considerable earnestness by those who wish to avoid the moral issue—we must consider the counterargument of the legal principle adopted by the United States at the time of the Nuremberg War Crimes trials. The official American position, submitted by Supreme Court Justice Robert Jackson, was quite simply that no citizen is bound to accept as legal and valid every act of his government, nor can he avoid responsibility for his conduct by placing responsibility on the government. This position was accepted by the Tribunal, and under it men like Albert Speer, Minister of Munitions, were found guilty. It is not necessary to argue that the CIA is violating international law; it is enough to recognize the validity of the principle that institutions, such as universities, are not precluded from inquiring into the credentials of such branches of the government as make demands upon them.

Whatever we may think about the larger place of the CIA in the scheme of national defense, we can scarcely avoid the conclusion that it is degrading for the university to lend its facilities, and a reputation painfully won over a period of 800 years, to cooperate in its own subversion. It is degrading for it to extend the hand of fellowship to those who are engaged in perverting its character.

Even those who are prepared to concede in principle the right of students to oppose corporate or military recruiting on campus, deplore the manner in which they have asserted, or demonstrated, that right. Almost everywhere student demonstrations have been accompanied by bad manners, and in some places by force and violence. Now it is very wrong for the young to display discourtesy in these situations, and quite intolerable for them to resort to violence, even the somewhat negative violence of refusing access to a recruiting-office room. Clearly the young should model themselves here on those who are older and wiser, model themselves on the spokesmen and representatives of our nation, on whom rests ultimate responsibility for the maintenance of an orderly society. What a pity they do not follow the example, in their protests, of distinguished statesmen like Senators Russell Long and John Stennis, who think all dissenters should be jailed; of presidential candidate George Wallace who thinks they should be shot; or of Rep. Mendel Rivers of South Carolina who thinks the proper response to flag burning is burning the Bill of Rights. What a pity they do not model themselves on official defenders of law and order like the police of Watts, Cleveland, Detroit, Newark and Philadelphia, or the US Marshals in Washington. How distressing they do not conform to the models of that military who try so hard to enlist them, "General-Bomb-Them-Back-to-the-Stone Age" LeMay, for example, or the Air Force officers who habitually fly over Communist China in violation of international law. How much wiser they would be if they studied the conduct of the CIA whose interests their deans so sedulously protect, and who have never been known to resort to violence, and who conduct their operations in some 60 countries throughout the globe with the nicest regard to the legal amenities. How it would improve their characters if instead of milling about the campus in futile demonstrations they resorted to their libraries and read how their government eschewed violence and championed law at the time of the Bay of Pigs invasion of Cuba, or of the intervention by Marines in Guatemala and Santo Domingo. How much wiser they would be if they studied the Kellogg-Briand Peace Pact, or the Charter of the United Nations and reflected on their own government's faithfulness in their commitment to these renunciations of war. But we should remember that students are young, and that they have not had the training and experience which has made their rulers such models of moderation and of reason.

On this whole matter of discourtesy and violence that so often accompanies demonstrations it is relevant to recall what the Rev. Samuel J. May—he was uncle to the Little Women—wrote to his friend the Rev. William Ellery Channing about the demonstrations of abolitionists against slavery: "You must not expect those who have left to take up this great cause [of abolition] that they will plead it in all that seemliness of phrase which the scholars . . . might use. But the scholars and the clergy and the statesmen had done nothing. We abolitionists are what we are—babes, sucklings, obscure men, silly women, publicans, sinners, and we shall manage the matter we have taken in hand just as might be expected of such persons as we are. It is unbecoming in abler men who stood by, and would do nothing, to complain of us because we manage this matter no better."

To this Dr. Channing answered in words that apply to demonstrators against the Vietnam war as against the abolitionists: "The great interests of humanity do not lose their claims on us because sometimes injudiciously maintained."

Indeed they do not. Yet more and more those in authority, in the academy as in government, are avoiding moral issues and taking refuge in questions of conduct or of manners. Instead of falling back on the familiar principle, "I disagree with what you say but shall defend to the death your right to say it," they substitute, "I may agree with you, but I disapprove profoundly of the manner in which you say it."

What is this silence that has fallen on the leadership of the university—presidents, deans, boards of trustees and regents alike? The leaders of the religious community have spoken out boldly enough—heads of great theological seminaries, distinguished theologians and clergymen. The scientific community has taken a strong stand on the moral issues of the war and of nuclear weapons, Nobel Prize winners, heads of great scientific organizations. The rank and file of the academic community, teachers, scholars, students, have seen that here are moral issues that must be faced, and have wrestled with them. But from Cambridge to Berkeley, from Madison to Baton Rouge, not a single president of a great university has taken a public stand on what is the greatest moral issue of our time.

Are they silent because they are bemused by the notion that with their position they take a vow of moral continence? They did not so reason in the past—not at the time of the two World Wars, not during discussions of the League of Nations, or of communism. Is it because they fear that if they spoke out like independent men, they would somehow "commit" their institutions? If so they are mistaken in fact and logic. No president can commit his university, which consists of faculty and students, to a moral position, or a political. No one supposes that a senator who speaks out somehow commits the United States Senate, or that a judge who speaks his mind commits the Supreme Court, or even that a business executive can commit his corporation and his stockholders to political positions. Why should presidents or deans indulge in the vanity of supposing that they can somehow commit great universities? Yet here they stand numbed by timidity, taking refuge from the obligation to confront great moral questions by escaping into the easy activity of applying petty disciplinary measures to students who embarrass them.

If presidents, deans, trustees and regents are unwilling or unable to protect and exalt the dignity of the university, they should be grateful to students who have remembered it and exalted it. If universities have refused to face the major moral issues of our day they should rejoice that they have, somehow, helped to produce students who are neither paralyzed nor timid, who are sensitive to moral issues and prepared to respond to them, however convulsively.

On this matter of recruitment, as on the larger issues of the relation of the academy to the moral problems which glare upon us from every quarter of the horizon, this generation of university presidents, so respectable, so cautious, may yet hear from their own students that immortal taunt of Henri IV: "Go hang yourself, brave Crillon; we fought at Arques and you were not there."

CHAPTER 9

ROTC: The Case of Harvard

Reserve Officer Training Corps programs on American campuses have been a source of controversy that predates the 1960s. ROTC, and particularly compulsory ROTC, has been the focus of many conflicts over the years, usually on the grounds that military training is a function incompatible with the spirit of the university. The Vietnam War revived the controversy, which had died down after the Second World War.

Since the story has been essentially the same everywhere, we have limited our account to one major institution—Harvard—where the battle was fought in 1968–69. We start with a memorandum from the Harvard ROTC Instructor Group of December 4, 1968, which was made public by SDS in February 1969. It warned that any negative action on ROTC by Harvard might be "precedent-setting," as indeed it turned out to be. In January 1969, *The Old Mole,* a Cambridge radical newspaper, published an article on ROTC challenging the "liberal position." The minutes of the Harvard faculty meeting in February 1969 record the range of views that were expressed, from total opposition to total support for the continuance of ROTC. The final faculty vote was for a resolution that abolished academic credit for ROTC courses, terminated faculty appointments for ROTC instructors, and removed ROTC from the catalogue; it stopped short, however, of abolishing ROTC. When the Harvard sit-ins occurred in April, SDS "liberated" and published two documents from Harvard administrators to President Nathan Pusey which discussed means of circumventing the faculty resolution. The publication of these documents, which had been confidential, was the subject of further controversy.

Resolutions similar to the one approved at Harvard were adopted at that time by Columbia, Dartmouth, and Yale. Since these resolutions posed conditions for the continuance of ROTC that were incompatible with existing federal legislation, the four schools ultimately decided that the line of least resistance was to terminate the ROTC programs by accepting no new freshmen recruits.

From a memorandum by the U.S. Army ROTC Instructor Group, Harvard University, December 4, 1968.

The Case for ROTC at Harvard

Q: Why is ROTC under attack at Harvard now?

A: ROTC is under attack at Harvard now because a small group of student extremists—a tiny minority of the student body—have played upon the inherent anti-war sentiment shared by a majority of peace-loving, traditionally isolationist Americans. The Vietnam war, grievous to virtually all of us, is the immediate source of their blanket denunciation of everything related to the military. They offer no alternatives when they propose destruction of the nation's armed forces. (Let it be understood beyond question that there is at present no acceptable alternate source of junior officer leadership if ROTC is driven from the college campus.) The radicals' reasons for wanting to destroy ROTC are patently contrived because they are exactly the same reasons that existed without challenge for 50 years before Vietnam clouded our vision and robbed our logic.

The anti-ROTC arguments in the excellent study done by the Harvard-Radcliffe Policy Committee are eminently logical when evaluated in the narrow terms of academic freedom. The arguments of the anti-war, moralist protest group are even less practical and convincing in terms of the real-life world. Both arguments deal mostly with technicalities from a very narrow point of view rather than with the hard realities of life and the broad spectrum of our national existence.

When pinned down, none of the radicals and their sympathizers will admit that the nation, in the presence of ruthless enemies, can afford to disband its armed forces. But the question of who is to man the armed forces is left unanswered. The traditional precept of a broad-based citizen-soldier army, with the dangers and sacrifices of military duty shared equally by all able-bodied men, is conveniently forgotten. There is no hue and cry to make the draft laws fair and equitable or to provide an acceptable substitute for ROTC, if indeed a substitute can be found.

How, in the presence of these facts, can there be any rational support for the destruction of ROTC? Surely there is some doubt that a gambit in the guise of academic freedom in the liberal arts milieu should not be allowed to destroy an important institution in our society without a reasonable alternative.

Q: What alternatives are available if the ROTC program is discredited or driven completely from the college campus?

A: There is no acceptable program in existence at this time to substitute for ROTC as a broad-based source of college-educated citizen-soldier leaders for our armed forces. About 45 per cent of all Army officers currently on active duty are ROTC graduates; 65 per cent of our 1st lieutenants and 85 per cent of our 2nd lieutenants come from the ROTC program. The Army needs 18,000 new 2nd lieutenants each year to meet normal attrition. We met that goal last year and expect to meet it again this year. For some years before that, we had serious shortfalls. There is little question that the current wave of anti-ROTC sentiment, unless reversed by exemplary action on the part of ROTC host institutions, will have serious impact upon ROTC production figures in the immediate future.

The anti-ROTC extremists apparently do not accept the criticality of ROTC to our defense establishment. They persist in the notion that the armed forces will continue to exist and perform their functions, somehow, without ROTC. The blunt truth is that Officer Candidate School (OCS) programs are not attractive to college graduates unless there is extreme pressure from the draft. One reason is obvious: the Army OCS volunteer must serve a three-year tour of active duty, not two years as in the case of the ROTC graduate or the college graduate drafted into the Army as a private.

What about officer training programs such as the US Marine Corps' Platoon Leader Program which requires no on-campus training for college students? That program is not popular because it requires two summer training camps instead of one, plus three years of active duty. College men are increasingly reluctant to give more than one summer of their college years to officer training.

An OCS program catering to high school graduates and college dropouts as a primary source of junior officers for the Army Officer Corps is unthinkable. The armed forces simply cannot function—nor should they be expected to function in our complex society—without an officer corps comprised largely of college graduates, just as most of our national institutions these days rely upon college-educated men for their leadership. Who is prepared to trust their sons—let alone the nation's destiny—to the leadership of high school boys and college drop-outs? Only the grossly uninformed or narrowly bigoted critic could fail to comprehend that the armed forces have a perfectly valid need for a fair share of the time and talents of the young Americans who have been blessed with a college education.

Q: What will be the effect if the various changes in Harvard ROTC programs being recommended for faculty action are approved?

FACULTY STATUS

In the matter of faculty status for service officers assigned to ROTC duty, this is a requirement of law. It follows that no one in the Department of Defense could possibly have the authority to waive that requirement. The Congress could change the law, of course, but the purpose of the provision in the first instance—insuring a respectable position and status for the ROTC program on every college campus, insuring that the program is not categorized as a college game—would be sacrificed. . . .

INSTITUTIONAL SUPPORT

In the matter of withdrawal of physical support—classrooms and administrative offices—by the institution, it seems quite clear that no military department could continue to operate a unit under such circumstances.

ACADEMIC CREDIT

With regard to academic credit, the services are all known to be most anxious to retain academic credit as a mark of prestige and a matter of ultimate inducement in attracting young men to the ROTC programs. All services are known to be most eager to "upgrade" their curricula to satisfy the demand for "college-level" subjects. All services have some flexibility in this regard and are anxious to work with host institutions in search of agreeable compromise ground. The ability to do this varies among the services, however, largely because the Army is wedded—for better or for worse—to a two-year active duty obligation. Without being grossly imprudent personnel managers, we cannot afford to take six months out of the two years—25 per cent of the ROTC graduate's productive time in service—to teach him the military skills which he must know in order to be an effective officer. With a three or four year active duty obligation to work with, our sister services can afford to teach their "officers" what is required to be an officer *after* they come on active duty. . . .

More important than any point thus far made is the role of Harvard University in setting a pattern of ROTC policy for the entire academic community. There are other colleges and universities where academic credit for ROTC is much more meaningful than at Harvard. Many of these institutions are big-production schools which can have a major impact upon Army officer procurement objectives. Harvard has a special obligation to the nation as a precedent-setting leader of the academic community. "As Harvard goes, so goes the Army ROTC program" might produce a disaster of real proportions if the ROTC concept is weakened and degraded nation-wide.

Article by Alan Gilbert, instructor in government, Harvard University, in The Old Mole, *Cambridge radical newspaper, January 13–26, 1969.*

ROTC: SDS Challenges the Liberal Position

As a result of student protests against the Vietnam war, the presence of ROTC has become an issue on the Harvard campus this fall. Some official university bodies . . . have voiced a limited opposition to ROTC which maintains the dominant liberal conception of the government, the Army, and the University. The SDS position, on the other hand, fundamentally opposes the present structure of American society and perceives the existing relations between these institutions in a new way. The differences between these two views may be summarized as follows:

High Harvard Standards

In the liberal view, ROTC courses, presently offered for credit, do not measure up to Harvard's high intellectual standards. Course credit should be withdrawn, but ROTC should be allowed to remain on campus as an extracurricular activity.

In the radical view, ROTC is bad because it provides leadership for an Army engaged in the suppression of just popular movements at home and abroad. Hence, ROTC should be abolished. It makes little difference to the Vietnamese or to American black people whether the Army secures "human resources" on college campuses in an extracurricular rather than a curricular fashion.

The liberal view portrays the University as a pure community of scholars concerned with the free pursuit of learning. Military education, directed by the Department of Defense (which appoints all ROTC instructors) degrades this rarefied conception of an independent academy. The liberal says that the military (or military education) can justifiably be considered in abstract, eternal terms outside the context of the Vietnam war and American imperialism.

Radicals view the university mainly in terms of its function in society: to inculcate the dominant ideology (and perhaps to produce some limited innovations in it) and train highly-skilled technicians and scientists; and secondarily, as a corporation maintaining profitable relations with its students and with American society at large.

In terms of the university's ideological functions, social science courses express the more-or-less explicit attitude that American democracy and American capitalism are good institutions (or at least not actively harmful ones) for Americans and other peoples, and that we should all be concerned about the "free world interests" which are in fact the interests of American business. Humanities courses tend to posit the existence of a great humanistic tradition in the minds of cultivated men. The masses, however, are not susceptible to such intellectual concerns, so learning must be kept alive in the sanctuary of universities.

This exclusive definition of humanism coincides nicely with the needs and interests of America's rulers, for they too are exclusive humanists (man being defined as his capital, if one has no money one has no desires, i.e., is not a man, on the sensitive register of the market).

In the power structure of the University, the main governing body is the Corporation. This body consists of 7 members who hold 1 chairmanship, 3 presidencies, and 33 directorships in major corporations. For such important businessmen running Harvard actively would be a waste of time and money.

Hence, they delegate the job to the Administration . . . The administrators view Harvard as an elite institution. Their admissions policies strengthen the already unegalitarian tendencies of American class structure, e.g., less than 4% of a Harvard entering class comes from household units earning less than $7,500 (the national median). The Administration approves the use of the University's vast resources in such enterprises as the power companies of the American South and in expansion into Cambridge. High tuition, the necessity for even well-off students to take low-paying university jobs and to keep wages low for the buildings and grounds workers, the effects of Harvard's presence in driving up rents in Cambridge—these are a few of the many ways in which Harvard's activities as a corporation hurt both students and workers. Harvard's administrators are men of the same class origins, education, and breeding as the Corporation executives. They are dedicated to perpetuating Harvard's usefulness to the American ruling class.

The question arises: If Harvard is that bad, what can radicals expect to accomplish in the University? Harvard is part of American capitalism. The nature of Harvard (i.e., the interests which control it and which it serves) cannot be changed short of a revolution which changes the nature of the society. But by building a strong radical student movement, it is possible to win limited victories, e.g., to abolish ROTC. Such a victory would not in itself change the nature of Harvard, but it could significantly affect the US government's capacity to carry on the Vietnam war. To the extent that one builds such a movement, some education also takes place at a university.

Liberal ideology encourages students to conceive of themselves as privileged beings above the conflicts of the real world, to remain "neutral", and hence, since these conflicts continue, to ally themselves with the dominant power. In the case of ROTC, liberalism justifies shadow-boxing over the withdrawal of credit while allowing ROTC to stay.

The radical position sees that students as well as working people at home and abroad are hurt by the functioning of the university. As against liberalism which says that students should be apolitical, self-interested, and neutral, the radical position says that students should ally with working people and fight against their common rulers. Thus, the fight to abolish ROTC aligns students with the people whom the American government oppresses.

Procedural Objections

When SDS challenges the liberal position as in fact a reactionary one, liberals resort to procedural objections. The university, they say, is above the realm of politics. Hence, the willingness of SDS to use tactics of "violent" confrontation in the university is in itself wrong. Given their definition of the university, liberals do not discuss the substance of the radical position; rather, they attack the tactics used by radicals and claim that the position itself is devoid of substance (e.g., they charge radicals with "mindless activism," "manufacturing issues," disrupting "normal" procedures, etc.)

Liberals then proceed to draw the conclusion that since radicals have no other purposes, they must be out to destroy the university; they must be "wreckers," "outside agitators," and "sons of Communists" (cf Dean Ford, *Harvard Today*, August 1968; Pusey, *Annual Report*, 1968; Dean Watson, *Harvard Crimson*, this fall) who "dupe" and "manipulate" more "wholesome" students.

In effect, liberals play on the image which many students have of the university as neutral, nonviolent, and rational in an attempt to divert student anger over the war, over the oppression of black and white working people, over their own situation, onto the tactics of radicals. Last year, in the aftermath of the Dow sit-in, for instance, the administration and the faculty sought to make the essential issue Mr. Leavitt's (the Dow recruiter's) "right of egress" from Mallinckrodt—he was kept an hour from his dinner—rather than the war . . . Similarly, in the case of ROTC, liberals say that SDS is attacking the basic civil liberty of students to join any organization they choose. They claim that the issue is not what the army does, but free speech and association in the University. Finally, liberals threaten the radicals: if you do fight seriously against oppression and violate the cardinal principle of free speech, what will protect you in the next McCarthy era? (Given the performance of liberals in the last one, this argument is an especially blatant example of bad faith. See Jared Israel, "Free Speech at Harvard," *Old Mole,* No. 2).

Radicals say: the only precedent created by driving ROTC off campus would be a good one—students should fight hard against imperialism. Such a precedent could hardly be turned against SDS. In fact, a strong student movement to drive ROTC off campus is the best protection radicals could have when liberals—because they are imperialists—try to destroy us.

Not Free Speech Issue

Radicals say free speech is not the issue; ROTC is an instrument of US Armed Forces engaged in a war against the Vietnamese people. The American Government's "right of conquest" is here counterposed to the Vietnamese people's right to rebel. But only one of these mutually exclusive rights is in fact a genuine right. The force which a robber uses to extort goods from his victim does not give him a right to those goods. The force applied to maintain social conditions in which the great majority live on the edge of starvation and are treated as animals and a small number of men live luxuriously (e.g., in Vietnam, both French colonialism and U.S. imperialism from Diem through Ky) cannot manufacture a right of conquest. The oppressed on the other hand have the right to try to forge a society in which they can live as men, i.e., a more egalitarian and autonomous society. They have, in other words, the right to rebel (what makes rebellion a right is that there can be no genuine, i.e., non-coerced agreement among the men who engage in it and who attempt to build a just society).

In many countries besides Vietnam, the US Army (and military aid and advice) shore up reactionary regimes. There is no "right" involved in these activities. Since ROTC is engaged in such activities, its "right" to recruit junior officers on college campuses can justly be suppressed. It is the right of conquest, not freedom of speech, what ROTC does, not what individual officers say, which will be suppressed by driving ROTC off the Harvard campus.

Misguided Patriotism

In addition, an attack on ROTC is not, except in the minds of desperate liberals, an attack on students in the ROTC program. Radicals believe that ROTC uses the real needs of such students, e.g., money to go to school, fear of the draft for an imperialist war, etc., to manipulate them into signing up. There is no genuine—only misguided patriotism—involved in a war of conquest or in service in the American army. We think, therefore, that many ROTC students can be won over to a radical position. . . .

Extract from the Minutes of Special Meeting of the Faculty of Arts and Sciences, Harvard University, February 4, 1969.

What to Do About ROTC

The President offered as a suggested method of procedure one which had been used at the meeting of January 21. Each of the four motions on the Docket would be introduced by an individual, who would speak to it, this to be followed by simple seconding without supporting remarks. After all the motions had been presented, the floor would be open for discussion. At the end of the meeting, the motions would be voted upon seriatim.

The Docket consisting of the following items was in order:

I. Professor Putnam will move
That the Faculty of Arts and Sciences recommend to the Governing Boards that:
1. Air Force, Army, and Navy Reserve Officers Training Corps be denied course credit.
2. Corporation appointments for Reserve Officers Training Corps instructors be abolished.
3. The Reserve Officers Training Corps be denied the use of all Harvard facilities.
4. Reserve Officers Training Corps training not be recognized by Harvard in any form, including that of an extracurricular activity or of a departmental course.

5. The Reserve Officers Training Corps Scholarships be replaced, where there is need, by commensurate Harvard Scholarships.

II. For the Student-Faculty Advisory Council, Professor Albritton will move

Whereas, The ROTC program is externally controlled, i.e. taught by professors who do not hold regular appointments and do not enjoy academic freedom as it is ordinarily understood, and

Whereas, The ROTC curriculum taken as a whole does not, in its substance, deserve to be included in the course offering of Harvard College.

Resolved: That the Student-Faculty Advisory Council requests the Faculty of Arts and Sciences to:

1. Withhold academic credit from any courses offered by the three branches of ROTC at Harvard in the future.
2. Request the Harvard Corporation to terminate the Faculty appointments of the present instructors of these courses as soon as possible after the end of the current academic year and to make no further such appointments.
3. Request the Harvard Corporation to withdraw the description of ROTC courses from the course catalogue and to cease the free allocation of space in University buildings to ROTC.
4. Provide scholarship funds where need is created by this Faculty decision.

(The above motion was passed by the Student-Faculty Advisory Council at a meeting on November 26, 1968)

III. For the Harvard Undergraduate Council, Mr. Wilcox will move

1. That the Faculty of Arts and Sciences withdraw credit from the courses offered by the three branches of ROTC (Reserve Officers Training Corps) at Harvard.
2. That the description of ROTC courses be withdrawn from the Course Catalogue.
3. That this Faculty request that the Corporation withdraw its appointments from instructors of these courses.
4. That this Faculty request the Corporation to withdraw automatic allotment of space in Shannon Hall reserved for the ROTC courses.
5. That these changes be effected beginning with the fall of

1969, affecting the four-year program and the Class of 1973, and the two-year program and the Class of 1971.

6. That any changes in the financial status of ROTC students as a result of this motion should be given special consideration by the Committee on Admissions and Scholarships.

IV. For the Committee on Educational Policy, Professor J. Q. Wilson will move

1. That students who wish to do so should have an opportunity to prepare themselves for military service while pursuing academic work toward their liberal arts or professional degrees at Harvard University.

2. That present arrangements with ROTC units offering courses for academic credit at Harvard raise questions of academic policy sufficiently serious so that

   a. The Corporation be requested immediately to open negotiations with regard to the present ROTC contracts to reflect the sense of this Faculty as outlined in item 3, and that

   b. The Dean of the Faculty be requested to appoint a special committee to assist and advise officers of the University involved in these negotiations, this special committee to report to the Faculty before the end of the academic year 1968-69.

3. It is the sense of the Faculty that revisions in the ROTC contracts should be made in keeping with the following principles:

   a. No course in military, air, or naval science shall be accepted by the Faculty of Arts and Sciences for degree credit unless it is sponsored by an academic department, committee or division responsible for concentration, or General Education courses.

   b. All courses accepted for degree credit by the Faculty of Arts and Sciences shall be directed by persons whose appointment has been recommended by an academic department, division or degree-recommending committee and approved by the Governing Boards.

(At its meeting on December 9, 1968, the Committee on Educational Policy approved this motion eight in favor, one opposed, one absent, the Chairman not voting.)

Item I on the Docket: Professor Putnam introduced his motion. One of the principal issues in the matter of ROTC was that of civilian-military relations. Some members of this faculty support ROTC, however reluctantly, because they feel that University training is a liberalizing influence on military officers. Better an ROTC officer corps, so this reasoning goes, than a wholly West Point trained one. The mistake here is an overemphasis on a secondary effect coupled with neglect of the primary effect.

Many of the worst aspects of the Vietnam situation, counter-insurgency, the totalitarian methods of the Diem regime, outrages against civilians, bombings, massive troop build-up and other war policies were suggested and defended, Professor Putnam said, by liberals, products, many of them, of a liberal university. Clearly a liberal education is no protection against dreams of empire, nor does it succeed in inculcating a non-manipulative and decent attitude toward mankind.

We cannot then affect, or cannot more than marginally affect, the foreign policies of the United States or the execution of those policies by having half of the career officers, and not the most powerful ones in any case, trained in a university. But we can affect those policies by building a powerful protest movement. Professor Putnam cited the success that such protest movements had had in forcing France to withdraw from Indochina and Algeria and the partial success in stopping escalation of the Vietnam war. In the latter cases in particular such protest arose among students and intellectuals.

Most of this Faculty, Professor Putnam believed, supported the anti-war movement, as long as it stayed away from the campus. Yet it cannot possibly stay away when the vast majority of junior officers are trained there, not only for this war, but for future wars like it. It is inconsistent to urge students actively to go out and protest the war, while continuing to train men for the very purposes that are being protested. A student and faculty movement whose result would be that ROTC was removed from every university would be a great force for change in America's foreign policy, a great force against this war and similar wars. We might even venture to predict the end of the war in Vietnam, long before

ROTC might have been totally abolished, or required to leave every campus.

The same argument holds for those who are worried about the needs of legitimate national defense. America will, of course, have an army and an officer corps, no matter what we do. This, Professor Putnam continued, makes it all the more imperative that the army, government, and business circles that make and back the Army's policies, be restrained from acts of foreign subversion, counter-insurgency, and military adventurism. We must have civilian control of the military, but the only kind of civilian control that has any real effect is the restraint exercised by a strong and vigilant anti-imperialist movement. Keeping ROTC at Harvard is not going to restrain militarism; separation of ROTC from Harvard may trigger a nation-wide movement which can have a real restraining influence.

The primary question, however, is not one of calculating political effects. The dominant question is a moral one. Is a contract between Harvard University and the Department of Defense for the production of junior officers right, fitting or proper? Should Harvard provide gratis, or even for hire, space to the Department of Defense? For Professor Putnam, and he hoped many other members of the Faculty would concur, the answer clearly was no.

Still, though the moral issues may be the dominant ones, they cannot be separated from the political ones. The reason such a contract is objectionable is because what ROTC does is objectionable; what ROTC does is objectionable because what the Army does is objectionable.

Professor Putnam then formally moved Item I on the Docket and this motion was seconded.

For the Student-Faculty Advisory Council, Professor Albritton presented Item II on the Docket. He began by directing the Faculty's attention to the first contention of the motion, namely that the ROTC program is externally controlled. Obviously it is, and must be even with the best will in the world. The officers in charge of the program at Harvard are not responsible for this, nor can they help it in the least. What courses in Military Science, for example, do, according to the current *Courses of Instruction,* is to prepare eligible male students for commissioning as second lieutenants in the U.S. Army Reserve. Naturally, it is going to be the Secretary of the Army in the last resort who decides how that shall be done. It is equally natural that the members of the three military departments should be officers under military discipline, who are in effect appointed to this Faculty by the Department of Defense. What is unnatural, surely, is that there should be military departments offering courses for academic credit toward the B.A. degree.

As to the second contention of the motion, that the ROTC curriculum taken as a whole does not, in its substance, deserve to be included in the course offering of Harvard College, the Student-Faculty Advisory Council's case does not rest on the suspicion that something uniquely wicked is going on in ROTC classrooms, or on the idea, which may be right or wrong, that ROTC courses are in general rather easy to pass. The question is, rather, whether the subject matter of the courses given by the military departments amounts to three subjects, or even to one subject, in such a sense that it should keep its place in the offering of this Faculty. The answer to that question, Professor Albritton said, is clearly no. What is offered by the military departments is on balance narrowly vocational or preᴌrofessional, if not professional training, which has no parallel elsewhere in this Faculty. The military departments would be obvious anomalies on that ground alone. No course-by-course examination is needed to see that fact about them. We have for good reason no departments of journalism, social work, business management, divinity, legal studies or police science. Why then do we have Departments of Military and Naval Science and Aerospace Studies? They have always been anomalies, and by now they are anachronisms.

Harvard College should be a college of liberal arts and sciences, not arrogant or closed, but a college of liberal arts and sciences, just that. This is not to say that military history, for example, or the political theory of military establishments, or their sociology, is not worth studying. But would it not be ludicrous to arrange for instruction in these subjects by inviting the Pentagon to supply us with a staff of officers under military control? As things are, Professor Albritton was willing to believe that much or most of what is taught by the military departments *should* be taught by officers under military control. But just in that measure he was unwilling to pretend that it should form a part of our curriculum.

In a great military emergency, we might think, rightly or wrongly, that some distortion of what we and our students are about here ought to be tolerated. We might have to bend to military necessity. But we are now in no such emergency. If there is any bending to be done, in response to terrible needs of our society, it should be in other directions. In the present situation of this country our posture of special concession to the armed forces is at best archaic and demeaning. We should simply get out of it, with what dignity we can muster, and we should do so unequivocally.

In that regard, among others, the motion proposed by the Committee on Educational Policy (Item IV on the Docket) seems too statesmanlike by half. Whatever its intention, it has an appearance of anxious solicitude for the possibility that this or that ROTC course—for that matter, this or that ROTC instructor— might plausibly be bundled under this or that departmental umbrella or rug. It does not even preclude the possibility that the present military departments should remain *in statu quo*, their courses "sponsored" by other departments, divisions, or committees and "directed" by persons whose appointments have been recommended by academic departments, a provision, it should be noted, which would not necessarily prevent these courses from being taught by the present ROTC staff. This concern to allow for the possibility of clothing the present ROTC program or something very much like it in academic gowns, so to speak, is misplaced.

What ROTC should be here, if anything, is precisely something very different from what it is now. As to what that should be, the Department of Defense, which is neither poor nor uninventive, can safely be left to its own devices. If we dismantle its academic apparatus here, it will learn to live with that fact and will, no doubt, propose other means of offering reserve commissions to Harvard students who want them. We can think about those means when they are proposed. The Student-Faculty Advisory Council was not prepared, nor was Professor Albritton, to reject every such proposal that can be imagined, every possible contract between the University and the Department of Defense for continuation here of some form of ROTC program.

This should not, however, be taken to mean that any such proposal that might be made would be found acceptable, whether by the Student-Faculty Advisory Council or by anyone else who thinks about it in the context of what a university is supposed to be and in the context of the present state of our society.

Referring then to the four specific actions which the Student-Faculty Advisory Council proposed that the Faculty take, Profes-

sor Albritton took note of the students currently enrolled in
ROTC programs. Solicitude for them is surely not misplaced, but
perfectly in order. There is, however, nothing in the motion of the
Student-Faculty Advisory Council that would force the Department of Defense to abandon those students. The only peremptory
section is the first which would withhold academic credit from
any courses offered by the ROTC at Harvard in the future. The
Department of Defense has lived with that elsewhere; no doubt it
will find a way of doing so here. The next two sections either include the proviso "as soon as possible," or imply it, the intention
being to make sure that no action is taken by the University so
precipitate as to throw out of the ROTC programs students who
are now in them.

Item III on the Docket: In presenting the motion for the Harvard Undergraduate Council, Mr. Wilcox explained that he did so
simply to provide a mechanism by which it could be placed formally before the Faculty. In the specific case of this ROTC resolution, it seemed unfortunate that a constituted broadly representative student governing body might, by default, be denied an
opportunity to have its resolution brought before this meeting.
Mr. Wilcox had therefore volunteered to place the resolution on
the Docket with the understanding that he would not speak on its
behalf. Item III on the Docket was then formally moved by Mr.
Wilcox, the motion being thereafter seconded.

Item IV on the Docket: Professor Wilson opened his remarks
by explaining that it was surely not the intent of the CEP * to attempt to find a way to defeat student interest, to turn aside another student challenge to Faculty government, or to devise some
mechanism whereby the whole matter could be swept under the
rug. Just the opposite. What the Committee on Educational Policy wanted to do was to find a way to meet these objectives, to
remedy the anomaly that ROTC is today, and to do this in a manner that is consistent with the policies of this Faculty, that does
not set a dangerous precedent, and that permits maximum flexibility, neither soliciting nor foreclosing alternative arrangements,
should the Department of Defense or other interested groups
choose to suggest them.

There is to be considered the exceptional action proposed or
implied by the other resolutions. This Faculty, sitting as a Com-

* Committee on Educational Policy.

mittee of the Whole, is being asked to decide that the content of all the courses of three departments of the Faculty are undeserving to be included in the Catalogue. Why should the normal tests of close scrutiny by the academic departments not be applied instead? If courses cannot pass this scrutiny, they cannot be offered, save as an extracurricular activity. No clear case has yet been made as to why we should make this general finding of fact, especially with no independent inquiry on the part of this Faculty or its usual fact-finding bodies: the academic departments.

Professor J. Q. Wilson next turned his attention to the third section of the Committee on Educational Policy motion. Let us assume, he said, that a status other than complete withdrawal or complete extracurricular status could be found and agreed upon. Let us suppose, too, that some courses acceptable to ROTC would be clearly labeled as extracurricular, while others would be given for credit. The crucial question is how will it be determined which courses may be given for credit. Under the CEP resolution, which is consistent with the traditional policies of this Faculty, no course can be given for credit unless it is sponsored by a department or a degree-recommending committee. Thus any course which might be acceptable for ROTC credit would first of all have to be sponsored by a regular academic department and would have to be approved by that department in the same way that any course counting for concentration in that department is approved. This course could either be one now in existence—taught by a regular member of the instructional staff, which course the ROTC authorities would accept as counting not only for the degree, but for the commission—or it could be a new course. If it is a new course, it could be taught either by a civilian or by a military officer.

If anyone proposed that a course for credit be taught by a military officer, that officer would be subject to the same tests of academic competence and freedom from outside control as would any nonmilitary instructor. In fact, we could safely assume that the tests would be even more stringent, that there would be the closest possible scrutiny. If, as has been suggested, no military officer can truly be free from academic control, and if that judgment is shared by the academic departments, then that means a military officer could not teach such a credit course. But, Professor Wilson said, he had heard no good reason why we should suspend or supersede the judgments of these departments and attempt to anticipate these conditions ahead of time.

Professor Wilson then explained to the Faculty the purpose of the special committee to be appointed under the second section, second paragraph, of the Committee on Educational Policy motion. This is not to be a fact-finding committee, but is designed to represent this Faculty as a partner, holding a watching brief, in the negotiations that will have to ensue if the Governing Boards accept the recommendations of the Faculty. The committee would presumably represent our interests, interpret the principles of the CEP resolution to the Department of Defense and the Governing Boards, and report back to the Faculty before the end of the academic year, or at such future dates as the negotiations may require. This Faculty will then once again have an opportunity to decide not only whether the arrangements are satisfactory, but also and most importantly, whether the academic departments which make up this Faculty, have seen fit to give any ROTC courses credit status and whether they have seen fit to give to any military instructional staff the right to offer such courses.

For the Committee on Educational Policy, Professor J. Q. Wilson then moved Item IV on the Docket and this motion was seconded.

The floor was then opened for discussion.

The Student-Faculty Advisory Council motion, Professor Meselson said, seeks on sound and important academic grounds to affect a clear and total separation between the membership and course offerings of this faculty and the membership and instruction of an outside body, namely the Reserve Officers Training Corps. In contrast, the Committee on Educational Policy motion seeks what would appear to be the reverse, that is to have some of the ROTC courses and some of the ROTC instructors more fully integrated into the regular departments of the University. This contrast is the central difference between the two resolutions.

The consequences of inviting ROTC officers into regular academic departments or of approving courses proposed by the ROTC have not, up to this point, been considered carefully enough. It is important that departments initiate appointments to this Faculty and that they conceive and initiate courses, not merely recommending and approving them. Only in this way can high standards of excellence in teaching and in membership in this faculty be maintained. To maintain this excellence is a responsibility that belongs to none but ourselves, a responsibility that we should not share.

The Student-Faculty Advisory Council motion would make that clean separation which is so very necessary. While the Committee on Educational Policy motion might result in the same end, it also might not, and this would be a far worse outcome than the present situation. It would be better to see a separate Department of Military Science than to see yoked together members of existing departments and persons from ROTC, or any other outside body. However, the rationale of the Student-Faculty Advisory Council motion, as embodied in the first two paragraphs, does not clearly enough state the considerations which should lead to a clear separation between departments within the University and outside bodies. The first paragraph does contain the central point, that is, that the ROTC program is taught by professors who do not hold regular appointments. A regular appointment is initiated, conceived, recommended, generally even paid for by the department. These appointments are not. On the other hand, it is improper, and possibly even dangerous, for us to try to decide as this part of the motion would have us do whether or not professors who do hold regular appointments might not, nevertheless, enjoy academic freedom. As we all know, this has been a problem in some places at some times, but how unwise it would be for us to establish the precedent of questioning whether a professor who does hold a regular appointment does enjoy academic freedom. Similarly, the second paragraph, which states that "the ROTC curriculum taken as a whole does not, in its substance, deserve to be included in the course offering of Harvard College," asks this Faculty to sit in judgment on course offerings of this Faculty, or it might, at least, be cited as a precedent for so doing. The statement, furthermore, has very little to do with real justification for achieving a clear separation.

It was with this sense that Professor Meselson made the following amendment to the Student-Faculty Advisory Council motion: That the first paragraph be amended so as to read, "Whereas the ROTC program is taught by professors who do not hold regular appointments," striking out the remainder of that paragraph, and in addition, the entire second paragraph. The amendment was thereafter seconded.

Professor H. S. Hughes, who favored the Student-Faculty Advisory Council motion, was opposed to the notion of the tidying up process which the Committee on Educational Policy motion seemed to imply. This tidying up of courses to perform a service function for a noneducational institution is simply inappropriate for a Faculty of Arts and Sciences. Putting what are now ROTC courses, or ROTC-type courses, under the regular departments or having a department certify military personnel as competent to teach is a solution which would offer the worst of all possible worlds. The implications of the Committee on Educational Policy resolution are less defensible intellectually and in terms of educational policy than what we have now.

It would be better to live with the *status quo,* that is, ROTC set apart so that we know exactly what it is. What the motion does is merely to shift responsibility; it shifts it to departments which are already laboring under more than their share of perfectly legitimate problems. The Faculty should not shirk its job; it should pass the Student-Faculty Advisory Council motion and present ourselves, the students, and the outside world with a clear-cut decision. . . .

The ROTC courses, Professor Huntington said, had frequently been referred to as anomaly. If they were anomaly, it was a procedural one more than anything else. They have crept into the Catalogue through some means now lost in history, but through a procedure quite clearly not the procedure by which any other courses get into the Catalogue. The basic point, therefore, is not whether we withdraw credit from the ROTC courses, but how it takes place.

The Committee on Educational Policy resolution goes to the heart of that issue. It makes the decision on how courses get into the Catalogue on procedural grounds; it does not attempt to judge the ROTC courses, for example, on whether they are wicked or easy or narrowly professional. As a Faculty we do not make that judgment about other courses, and neither the Faculty nor the Student-Faculty Advisory Council are in a position to make that judgment about the ROTC courses. Whether or not the ROTC courses should be given credit or should be in the Catalogue and the very complicated issues of quality and outside control are all matters which can only really be decided by the departments of this Faculty. These are the units of the Faculty which we rely upon to make these decisions with respect to all other courses and to all other appointments. Therefore, in regard to ROTC we ought to follow our usual procedures, remove the procedural anomaly and insist that the departments confront the issues posed here. If the ROTC wants to propose an engineering course for the Division of Engineering and Applied Physics, or a strategy or Defense organization course for the Government Department, or a military history course for the History Department, the departments will take action on them as they deserve.

Professor Sutherland reminded the Faculty that the ROTC program has been at Harvard for a little over half a century. Nothing in the forty-seven years with which he had been familiar with the ROTC program had persuaded Professor Sutherland that somehow the presence of this form of instruction at Harvard was bad or prejudicial. It seemed to him, and here he drew on personal experience, highly desirable that men serving in the military should have the wisest, best educated, best equipped, firmest and most kindly officers that can be found. Any question of the elimination of our armed forces is an interesting but utterly vain dispute. This being so, the more people like our graduates and graduates of our sister universities and colleges throughout the country, who will have responsibility for our young men the better it will be. While admittedly the ROTC program is different from the programs of other departments in the University, there is no reason why we should treat it as a pariah among us. It has done much good to Harvard in this past half century. Let us hope that we may not lose the advantage of this system and that it may continue here.

Professor Wylie felt that the most important problem had not been talked about at all. As Professor Wald had said at a previous meeting (December 3, 1968), it is our army and this is true. What we have done though is to neglect our duty, to let our army get out of hand. We now have to do something to limit it. What can we do? We can set an example in an extremely important matter. It is not only a question of the military-industrial complex, which must be brought to heel, but an educational problem as well. The war is having an effect on our students and because of that is driving a wedge between them and the Faculty. While our individual votes in national elections may count for very little, they do count for considerably more in this Faculty. It was with these thoughts then that Professor Wylie urged the Faculty to vote favorably for Professor Putnam's motion, and barring that, for the Student-Faculty Advisory Council motion and the Harvard Undergraduate Council motion in that order. He was strongly opposed to the Committee on Educational Policy motion, labeling it smooth and a sham, something which could only cause students to lose respect for the Faculty.

The issue, Professor Deutsch remarked, is not alienation from the United States, its government, or its defense services. Many of the most radical students are alive today because there was a United States Army in the World War II. On the other hand, we must remember that ROTC departments in the past have not been considered purely academic ones, nor have their offerings ever been considered as primarily an intellectual program. These departments have always been an anomaly in the type of university which over the decades Harvard has become.

The reasons for making special arrangements and special concessions to the ROTC program are not as convincing now as they were five, ten, or twenty years ago at the time of World War II or even of Korea. Today, these reasons no longer convince a significant part of our students, nor, no doubt, a significant part of this Faculty. They have now become divisive. The special arrangements of disguising ROTC as an academic program in an academic department are no longer valid, although this is not to say that the positive functions of ROTC cannot be carried on as an extracurricular activity for those who wish to commit themselves to it.

We should, therefore, abolish this special exception which has outlived its usefulness. We need defense but we must put limits on the militarization of our communities and our culture. This Faculty has a responsibility in these matters. It was with these thoughts that Professor Deutsch recommended acceptance in principle of the Student-Faculty Advisory Council proposal, the details to be worked out by appropriate committees.

The President asked the Faculty whether it was prepared for the question and response was overwhelming in favor of moving to it. The vote then was taken on each motion in order, those in favor being first asked to stand, followed by those opposed. The first motion which was Professor Putnam's (Item I on the Docket) lost, this being clear without an individual count. Professor Meselson's amendment to the Student-Faculty Advisory Council motion was in order before that motion could be voted upon. Professor Meselson asked Professor Albritton whether he would be willing to strike the entire preamble of the Student-Faculty Advisory Council motion (the first two paragraphs beginning "whereas"), but Professor Albritton felt that he could not do so without instruction from the Student-Faculty Advisory Council. Professor Meselson's amendment was then voted on as originally presented, and this amendment was carried by 116 in favor to 100 opposed. The Student-Faculty Advisory Council motion (Item II on the Docket), as amended, was next put to a vote, and it passed by 207 for to 125 against. The third motion which had been presented by Mr. Wilcox for the Harvard Undergraduate Council (Item III on the Docket) had no more than two or three people rising in its favor. Finally, the ballot was taken on the Committee on Educational Policy motion. This motion lost, there being only 112 favorable votes, approximately the reverse of the vote on the Student-Faculty Advisory Council motion.

The meeting adjourned at 6:02 p.m.

Robert Shenton, *Secretary*

Two letters to President Nathan Pusey of Harvard, both sent in February 1969, both taken from files by demonstrators in April 1969 and published that month in The Old Mole Strike Special (*Numbers 2 and 3, April 13 and 14, 1969*). *The first is by Franklin L. Ford, Dean of the Faculty of Arts and Sciences, the second by Fred L. Glimp, Dean of Harvard College.*

Two Confidential Letters

February 11, 1969

CONFIDENTIAL

Dear Nate:

Having just written you the necessary report of this Faculty's vote of last Tuesday concerning the ROTC, I should now like confidentially and informally to set down a few thoughts of my own.

As you know, I disagree with many of the particulars, and virtually all of the spirit, of the resolution passed by my own Faculty. This is not a pleasant situation in which to find oneself, especially since in discharging my duty to make public that resolution, I have inevitably been identified by many outside critics as one of its proponents. However, I am here underlining my own attitude only to be sure that neither you nor any other member of the Governing Boards is in any doubt about it.

` . . . All that was needed from the Faculty was a general statement of direction, accompanied by a request for the creation of a committee to negotiate details.

What we have instead is a very badly framed, gratuitously unpleasant and basically confused pronouncement. . . . But what bothers me most is the underlying theme of the entire resolution, a desire to go on record against all things military, unaccompanied by any rational evaluation of the effects of such action on a large number of non-militaristic people, upon vast questions of foreign policy (which effect I should suppose to be just about nil), and upon the public standing of this University (which effect, by contrast, I can well imagine being massive).

One more word of background. The so-called "CEP alternative" was not in my opinion a very good one. Quite by accident, the two meetings at which it was drafted were both ones I had to miss—the first because of a conference in Italy, the second because of the flu—so I was left in the position of not being able to defend a formulation which seemed to many people unnecessarily and perhaps even intentionally, oblique. Yet it struck me as unthinkable that I should repudiate the work of my own principal advisory committee. So much for this period of what I hope will turn out to have been only temporary impotence.

As to where we go from here, that is obviously something for you and the rest of the Corporation to decide. It is not my intention to try to guess that body's reactions or its views as to viable options. However, I should feel irresponsible if I did not suggest very briefly what any of several *possible* reactions might represent, as appraised from my particular angle.

(1) The Corporation might, though I doubt that it would, flatly reject the Faculty's recommendations as unacceptable. The trouble here is that interwoven among points with respect to which the Faculty's competence is questionable, to say the least, are other points, having to do with the curriculum as such, where delegation of responsibility to the Faculty has been virtually complete.

(2) It might be that a request for expressions of opinion from other Faculties of the University, especially that of Law, would remind people both inside and outside the institution that this is truly a university-wide problem. Such referral, however, might only make things worse unless Derek Bok were able to say with some certainty what his assembled colleagues would do—and the last time I talked to him, he just was not sure.

(3) The Corporation might decide, purely on the strength of the vote from Arts and Sciences, to open exploratory discussion on

behalf of the University with the three service Departments in Washington, perhaps using an advisory committee drawn from *all* the Faculties involved. Thereafter, if some clearly non-negotiable point emerged—such as the title of Professor for the head of each unit, as an absolute requirement for the maintenance of such units at the University—the negotiators could come back to the Faculty of Arts and Sciences, either with a question as to how to treat that condition or with a flat announcement that the Corporation *would* offer professorial appointments to the ROTC unit heads, quite outside the structure of this Faculty.

(4) The one other alternative I have been able to conceive would be a decision not to accept these recommendations from the Faculty of Arts and Sciences in *their present form,* but instead to refer them back to the Faculty for whatever additional work and discussion is required to make them usable as a basis for further action. This course would occasion loud squeals; but there are two things to be said for it. First, the SFAC [Student Faculty Advisory Committee] resolution was badly drafted—and I know that at least some of the Faculty members who voted for it were aware of its imprecision. Second, because of this bad drafting, we are left with no reliable notion as to how many members voted on the basis of vague emotionalism and how many others voted because they find the present departmental-curricular situation genuinely anomalous. At the very least, it would help to have the questions put separately, so that one might have some idea of what kind of Faculty opinion he has to deal with.

Finally, having jotted down these quite candid thoughts without presuming to go very far in elaborating or grading them (though my own preference for the fourth alternative just cited must be apparent), let me add one final reflection which is as necessary to state clearly as it is difficult to state tastefully. This has to do with my own position as Dean.

. . . On issue after issue this winter the Faculty has disregarded the recommendations of its own committees and its own administrative officers, preferring to substitute the quickly formulated product of emotional debate for a considered judgment by people—including many besides myself—who had tried to weigh all the arguments heard at the Faculty meeting, and a number of others as well.

Somehow, without seeming to threaten in any egocentric way, I feel I must get before the Faculty the simple truth that in the atmosphere created by recent meetings it will be virtually impossible to hold the services of a Fred Glimp or a Chase Peterson or the remarkable hardworking professors who make it equally clear that in such an atmosphere it will be completely impossible for anyone who also cares about teaching and scholarship to justify what seems to be an increasingly futile effort to represent his colleagues as Dean of Faculty.

Yours sincerely,
Franklin L. Ford

February 14, 1969

Dear Nate,

Yesterday I had a long and potentially encouraging talk with General C. P. Hannum, Deputy Director of Individual Training for ROTC affairs. He feels there is a good chance that the credit and teaching-appointment aspects of the Faculty's February 4th action can be accommodated by Army ROTC in some way.

His first point, which he was anxious to have relayed to you, is that the Army will need some time. For some eight months now, General Hannum has been working on new plans for ROTC. That work has produced two projects. The first is a policy paper on academic credit—the gist of which is Hannum's view that the Army simply can't expect to require academic credit for strictly professional military subjects. If an institution, for reasons of its own, wishes to give credit, fine. So the policy paper recommends that credit for strictly military courses be a matter of institutional choice. The paper is already well along in military channels; the Army Chief of Staff has approved it and it is now in the office of the Secretary of the Army.

The second paper is a detailed draft of a new plan, which will be something like the following:

a. Purely professional subjects will be kept to a minimum (Hannum hopes 1 hour a week for freshman and sophomore years, 2 hours a week for juniors and seniors). Credit may be urged, but it will not be required—institutional choice.

b. Basic academic requirements will be outlined (math, psychology, economics, English, history, etc.). Thus part of ROTC requirements would be met by taking the College's courses. Hence the condition of giving academic credit would be met.

c. The professor of military science would have flexibility to work with his institution to translate the basic academic requirements into the college's existing courses.

This detailed plan has a good deal of unofficial support, but General Hannum has not yet started it through channels. He hopes it will have been approved sufficiently to begin negotiations with individual universities by mid-April, to be implemented "normally" by September 1970. However he expects that "at a few" institutions the new plan could be put into effect for September, 1969.

Hannum is very anxious that this be kept confidential until mid-April. He has a great deal of work yet to do with the complex parts of his own constituencies. He hopes, for example, that we can urge the other Ivy colleges to delay requests for actual negotiations until late April, but without going into much detail beyond saying that we understand that a new and helpful basis for negotiations may well be in force by then. I said it would be hard to convey that limited message but that we would try. (How?)

Regarding appointments, General Hannum feels there is somewhat more flexibility in the title and the relationship of the professor of military science than might appear to be the case. He has checked "visiting professor" with Army lawyers and they say it would meet the requirements of the law. The important substantive elements from Hannum's point of view: (a) the title could, perhaps should, indicate the non-tenured character of the appointment; (b) there could be flexibility in the status and voting privileges of the officer (perhaps appointment to and voting on a university-wide committee on ROTC programs); (c) the appointment should convey some sense of hospitality and standing.

We spent almost all of our time talking about those two issues. Brief talk about the others indicated that resolving the "course catalog" issue is difficult but probably not impossible. A decision to cease free use of space would be very difficult.

One final point about similar matters with the Navy. My personal impression is that there is some chance of our reaching an acceptable agreement. The key, I think, is convincing the Navy that our imperious style of making this change was not meant to be a slap at a proud service, that in fact we want to make changes in a program which a majority of the faculty and the other elements of the University are deeply concerned to keep at Harvard.

The Air Force is hard to read right now.

Sincerely yours,

/s/ Fred

PART IV

RACISM
AND THE
UNIVERSITY

Universities in America, particularly those outside the south, have long prided themselves on being centers of opposition to racism. Particularly since World War II, most overt discriminatory practices have been eliminated; fraternities that discriminated, for example, have usually been forced either to eliminate such practices or leave the campuses. The civil rights movement attracted widespread support from the American university community. And one concrete measure of the support of the liberal university for the fight against racism was the decision major American universities made in the mid-1960s to recruit more Negro freshmen.

It was with considerable surprise, annoyance, and dismay, therefore, that the liberal university found itself under attack for racism by their new Black students. Furthermore, the charge was difficult for the liberal university to credit. They found themselves charged, not with overt acts of discrimination, but with something they had never previously heard of—"institutional racism." It has taken several years of struggle by Black students to get the liberal university even to acknowledge that there is any substance to this new concept. The charge, in general, and its detailed manifestations are the subject of the following chapters.

CHAPTER 10

Institutional Racism, Admissions and Housing

Most white Americans still conceive of racism as a set of attitudes, but attitudinal racism is only its most blatant form. What Black students found in the liberal university was that even if discriminatory attitudes were eliminated, racism persisted. Blacks were still "getting the short end of the deal."

The admissions question is illustrative. Given the disadvantages most Black students start out with—poorer educational facilities, the need to spend time working rather than studying, lower family income and higher unemployment, nutritional deficiencies, inferior health care, primary and secondary school teachers who do not expect them to succeed—it is inevitable that when the same admission standards are applied to white and Black alike, the number of Blacks admitted will be low. The standards were established with the experience of white middle-class students in mind. Conscientious admissions officers might apply those standards without the least intent of discriminating against blacks; it did not matter. Racism was not the product merely of attitudes. It was institutionalized—built into the society at all levels.

The chapter opens with a series of documents from Northwestern University, where in May 1968 Black students occupied and barricaded an administration building over a set of seven demands.* Here we include the statements exchanged between the students and administration regarding three of the demands: a policy statement from the university opposing racism and acknowledging that Northwestern had been a racist institution; a guarantee that all forthcoming freshman classes would consist of ten per cent Black students; and a pledge for a separate Black living unit. After the university initially rejected the demands, the students reissued them in stronger terms and finally negotiated a settlement with the administration. The settlement included an acknowledgment that Northwestern had throughout its history been "a university of the white establishment"—an obvious fact, but nevertheless a milestone of sorts. The administration also agreed to grant a separate living unit to those Black students who wished to live apart.

The public debate on these issues has divided both Blacks and whites in America. Following the Northwestern material are statements by Julian Bond, Georgia state senator, and Roy Wilkins, executive director of the National Association for the Advancement of Colored People. Bond supported the Black students, while Wilkins voiced strong opposition to separate living arrangements or separate educational facilities, which he called "Black Jim Crow."

On the admissions issue, Vice President Spiro T. Agnew denounced the "methods by which unqualified students are being swept into colleges on the wave of the new socialism" as a "threat to educational standards." In a defense of open admissions, educator John Holt challenged the views of men like Agnew, asserting "that the admissions problem of our universities is not a real problem, but a manufactured one." Holt attacked the basic notion of institutional standards upheld by universities that "have come to think of themselves as private clubs."

* For the full set of demands, see Appendix A, Volume II.

Northwestern

From a petition prepared by Black students at Northwestern University, April 22, 1968.

Black Student Demands

We, the Black students at Northwestern University, have found the academic, cultural, and social conditions for us on campus deplorably limited. In order to counteract the physical, emotional, and spiritual strains we have been subjugated to, in order to find some meaning and purpose in our being here, we demand that the following conditions be immediately met:

I. POLICY STATEMENT:

We demand, firstly, that a policy statement be issued from the administration deploring the viciousness of "white racism" and insuring that all conscious or unconscious racist policies, practices, and institutions existing now on campus will no longer be tolerated. This statement should make it clear that Northwestern is willing to go to any extent to enforce such a policy and also to protect the interests of the Black students on campus who have been negatively affected by such racist attitudes and practices. Furthermore, this statement should express Northwestern's readiness to exert its influences, both political and financial, in uprooting racism in the city of Evanston.

II. ADMISSION:

Considering that Black people account for 12% of the total American population, we demand that Northwestern initiate a project which guarantees the gradual increase of the number of Black students to a more "realistic" figure which we shall decide. We demand also that we have some say in the development and initiation of such a project with Black students of our own choosing on the steering committee. We further demand that at least half ($\frac{1}{2}$) of each year's incoming Black students be from the inner city school systems.

As for now, we demand a complete list containing the names of *all* Black students enrolled at Northwestern as of Fall Quarter 1967. . . .

IV. HOUSING:

We demand that the University provide a living unit(s) for those Black students who want to live together. We demand that immediate action be taken to provide such a unit(s) by Fall Quarter 1968.

Inasmuch that Black freshman women do not usually room with each other, we demand that they receive the same treatment as their white roommates. In the past, upon receiving room assignments, a white girl or her parents have been allowed to object to having a Negro for a roommate and upon either of their requests, a shift in room assignments took place. We contend that if the girl or her parents wanted to be assured that she would not be rooming with a Negro, she should have stated on her housing form her preference of a Caucasian roommate to a Negro one. Black students did not even have the option to request another Black student for a roommate. We were told from the start that it was the University's intention to split us up and that we would not be allowed to room with each other.

Due to contradictory (racist) housing policies and practices, to the definite differences in social and cultural differences between us and our white roommates, and to the general tenseness of the racial situation, we demand that this Black living unit be made available to us by Fall quarter to help alleviate some of the tension of being "a Black student at a white university."

From a statement signed by Roland J. Hinz, Vice President for Student Affairs, Northwestern University, April 22, 1968.

Administration Response

I. Racism of any character has no place at Northwestern which as a University is an institution where tolerance and mutual respect are essential to the educational process and for the dissemination of knowledge. The University repeats that in the admission of students, the appointment of faculty and staff, and in the operation of all its facilities, such as housing, dining halls, libraries, placement offices and the like, no discrimination on the basis of race, religion or color can be countenanced. The University deplores incidents which have racial implications, and asserts its determination to prevent any such events and to use its authority to employ disciplinary measures against those who violate the rights of others.

Increasing efforts will be made to improve the social and cultural welfare of all students in ways which will better prepare them for the roles of professional leadership which are in keeping with the educational objectives of a university.

To this end, and pending receipt of reports from existing University Committees now considering these problems, a special University Committee on Human Relations will be established to consider the grievances wherein the human rights and dignity of students have been violated, to continually review all facets of the university life, and recommend new policies and procedures which will bring our student environment in line with Northwestern's national and international responsibility. While the membership of this Committee has not yet been determined, appointments will be made after consultation with all elements of the university community.

The University Discipline Committee (UDC) has recently completed an intensive study of the racial problems of black students on campus, and their aspirations and search for identity within the university and the community. This report has just been released for publication. The Committee on Human Relations will be asked to develop programs and recommendations which will implement the objectives of the UDC report.

While the crises which confront the nation and the university warrant the depth of this concern, it is essential that all members of the university act responsibly and with accountability in helping achieve the objectives of equal rights and dignity for all.

II. ADMISSIONS

Since the summer of 1965, the University has made a substantial effort to change the composition of the undergraduate student body. The change has been from a homogeneous student body to a student body which is representative of the many different subcultures of our society. The forces necessary to bring about this change were (1) increased recruitment efforts in a variety of high schools serving populations which traditionally had not been interested in the University in the past and, (2) a substantial increase in the University's financial aid program.

One result of this effort was the matriculation of 54 black students in the entering class of 1966, in contrast to 5 black students in the entering class of 1965. At least 35 of these students were from inner city high schools. In the fall of 1966, recruitment efforts were intensified in predominantly black areas. The results were more applications from these areas, more admitted students from these areas, but a nominal matriculation increase over the previous year. For example, 50 students from inner city Chicago schools were accepted for the fall of 1967, but only 31 matriculated. In 1966, 36 students were accepted from these same high schools and 35 students entered. Greater competition from other colleges and universities has affected the percentage of students who have entered the University. In the fall of 1967, the admission recruitment efforts were further intensified to include the inner city high schools of Chicago, St. Louis, Milwaukee and Gary, Indiana. In addition, the University has coordinated its efforts with the Cooperative Program for Educational Opportunity, the National Scholarship Service Fund for Negro Students and the National Achievement Scholarship Program.

These efforts resulted in more applications than in the year 1967 and the acceptance of approximately 100 black students to the entering class of 1968. The matriculated number will not be available until the end of summer. According to a recent article in *Newsweek*, Northwestern has accepted more black students to the entering class of 1968 than any other major private university. The University will continue to increase its efforts in the inner city school systems and will continue to admit to the University those students who have a high probability of success at Northwestern. In terms of actual percentages, at least 50 percent of those admitted black candidates for admission have attended high schools serving the inner city. There is no reason to believe that this percentage should change with the University's intense interest and efforts in this area. The University will welcome the support of its black students in University admission activities.

In the spring of 1967, the University held a series of meetings with interested black students to discuss campus, summer program and admission problems. The Admission Office now seeks to formalize such meetings in order to acquire better counsel from the University's black community regarding the recruitment of black students. It is requested that a committee be appointed by the black student community to assist in University admission activities. One of the most immediate needs is to develop procedures to assure that a greater percentage of those black students accepted enter the University. Students selected to serve on such a committee should be undergraduate students. This is consistent with the University position in asking undergraduate students to participate more fully in the decisions governing those elements affecting student life.

The University further will provide the black community of Northwestern with the names of all black students who are known to the administration. In addition, the University will provide a list of names of all entering black students to the black community when all names of all entering students become available to campus organizations. . . .

IV. HOUSING

"The housing policy of Northwestern University is not predicated upon any consideration of race, color, or creed of the applicant. All roommate assignments will be considered binding for all parties throughout the first academic quarter." The foregoing is a direct quotation from the Housing Information statement which is sent to all new students. The University Housing Committee added the second sentence at its meeting in January of this year. Freshmen roommate assignments will not be changed during fall quarter. Thereafter, changes will be made by the Housing Office when possible and only upon the consent of all parties.

In addition, all landlords wishing to list a rental property with the University have been asked to sign a statement which specifies that they "agree to offer without regard for race, color, or creed the facility listed." In addition, they are sent a copy of the Housing Policy Statement.

While we can understand and appreciate the frustrations that lead to the demand for black living units, the University cannot accede to this request. For one thing, the University is living with a severe shortage of on-campus housing which in itself limits the policy options which are open to us. Given the need to house freshmen on campus, there are not enough spaces left over to permit the University to give any one group of students special exemption from the normal room assignment procedures.

The most important reason, however, for denying this request lies in the function the residence hall serves in the educational program of the University. The residence hall is far more than just shelter and a place to escape from the daily academic routine. Rather it is a place where students learn from each other and thereby further the educational process in which this institution is engaged. This function of University housing depends on a mixture of student types which cannot be achieved if certain groups are segregated from the rest of the living environment.

While the University believes there is much that must be done to accord the black student the rights and respect on this campus that he deserves, it strongly believes that organizing separate living for black students is self-defeating and cannot contribute constructively to the academic purposes for which the University exists.

The University will take every step it can to provide housing for black students wishing to live on campus. Black students wanting to live off-campus are urged to use University off-campus housing directory services and to report to those services all cases of suspected discriminatory renting practices so investigation and follow-up action can be taken by the committee on housing discrimination.

From a second statement by Black students at Northwestern University, in response to Roland Hinz's statement, April 1968.

Still Stronger Demands

Having rejected the basic principles on which our demands were based, the administration has forced us to speak for the last time on those matters discussed at the meeting of Wed., April 24, 1968. We demand that such action be taken to meet this, our final list of demands. The University must show itself flexible enough to take in the "peculiarities" of our culture and background. The only way, we feel, the University can display its understanding and flexibility is by the immediate approval and implementation of those demands submitted by the Black student body on April 22, 1968.

I. POLICY STATEMENT

Northwestern cannot begin to deal effectively with racism on this campus until it first realizes and openly acknowledges the existence of racism in American society. For this reason we reject the statement given to us in response and demand that a "new" policy statement be issued and made public from President Roscoe Miller asserting that the racism of American society which has penetrated all American institutions has also penetrated Northwestern University, and has thus affected the social and academic life here.

This statement is to include a declaration that the University is attempting to provide a multi-racial and cultural society within the university walls and that any racist attacks and/or abuses shall be considered in direct opposition to the University's goals and a danger to the peaceful existence of such a society. The extent of this danger is such that the perpetrator shall be immediately excluded from this institution.

In order to alter the racist structure of this University, a change has to take place in the judiciary structures, attitudes, and practices. As of now, the University Disciplinary Committee is ineffective in dealing with racism on campus (examples include the Fiji incidents and the many encounters with Sigma Chi). We demand that this judiciary be changed and implemented to bring about swifter and fairer decisions, or that a special judiciary be created to deal with these special cases.

On acknowledging the racist structure of this country and this institution, Northwestern is committed to understand the negative effects of racism on Black people and other oppressed people. The entire concept of justice has to be reevaluated for this reason. Justice for Black people at this time does not mean equal treatment before a law or rule which is insensitive to our oppressive position in this country. We contend that justice for Black people means that extra consideration and efforts are to be made in order to balance the effects of racism. This means in effect that the U.D.C. decision to place 3 white students and 2 Black students on disciplinary warning is not justice and is thus unacceptable in our eyes.

Our experience in America has not been characterized by justice in any way. No white institution can right our hundreds of years of history and experience by suddenly treating us the same as white people (only at those times when it is strategic to do so) and call it justice and equality. No matter how one looks at it, idealistically or realistically, Black people know that we are still getting the short end of the deal. A new basis for administering justice must be developed and put into effect and it is with this that U.D.C., or any new judiciary which intends to deal with racism, has to concern itself.

The only concrete response from the administration was the establishment of a special University Committee on Human Relations. However, we are not satisfied with that response and demand the right of the Black student community to approve all appointments to this committee and to determine at least 50% of these appointments.

II. ADMISSIONS

We understand that Northwestern has suddenly made a "substantial effort to change the composition of the undergraduate student body." However this statement or any of the others which followed says nothing about a guaranteed increase of the number of Black students at Northwestern. We demand that each forthcoming freshman class be 10-12% Black and that it will be financially feasible for all those Black students accepted to come.

We demanded that 50% of each year's incoming Black students be from the inner city school systems. The administration emphasized that in the past the Black enrollment contained at least 50% from the inner city and ended with the statement "There is no reason to believe that this percentage should change." In lieu of this statement there is no reason why we should not be given a guarantee that this percentage will remain the same.

We agreed that a committee will be appointed by the Black student community to assist the Admissions Office, especially in the area of recruitment. We demand that there be no restrictions placed on our selections, that this committee be in a salaried position, and that it have shared power with the Office of Admissions and Financial Aid in making all decisions relevant to Black students, including decisions on which Black students are to be admitted.

The University has agreed to provide us with the names of all Black students who are known to the Administration as well as a list of all entering Black students. We demand a list of all Black students accepted as well as those entering with information relevant to our purposes such as residence (city and state). We further demand that such lists be compiled and turned over to F.M.O.* for each subsequent freshman class.

In addition, the University agreed to arrange a meeting between us and the incoming Black freshman. . . .

IV. HOUSING

As taken from the University's reply to our demands of April 22nd: "While we (the administration) can understand and appreciate the frustrations that lead to the demands . . ." We, the Black students of Northwestern, cannot *appreciate* the *frustrations* that led to making these demands. How the University can claim to understand our problems and/or frustrations and not concede to our demands is beyond our comprehension!

The University might be living with a severe shortage of on-campus housing. However, this does not affect us in that a Black living unit would not necessarily call for additional space, only the relocation of students.

Furthermore, the Administration contends that the most important reason for denying this demand lies in the function the residence hall serves in the educational program of the University. "(The residence hall) is a place where students learn from each other and thereby further the education process in which this institution is engaged. This function of University housing depends on a mixture of student types which cannot be achieved if certain groups are segregated from the rest of the living environment." Why, we ask, are the fraternities and sororities exempt from this educational program?

The University evidently helps to support living units (fraternities and sororities) on this campus which are in direct opposition to the above quoted University policy. Therefore, the University should have no objection to supporting another living unit (Black) without this educational program. . . .

If the University genuinely believes that a Black living unit would be in direct conflict with their program and/or basic university policy, then we demand that the University should make a

* For Members Only, an organization of Black students.

policy statement condemning the existing living units of this sort (i.e. fraternities and sororities) with a commitment to get rid of them immediately. Otherwise, on the basis of this argument, we restate our demand that the University provide us with a Black living unit.

From the agreement between the Afro-American Students Union, FMO, and a committee representing the Northwestern University administration, May 4, 1968

The Negotiated Settlement

I. POLICY STATEMENT

Northwestern University recognizes that throughout its history it has been a university of the white establishment. This is not to gainsay that many members of its administration, its faculty, and its student body have engaged themselves in activities directed to the righting of racial wrongs. It is also true that for many years a few blacks have been members of its administration, faculty, and student body. But the fact remains that the University in its overwhelming character has been a white institution. This it has had in common with virtually all institutions of higher learning in the United States. Its members have also had in common with the white community in America, in greater or lesser degree, the racist attitudes that have prevailed historically in this society and which continue to constitute the most important social problem of our times. This University with other institutions must share responsibility for the continuance over many past years of these racist attitudes.

A few years ago, the Northwestern administration became increasingly concerned with the problem of doing something to improve race relations and to provide educational opportunities in greater measure than ever before for the black people in its community. Within a relatively short period the number of black students, though still small, has grown to the point at which it can now be said that there is a definite, significant, and important black community within the larger community of the University.

Despite the difficulties of understanding that have attended this process, we mean to and shall approach our problems constructively in this area. We wish to face these new challenges and to enhance, both quantitatively and qualitatively, the role of black men and women in the activities of the University at all levels.

The events of this week, which have given us new and broader insights, have led us to a reappraisal of the attitudes with which we confront these problems. For many of us, the solution has always seemed to be one of simply obliterating in our laws and in our personal relations the distinction between the races: that is, if only man would ignore in his human relations the differences in skin colors, racial problems would immediately disappear. We are now learning that this notion does not come fully to grips with the problems of the present turbulent period of transition. In short, this means that special recognition and special concern must be given, for some unspecifiable time, to the black community that is emerging within our institution.

Accordingly, we cannot be complacent with institutional arrangements that ignore the special problems of black students. An important and difficult problem is that of an essentially white leadership coming to understand the special needs and feelings of the black student, as well as the difficulty arising because the black student does not regard the white university authorities as capable of appreciating all of the nuances of his decidedly separate culture.

The University therefore accepts the basic sentiments expressed in the black students' petitions, and urges the following in addition: that there be established a special Northwestern University Advisory Council as an instrument of University administration to function at all administrative levels as the administration deals with problems of the black community related to the University. We believe that membership on this council should consist only of black leaders who have distinguished themselves within the black community in educational and professional affairs. This council, to consist of ten (10) members, should be chosen by the University administration from a list of twenty (20) nominees to be made by the black members of the University community. We believe that the insight and the advice of this council will be valuable in assuring that the University will be more responsive in reacting to the particular needs of its black students.

An urgent function for such a council would be to recommend to the University what changes in its procedures are needed to handle better the problems of black students. We believe that such a council could play in future years an important role in recommending the selection of members for the newly appointed University Committee on Human Relations. But until the council is formally constituted, the President will appoint a University Committee on Human Relations and will make appointments in a way that elicits and recognizes the views and recommendations of the black students. The University will inform the black student community of the date by which recommendations for membership on the Committee must be submitted.

The University also recognizes in the matter of student discipline that the intent of disciplinary action is to improve the standards of personal conduct rather than to punish *per se,* and it recognizes that in this purpose it is necessary to take account of the racial, cultural, and personal characteristics of all students concerned. In keeping with this principle, the Administration will instruct the University Discipline Committee to review the case growing out of the December 2 incident. It also agrees with the complaint that the judiciary function must proceed as rapidly as is consistent with the justice of decisions. All ways of expediting the judiciary process will be pursued.

II. ADMISSIONS

We acknowledge and respect the black students' desire for a guarantee of an immediate proportionate representation in Northwestern freshman classes. We cannot in good faith offer such explicit guarantees and wish to explain why. Hitherto, we have confronted three major problems in this regard: recruitment, competition from other colleges and universities, and support for a program of financial aid to black students.

The University welcomes assistance in resolving these problems from black students at Northwestern and from any other interested quarter, but especially we welcome assistance on recruitment and related issues, including admissions criteria for black students.

It is hoped that in the future, through the combined efforts of the black students and the Office of Admission, a greater number of applications will be received from black high school students.

If such efforts are successful, it is realistic to assume that the black community in the nation at large will soon be proportionately represented in the Northwestern student body. It should be noted that the University has received the following number of applications from black students in the past three years: in 1965–66, seventy; in 1966–67, ninety; and in 1967–68, one hundred-twenty. The Office of Admission will provide an annual progress report of the number of black students who have applied and who have been accepted by the University.

The Office of Admission of the University is committed to increase the number of black students at Northwestern as rapidly as possible, and to seek at least fifty percent of these students from the inner-city school systems. The University is further committed to intensify present recruitment efforts in order to assure such an increase. Although the University is committed to accelerate the increase, it is unable to cite a specific number because of ever-increasing competition from other colleges and universities.

In pursuing this goal of a guaranteed increase in black students the Office of Admission will welcome a committee of black students selected by the black community to advise, assist and counsel the Committee on Admission. The faculty Committee on Admission prescribes policy governing the philosophical concerns of admission, for example, it determines criteria for admission. In the daily operations of the admission office black students will be asked to provide direction as to which high schools, other institutions or persons the Office of Admission should contact. In addition, black students will be asked to advise with respect to the admission and financial-aid candidacies of individual black applicants and on other operational concerns as they arise. Salaried positions in the Office of Admission will be created for such students who assist in student recruitment.

The University, however, cannot permit students to make individual admission decisions. The evaluation of a candidate's folder is confidential and is a privileged communication between the candidate and the Office of Admission. The University is legally and morally bound to honor such privileged communication.

The Student Affairs Office of the University routinely provides lists of students to campus organizations. A list of all black students, as far as they are known to the Student Affairs Office, will be provided to F.M.O. Such a list will include names and addresses of presently enrolled black students and those accepted in each entering freshman class.

We agree that an orientation program will be arranged for entering black students. For students entering in the summer program, block-time will be allocated for scheduled meetings and programs which will be organized and conducted by an orientation group selected by the black student community. Similarly, two days will be arranged at the beginning of the fall quarter for the orientation of entering black students. A minimum amount of $500 will be made available for these purposes. . . .

IV. HOUSING

While reaffirming our previously stated belief that a mixture of student types should characterize living arrangements within the University, we have modified that position in response to two impinging influences: one is the distinctiveness of existing racial concerns; the other is the admitted inconsistency between the ideal of nondiscrimination in housing and the recognized practice of discrimination that exists in certain living units of the University.

Accordingly, starting with the Fall of 1968, the University will reserve separate sections of existing living units of the University in which black students, upon their individual requests, will be housed.

Moreover, the University will move toward providing separate housing units for black male and female students, and will inform the black students of progress in this direction during the Spring Quarter of 1969.

From statement by Trustees of Northwestern University, May 14, 1968.

A Partial Disavowal

The preamble of the agreement of May 4, insofar as it is interpreted to impute to the University hostile and antagonistic 'racism,' is wholly unacceptable to the Board. In fact, the Board decries racism in any form. It is proud that Northwestern University is in the forefront of those educational institutions which offer educational opportunity for all qualified applicants, without discrimination on the basis of race, creed or color.

The Public Debate

Address by Julian Bond, Black member of the Georgia state senate, to the American Council of Education, October 10, 1969.

The Failure of the White Minority

The crisis in race that exists on the college campus is of course only a reflection of a larger, more serious crisis in the country and, indeed, throughout the world.

The roots of the crisis are as old as the world itself; they involve the continuing failure of the white minority of peoples of the world to share power and wealth with the nonwhite majority.

That struggle has been in the streets of every city in this country, both violently and non-violently. It is a part of the struggle that inspired Fidel Castro to overthrow a dictator in Cuba, and it is the same struggle that is inspiring the patriots of Vietnam to continue, successfully, it seems, their 20-year-old struggle to resist foreign domination of the homeland.

That it should come to the college campus is not at all unusual; here, after all, are the people who have been told since the day they graduated from high school that the earth is theirs for taking, that they are the inheritors of tomorrow. Who is to blame if they believe it? That it is spreading downward into high schools and even elementary schools is not surprising either.

It ought not be surprising that young people who learned how to organize the poor and powerless in the Mississippi Delta would transfer their expertise to the powerless at Berkeley and Cornell.

And it ought not be surprising that race has played a large part in the continuing struggle of man against man.

To tie today's on-campus unrest only to yesterday's off-campus protests is unreal, however. There is a great deal more at stake than that.

A great deal has been made by some scholars and pollsters of the difference in the demands of black and white student activists. The whites want revolution, the experts say, while all the blacks want, despite their revolutionary rhetoric, is reform, a chance to bend the established system to their own ends, which are as safe and as ordinary as those shared by the rest of middle-class America.

Therein lies, I think, the conflict present in the black mind on the American campus. The black student is torn between the need for a regular, formal education, part of the socialization process that we are told everyone needs in order to seek an acceptable role in society, and his need to carve out a new education experience, one that is meaningful to him as a black person.

A young girl, a student at Tougaloo College in Mississippi, summed up this feeling when she wrote of her reaction to learning that Tougaloo and Brown University had entered into an educational compact, with Brown acting as big brother.

"We argued," she wrote, "that Tougaloo could do better, that we did not have to pattern ourselves after Brown or any of the Ivy League schools, that we had a unique opportunity to make Tougaloo a revolutionary institute of learning. We questioned the notion that places like Brown offered a superior education; we felt in fact that they dealt in miseducation. We felt that if schools like Brown had been truly educating their students then the state of the country and the world would be a lot different."

The dilemma of whether to change the Tougaloos of the world or to get what can be gotten from the Browns is the continuing one among young blacks.

The demand for a black dorm or an Afro-American center is a part of this dilemma. The unscholarly attacks on black educational institutions by scholars who should know better are a part of that dilemma.

So the current and future course for those blacks interested in solving—or rather eliminating—the crisis of race is unclear.

One has to realize that it is educated and civilized man who has put us where we are today. The rape of Vietnam was not begun by high school dropouts, but by liberally educated men. The pollution of the air and water is not carried out by fools and idiots, but by men educated at the best scientific and technical centers. The ability to shape a society that spends nearly $100-billion on conquering space and dominating the globe militarily comes from men of genius, not from men whose minds are limited.

Civilized man, or educated man, is supposed to solve his problems in a civilized manner.

But the problems of the 20th century are so vast that many have quite properly been urged to seek uncivilized solutions to them. These problems include the poisoning of the air and water; the rape of the land; the new colonialization of peoples, both here and abroad; the new imperialism practiced by Western democracy, and the continuing struggle of those who have not against those who have.

With the birth, 200 years ago, of the colossus called the United States, rational and educated men began to believe that civilization stretched to its highest order had begun. Building on a heritage of revolution, expressing a belief in the equality of most, if not all, men, this new democracy was to be the highest elevation of man's relations, one to the other, and a new beginning of decency between nations.

Civilization, as it was then defined, included imposing limitations on war between nations, encouraging the spread of industrialization, the civilizing of so-called heathen elements, the harnessing of nature for the benefit and pleasure of man. It was believed generally that man's better nature would triumph over his base desire to conquer and rule and make war, and that intellect, reason, and logic would share equally with morality in deciding man's fate.

Of course it has not been so. Man still makes war. He still insists that one group subordinate its wishes and desires to that of another. He still insists on gathering material wealth at the expense of his fellows and his environment.

Men and nations have grown arrogant, and the struggle of the 20th century has continued.

And while the struggle has continued, the university has remained aloof, a center for the study of why man behaves as he does, but never a center for the study of how to make man behave in a civilized manner.

Robert M. Hutchins, former chancellor of the University of Chicago, describes the present-day university thusly: It was hoped "it would lead the way to national power and prosperity . . . become the central factory of the knowledge industry, the foundation of our future. [But it became] . . . the national screening device through which individuals were to be put in the proper productive relationship to the national program of power and prosperity.

"[But] the world has moved too fast for the university. The leaders of the younger generations see that the problem is not to get wealth and power; [nations] have enough of those already. The problem is justice, or what to do with wealth and power. An institution that evidently has little interest in this question cannot command the allegiance of the young."

That the allegiance of some of the young is not with the university but with the oppressed and downtrodden is evident. Every continent has seen its young rise up against the evils the university is supposed to teach them how to destroy, and many have risen up against the university itself.

Despite its goal of producing individuals who know their relationship to be managers of the new industrial and technological society, the university has thankfully, probably against its desires, produced a new crop of people, a group of activists whose current demands on the university will hopefully be expanded to include assaults on the foundations of a society which has perverted education to reinforce inequity.

So then it is the entire fabric of education that is being attacked, its purpose, its ends. All black students have done is allowed their demands to be colored by their race.

Why should we not demand amnesty, the young ask, when you have allowed yourselves amnesty for over 300 years? Why should we negotiate, they ask, when you have received it since you came to power? Why should we not use weapons, when you have used them time and time again against us? Why should we be accused of tearing down the university and having nothing to put in its place, when you have torn down Vietnam and left the ghetto standing?

Why should we not have a black house on campus, the blacks ask, when the Methodists, Episcopalians, Jews, and Catholics often have theirs?

Why shouldn't we take over a building and evict the deans? Isn't every big-city university, in connivance with urban renewal, doing the same thing to entire families on a permanent basis every day?

Why should we not learn about ourselves, the blacks ask? Haven't we been made to learn more than we ever wanted to know about you?

Why shouldn't any and every black high school graduate be admitted freely to this college, the blacks ask? Aren't they being taught by your graduates, and therefore shouldn't they have learned what it takes to fit in here?

Why should Dow Chemical or ROTC be on campus, the students ask? We are not here to learn to make napalm or to learn how to be soldiers. This is not a vocational school for *any* employer. Or at least it should not be.

This ought to be, the students say, a center for the shaping of civilized man; a center for the study of not just why man behaves as he does, but also a center for the study of how to make him behave better.

To do this, the university must rid itself of several old notions. First of all, higher education can no longer be regarded as a privilege for a few, but must be seen as a right for the many. None of the rhetoric of the past several years about an education for everyone really approaches this aim; higher education is still an elitist and largely white preserve in America today.

In an age when education itself is being questioned, to permit or even to require that everyone receive a piece of parchment which will establish that he knows what millions of people already know with little profit to mankind will not suffice; it is simply not enough and simply will not do.

What is it then that is lacking? What is there beyond four years of compressing all the world's knowledge from lecture notes to the little blue book?

For the blacks, it must be more than Swahili lessons and Afro-American centers, although these have their place. For white universities, it must be more than raiding Southern black schools and taking their most talented faculty and students. For the black school it must be more than pride in blackness.

A writer in *The Center Magazine* described the school's failing function. He wrote: "Students are encouraged to relinquish their own wills, their freedom of volition; they are taught that value and culture reside outside oneself, and must be acquired from the institutions, and almost everything in their education is designed to discourage them from activity, from the wedding of idea and act. It is almost as if we hoped to discourage them from thought itself, by making ideas so lifeless, so hopeless, that their despair would be enough to make them manipulable and obedient."

While the university may have bred despair, it thankfully has not bred obedience. Violence occurs where there is no politics; while there is no politics of race, or rather while there is no anti-racist politics in the university, violence—physical and intellectual—will flourish.

Until the university develops a politics or, in better terms perhaps for this gathering, a curriculum and a discipline that stifles war and poverty and racism, until then, the university will be in doubt.

If education is a socializing process, in our society it has prepared white people to continue enjoying privileged traditions and positions, while black people, through it, have been programmed for social and economic oblivion.

Today's black and white students see this. They see the university nurturing war and directing counter-revolution; they see their professors employed in the Pentagon; they see their presidents serving on commission after commission investigating and recommending last year's solution to the last century's problems; they see the university recruit ghetto students with substandard backgrounds and then submit these students to standards of white, middle-class America.

They believe, as does the Tougaloo student I quoted from earlier, that "the task for black students and black Americans is much greater than trying to change white institutions and their white counterparts in the South. The task is to create revolutionary institutes of learning. The act of trying to be a better person, of trying to imagine and create humane institutions is formidable, but we have no other alternative. We must have a prototype from which to build a good society.

"The point which I make is an old one: that revolution is not only the seizure of power, but is also the building of a society that is qualitatively better than the one we presently live in."

But perhaps what the university's response ought to be in sentiments like that is best expressed in the words of the late W. E. B. DuBois, words written almost 50 years ago.

Dr. DuBois said: ". . . We believe that the vocation of man in a modern, civilized land includes not only the technique of his actual work but intelligent comprehension of his elementary duties as a father, citizen, maker of public opinion . . . a conserver of the public health, an intelligent follower of moral customs, and one who can appreciate if not partake something of the higher spiritual life of the world.

"We do not pretend that this can be taught to each individual in school, but it can be put into his social environment, and the more that environment is restricted and curtailed the more emphatic is the demand that . . . [man] shall be trained and trained thoroughly in these matters of human development if he is to share the surrounding civilization." Or, indeed, if there is to be any civilization at all.

Article by Roy Wilkins, Executive Director of the NAACP, in Newsweek, *February 10, 1969.*

The Case Against Separatism: "Black Jim Crow"

In the 1920s in Kansas City, Mo., I learned a lesson that I never forgot. It has come home to me forcibly these past twelve months in the demands of 1968–69 Negro college students for autonomous black units on some of their campuses. A Kansas City school-bond issue for the then racially segregated town provided $985,000 to build an athletic plant and field for a junior high school for white students—and $27,500 to convert a factory building into an elementary school for black children.

This was the ugly face of segregated education. The system must not be revived. It must not be invited back at the request, nay, the ultimatum of black students themselves.

No person who has watched the halting march of Negro civil rights through the years can fail to sympathize with the frustrations and anger of today's black students. In their hurt pride in themselves and in their outrage, they have called retreat from the tough and trying battle of a minority for dignity and equality. They don't call it a retreat, of course. They have all sorts of fancy rationalizations for their course. They renounce "white middle-class values" so they can refuse logically to be judged by the standards of the times and of the place they live in. Every black dissenter is an Uncle Tom and every white one a racist. Vituperation, not reason, is invoked.

They say they need to get together in their own dormitories to build a common strength. After they are strong and sure of themselves they will be able to meet other groups as true equals.

Who can declare them completely wrong? Certainly they are right about the strength that comes from being with their brothers. Certainly they are right about the usefulness of a study of Afro-American history and culture. They are right, also, in calling for increased enrollment of Negro students and in requesting more black faculty members. But in demanding a black Jim Crow studies building within a campus and exclusively black dormitories or wings of dormitories, they are opening the door to a dungeon. They do not see that no black history becomes significant and meaningful unless it is taught in the context of world and national history. In its sealed-off, black-studies centers, it will be simply another exercise in racial breast-beating.

To oppose black academic separatism is not to ignore black youth or to be unmindful of the spirit displayed by so many of them. They must be heard and they are heard; I have talked on numerous occasions with student groups, some members of which were not Wilkins cheerleaders. But it would be an abdication of responsibility, to them and to those who will follow us both, to acquiesce in a course which we know to be wrong, solely to avoid their criticism.

The key word in the current spate of similarly worded demands of black students is "autonomous." No university administration faithful to its trust can grant this. There is substantial informed opinion that tax money cannot be used to set up racial enclaves within campuses. I am sure that sooner or later a court test would arise. And all this is apart from the practical difficulty that it costs more money to establish real studies centers than most colleges can afford and that the qualified personnel—black or white—is simply not available at this time.

The demanding students might well find themselves saddled with a poor substitute for a center, foisted on them by an administration ready to buy peace at any price. Thus would segregated education once more run true to form.

An alternative with good chances of success would be to concentrate as a beginning on two centers of genuine stature, one on the East Coast and one on the West. The financing and staffing of two such university-based institutes would not be an impossible task, and they would draw not only on their own resident scholars but on exchange and visiting personnel as well. Meanwhile, valid courses in Afro-American history and culture should be established at all good colleges and universities to the extent that qualified faculty, black or white, can be found. Also, it should be the immediate task of every school claiming to be a school to provide an extensive library on the Negro past and present, in Africa, and in the New World.

Incidentally, the familiar "reading course" should not be disdained; after all, my generation had no "black-studies" curriculum—but we found ways to learn about ourselves and our past.

Speech by Vice President Spiro T. Agnew to a Republican state-wide fund-raising dinner in Des Moines, Iowa, April 14, 1970.

The Threat to Educational Standards

Tonight I hope to cover more completely a subject touched upon in my Lincoln Day remarks in Chicago—the disturbing trends in administrative and admissions policies of America's colleges and universities.

With regard to the determination of curricula and the hiring and firing of college professors, I stated in Chicago that the desires of students should not be the controlling factor. However, it cannot be validly argued that students' views on these matters are of no value in making educational judgments. Students, the consumers of knowledge, are in a unique position to assess the effectiveness of educational policies. Therefore, their views should be considered and be an ingredient of final decisions by the educational establishment.

From the light of experiences in the last decade, it would seem to me that Prof. Sidney Hook hit the nail on the head in his recent book, *Academic Freedom and Academic Anarchy.* He stated:

". . . There are no compensating advantages in the risks incurred when students are given the power of educational decision.

"That is why with respect to the . . . demand for student rights, we must say: 'Consultation, yes—decision, no.' "

Tonight I want to give you my views in greater particularity on the subject of college admissions, and this time I come armed with supportive quotations from distinguished administrators who are equally concerned about this problem.

The American system of colleges and universities is the envy of mankind. It belongs not just to the professional educational community, but to all of us. When decisions begin to represent a definite trend that may drastically depreciate those national assets, then all of us have an interest at stake; all of us have a right to be heard—indeed, a duty to speak.

When one looks back across the history of the last decade—at the smoking ruins of a score of college buildings, at the outbreaks of illegal and violent protests and disorders on hundreds of college campuses, at the regular harassment and interruption and shouting down of speakers, at the totalitarian spirit evident among thousands of students and hundreds of faculty members, at the decline of genuine academic freedom to speak and teach and learn—that record hardly warrants a roaring vote of confidence in the academic community that presided over the disaster.

We in public life who criticize, however, should make that criticism constructive. This I intend to do. I feel as much as anyone that there should be expanded educational opportunities for deprived, but able, young people in our society. The difference is that I favor better preparing them—with additional governmental assistance—in some form of prep school rather than tossing them into a four-year college or university curriculum that they are not equipped to handle. And I do not feel that our traditional four-year institutions should lower their sights or their standards for the sole purpose of opening their doors wider.

Now, there are two methods by which unqualified students are being swept into college on the wave of the new socialism. One is called a quota system, and the other an open admissions policy. Each is implemented by lessening admission requirements. They may be equally bad.

Under a quota system, a specific percentage of the student body must consist of minority or disadvantaged students regardless of whether they can meet the existing standards for enrollment. If they do not apply, they must be recruited.

Under an open admissions policy, a college deliberately opens its doors and expands its enrollment despite the inability of many of the applicants to meet minimum standards.

There are distinguished, even brilliant, men with grave reservations about the wisdom of either of these policies. The historian Daniel Boorstin is one of them. Speaking in Tulsa last June, he carved his views in sentences more emphatic than my own:

"In the university all men are not equal. Those better-endowed or better-equipped intellectually must be preferred in admission, and preferred in recognition. . . . If we give in to the armed demands of militants to admit persons to the university because of their race, their poverty, their illiteracy, or any other non-intellectual distinctions, our universities can no longer serve all of us—or any of us."

Professor Boorstin argues his case on behalf of the integrity of the university, but there are also other arguments against racial quotas, not the least of which is that of simple justice.

For each youth unprepared for a college curriculum who is brought in under a quota system, some better-prepared student is denied entrance. Admitting the obligations to compensate for past deprivation and discrimination, it just does not make sense to atone by discriminating against and depriving someone else.

Another argument against easy admissions was summed up in the testimony of Dr. Clark Kerr of the prestigious Carnegie Foundation's Commission for the Advancement of Teaching in testimony before the House Education Committee. [Mr. Kerr is chairman of the Carnegie Commission on Higher Education, supported by the Carnegie Foundation for the Advancement of Teaching.]

He said:

"Some institutions have brought in students too far below the admissions standards with the result that it ended up in frustration for the student. . . . It's bad policy to start someone on a path when you know he can't reach the end of the road."

Is it understandable that I wonder why the remarks of Kerr and Boorstin were greeted with respectful editorial silence by the same tribe that came looking for my scalp after Chicago?

We can see the visible results of weak and insufficiently defined educational policy in the growing militancy of increasing numbers of students who confuse social ideals with educational opportunities. John Roche, a former special consultant to President Johnson, a syndicated columnist and a professor at Brandeis, observed the phenomenon on his own campus. In my opinion, he analyzed it correctly. Last year he wrote as follows about the violence emanating from black student militancy:

"Sociologists and others have had a field day explaining the sources of this behavior, but I do not believe the problem at Brandeis, San Francisco, Swarthmore or wherever trouble has erupted is terribly complex. We created our own difficulties the day we (and I mean the liberal academicians) decided that a college or university should double as a settlement house. Once the decision was made that Negro or 'culturally underprivileged' youngsters should be admitted to first-class colleges, without the usual prerequisites, the escalation began. . . .

"All this special black admission business has, of course, been conducted with a brass band, as college and university administrators and faculties congratulate themselves on their radicalism, on their willingness to rise above white racism. In fact, what has happened in most instances that have come to my attention is sheerly cosmetic: nobody has actually worried about the anguish of the poor Negro kids who have been dumped into a competitive situation, have been thrown with inadequate preparation into water well beyond their capacity to swim."

In criticizing my views on racial quotas following my speech in Chicago, the Cleveland *Plain Dealer* said:

"In the prestigious Ivy League, the schools admitted freshman classes last September that were 10-per-cent Negro. . . ." And it added approvingly, "This represented a huge increase in black enrollment."

But, is this a really good thing—and if 10 per cent is good, would 12 or 15 per cent be better?

President Clifford Lord of Hofstra, in a speech last December, aired his own doubts about a policy of "open admissions":

"This can be a very expensive process for the private institution, financially and academically," he noted. ". . . There is the additional and critical question of the educational desirability of mixing those who are qualified by modern standards for work in a particular institution and those who come in under an open enrollment program."

A Ford Foundation education expert, Mr. Fred Crossland, registers more than just doubts; he thinks this 10-per-cent quota today is impossible to attain.

According to the Office of Education, though blacks constitute about 12 per cent of our college-age population, they account for only 6 per cent of all high school graduates. Mr. Crossland adds that only about half of this 6 per cent is capable of handling a college curriculum. Where does this leave the *Plain Dealer's* 10 per cent? Says Mr. Crossland:

"Given present standards, it's preposterous and statistically impossible to talk about boosting black enrollment to 10 per cent even over the next five years."

What makes Mr. Crossland's unequivocal statement so timely

is that just two weeks ago—after 12 days of heat from striking black militant students at the University of Michigan—President Robben W. Fleming agreed to nearly all their major demands—the first of which was for a 10-per-cent black enrollment by 1973.

Now let me read you what a distinguished member of the Michigan faculty said about the president's action. He is Gardner Ackley, the economics professor who served as chairman of President Johnson's Council of Economic Advisers. According to the Ann Arbor *News*, this is what Professor Ackley told a faculty meeting:

"This has been a very tragic year . . . which has seen the beginning of the destruction of this university as a center of learning. . . . It is being destroyed by its own faculty and administration."

The university's administration, he said, is "unwilling or unable to resist the destroyers. . . . However ridiculous or worthy the cause, it will win in proportion to the willingness of its supporters to disrupt the life of the university.

"University facilities are now available for . . . promoting any cause, no matter how obscene or revolting.

"There is no reason. There is only power."

According to the Ann Arbor *News*, Professor Ackley received a standing ovation; and there were shouts of "Bravo" from his colleagues.

The surrender at Ann Arbor is not dissimilar to the tragic surrender of Italian academic and political leadership to the demands of rebellious students two years ago for open admissions to the universities of all high school graduates.

The results have been instructive, to say the least. Measured in diplomas granted annually—the number has jumped, in just a few years, from 28,000 to 40,000—the reform is a success. But these are bargain-basement diplomas—and today Italian employers advertising for college graduates are careful to specify that the degree must date back to 1967.

In a few years' time perhaps—thanks to the University of Michigan's callow retreat from reality—America will give the diplomas from Michigan the same fish eye that Italians now give diplomas from the University of Rome.

President Lord of Hofstra, who, as I stated earlier, expressed his serious reservations about mixing "open enrollment" students and academically qualified students, feels nevertheless that this might be a good policy—for institutions other than Hofstra. Is it with tongue in cheek that he said:

"It seems to me that the wholly or largely tax-supported institutions such as the State University or the City University have got to pick up this ball and carry it. . . ."

One gets the distinct impression that Hofstra will not be picking up the ball and carrying it any time soon.

But the public institutions are not without impassioned defenders—like Irving Kristol—who believe it a major tragedy to impose upon quality institutions of higher learning, such as the city colleges of New York, a social burden of assimilation and uplift that they are neither designed nor equipped to shoulder.

Writing in the *Public Interest* last November, he warned:

". . . Black militants are demanding that many more (and eventually all) black students who are graduated from high school be admitted automatically to the city colleges regardless of grades or aptitude, or whatever and (New York's Upper East Side and Suburban Elite) which in any case sends its youngsters out of town, think it is being 'constructive' when it meets this demand at least part way—*i.e.*, when it grants to poor black youngsters a college diploma in lieu of a college education. . . .

"The city colleges," continues Professor Kristol, "are one of the most valuable—perhaps the most valuable—patrimonies of New York. The Jews took them over from the WASP's and used them to great advantage; the Irish and Italians are now participating and benefiting; the Negroes and Puerto Ricans will very soon be in a position to inherit this remarkable system of higher education. But as things are going now, their inheritance will be worthless."

These institutions—the widening avenue of advancement for the young natural leaders in New York's community—are, in his words, ". . . being transformed—degraded is not too strong a term—with the approval and consent of the elite, into four-year community colleges, with all academic distinction being remorselessly extinguished."

If these quality colleges are degraded, it would be a permanent and tragic loss to the poor and middle class of New York, who cannot afford to establish their sons and daughters on the Charles River or Cayuga Lake. New York will have traded away one of the intellectual assets of the Western world for a four-year community college and a hundred thousand devalued diplomas.

The central mission of higher education is intellectual, argues Dr. Lincoln Gordon of Johns Hopkins.

To the extent universities deviate from that objective, we are devaluating a national asset that many foreign leaders believe has given America a unique advantage over the nations of the world.

I agree with Dr. Gordon. Any attempt to subordinate the great universities of this country to social goals for which they are ill-designed and ill-equipped can only result in tragic losses to both these institutions and the nation.

Perhaps the country has already marched too far under the banners of the slogan, "Every Man a College Graduate," to abandon it now. But maybe not. Perhaps there remains a "via media," a middle way, that will both preserve the integrity and quality of America's colleges—and advance the cause of minorities and the disadvantaged.

Assuredly, the first step along such a road was taken a few weeks ago by President Nixon when he called on the nation to make an historic commitment:

"No *qualified* student who wants to go to college should be barred by lack of money. That has long been a great American goal: I propose that we achieve it now."

Certainly, no young man or woman with ability and talent should be denied, by the ancient and traditional barrier of poverty, the opportunity to advance to the limits of his capacity. Not in this wealthy country in 1970. To allow that to happen is to tolerate an unnecessary individual tragedy which, when multiplied, amounts to a national tragedy.

Nor can we let talent go unnoticed. A perpetual national search should be conducted to locate within every community every child of ability and promise. When located, they should be given special attention—to advance them to limits of their potential and to prepare them for leadership in their communities and in society.

We must also recognize the needs of the unprepared and under-achieving child and of those who do not begin to show promise academically until later in high school. Where necessary—and it is often critically necessary—substantial programs of compensatory education must be developed. Extra summers of study, extra years of academic preparation must be provided at public expense. For there can be no doubt that we must compensate for the deprived environment.

For these students I believe we must have more community colleges and special preparatory schools, to insure to the late-blooming, the underprepared, and the underachieving student every educational opportunity.

But I make this distinction: preparatory and compensatory education do not belong in the university. Students needing special educational services—who do not meet the standards and requirements of institutions of higher education—should not be encouraged to apply—in the first instance—to such institutions.

Rather than lower the standards of higher education, we must raise the level of the student's preparation and achievement, so that he may not only one day take his place in the colleges and universities of this nation, but successfully hold that place in active, healthy competition with other students.

This, I believe, is the kind of commitment that can and must be made to balance the scales and insure full equality of educational opportunity.

But a firm commitment to equality of opportunity must not result in the dilution of that opportunity. For colleges and universities to deliberately draw into a high academic environment students who are unqualified intellectually or whom the primary and secondary schools have conspicuously failed to prepare is to create hopes which are doomed to disappointment.

Moreover, the cluttering of our universities, already too large in many cases, through the insertion of high-school-level semesters for the accommodation of those unqualified for the traditional curriculum is a major cause of campus inefficiency and unrest. The number of students on college campuses has increased by 400 per cent in three decades and is expected to reach nearly 10-million within five years. In 1940 only two universities in the country had more than 20,000 students; today, 60 universities can claim that dubious distinction.

Rising student enrollments have been forced to exaggerated heights by a combination of underlying social pressures. Within the awesome statistics of bigness lie the heart of the justified complaints of many college students today—complaints about absentee professors—about the plastic facelessness on campus—about the decline and disappearance of the personal teacher-student relationship—about ill-equipped graduate students teaching courses for which undergraduates have paid $60, $70, and even $80 a credit—about being matriculated, administrated, graded, and graduated by computer.

I do not accept the proposition that every American boy and girl should go to a four-year college. Even now, with nearly 8-million students on the campuses of this country, there are tens of thousands there who did not come for the learning experience and who are restless, purposeless, bored, and rebellious.

College, at one time considered a privilege, is considered to be a right today—and is valued less because of that. Concentrations of disoriented students create an immense potential for disorder.

The chairman of the sociology department of Columbia University, Professor Amitai Etzioni, recognizes the phenomenon, deplores its inevitable and undesirable by-products—the depersonalization of the campus and the threat to academic quality because of massive enrollments—but sees no certain solution.

Writing recently in the *Wall Street Journal,* he contends that the lowering of admission standards results in the presence on campus of pressure groups with "a social ideology and a political organization to further demands for easy promotion and guaranteed graduation.

"If one tries to enforce select admission or academic standards, he risks being labeled a racist, and he lays himself open to campus-wide attacks. . . .

"The goal of college education for everyone is now too widely endorsed both by white middle-class Americans and minorities to stop the high-schoolization of colleges simply by trying to uphold the old standards. . . .

"If we can no longer keep the flood-gates closed at the admissions office, it at least seems wise to channel the general flow away from four-year colleges and toward two-year extensions of high school in the junior and community colleges."

And, of course, that is what should be done.

Consistent with this philosophy, I favor the sort of procedures in high school that screen out the best students and make greater demands upon their greater talents.

In some areas, such ideas have been discarded as reactionary. But if we accept Jefferson's concept of a "natural aristocracy" among peoples—then that is as true for every race and community of man. It should be our objective to find, to nurture, and to advance that natural aristocracy through the rigorous demands of intellectual competition.

To require a student of genuine ability to sit for hours in a classroom with those neither able nor prepared, and to permit him to be intellectually stalled at the level of the slowest, is a cruel waste of his God-given talents.

In Washington today there is a single black high school—Dunbar—which once trained this natural aristocracy with unrivaled success. Two decades ago, 80 per cent of its graduates went on to college, a higher percentage than any other school in the District of Columbia. That high school numbers among its graduates federal, district, and appellate judges, the first black general in the American Army, and a United States Senator.

After the Supreme Court decision of 1954, however, this school under prevailing educational nostrums was allowed to become just another school in the inner city. Today, it ranks at the bottom of District of Columbia schools in the percentage of graduates going on to college.

In my opinion, Dunbar High School was sacrificed by the levelers and the ideologists on the altar of educational egalitarianism —and I cannot believe that the black people of the capital or the nation are better for the loss.

My remarks here tonight have been extended—I am sure they will also strike some of my critics as pure heresy. As soon as they come clacking off the news wires into the horrified city rooms of the East, my friends on the editorial pages will start sharpening their knives and dancing around the typewriters. I ask no favors —but make one recommendation. Read my remarks through, just once at least, before turning to the keyboard. Sometimes, that can improve the editorial.

From an article by educator John Holt, entitled "The Radicalizing of a Guest Teacher at Berkeley," in The New York Times Magazine, *February 22, 1970.*

In Defense of Open Admissions

. . . Nothing worth saving, or worth having, in the university is seriously threatened by the demands of even the most radical students. Indeed, in their efforts to get agreement from the university, the Third World people at Berkeley very quickly watered down their original demands to the point where I, for one, felt they were nowhere near radical enough.

One of the student demands that most terrified the university, and at first most puzzled and startled me, was the demand for open admissions.

During the strike I thought about this a great deal, and it is worth saying again that it was the fact of the strike, and only that, that made me think about it. Indeed, I felt the strike as a kind of pressure on my mind, often an unwanted pressure. I often wished angrily that they would get the thing settled and over with so I could again think about what I wanted to think about. It was not really until the strike ended, and even after I left Berkeley altogether that I began to realize that what the strikers wanted me to think about were indeed the things that I ought to be thinking about.

There is no more crucial question in our society than this question of relationships between the old and the young, between educational institutions and their students, between the people who hold effective power in our society in and out of universities and the young people who increasingly demand to be given more and more of it. The revolt of the young, or the battle between young and old (look at it how you will) is the most important question of our time, and on the way we resolve it or fail to resolve it will probably depend, more than on any other one thing, our society's prospects for survival.

But I was puzzled by the proposal for open admissions. I found myself thinking, if anybody could get into the university, why wouldn't ten thousand, twenty thousand, a hundred thousand people come here, and if they did, what would the university do with them? And I began thinking freshly about a question that people have been asking me many times in my lecturing on education. Hundreds of teachers and parents have said to me, "If children are educated the way you want, if they can learn whatever they like in the way it seems best to them, how are the colleges going to solve their admissions problem?"

My answer was usually that I did not consider the solving of the college admissions problem a high-priority question, for me or even for the elementary or secondary schools of this country. I usually followed this by suggesting one or more ways in which colleges might, by my lights, improve their admissions procedures so as to make places available to students of a much wider variety of talents and backgrounds. But I accepted almost without realizing it the assumption on the part of my hearers that a college must make decisions about who *can* come in and who *cannot*. After all, their facilities are limited, aren't they? They can't take in everyone, can they?

Then one day I found myself thinking of the Boston Public Library, which I go to quite often, more to borrow classical records than books. Here is what must certainly be called an educational institution. Yet it does not make decisions and judgments about who can come in and who cannot, and—what is more important —who is good enough to come in and who is not. It simply says like libraries everywhere, "Here are some facilities—books, records, films, exhibits. If you want, come in and use them, as much as you want, as long as you want."

I thought of many other educational institutions that serve society, none of which exclude anybody, and it suddenly occurred to me that the admissions problem of our universities is not a real problem but a manufactured one—that is, it exists because the universities want it to exist, not because it has to.

Why shouldn't a school, college, or university be like a museum, a library, a concert hall, a lecture hall, a sports facility? Why shouldn't it, like them, say to the public, "Here is what we have to offer you: here are the possibilities. If they appeal to you, come in and use them, for as little or as long as you like"? If more people want to get in than there is room for, let them handle this situation the way a concert hall or theater handles it. Why not hang out a sign saying "Sold Out—next performance tomorrow afternoon, next week, next month, next year"?

If a student wanted to take a course with Professor So-and-So and there were hundreds of other students wanting to take the same course, why not let him make the kind of choice that someone makes who wants to see a very popular play? Let him either, in effect, wait until there is an opportunity to get in the course, or, if that seems like too long a wait, think about getting the same sort of information or help somewhere else. If I want to see a doctor, and someone says that he has so many patients that I won't be able to see him for four months, the sensible thing to do is find some other doctor, maybe not quite as good but with fewer patients.

Let the student worry about overcrowding. The university can say, we can provide university housing for so many thousand students; after that, people will have to find their own. Large numbers of students at Berkeley and other state universities do in fact live off campus. This often makes housing both scarce and expensive, and this may in turn make a student decide that a particular university is or is not a good place to go. But let this be his worry, not the university's. If the housing, facilities, and courses at one university are terribly crowded so that desirable courses are hard or impossible to get into—as indeed they are now in many cases at places like Berkeley—the student can decide either to try to wait it out or to go somewhere else.

Nor is there any necessary reason why universities should worry so about qualifications. This will seem startling at first. But after all, when I borrow a book or record from the Boston Public Library, nobody gives me a quiz to be sure I will understand it. It's up to me to decide how I want to spend my time and to run the risk of wasting it. Similarly, if I go to the Boston Symphony to hear a piece of difficult modern music, nobody examines me in the hall to make sure I'm educated enough to appreciate it. I pay my money and I take my choice. If I go home later feeling angrily that it was a waste of an evening, all right, that's my tough luck. But why should anyone else make this decision for me?

It is perfectly true that universities of this kind would be in important ways different from the ones we know today. The universities as they exist have come to think of themselves as private clubs. They are in a race with each other for prestige, which is quickly translated into money and power—the professor from a prestigious university has more chance of getting a big foundation or government grant than a professor from some less prestigious one. Therefore, they have an interest in convincing the world that their club is harder to get into than anybody else's. At the same time, they try to convince the oncoming generations of students that membership in this club will in the long run prove more valuable—again in terms of power and money—than membership in any other. That is what creates the admissions problem. I make a great many people think that my club is the one to be in, and then I stand at the door and tell large numbers of them that they aren't good enough to get in.

On the other hand, since the Boston Public Library isn't trying to convince people that because it is harder to get in it is a "better" library than the New York Public Library, it doesn't have to urge large numbers of people to come to it because it is the best, and then put somebody at the door turning most of these people away because they aren't good enough to get in.

The universities that consider themselves superior have an enormous investment, financial and psychological, in the notion of their own superiority, and I don't expect them to give it up quickly or lightly. Given its present concerns, which do not for the most part have much to do with education, I can understand why the University of California should feel threatened by the demand of the Third World students that they open their doors to any Third World people who want to come in, and I can understand their wanting to resist this demand as much as they can.

As long as universities are interested in prestige and power, they will want to go on saying to the world that people are coming to them because they are so good, and that they are turning away most of their applicants or supplicants because they in turn are not good enough. But a university truly dedicated to education, to the spreading of knowledge, skill, and—most important—wisdom to all who wanted or needed it, would think in other terms.

People ask, what about the granting of degrees? If anybody who wants can come to a university and there study as much or as little as he wants, how will the university issue its credentials? I don't think the university ought to be in the credentials-granting business. Why should our universities be hiring halls for business and government? It does not seem to me to be a vital or necessary or even acceptable part of the process of education. In any case, people even now take courses in the extension divisions of universities and, depending on the length of the course, get a certain number of credits for work done.

There's no reason at all why people could not over a number of years take courses in an assortment of universities, depending on where they lived and who they wanted to study with, and simply have some kind of certificate listing the total number of credits they had collected. In any case, there is plenty of evidence that educational institutions do not and cannot teach competence. Since they don't and can't, why go on any longer with the pretense that an academic degree is a certificate of competence? All it shows or can show is that such-and-such a person has taken so many courses and played the school game for a certain length of time; it says nothing about what he will or will not be able to do in his later working life.

The prestige universities have worked hard, for reasons already given, to convince employers and the public at large that their degrees are indeed certificates of exceptional competence and worth. They have to do this to create among the students a demand for these degrees and among employers a demand for holders of them. But it is a con, and there is really nothing in it. If the universities grew interested in education they could give up this fiction along with others.

To the dissatisfied, the universities like to say, in one way or another, "If you don't like our rules, you don't have to play our game." This seems the height of reasonableness. It is nothing of the kind. The universities, which in other circumstances like to think of themselves sometimes as exclusive clubs, sometimes as temples of the higher truth and learning, are comparing themselves here to any kind of store. You go to the supermarket, pay some money, walk out the door with a little food. If you don't like their food or their prices, you don't go to that supermarket; you go to some other. In the same way, the universities say, we offer certain kinds of learning, skill, and money-attracting credentials, in return for a good deal of the students' money and time.

The trouble with this—and it should be obvious to anyone who takes half a minute to think about it—is that the stores we trade at do not exercise the kind of influence and pressure on our lives that the universities, singly and collectively, exercise on the lives of their students. The supermarkets do not post people at the door deciding whether or not I am good enough to get in. Nor do they stamp on my forehead in indelible ink for the world to see whether or not I *was* good enough. They do not grade me like the meat they sell.

The universities, on the other hand, do exactly this. They have arrived at a situation, and to a considerable extent contrived it, in which their opinion of a young person determines to a very large degree what that person can or cannot do, will or will not become during the rest of his life. There is probably no other single institution in society, even the armed forces, which has as much to say about our lives. (The armed forces, it is true, can put a man in a position where he may be killed or injured, but once he gets out of their hands, so to speak, they don't cast much of a shadow over his future.)

Our young people start living under the shadow of universities almost as soon as they're born. What the universities want, what they think is good, bad, valuable, valueless, certainly determines and creates the kinds of pressures that our young people live under beginning as early as age 3 or 4. Our young people spend a very large part of their time, even before they go on to college, doing what the schools think the universities want; they go on doing what they want while they're at the universities, which may be anything from four to heaven-knows-how-many years; and, as I said before, they carry on them for the rest of their lives whatever sort of brand the university has chosen to put on them. Their demand—that since universities exercise this enormous control over the lives of their students, students should have something to say about them and the way they are run—seems to me to be altogether right and just.

If universities want to say to our young people in effect, "We are just a gathering of scholars doing our thing; please stop bothering us and interfering with us, and let us do our own thing the way we want," then they have got to get their feet off the collective necks of the young and give up the extraordinary and unjustifiable power that they have acquired over their lives.

CHAPTER 11

Black Studies

A central demand of Black students has been for curricular revisions, for the institution of new fields of study, namely, "Black
Studies." Elliott Moorman, a Black student leader at Princeton,
argued that the existing curriculum of American universities was
essentially "an Anglo-American studies program." At the University of Wisconsin, the official faculty-student Committee on
Studies and Instruction in Race Relations issued a report in
March 1969, in which the majority provided a rationale for "Afro-
American Studies." Troy Duster, a Black sociologist at Berkeley,
put the case even more strongly, by employing the "colonial analogy" and arguing in favor of a "non-Western" kind of education
for Black students.

There were skeptics nonetheless. W. Arthur Lewis, a well-
known Black economist, argued that Black Studies was marginal
in the fight against discrimination and not "the road to the top."

From an article by Elliott Duane Moorman, President of the Class of 1971 at Princeton University and an active member of Princeton's Association of Black Collegians, in Saturday Review, *June 21, 1969.*

The Benefit of Anger

Of the myriad of ethnic groups to enter the American ethnic "melting pot," none has historically suffered more of a near desertion by its best, most qualified leaders than the black community. For scores of years being a relatively successful black man in America necessitated a de-emphasis of all that you were and an often ludicrous yet desperate attempt to be, or at least appear, white. One worked hard at assuming white lingual and grooming patterns, studied the white value system, and kept silent on race issues. One either rejected or enjoyed clandestinely Negroid cultural preferences, which very often when they surfaced caused shame and embarrassment. The irony assumes tragic proportions when one considers the virtual devastation in young black children of any readily distinguishable and identifiable cultural heritage, a legacy jealously and legitimately guarded by the Italian-, Jewish-, and Irish-Americans.

Black America's young, with its leadership reservoir depleted and its culture and heritage devastated, have educational needs one dimension beyond those of the average American student. College must create a black leadership group that readily and permanently identifies with, and is culturally proud of, other black Americans in order to counteract the negative influences produced by centuries of Uncle Tom survival tactics that still plague the race. Hence the need for Afro-American studies, black student groups, and the black experience in general—at both black and white universities.

There is, then, a dual imperative for a college educating black people: the normal educational function of creating questioning, restless, dissatisfied students, and the added dimension of providing for heritage identification and enculturation. It cannot continue to churn out year after year acquiescent, quiet, satisfied members of the black bourgeoisie, as many American colleges now do.

There is no question that this line of reasoning implies that the

educational needs of black Americans are different from those of
the white student community, but the needs of both can be served
in a single institution. We must now, if we will really create a generation of intelligent, capable black leaders, stop anesthetizing
ourselves with heartwarming talk about forgetting our differences
and emphasizing our "common humanity." Where was our common humanity when the teachers of black people were slave trad-
ers, when the books were bullwhips, when the classrooms were
cotton fields? We need to recognize the sociological, cultural, and
historical differences that the collective American psyche has imposed on black and on white, and to serve the particular needs of
each. And service of these particular needs does not necessarily
imply creating a situation of confrontation and conflict. Creative,
constructive dissent is endemic, indeed fundamental, to this country. And creative dissent can spring only from constructive
anger. . . .

Another argument may be that there is no special consideration
given to the particular needs of white students; there are no
"Anglo-American" courses or studies programs, no Anglo-American youth groups, no all-white dormitories. And I respond that
the actual curriculum of most predominantly white universities *is*
an Anglo-American studies program: the study of the culture and
heritage of the American ideal as it has unfolded in the several
disciplines—American politics, history, sociology, music, drama,
the life sciences.

How many American colleges have American civilization programs? Literally hundreds. And the athletic teams, fraternities,
special interest groups, and a host of other college activities become—either by accident or by intention—all-white Anglo-
American groups that, in a very real sense, exist for the preservation and enculturation of the American heritage in the student. It
may be called "good sportsmanship" or "fellowship" or "camara-
derie"; it's essentially the preservation of some of the values of the
American experience that have proved to be worthwhile. And all-
white dormitories? They exist, again either by accident or by design, and in large numbers across America. Because such groups
are so much a part of the college structure, they are not labeled
"separatist" or "polarized"; yet, black student groups contribute
no more to the polarization of attitudes than do these Anglo-
American groups.

When black-initiated college disorder and disruption are viewed in this way, it becomes evident that such events clearly represent the healthy functioning of the highest ideals of the American university. And the anger that this functioning produces has historically proved to be one of this nation's greatest assets in terms of fostering constructive change. But, granting this thesis, where does that leave the black student? Does it predict that the university structure will come crashing down under the righteous indignation of its black students? Is the destruction of the university inevitable? The answer to this is, for the most part, dependent on the *response* of both those in university administrative positions and in governmental positions. Will academicians respond with complacent mediocrity? Will they respond (as in many cases they already have) with helmeted state troopers? Will they respond with the traditional historic banalities? Or will American educators respond with an honest and searching effort to identify the causes of campus unrest, and attempt to act upon these findings? . . .

At predominantly white institutions, it seems to me, a positive response is not difficult to frame. Rather than seek to crush black anger, the academic community should seek to keep the anger constructive. This can be done by taking a general attitude of cooperation and willingness to understand, and to make special attempts to accommodate student needs by providing the financial and technical assistance necessary to implement such changes as black studies, by increasing minority recruitment and admission, by hiring more black faculty, and by attempting to create an atmosphere of mutual trust and confidence. Massive police intervention can only serve to increase polarization and distrust and to convert constructive anger into vengeful and spiteful wrath.

At predominantly black institutions, the administrators would do well to view the gem they hold for what it can be: an institution uniquely equipped to create and develop a proud, aware generation of black leaders. A black college can, in the least dramatic sense, become a vehicle toward freedom, a vehicle toward meaningful knowledge—a vehicle toward black anger. Once the administrators view the black college for what it can be, then they must pattern their responses accordingly: an outpouring of all resources—financial, moral, and intellectual—toward meeting the *real* needs of black people today, not the illusory need of a one-way admission ticket to the comfortable black bourgeoisie. This response becomes critical, since most black students are in all-black colleges.

The future? It is what the colleges themselves—faculty, administration, and students—wish to make of it, in terms of constructively responding to the needs and moral imperatives of each other. Negative responses may well mean destruction.

From the majority report of the Committee on Studies and Instruction in Race Relations, University of Wisconsin (Madison Campus), March 3, 1969, signed by both faculty and student members.

The Rationale for Afro-American Studies

The important role of Afro-Americans in the shaping of these United States has been seriously ignored and quite often distorted in the curricula of this and other universities. University professors have contributed to the perpetuation of ignorance and distortion about the black man and his past. Moreover, it is only very recently that American publishing houses have set about the task of re-making the image of the black man as traditionally portrayed in books intended for schools, colleges, and universities. The study and teaching of Afro-American subjects must be approached from a new perspective. The aim of such an approach should be the systematic and coordinated presentation of this neglected corpus of human experience. It is essential that this effort be undertaken by individuals who have an expertise in the subject matter, who have an overriding commitment to the subject; that is, by individuals who are not cursorily interested in Afro-American studies but who are eager to devote the better part of their research and teaching toward the reconstruction of the Afro-American past, and the understanding of the black man's role in contemporary society. What is needed is a core of courses taught by concerned individuals who will be able to convey to black students and white what it means, and has meant, to be a black man in a white society. What is required is that no student, black or white, should leave this University without a deep appreciation and understanding of the problems of a multi-racial society; of the contribution of black men and women to the shaping of American culture; of the psychological and social difficulties of second-class citizenship; of the pain and suffering of decades of social ostracism; of the educational and economic effects of racism and racist institutions. What is essential is that black students and white should not leave this University without some knowledge of the Afro-American cultural and intellectual tradition; of the nature and character of a black subculture traditionally segregated from the mainstream of American life; of the metamorphosis of black identity through periods of slavery, emancipation, segregation, integration, protest, and revolt; of the Afro-American and his cultural and intellectual roots—that is his historical evolution in Africa and the New World; of the origin and nature of Afro-American institutions, the family, the church, the school, and the press; of the nature and history of the Afro-American's struggle for survival, as specially seen through movements of social and political protest. For it can be genuinely stated that without such knowledge, fundamental and integral to the American experience, such students will not have received in this University a truly "liberal" education.

The social science and humanistic disciplines within the University stand to gain from such a growth of Afro-American studies, and from the development of concomitant research facilities in these areas. It may be necessary for these disciplines to reexamine their assumptions about the American social system in the light of increased knowledge of communities, institutions, and cultures which have so long been ignored. Such research and teaching is necessary if we are to improve our ability to understand and deal meaningfully with schisms in American society which have become evident in recent years. This will be fully consistent with the University's long history of concern with problems of the state and nation.

Article by Troy Duster, Black associate professor of sociology at the University of California, Berkeley, in The Daily Californian, *February 20, 1969.*

The Third World College and the Colonial Analogy

In the middle of the nineteenth century, when the British held control of India, a debate arose about the kind of education the Indian elite should receive. There were some Englishmen who argued for a resurrection of traditional Indian education, the study of classical Indian history, Indian literature, and Indian institutions. They were opposed by Englishmen who believed that the only real education was one based in Western civilization, and more particularly, at Oxford. This faction, led by Lord Macaulay, won the debate.

Macaulay is an important figure, for his victory crystallized the development of higher education throughout the whole British Empire, and radically affected the way in which the French and Dutch were to proceed. In brief summary, the Western countries decided to train the elites from their colonies with Western higher education.

Most of the colonial elite swallowed the package whole, undigested, just as most students now unthinkingly take notes in class without digestion. These men, dressed in English gowns at Oxford or at the English-style home university in the colony, drank their port and brandy, and discussed humane letters of the West. Occasionally, however, one or two here and there did some critical careful reading.

They not only read Locke and Paine, they thought about it and compared it to reality in the colony. Thus, Gandhi, Nkrumah, Kenyatta, and many other Western-trained colonial elite became disgruntled reformers and revolutionaries because they took Westerners to task for preaching the equality of man, then institutionalizing inequality in the colony.

For the most part, however, the Western-trained colonial elite were a rather docile group. ("Toms" come in all colors and cultures, in both sexes and in all ages.) By their training and education, they were oriented to the West.

Western standards of success and excellence were assimilated as their own standards. Even the revolutionary elite, such as Gandhi and Nkrumah, were to some measure victimized, if we can call it that, for their vision of excellence and equality was often a Western one, and was not grounded in Indian or African soil or culture. (Gandhi was inspired by Thoreau. Nkrumah was trained by U.S. intellectuals.)

Thus, even the revolutionary colonial elite, while bursting with fury and indignation, were so much Western-trained after all those years in London and Paris that they were lacking in systematic knowledge about the indigenous problems of their own cultures. Freedom they could cry, and the colonial yoke they could burst, but I repeat, even these men were Western-trained.

They knew of Socrates and Marx, not of their own economies, cultures and social and political institutions. How could they?

In the discussion and controversy over the Third World College, the colonial analogy deserves to be taken more seriously:

The Academic Senate and the Regents will join to argue that there is only one kind of real education for the black elite, the Mexican-American elite, the Asian elite, or any ghetto elite. The Academic Senate follows Macaulay.

The debate over Black studies behind closed doors has taken the form of the argument expressed in the middle nineteenth century: "Is it possible that there is another kind of education, with other standards?" "Well, now, perhaps Black Studies, but the faculty and staff of such a department must be Western-trained black elite. They must be from Harvard, Columbia, Princeton, Berkeley."

Here is the heart of the conflict on the Berkeley campus now, across the Bay at San Francisco State, and increasingly to be heard at other major urban campuses. On the issue of who is to staff such programs, on the issue of how the curriculum is to be oriented, on the issue of "autonomy and control," we can find a different level of insight in the colonial analogy. The students often speak in such abrasive and abusive terms that "civil men" dismiss them out of hand, and either misunderstand them or, having understood, malign them. I am myself a Macaulay product. Accordingly, these men of letters are attuned to listen more carefully when I speak.

The analogy takes both a personal and a political turn. Just like a disgruntled and even outraged colonial elite that spent long years in London or Paris, while I can try to help break the yoke of oppression that lets mace be sprayed in paddy wagons, my "Macaulay education" has ill-equipped me or any other person in my general position to do the specific job that must now be done.

That does not mean that I despair of my utility, for I have never accepted the artificial and mindless separation of ideas and action. There is something fundamentally important about the way problems are isolated by the ideas chosen to characterize them. I see a need for approaching and formulating the problem of higher education of Third World students that orients toward their local communities (read ghetto, read colony, read whatever you like, but know that one-third of this state is living now in communities isolated by color and culture, isolated from the Western whites).

I do see the need for Third World student leadership to emerge that is not already "too far gone" down the road to Macaulay's victimization. Too far gone, that is, to be given a role in carving out new criteria of excellence. The Western-trained colonial elite will only set up a new college based on the one model they have "for too long" experienced.

From an article by Professor W. Arthur Lewis, Department of Economics, Princeton University, in The New York Times, *May 11, 1969.*

The Road to the Top Is Through Higher Education—Not Black Studies

The road to the top in the great American corporations and other institutions is through higher education. Scientists, research workers, engineers, accountants, lawyers, financial administrators, presidential advisers—all these people are recruited from the university. And indeed nearly all of the top people are taken from a very small number of colleges—from not more than some 50 or 60 of the 2,000 degree-granting institutions in the United States. The Afro-American could not make it to the top so long as he was effectively excluded from this small number of select institutions. The breakthrough of the Afro-American into these colleges is therefore absolutely fundamental to the larger economic strategy of black power.

I do not mean to suggest that the most important black strategy is to get more blacks into the best colleges. Probably the greatest contribution to black advancement would be to break the trade-union barriers which keep our people out of apprenticeships in the building and printing trades, and prevent our upgrading or promotion in other industries. The trade unions are the black man's greatest enemy in the United States. The number of people who would be at the top, if we had our numerical share of the top, would be small. Our greatest task, in terms of numbers, is to con-

quer the middle—getting into skilled posts, foremen's posts, su-
pervisory and white-collar jobs—through better use of apprenticeships, of the high schools and of technical colleges. I am going to
discuss the universities not because this is numerically important,
but partly because it has become so controversial, and partly because if we did conquer the top it would make much easier the
conquering of the middle—both in our own minds, and in other
people's minds, by altering our young people's image of themselves and of what they can achieve.

What can the good white college do for its black students that
Howard or Lincoln or Fisk cannot do? It can open the road into
the top jobs. It can do this only by giving our people the kinds of
skills and the kind of polish which are looked for by people filling
top jobs. To put it in unpopular language, it can train them to become top members of the establishment.

If it is wrong for young blacks to be trained for the top jobs in
the big corporations, for top jobs in the government service, for
ambassadorships, for the editorial staff of *The New York Times*
and so on—then there is little point in sending them to the best
white colleges. On the contrary, if what one wants is people
trained to live and work in black neighborhoods, they will do
much better to go to the black colleges, of which there are, after
all, more than 100, which know much better than Yale or Princeton or Dartmouth what the problems of black neighborhoods are,
and how people should be trained to handle them. The point
about the best white colleges is that they are a part, not of the
neighborhood side of American life, but of the integrated part of
American life, training people to run the economy and the administration in the integrated part of the day before 5 P.M.

But how can it be wrong for young Afro-Americans to be
trained to hold superior positions in the integrated working world
outside the neighborhood when in fact the neighborhood cannot
provide work for even a half of its people? Whether we like it or
not, most Afro-Americans *have* to work in the integrated world,
and if we do not train for superior positions there, all that will
happen is what happens now—that we shall be crowded into the
worst-paid jobs.

If one grasps this point, that these 50 colleges are the gateway
to the superior jobs, then the current attitudes of some of our
black leaders to these colleges is not a little bewildering. In its

most extreme form, what is asked is that the college should set aside a special part of itself which is to be the black part. There will be a separate building for black studies, and separate dormitories and living accommodations for blacks. There will be separate teachers, all black, teaching classes open only to blacks. The teachers are to be chosen by the students, and will for the most part be men whom no African or Indian or Chinese university would recognize as scholars, or be willing to hire as teachers.

Doubtless some colleges under militant pressure will give in to this, but I do not see what Afro-Americans will gain thereby. Employers will not hire the students who emerge from this process, and their usefulness even in black neighborhoods will be minimal.

I yield to none in thinking that every respectable university should give courses on African life and on Afro-American life, which are of course two entirely different subjects, and I am very anxious to see such courses developed. It is, however, my hope that they will be attended mostly by white students, and that the majority of black students will find more important uses for their time; that they may attend one or two such courses, but will reject any suggestion that black studies must be the major focus of their programs.

The principal argument for forcing black students to spend a great deal of their time in college studying African and Afro-American anthropology, history, languages and literature is that they need such studies to overcome their racial inferiority complex. I am not impressed by this argument. The youngster discovers that he is black around the age of 6 or 7; from then on, the whites he meets, the books he reads, and the situation of the Negro in America all combine to persuade him that he is an inferior species of Homo sapiens. By the time he is 14 or 15 he has made up his mind on this one way or the other. Nothing that the college can do, after he reaches 18 or 19, is going to have much effect on his basic personality. To expect the colleges to eradicate the inferiority complexes of young black adults is to ask the impossible. And to expect this to come about by segregating black students in black studies under inferior teachers suggests some deficiency of thought.

Perhaps I am wrong about this. The proposition is essentially that the young black has been brainwashed into thinking himself inferior, so now he must spend four years in some place where he will be re-brainwashed into thinking himself equal. But the prospect that the 50 best colleges in the United States can be forced to take on his re-brainwashing operation is an idle dream. Those who are now putting all their energies into working for this are doomed to disappointment.

We are knocking our heads against the wrong wall. Every black student should learn some Afro-American history, and study various aspects of his people's culture, but the place for him to do this compulsorily is in the high school, and the best age to start this seriously is even earlier, perhaps around the age of 10. By the time the student gets to a first-rate college he should be ready for business—for the business of acquiring the skills which he is going to be able to use, whether in his neighborhood, or in the integrated economy. Let the clever young black go to a university to study engineering, medicine, chemistry, economics, law, agriculture and other subjects which are going to be of value to him and his people. And let the clever white go to college to read black novels, to learn Swahili, and to record the exploits of Negro heroes of the past. They are the ones to whom this will come as an eye-opener.

This, incidentally, is very much what happens in African universities. Most of these have well-equipped departments of African studies, which are popular with visiting whites, but very few African students waste their time (as they see it) on such studies, when there is so much to be learned for the jobs they will have to do. The attitude of Africans to their past conforms to the historian's observation that only decadent peoples, on the way down, feel an urgent need to mythologize and live in their past. A vigorous people, on the way up, has visions of its future, and cares next to nothing about its past.

My attitude toward the role of black studies in the education of college blacks derives not only from an unconventional view of what is to be gained therefrom, but also from an unconventional view of the purpose of going to college. The United States is the only country in the world which thinks that the purpose of going to college is to be educated. Everywhere else one goes to high school to be educated, but goes to college to be trained for one's life work. In the United States serious training does not begin until one reaches graduate school at the age of 22. Before that, one spends four years in college being educated—that is to say, spending 12 weeks getting some tidbits on religion, 12 weeks learning French, 12 weeks seeing whether the history professor is stimulating, 12 weeks seeking entertainment from the economics professor, 12 weeks confirming that one is not going to be able to master calculus, and so on.

If the purpose of going to college is to be educated, and serious study will not begin until one is 22, one might just as well perhaps spend the four years reading black novels, studying black history and learning to speak Fanti. But I do not think that American blacks can afford this luxury. I think our young people ought to get down to the business of serious preparation for their life work as soon after 18 as they can.

And I also note, incidentally, that many of the more intelligent white students are now in revolt against the way so many colleges fritter away their precious years in meaningless peregrination from subject to subject between the ages of 18 and 22.

Any Afro-American who wishes to become a specialist in black studies, or to spend some of his time on such work, should be absolutely free to do so. But I hope that, of those students who get the opportunity to attend the 50 best colleges, the proportion who want to specialize in black studies may, in their interest and that of the black community, turn out to be rather small, in comparison with our scientists, or engineers, accountants, economists or doctors.

CHAPTER 12

The Black University

The demand for Black Studies in white universities has had a parallel in predominantly Negro colleges: the demand for a Black university. "Black body, white mind," issued by *Student Voice,* a Black publication in Atlanta, accused Negro educational institutions of having "embraced the concept of white supremacy," and called on such institutions to "break out of the mental barriers posed by Western (the U.S. in particular) education." Professor Edgar Beckham, speaking for the National Association of Afro-American Education, envisioned the Black university as an institution that would have both "autonomy" and "committed responsiveness to the Black community."

At Fisk University, Black students drew up a statement setting forth the basic principles of the Black university, defining it as "an institution structured, controlled, and administered by Black people, devoting itself to the total cultural needs of the Black community."

The Trustees at Howard University, faced with similar demands, were unmoved.* They refused to change what they saw to be Howard's historic mission to stand against discrimination.

---

* For text of student demands, see Appendix A, Volume II.

Article in Student Voice, *a publication of the Student Non-violent Coordinating Committee, Atlanta, Ga., 1967.*

Black Body, White Mind

"Cooperation—Not Competition: Community—Not the Individual."
From Poolhall Address Delivered at It, Mississippi, February 2, 1960.
"Keep your cue-stick chalked."
—*Junebug Jabbo Jones*

Education, as it is now constituted, is a disruptive force to the needs of Afro-Americans and the Afro-American community. To focus on this thesis, it is necessary to discuss the beginnings and history of Negro education.

The first schools black people attended were slave-breaking schools where black men, women, and children would have their spirits broken in order to make them into obedient servants of their white masters. The history of our education in the United States cannot be separated from this fact.

In Africa, Asia, etc., education grew out of what people had to do in order to survive and the need for one generation to pass on to the next the knowledge acquired through experience. But in America where white men and black men met, this was not the case. In America, some men were taught to be masters and others were taught to be slaves.

Mass education in the United States grew out of the need to rationalize racism and exploitation in the United States. It is important to understand this if we are to begin to effectively deal with the problems of education we face today.

The first Negro colleges were set up for the half-breed or "illegitimate" children of white slave owners. The white man understood then, as he does now, the necessity of splintering the Afro-American community. The most effective mechanism for affecting this has been the taught and bred-in orientation toward a white culture projected as superior.

There are many historical examples of how Negro educational institutions have abdicated their responsibilities to the Afro-American community and embraced the concept of white supremacy. During its early days, Howard University required you to submit a picture of yourself before you were admitted. Of course, the picture established your color credentials. "If white, all right; if black, get back"; along with the "palm test"—the palm of your hand had to come damn close to the color of your face in order for you to get in.

At Fisk University, the Fisk Jubilee Singers were "happy and satisfied" educated darkies in the finest of white cultural traditions, and to this day are acclaimed for establishing much of the prominence and validity of Fisk University. They sang before Queen Victoria of Britain (which at that time was the major colonial force oppressing our colonial brothers and sisters around the world—"the sun never sets on the British Empire," "take up the white man's burden," and that sort of rot)—and were acclaimed great because they sang by white standards (four part harmonies, rounded tones, and proper diction), and didn't pat their feet, shout, and get happy—ya'll know, embarrass the race.

Booker T. Washington and his policy of accommodation is another example of Negro education. Tuskegee Institute was attempting to provide Negroes with "industrial education." At the beginning of the 20th century, the industrialists who financed Booker T. knew industrial education was not going to do the black man any good. It was outdated and could only keep the black man in tasks of menial, servile labor. Today, there is a statue of Booker T. on Tuskegee's campus in which he is supposedly raising the veil from over the head of a young Negro who is kneeling. At least some people say that he is raising the veil; probably he is lowering it. But, supposing that he is raising it, that statue stands as a symbol of the fact of Booker T.'s acceptance of the concept of Afro-Americans' inferiority—that Afro-Americans had to be raised and uplifted to the level of whites. In other words, Booker T. was a white supremacist. (An insidious example of the white war to annihilate feelings of blackness is found in the number of Negro schools named Booker T. Washington.)

At every level the history of our education has been motion toward white standards of culture, or a white posture, which was somehow supposed to be superior. Educated Negroes were set up as a separate class, the model toward which the community should aspire in order to be considered "civilized" or on the way to progress. Negro progress is measured by its closeness to total imitation of the white model.

Another example of the orientation toward whiteness is reflected in the orientation of freshmen males at Howard University. On the first night of residence, freshmen males are gathered at the top of Drew Hall and warned of the dangers of the surrounding community of northwest Washington. "Block boys" beat up Howard men, rape girls, and steal, the students are told. They are further told that if they are to go out at night (to be avoided if possible), to try not to go out alone. Avoid community parties. Always, the posture of the University is how to defend yourself from that savage, wild uncivilized community. They are saying, in fact, "you're better than those niggers. You might get your picture in *Ebony Magazine.*"

This is a double tragedy because 1) Howard University students are subject to all the above dangers. Howard is an alien in what could be a responsive community; and 2) given what it is oriented to, it seems impossible for Howard to change itself in order to become relevant to the needs of the Afro-American community around it. Therefore, it stands as a source of frustration in the eyes of the Afro-American community that surrounds it subject to the hostility that flows from what it (Howard) denies.

Howard is typical of Negro schools. To describe them in terms of what they really are is to call them islands of whiteness in a sea of blackness. These schools relate to the white community and feed individual Negroes into the white community. That is, they teach these individuals how to step on the backs of their black brothers, "up" towards whitey, and/or act as a buffer and transmit the white message and culture into the Afro-American communities. In a real and profound sense, Negro schools are only important as they relate to the white community. They tell the Afro-American people that you are inferior; that you have nothing to offer; that you are not worth giving anything to. Negro educational institutions are very much vulnerable to questions from Afro-Americans as to why they should be allowed to exist if they continue to play such a destructive role in our community.

If we accept the position that Negro schools are white-oriented and geared not to the needs of Afro-Americans but to the needs of white supremacy, then to examine Negro education is also to examine, in part, the nature of education in this country. The idea of education as a magic key that unlocks the door, that gives you entrance into the chamber, that has the buttons that run things, is a myth. The education that we get is designed to keep us in our place. For instance, in October, when Stokely Carmichael was invited to speak at Fisk as a guest speaker by students involved in the honors program, the white people of Nashville put pressure on acting Fisk President James Lawson to cancel the engagement. Knuckling under to pressure, Lawson cancelled the engagement on the supposition that Carmichael's presence would be disruptive to the campus and the city of Nashville.

We have to understand that education is exclusive. The persons who are educated or the children of the persons who are educated have the best chance of being educated. That circle does not expand very much. In white society, class is important to this exclusiveness. In the Negro community, caste and class are key to this exclusiveness. And, as you know, those closest to white are of the highest caste.

Education as a key in running things in the country is also a myth. The country is run informally, and the first requirement is not a college degree but a white skin. How many presidents of major corporations have you seen advertised for? They are bred. They meet certain social, as well as educational requirements. If you have a college degree, it is because it's required socially these days. And us scuffling niggers is just out here, believing all the stuff that the man says about "get a degree and work your way up," like the brother in Ralph Ellison's *Invisible Man* who on seeing the contents of an envelope given him by the president of what might be Tuskegee, saw: "Keep this nigger running."

The motion of the so-called civil rights movement around the question of education has been on the assumption that Negro schools were inferior in this society. The facilities were poor for the teachers. The teachers were poor for the students. The students were culturally inferior. Finally in 1954, the U. S. Supreme Court decided that us porr cullud folks could go to the white superior schools. They did it for us, they say. However, in many respects the 1954 Supreme Court decision marks a new stage in the United States program of International Pacification. Faced with a world-wide struggle against western imperialism, the U. S. had to project an appearance of resolving the contradiction between its claims as a representative of "democracy" and "freedom" and its domestic policy of racial exploitation. Needless to say, the hypocrisy of that move is reflected today in both the Vietnam war and the situation of Afro-Americans.

The white schools decided to integrate with "all deliberate speed." That is, about 4 or 5 years apart. We were supposed to be most appreciative of this opportunity opened up to us through the "good" graces of white society. Hallelujah, we could all go to white schools.

We began to feel as if we had to push as many Negroes as we could into these schools, in order that they get the information that we felt whites were getting. This was vitally necessary to functioning in white society. The whole Afro-American community was kept in motion, directing our energies toward the responsibilities necessary to allow individuals from our community to function in the white man's society.

Several things happened in regard to this integration effort. There was massive resistance, especially in the south and in the north when we came in masses. Formerly all-white schools became all black. We began to realize that if we ever wanted to integrate with the whites, we would have to chase them all over the country. The south, in many instances, put up physical resistance. In order to *make it easier on the whites* in some northern areas, it was proposed that a few black students be bussed out of the ghetto before dark. Sort of a daytime whiteness attempt. And in the south, we were asked to ignore spit in our faces, mobs around our children, and bombs thrown at our homes.

On the college level, the effort of Negro colleges is to become as "good" as white and, therefore, schools like Harvard, Yale, etc. are being used to evaluate the needs of Negro education. One result of these kinds of evaluations is that the president of Howard University has recommended that within five years or ten years, Howard become 60% white in order to become more able to compete with the white schools. In essence, he was saying that it was impossible for a Negro school—that is, a school for those of African descent, a black school, to measure up to white schools; therefore, these schools must be flooded with whites, whose presence, by definition, would bring superiority.

Another development in regard to Negro colleges is the concept of pairing. Princeton takes responsibility for Miles, the University of Michigan for Tuskegee, Brown for Tougaloo. These schools would correct standards, design a better curriculum in terms of national educational standards. Whiten them. Brothers and Sisters, "First there is a tragedy, then there is a farce."

The deep crisis in education that we face today flows from a much broader and profound political problem that pervades every segment of the black community. In a phrase, we blacks control none of the resources and institutions in our communities.

And until we begin to move to exercise this control over our lives, anything else is an exercise in futility.

Education consists mainly of two factors: indoctrination to a certain point of view (e.g., the slaves were civilized by being brought here; the Indians were savages and destroying them was taming the west); and the accumulation of factual information (e.g., the sun is in the sky; water is wet). However, our indoctrination in many respects determines what is factual. For example, you would laugh if we said that England wasn't discovered until the first time Sékou Touré, President of the African country of Guinea, first set foot there, but we accept the idea of Columbus' discovery of America, despite the fact that people were here to meet him.

Columbus, a poor navigator at best, accidentally got here trying to get to India, and he died thinking he had made it to India.

We are only educated in our schools, but the white attitude also breaks into the Afro-American community through television, radio, movies, and magazines (both white and white-aspiring— dig *Ebony*), through advertising such as Nadinola, Silky Straight, and the white knight that drives out dirt. In fact, we are overwhelmed.

It is safe to say that every device for indoctrination including institutional education is used to lock us mentally within the white prison of western civilization.

If we are to survive, we must break the chains that bind our minds and bodies within the prison of western civilization. We must, therefore, build within our communities educational institutions that allow us to locate and utilize in our own interests the resources that we have as a people. This effort, which we must all commit ourselves to, will be resisted, as it has been historically by this country and her sister countries of the West whose commitment to the protection of white supremacy prevents an understanding of human rights and needs.

We want to begin now to break out of a very negative concept of ourselves and of our possibilities taught us as a result of our American captivity. We should understand that while there is world-wide oppression and exploitation along color lines, there is strength for us in the struggle against the oppression. For we, the oppressed, represent 87% of the world's population.

We have outlined a description of white cultural and educational domination and many of you must be asking by now, how do we deal with this?

How do we move as Afro-Americans to meet our educational needs? Let us begin to think of a school, international in its scope, yet parochial in that it is aimed at the needs of Afro-Americans colonized within the United States.

The thrust of such a school would be to break out of the mental barriers posed by western (the U.S., in particular) education. There would be a positive and a direct effort to relate to Africa, Asia, and Latin America. Language as a basic communication tool would be very important. Emphasis would be put on these languages: Swahili and French in terms of Africa; Spanish in terms of Latin America; Chinese and Japanese in terms of Asia. Coupled with this language learning process would be travel to countries in these areas to begin to break through the overwhelming mental effect of a life within the American society whose every function is controlled by whites.

We need to begin to conceive of our community in a different light. Instead of a place to escape from, we must now see our life, work, labor, and love in terms of that community. With this different attitude toward our community in terms of our life work, we must begin to get specific technical skills directly relevant to the Afro-American community. Specific technical skills gotten by individuals should be seen as community resources rather than individual profit; for the true profit of the individual flows from the profit of his community. Medical care and health, for example, would be organized as community programs, not as lucrative private practices. Technicians would see as part of their work, the organizing and encouragement of their communities to tap its own resources in its own interests.

For the final analysis, education is not a gathering of intellectual skills, but a preparation for participation in living; and life is lived with people and community.

Integral to the purpose of this kind of school is the shedding of our inability to understand in anything other than western cultural standards. The West is not *the* culture, but *a* culture—one of many and in many ways more primitive than most.

We, as Afro-Americans, must choose on which side of the color line we stand. We have, in fact, only one choice. The choice is made by the color of our skins.

LET US NOW PREPARE.

From a speech by Professor Edgar F. Beckham, Black assistant professor of German, Wesleyan University, to the College Entrance Examination Board as part of a program on "The Black Agenda for Higher Education" during its annual meeting, October 1968.

What We Mean by "The Black University"

The black university, as it was conceived by a task force at the Chicago meeting of the National Association of Afro-American Education last June, can be the instrument for neutralizing the tensions which have characterized deliberations on black education by black people. It can be the instrument for merging long- and short-range goals, for finding unity in diversity, for establishing an educational model to serve both as a conceptual framework and as a concrete object for action. The black university, as the task force saw it, will be a center for the production of new knowledge about black reality and a major device for the dissemination of that knowledge. It will celebrate the legitimacy and the worth of the experience of black people and will incorporate the expertise created by that experience into programs designed to educate black people about themselves. It will be a research center, a teaching center, and a focal point for black community organization. But its most comprehensive function will be the creative one of generating the intellectual apparatus, the new values, concepts, and criteria, the models, the policies, and the procedural guidelines which must inform and support the black man's new perception of himself.

The black university is when black people join together and do something profoundly educational for themselves. The black university is when black students and educators reject the conditioning of white America and resolve to recreate themselves. The black university is when the community of black teachers and learners weaves into the fabric of black education the ties that join it to black people everywhere.

There are a number of immediate objectives of black education which were discussed in Chicago. I'm going to run through them very quickly because we're somewhat short of time. But I want to preface that list with one or two remarks. Since the black university is the primary goal of educational planning in the black community, all interim planning for the alleviation of current problems should be based, as is the black university itself, on the principles of autonomy and community commitment. In other words, our immediate objectives should remain consistent with our long-range goals.

We know, for instance, that at present, virtually all black students in the United States are being educated in an environment which is hostile to their development as members of the black community. They are being trained to participate in a society to which they do not fully belong, and are alienated from the people to whom they owe primary allegiance. That situation has to be altered so that rapidly increasing numbers of skilled black people will be available not only for the building of the black university but for the revitalization of the entire black community. Alterations and modifications are admittedly revisionist in intent, whereas the black university is a revolutionary concept. But the presence of so many thousands of black students in institutions which are not black dictates that revolution and revision proceed simultaneously. And they can, provided that all attempts at revision are informed by determined adherence to the revolutionary goals of black autonomy and committed responsiveness to the black community.

In discussing the specific purposes of black education, purposes which would be answered by the black university, we talked in Chicago about the overall purpose—namely, to liberate and realize collective black potential and to establish the relevance of black potential to the reality of all black people.

We discussed ways to fulfill a number of kinds of potential— economic potential through technical training, political and social potential through training for social change, intellectual and cultural potential through the development of the critical faculties and creative abilities of black people. The outline which was developed in Chicago was by no means exhaustive or comprehensive, but it does represent the ideas which were presented by members of the task force working on that particular problem.

We also talked in Chicago about a number of structural considerations of the black university. The primary characteristic of the black university's development will, of course, be change—creative change—which will parallel the evolution of the black community. But if the assumption holds true that the black university represents symbolically all black efforts at education, then we have an incipient black university now in our present institutions, though it is decidedly ill-formed and in serious need of corrective treatment.

There are a number of treatments which I'd like to suggest, and I think that these are particularly important for people who are associated either with predominantly white institutions or those who are associated with Negro institutions that have not yet committed themselves to the black community and its development.

In the area of admissions policies and procedures, there is a need for complete review and revision of admissions policies, including the development of new procedures for recruiting, revised admissions criteria, and improved follow-up programs. One of the key recommendations that was made in Chicago was for the inclusion of black people on the staffs and committees which select students for admission, with the aim of having black people (black students, black faculty, and black administrators) exert controlling influence in the selection process. Such control would illustrate the black university as an implicit goal of all black educational efforts. The black university begins to exist whenever and wherever black people control educational policy, process, and procedures.

I'm going to skip over some of the other specifics and come to what I feel for the College Board is the primary consideration: that is the curriculum. Last spring at a symposium held at Yale University sponsored by the Black Student Alliance, four phases in the development of black curriculums were discussed and outlined. First, blackening of existing courses by including material related to the black experience; second, the addition of black courses; third, the creation of black studies programs; and fourth, the development of major research efforts to fill the gaps in our knowledge of black people. It cannot be emphasized enough, I feel, that the same principle of autonomy and community commitment apply throughout the discussion of the black university. Old courses should be blackened, and new courses designed by black people. They should be taught by black people, and they should be relevant to the needs of the black community. But it is precisely in the area of curriculum development that we find the only point of possible conflict between long- and short-range goals, between the model of the black university and our current revisionist efforts at our respective institutions.

The problem is in the area of staffing, or put another way, in the efficient exploitation of available resources. Simply stated, if the black community spreads its best teachers and scholars in token fashion among predominantly white and uncommitted Negro institutions of higher learning, we will not be able to implement the concentrated and intensified programs of education and research which the black university needs. I think that a case in point is in this morning's *New York Times* which reported that Cornell University is seeking the nation's best black teachers and scholars.

Without being privy to the program as written by Cornell and having only read *The New York Times* article (although I don't want to suggest that my opinion of *The New York Times* is as low, let us say, as Mr. Wallace's). I would still suggest, just off the top of my head, that neither Cornell University, nor Harvard, nor Yale, nor Princeton, nor Columbia, nor Wesleyan University where I teach—none of these places—is the place where the best black teachers and scholars should be. Not at this time. In fact, I can't conceive of a time when they should be there. The solution which I would propose is a compromise made necessary by a realistic appraisal of current needs. There is simply not enough room in the Negro institutions for the thousands of black students currently enrolled in predominantly white colleges and universities. Because of the large numbers of black students in predominantly white institutions, black curricular programs do have to be developed there. But the draining off of black educational resources has to be held to a minimum.

The key to the compromise, I think, is inter-institutional cooperation which would involve not only a sharing of teaching staffs but the sharing of students as well. It would not be in the best interests of the black university for such institutions as Yale University, Wesleyan University, University of Connecticut, University of Hartford, Connecticut College for Women, and Trinity College, all of which are located within a few miles of each other, to establish individual programs in black literature, black art, African languages, and black social sciences. Such institutions should be encouraged to divide the educational labor and share the educational problems. I really don't feel at this point that it's necessary to go into any more detail on that. I think that for these institutions it's a matter of getting together and coordinating the efforts over as large a geographical area as possible.

I hope that these remarks have given you some insight into the way many black people, certainly a large percentage of the thousand people who attended the Chicago conference, look at the black university, at its potential, and at the variety of ways in which it might be realized.

A letter to the editor of Liberator *from Black Students at Fisk University, published February 1970.*

Basic Concepts of the Black University

We, the students of Fisk University, have finally come to the realization that in order to bring about a major change in our university's philosophy, direction, and its structure, we must unite our own forces and pool our resources.

Our objective is to make Fisk a *Black University*. Education at Fisk University should be geared toward preparing its students for participation in the Black community. It should not only provide us with skills but with Black consciousness which will bring about commitment on the part of Fisk students to work with and for Black people.

With this in mind, we hereby state the basic concepts of the Black University:

(a) A Black University is an institution structured, controlled, and administered by Black people, devoting itself to the total cultural needs of the Black community. A Black University is where all departmental and administrative heads are Black. (Black people are people of African descent: they are people who work positively and without equivocation for Black liberation.)

During slavery, Black people were forbidden to hold meetings or engage in any functions, social, religious, or educational, which were not controlled or watched by white people, for the sole reason that progress for Black people meant loss of control over Black people by the white man. The white man has sought control of Black people since they were captives; the white man sought to obtain free labor for his plantations, and now he drafts Black men to fight in illegal wars. There are no Catholic leaders in Jewish organizations or institutions; Black people do not lead Polish organizations or institutions. Therefore, there can be no white leaders in Black organizations or institutions.

(b) A Black University is an institution set up to deal with the skills necessary for Black existence. There is a need for knowledge of chemistry, physics, mathematics, biology, micro-biology, engineering, medicine, industry, social sciences, art, drama, etc. All skills acquired for Black existence can be used anyplace where *human beings* exist. *Blackness* means *humanism.*

(c) A Black University is an institution that addresses itself completely to Black liberation, identifying all Black people as Africans under the ideological concept of Pan-Africanism. The concept of Pan-Africanism is an ideological definition predicating Black unity. It says, in essence, that all people of African descent are one. They are one in their ancestry, and in their struggle against White-European aggression and repression. Pan-Africanism is an idea that emphasizes respect for human dignity and human personality. It rejects white racism and Black chauvinism.

(d) A Black University is an institutional structure that addresses itself completely to Black liberation. In a Black University there is no problem of accreditation. Such a university will be functional just as Brandeis University, Yeshiva University, London University, and the University of Paris are, all of which are run and controlled by white people. An accredited institution must have scholars recognized in all disciplines. Here at Fisk University, and around the nation, we have Black scholars who are recognized and accredited. Therefore, the question of accreditation is not an issue in a Black University.

In a Black University there will be divisions equivalent to what are presently called departments at Fisk University. In these divisions there will be majors and graduate programs and professional programs.

A Black University is open to all people who subscribe positively to Black liberation as defined by Pan-Africanism.

Statement of the Board of Trustees of Howard University, October 22, 1968.

A Policy Statement on the Black University

The faculty, students, employees, alumni and friends of Howard University are entitled to a clear-cut delineation of the purposes and aims of the University at all times, but particularly at this time when there is so much discussion of Howard as a black university.

To that end, the Board of Trustees of Howard University makes the following policy statement:

Howard University was founded primarily for the education of disadvantaged black people and throughout its history has sought to fulfill that purpose. It still intends to carry it out. But nothing in Howard's history or its Charter will support a black university, if by that is meant a university operated by black people alone and serving only black students. In fact, the first four students at Howard were white and for one hundred years, the University has never discriminated against persons on account of race or color, and it does not now intend to do so. This is not only the policy of the institution, but it is also the law of the land.

Howard University is not only dedicated to the teaching of black people but also has a deep commitment to the study and teaching of the history, culture, and life of the black people in the United States and Africa. It is a university determined to teach pride in the black man and his multifaceted achievements, in his music and culture, and in himself as a personality.

In any sense of exclusiveness along racial lines, or of an abandonment of our rich history, or of restrictions of freedom of speech and association, Howard is not destined to be a black university. Not only is this contrary to our history, but it would not be the exercise of good judgment. The insistence by a minority (or even a majority) of students for the establishment of an exclusive black university at Howard is error. It is too late in history and in the structure of our general society to establish such goals or aims. The promotion of knowledge about the black people, African history and culture, and the contemporary role of disadvantaged people is not antithetical to the educational enterprise; but an exclusive concern and/or control in education by color restriction in language and meaning is a forfeiting of the long struggle to achieve entrance into the mainstream.

Certainly we agree with the idea that we should increase our services to and our interests in the black man and his problems. We should seek in our research to aid him in financing his own community, in rehabilitation of the ghetto, in improvement of his schools, in making life safer for him and in moving him into the mainstream of American business activity. But at the same time we must continue to carry on the other parts of the role of a university—teaching and doing research in a non-racially discriminating fashion and setting.

The University is firmly of the opinion that we are the last people in America who should espouse restriction on thought or speech. Within this framework, we believe Howard's next one hundred years will be greater and more constructive than its first one hundred years.

CHAPTER 13

Black Identity
in the White University

One of the ironies of the contemporary American scene, as many have observed, is that, at the very moment when many whites are at last giving nominal acceptance to the ideal of integration, Black Americans are now asserting the need for their own autonomous cultural institutions.

But Blacks are not completely agreed on the issue of cultural identity. At Columbia, two students, Oliver Henry and William W. Sales, Jr. debated the matter publicly in the student newspaper, the *Columbia Daily Spectator.* Henry styled himself a "Negro student" and criticized those who called themselves "Black students." He questioned their methods, their goals, their style. Sales, a "Black student," answered Henry sharply, calling his arguments a "veiled apology" for the "Black bourgeoisie."

The question of Black identity has arisen over certain symbolic actions. At Purdue University, for example, the issue was posed when Black cheerleaders gave the "Black salute" during the playing of the national anthem at a basketball game. The Purdue administration was outraged and threatened discipline. We include a column from the *Purdue Exponent* defending the Black salute, a statement from a Black Purdue student, and a denunciatory letter to the editor by another student.

The chapter—and this part of the volume—ends with a round-up discussion at Yale, where four members of the Black Student Alliance were interviewed by the *Yale Alumni Magazine* in early 1969.

Article by Oliver Henry, student, in Connection, *the magazine supplement of the* Columbia Daily Spectator, *student newspaper, Columbia University, March 11, 1969.*

A Negro Student's Observations on Blacks

Unrest and discontent characterize Negro student communities on campuses throughout this nation. The unrest manifests itself both internally and externally; the discontent stems from the conditions in which many of these students have been forced to live. For today, the majority of Negro collegians come from ghettos, and it makes little difference whether the specific ghetto was Bedford-Stuyvesant, Watts or the south side of Chicago. These students know from first-hand experience the world of the ghetto which, to a large degree, represents the life of most Negro Americans: poor educational institutions, poor health facilities, poor transportation services, poor everything. The shadow of the ghetto world follows many to the college campus. In their new situation—in fact, in their new life—some find a new freedom. Yet at the same time, most contemporary Negro students do not wish to forget their past while merging into the university scene. Indeed, many use their new freedom with its consequent permissiveness in furthering actions ostensibly directed toward so-called "black liberation."

In many cases, these actions are directed against real grievances and, whether or not recognized, symbolize an indictment of the whole structure of American society, a structure which has until recently countenanced the conditions in which most Negro Americans live. Many students have grown tired of this society and of its institutions. And, for many, the college or university represents but another "white racist" institution whose real function is the "destruction of the black mind." And the campus with its tradition of tolerance, of free inquiry, of personal freedom, provides a setting in which many students can engage in activities, formulate "plans for the liberation of black people." Thus many Negro students who, only recently freed of the confines of the ghetto, with the opportunity of a lifetime before them, suddenly become "Black students." Their goal is no longer academic success or a broad-gauged college experience or even post-college economic advancement; for, as black students, they see these goals as but tranquilizers, as binds in which, if they allow themselves to become entangled, "whitey" can continue to control their lives and through them the lives of all black people.

The new black students reject academic success, liberal education, and economic advancement as significant goals of their college years. And these blacks join, or are converted to, a movement whose goal is "the liberation of black people by any means necessary." These are strong words, but they are usually pronounced by those without power to make them meaningful, for those with real power do not have to engage in bravado.

Having rejected "whitey's" allurements yet still within the university, black students become frustrated. For the real struggle aimed at improving conditions for the masses of Negro Americans exists outside the university. But the attainment of those skills which, in the long run, might be beneficial in the continuing effort have been cast aside by black students as meaningless, without merit, unworthy of their time and energy. They see standards of merit and achievement as irrelevant both to themselves and to the lives of all black people. Therefore, instead of wasting time studying mathematics, chemistry, European History or English, they devote themselves wholly to Fanon, Carmichael, Malcolm, and to meetings of the black students' organization where they plan for the revolution: "It will come tomorrow if we only believe, plan, discuss, and demand enough."

But black students soon realize that the real revolution exists not on the campus but in the larger society. Thus, in order to be relevant to their people, they must wage a form of revolution on campus. They do so in their "demands" for Afro-American Studies Programs wholly controlled by blacks, black faculty and coaches, black student lounges, black dorms, "soul food," and quotas for black student admissions. Their revolution is against the university in which they are supposedly forced to adhere to "white standards." And this confrontation commences with incendiary rhetoric, the issuing of non-negotiable "demands," and the seizure of university buildings. Victory lies in the capitulation by those in power to their demands, for such represents a victory against white society, one which hopefully will lead to a better life for Negro Americans.

Perhaps these black students are right; but some students, Negro students, today a minority, question the methods, the goals, and the style of their erstwhile brethren.

Negro students believe in academic success, in individual merit, achievement, and responsibility, for they realize that those more fortunate must prepare themselves for the continuing revolution that exists outside the ivied walls of academe. These students see the way toward improvement of the terrible conditions in which the masses of Negro Americans live through "learning just what white students are learning." Their revolutionary commitment is not based solely on an emotional reaction to the Negroes' plight, but rather on an emotion tempered by intellect. The continuing struggle must and will be waged, but, before even the possibility of victory, weapons must be stockpiled. And Negro students see trained minds as the vital weapon, as the real resource that will aid in making life better for the majority of Negro Americans.

This view stems not from a movement, but from a sense of personal outrage and responsibility. And though many aid in countless ways the advancement of their less fortunate brethren, Negro students know where the real revolution lies. They see college as an opportunity in which they can gain the knowledge and skills necessary for meaningful participation in the ongoing struggle. And they are prepared to meet white students—indeed, white society—on its terms because that society will determine whether the revolution takes on a relatively peaceful tone or descends into an awful violence which can only mean doom for Negro Americans.

Thus Negro students work for success measured in terms of so-called "white standards" because these are the standards of a society that their people, as much as any others, helped to build. These students will not be forced out. Negro students desire the transformation of American society from one of limited opportunities for some and the sky for others to one in which all men will have the opportunity to become all that they can, regardless of pigmentation.

In this light, with this view of the revolutionary goal, Negro students question the current black happenings, for they see many of these as counterproductive to the achievement of an equal opportunity society . . . if in fact a society of equality of opportunity, one without delimitations and restrictions imposed by color, remains the goal to which black students are committed. Negro students desire the end of the color line; and thus they reject color as the criterion for judgment of any man. These students question the establishment of admissions quotas, dorms, and curriculum based on race. Negro students know that Negro Americans have been subjected to the "awful shadow of the veil" for too long. And they view many of the "demands" made by black students as representing a new segregation, a revivification of the color line, a new veil to opportunity.

While black students demand separate Afro-American History courses in university curricula, Negro students work for the inclusion of the Negro in American History where he, as an American, belongs. They question the establishment of courses which would further segregate the Negro American from the mainstream of American life and thought. In the whole area of curriculum, Negro students want no "academic ghettos."

While black students seize buildings and demand separate living and eating facilities, Negro students urge that students, all students, be allowed to live and eat as they choose; and further that university officials refrain from making concessions to blacks which would result in the creation of an atmosphere in which Negro students might be forced because of social pressure into making "choices" which could only limit, only divert them from achieving those skills without which no revolution is possible: knowledge, ability, and character. In the fullest sense, these fundamentals can only be obtained through a college experience as broad gauged, as free as possible. This necessarily means, where possible and where freely chosen, living, eating, competing, and working with white students; for these current students will tomorrow comprise the citizens and decision-makers of an American society in which Negroes will live. And the revolution, the real revolution, the one that takes long hard preparation, unshackled ability, tireless effort, and much time is not coming tomorrow. While black students have copped out of this revolution, Negro students know that for them it has only begun. While black students busily issue "demands," hold rallies, indulge in countless meetings, attract publicity and foundation and university funds,

Negro students deeply committed to the real task find themselves in an unenviable position, for they must struggle for the real revolution against university administrators who, pandering to the whims of the moment, capitulate to the "demands" of blacks which delimit not only themselves, but all students. Negro students must fight for the real revolution against white students who, paralyzed by guilt complexes, countenance anything, any idea espoused by the loudest, the most boorish black. Finally, they must oppose their brethren who have, though emotionally committed, not only lost sight of the real goal, but who have rejected either consciously or unconsciously the prerequisites to its achievement.

The unrest and tension which characterize Negro student communities throughout the nation are signs of "an ostracized race in ferment." Out of this ferment many directions will emerge and have emerged. While black students seem intent upon forcing all Negroes down the path toward a new segregation, toward a renewal of the closed society, Negro students seek to maintain equality of opportunity in a free society as the goal of Negro Americans. To a large extent, which road predominates will depend upon which faction white America supports through action of inaction. To Negro college students, the future appears dim, for on all sides white administrators, students, and decision-makers, seem intent upon conceding to black students' demands for separatism, for a renewal of racial exclusivism, for the maintenance of the color line. But, to the end, Negro students will and must oppose these new trends toward segregation, these new chains for Negro Americans.

Paragraph-by-paragraph refutation of Oliver Henry by William W. Sales, Jr., student, in the Columbia Daily Spectator, *March 14, 1969.*

Response to a "Negro Negative"

Oliver Henry's article, "A Negro Student's Observation on Blacks," which appeared in Spectator's March 11th supplement, is the first systematic presentation of the views of the Black student minority that he represents. My detailed response is offered in the hope that a clarification of the contradictions within the Black student community will go a long way toward eliminating these internecine contentions.

While it is true that "The shadow of the ghetto world follows many (Blacks) to the college campus," it is equally true that these campuses represent much less a "new life" or a "new freedom" than at best a subtle extension of the institutional racism of that ghetto. Far from possessing a "tradition of tolerance, of free inquiry," and "personal freedom," the American university and especially Columbia are repositories of racist European values and attitudes.

John W. Burgess, who founded both the political science department and graduate education at Columbia in the late 19th century, instituted the concept of Anglo-Saxon supremacy into the very fabric of the American university. Burgess, an apologist for Jim Crow and Manifest Destiny, had this to say about Blacks in his book on Reconstruction: "A black skin means membership in a race of men which has never of itself succeeded to reason, has never, therefore, created any civilization of any kind." Professor Gosset in his book, "Racism: The History of an Idea in America," informs us that Burgess' students assumed commanding positions throughout the best universities, one of his disciples being Nicholas Murray Butler, who held sway over the fortunes of Columbia from 1902 to 1945.

As C. Wright Mills noted in his pioneering study, "The Power Elite," the necessities of the "cold war" have resulted in the incorporation of the university into the military-industrial complex, the operative arm of the power elite, for reasons of efficiency and security. Within this military-industrial complex, the university trains men and women for future jobs in corporations and the military. Therefore, the American university is in the service of the "power elite," who run it on a profit-loss basis as they would any other corporation. The ideology of this elite still conforms to the tenets of the "Teutonic-Origins Theory" of John W. Burgess and is therefore racist.

A Black student cannot merge "into the university scene" without consciously striving to forget his past, since the WASP dominance of that institution is, of itself, institutionalized racism, which assumes more blatant and overt form in the actions of the campus security guards toward Black students. Rather than explain militant Black student action as putting to "use their new freedom with its consequent permissiveness" it can more correctly be explained as a response to overt and covert campus racism.

The actual programs undertaken this year by BOSS [Barnard

Organization of Soul Sisters] and SAS [Students' Afro-American Society] belie the assertion that "new black students reject academic success, liberal education, and economic advancement as significant goals of their college years." In fact, the organizational efforts of SAS and BOSS [reflect] a realization that through group action each individual Black student can more successfully compete for the traditional goals of students. Recruitment programs undertaken by BOSS and SAS in eight cities are geared to expanding the benefits of academia to larger numbers of minority group youths.

Black students realize that the traditional educational goals, while worthy of individual pursuit, neither fulfill the individual needs of Blacks, nor prepare them adequately to deal with the oppression to which they and their community are subject. Success within the present educational structure is not indicative of real learning or preparation for relevant action in the Black community. If Mr. Henry really interacted with white students, he would no doubt find that the majority of white students are rejecting the narrow educational life style to which he aspires. Militant Black students do not repudiate the study of mathematics, chemistry, European history, or English but utilize the works of Carmichael and Hamilton, Fanon and Malcolm X, in order to put these disciplines in a perspective relevant to the struggle of Black people against racist oppression. A Black student by studying his people adds depth to his understanding of the traditional academic disciplines. The question is not one of repudiating standards per se, but of setting standards of merit and achievement relevant to ending the oppression of the Black community.

It is patently ridiculous to believe that the "real struggle aimed at improving the masses of Negro Americans exists outside of the university." The American university is not an "ivory tower" but a colossal corporate behemoth which pursues a policy of domestic imperialism toward its surrounding community. A Black student must deal with racism wherever he finds it, whether it be Columbia's expansion into Harlem at the expense of that community or the development of anti-personnel and "population control" weaponry by IDA or Operation Spicerack which is used against the liberation struggles of non-white peoples everywhere.

It is unfortunate that the author scores Black student demands without ever dealing with the problems to which these demands are addressed. Actually when Black students and the Harlem community linked up to resist Columbia's Jim Crow gym, Mr. Henry was notably absent. Maybe he was as repelled by the tactic of seizing university property as we were by Columbia's theft of public park land.

The author initiates the discussion of his ideology by reaffirming Dr. DuBois' concept of the "talented tenth." A cursory reading of "Souls of Black Folks" will prove beyond a doubt that DuBois did not think this talented tenth could be solely developed within the "walls and halls of ivy." No Black student disagrees with combining compassion with a well-honed intellect. We must, however, train ourselves into serving the Black community by taking advantage of those experiences accessible only through intimate contact with the Black masses. By so doing, the Black militant student tempers his knowledge of white academia with the realities of the Black experience. If the university has traditionally trained the leadership of this country, then it is teaching racism, for that leadership has been responsible for creating and perpetuating unabated racism domestically and internationally. Thus, for Black students to learn "just what white students are learning" is to learn to continue the oppression of their people and in so doing, to commit suicide.

To meet white society on its terms is to capitulate in the face of intimidation before the battle is joined. Whites, it is true, may largely determine the violent or non-violent nature of the struggle but they can and have done this independently of Blacks. In fact, they have already opted for violence as can be seen by the institutional racism Carmichael and Hamilton's "Black Power" has so aptly highlighted as the essence of the ghetto.

Blacks have built this society but they did not design it and have had no say in its present structure. This is the essence of separation which has been a fact of American life since 1619. While the author says, "These (Negro) students will not be forced out," in actual fact they are outside trying to get in and this is the essence of their problem. It appears that the "Negro student" is trying to make America what it can't be by its very nature. These students are believers in the myth of equal opportunity based on individual achievement within the melting pot of America. Harold Cruse has exposed this naivete in "Rebellion or Revolution":

"The historical development of the relationship between the races in America has cultivated a strange and unique pattern of intergroup psychologics between Negro and white of various castes and classes. Many Negroes, especially those who aspire to leadership of one form or another, and the majority of whites have shown a very perverse tendency to overlook or deny exactly what America is as a nation. America never was the all-white nation that the national psychology pretends. America is and always was multi-racial, multi-national, and culturally pluralistic. People who try to deny this fact with talk about Americans all speaking the same language or sharing the same customs are merely propagating the myth about 'assimilated Americanism'."

Survival in America is based on ethnic power, not assimilation.

In regard to curriculum, Black students have demanded relevant Black history courses. It is not our intention to blacken white history. Bill McAdoo is correct in asserting that "The history of Black America is not identical to the history of white America, even though there is an organic developmental relationship between the two. The history of the oppressed is never identical to the history of the oppressor: the history of the slaveholder can never be the same as the history of the slave." The history of Black America began in Africa, while the history of white America began in Europe. The various European émigrés who arrived in North America as free men eventually formed one people. The different peoples who were brought here in chains grew to become "another separate captive people, upon whose back America was built from its inception." The idea that relevant Black courses will establish an "academic ghetto" shows a profound inferiority complex on the part of the author.

No Black student demands infringe on the freedom of choice of other Black students, but broadens the range of choice. Blacks need to be able to interact with each other as well as with whites if not more so. Why are all demands which give legitimate power to Blacks called "separatist"? There must be something in the white psyche which alienates whites from Blacks with power, from Blacks, therefore, with manhood. I think everyone would like to know of this "real revolution" of which Mr. Henry speaks. Can it really be revolutionary for "Negro" students to struggle against university administrators and white students who concede power to Blacks? Can it really be revolutionary to struggle against your brother assuming power? (Yes, Black and "Negro" students are brothers since our Blackness is determined, not by our ideology, but by our membership in an oppressed minority.)

Hopefully, a single and correct direction will emerge out of

Black ferment directed at ending the oppression of racist America. Everyone "doing his own thing," which seems to be Mr. Henry's ideology, is not revolutionary, but the same old anarchy characteristic of the "Negro" community's inept response to racism. Racism is not the result of every white man "doing his own thing." It is institutionalized and thus our movement must be the institutional expression of the whole Black community. . . .

In summary, I would say that the position of the "Negro student" is a veiled apology for the class aims of what E. F. Frazier called the "Black bourgeoisie." What "Negro students" are afraid of is the fact that the activation of the masses of Black students and Black people in general will erode their bargaining position with the white power structure. "Negro students" don't want to increase the number of Blacks competing for power and wealth in America. Black student activism is viewed by them as a betrayal of the class goals of the Black bourgeoisie. Their position represents a fundamental fear of the Black masses which is an extension of their own self-hate complexes.

This fear has been given concrete expression by the author himself who has on occasion argued that Black people were inherently inferior and that the Black middle class could be of service to the ghetto only at a distance. Black students recognize that the ultimate bonds of unity are not with their class but with their people since all Blacks regardless of class are subjected to racist oppression. We believe in Power for Black people.

Purdue: The Black Salute Case

Article by Sharron Saveland, Assistant City Editor, The Purdue Exponent, *student newspaper, Purdue University, November 20, 1968.*

The Black Salute:
An Expression of Identity

Saturday afternoon, Homecoming Weekend. The "All-American" Marching Band had spread its ranks the length of the stadium floor and the majorettes had struck a position of attention at the drum roll announcing the Star-Spangled Banner.

Players removed their helmets, Gimlets and Reamers doffed their pots, coaches and photographers stood along the sidelines with hats crushed to their sides.

It is likely that the attention of most of the crowd was focused on either the spectacle on the field, the ocean of people in the stands, or the "clear October sky" above. But some may have glanced toward the sidelines and seen two black cheerleaders standing with fists raised in the air and heads bowed.

The more astute observers perhaps recognized the similarity between this pose and the one struck by black athletes Tommie Smith and John Carlos during the playing of the national anthem at the recent Olympic Games.

This gesture is the now famous Black Salute—a fist raised in challenge, a head bowed in shame—which led to the suspension of the two black medal winners from the Olympic team for "untypical exhibitionism."

Smith and Carlos had finished first and third in the 200 meters. As they mounted the victory stand to accept their awards, each wore a black glove and black socks. Smith had a black scarf around his neck.

Explaining the symbols, Smith said, "The black right glove symbolized power, the left black glove symbolized black unity, the scarf symbolized blackness and black socks symbolized our poverty."

At a press conference afterwards, Smith and Carlos emphasized their protest of the blacks' position in America. "When we arrived there were boos. We want to make clear that white people seem to think black people are animals doing a job. We want to tell Americans that we are not animals or rats."

Following this display, the two runners were given a notice by the U.S. Olympic Committee that they had 48 hours to pack their bags and move out. It was reported that the USOC at first wanted to keep the sentence light, no more than a censure, but the International Olympic Committee demanded more.

In one version of the still untold story, the IOC dangled the possibility of expelling the whole U.S. team, saying it could not let such an abuse of the Olympic rules against political activity go unpunished.

The uproar lasted a day with newsmen and photographers chasing after the two runners and conducting whose-side-are-you-on opinion polls. The last word from Carlos was that he intended to sue the U.S. Olympic Committee.

The salute has been adopted at Purdue by the Black Student Action Committee of the Afro-American Forum (formerly the Negro History Study Group).

"While we do not require that all black students make the salute, we feel they should have a right to make it if they feel that it is a part of their identity," said a spokesman for the group.

There are those who look upon the Black Salute as an act of disrespect, and even contempt, for the American flag and the national anthem. Smith and Carlos were booed by those who saw the clenched fist as a symbol of black power.

Black students at Purdue look at the salute differently. To them it is an expression of unity. Self-identity is being sought through group pride and cohesiveness.

"We do not mean this as a gesture of defiance, but feel we have a right to express ourselves in this manner," the spokesman said.

The Black Salute is but one token of a new attitude reflected by black students both on this campus and on others across the country, evidence of a "turning inward" process which the group is undergoing.

It used to be that blacks who attended "white" universities disavowed their blackness as much as possible and tried to assimilate with the white community, adopting its standards and values.

Today black students no longer feel it is essential to adopt the values of whites when these values have little or no meaning for them.

They are acknowledging the differences which exist between the races and asserting these differences with pride.

They ask the white community to acknowledge their right to express themselves.

Statement by "A Black Purdue Student," published in The Purdue Exponent, *November 20, 1968.*

Sharecropper of the American Dream

The Black Salute embodies a disenchanted pride. It is the sorrow of knowing that one is a sharecropper of the American Dream. It is the pride that comes in knowing the potential of men . . . of knowing that we can make America what America must become. Freedom . . . bravery . . . they go hand in hand. So though our salute has ambiguous meanings to some people, yet will we not abandon it. The identity of a people is embodied in the bowing of the head and the raising of the arm. Unless America bows her head in shame at the atrocious acts she commits against humanity, then never can America be free.

But the hope, the dream, the promise that belong to all Americans will, with its blessed realization, resurrect America to heights never before achieved by any people. And this is what we want so let that be our common goal, by recognizing our patriotic participation through the Black Salute.

Letter to the editor, The Purdue Exponent, *December 4, 1968. (No signature.)*

'Ole Black Action'

In answer to the article "The Black Salute . . . expression of identity" and the explanation by A Black Purdue Student and to "all Blacks" on this campus:

The black salute is just as revolting as the other so-called black "unity bits"—the "natural" hair and the "soulfulness" idea. Take one good look at Purdue's black students and you will see a group that has everything except "unity." While the males spend their waking hours chasing white girls, the girls "poke" fun at other blacks who don't meet their standards of dress. One recently described another as "The big-mouthed girl that's black as a shoe."

As for the black cheerleaders (who were placed on the squad by the Dean), just who are they identifying with? The fact that they have accepted the cheerleading position means that they want to identify with whites. Why don't these students express themselves at ALL BLACK UNIVERSITIES? While these rather "pathetic" young adults struggle with self-identity, and other gestures to express themselves; while they flutter about, too filled with "ole Black Action" to speak to another Black; there are those of us who are proving that we can compete in the classroom—and tell me please—what is your reason for being at Purdue?

If you really want to test the willingness of these students to be Black, just talk to them about their families, and 4½ out of 5 will

proudly admit that he has a white grandmother or is 75% Indian
—anything other than what you're looking at—BLACK. The real
farce is that while most of these "young, tender minds" are
searching for their history and refusing to adopt the values of the
whites, the white student is moving ahead academically to
lengthen the "already wide gap." I'm not against unity of Blacks
but I'll have to see more positive indications than Purdue's Blacks
have exhibited.

NAME WITHHELD UPON REQUEST

Interviews in the Yale Alumni Magazine (YAM), *published in May 1969, of
four members of the Black Student Alliance at Yale: Armstead L. Robinson,
Raymond S. Nunn, Glenn E. deChabert, Larry E. Thompson.*

On Being Black at Yale

YAM: Since Yale is a predominantly white community, what
kinds of problems does that present for the black student here?
What kind of effect does this environment have on black students,
and what kinds of responses does it call for?

Robinson: There's a fundamental contradiction between being
black and being at Yale. Yale by definition is white; in many respects it is the epitome of whiteness. To be black here—to be
aware of all the things whiteness has meant for black people and
to be asked to submit passively to being coddled by the white
power structure, being paid to come, is a fundamental contradiction for anyone with a positive black identification.

deChabert: The basis for it is the separation in society. The majority of the black students here come from a home environment that
is a black one, and they come into a home environment here that
is a white one. So from the outset they're confronted with problems simply by having to deal with a different kind of environment than they've dealt with for the past 19 years. They have to
examine their relationship with that environment and whether or
not they have anything to gain from it. This is a problem that
reaches into the social thing and into the academic thing of studying. Black students have to let it be known they have a cultural
identity of their own; the problem is using their identity as a positive force in terms of what they consider to be the negative force
of the white cultural identity at Yale.

Nunn: When I look at Yale and its educational process and the way it operates against blacks, I am struck by the overlap between the cultural and the academic—you can't separate them at all. You look at Yale in a social context from the moment you walk in here. Yale is the epitome of white, Anglo-Saxon, high Protestantism. I don't think it's possible, ever, for a black student to have a total positive identification with Yale. It's the power elite if you want to call it that. I could never walk around the Old Campus and consider myself "a Yale man"—in my freshman year or five, even 20 years after I graduate from here—because I know what a Yale man is and what his position in society is, and his position is one which is definitely counter to mine. Where he is in the establishment is certain to be the place where I'm not. At best, for me personally, all I can see is a momentary and reluctant participation in a social setting which is not my own.

Robinson: I suppose the immediate question that pops into everybody's mind is, If Yale is all that hostile, why do you come? If you come, why do you stay? Speaking personally, I came for a lot of reasons. First, I really didn't know what it was going to be like and I naïvely assumed that life here would be better than it was at home. I'm from the South and I assumed that life here would be different, that the white people wouldn't be as nasty as they were at home. So you get here, begin, and then discover the old headaches; Yale is white and anti-black. Do you transfer if you find that it is hostile? Well, you find yourself in an institutional bind in many ways. You find that your soul may have been bought. Yale made it possible for me to go to school cheaper than it would have been for me to stay at home. That doesn't make the problem of being black any easier, to realize that in many ways when you get here you're almost forced to stay. What you find among blacks is a determination to change the Yale environment to the degree that other blacks can find it more hospitable than it was when you got here. For example, I came here five years ago and there is no question in my mind that Yale is more hospitable to blacks now than it was then.

YAM: How much is it a question of numbers and the need for a sense of community within the community?

Robinson: That's obviously the beginning. My class was the biggest one in Yale's history. We had 14 blacks (out of 1,050 freshmen) and we said that just wouldn't make it. They had separated us, spotted us around so there was one for each college. We found each other because we were lonely. Now it's becoming easier, for example, to have a black roommate on the Old Campus as the number of blacks increases. Also the whole question of Afro-American studies was simply a rebellion against implicit racist assumptions that Yale courses had had. The courses were designed for the white people, and we couldn't find courses that had anything to do with us. We said this nonsense can't be, and demanded that either Yale reform itself and become a place blacks can find hospitable or else not have any blacks at all.

YAM: Of course there have been few precedents to work with anywhere in setting up Afro-American studies programs. On other campuses, if not at Yale, students advocating such programs are sometimes branded anti-intellectuals. Is this because of what you might call the high "relevance quotient" of such courses?

Robinson: The definition of intellectualism up to this point has been racist, it has been a definition which excludes blacks from consideration in intellectual issues. It's an a priori assumption that blacks have done nothing that is worth learning so we should consider white things. In one sense our demands to include blacks is the epitome of intellectualism; we're demanding that in fact the things which should have been done *be* done.

deChabert: Rigor in courses—even from the white point of view—needs to be redefined because a course may be very influential in determining someone's climate of thought at a particular time and yet not be a course that requires petty things like examinations and papers on a very frequent basis. Black people understand, I think, that if they have a course that is of value, no matter what the requirements, they will do the work purely as a matter of self-interest. Black people aren't asking for courses where they can go into the class and as a result of their environmental experiences be able to pull an honors or a high pass without any work; they're not asking for courses where it's established that once you get into them, then you have an easy way to go. They're asking for courses that could lead to something better in terms of their own thought. I don't think the Afro-American studies major, the way it's set up, will tend to make anything easier for those black students who take the courses, because there will be a lot of work required. I see that as being beneficial to black people in terms of their ability to cope with research and so forth, which are things they haven't had the opportunity to do, so their ability wasn't tested.

Robinson: Rigor needs a fundamental redefinition. I think one of the real problems of American education today is that you define rigor in terms of pedantic things like making a 96 as opposed to an 89. That's not what learning is supposed to be about. I hope that the Afro-American studies program can begin a movement away from defining rigor in terms of how many pages long your paper is as opposed to the quality of thought contained in the paper. I'd like to define rigorous courses as courses which are challenging, interesting. This may mean that you have a year course with one book you consider in depth, or you might have 20 books. The only question is how well you deal with the issues that the course is supposed to be concerned with.

Nunn: The push for black studies at Yale, and from what I can see, on other campuses too, is a push to elevate if you will the efforts of intellectuals in the area of black studies. One of the things that black studies is going to do will be to demand that people focus on what they are saying about black Americans. Traditionally any white person who did a minimum amount of research could pass as an authority on black America, and so could any black man for that matter. You didn't have to do any real research; you didn't really have to examine what you were saying. What we're calling for now is for people to do some really intensive reflection about what black America is, what our role in America has been, what we've done, and so forth. That's rigor, and that means a lot of people who have passed for authorities will be severely questioned.

deChabert: I think the main question here is relevance. The way in which people in general attack their work at the so-called top institutions has always been dependent on whether they thought the subjects they were taking were relevant. Insofar as these institutions were white institutions, any subject a white student took was in essence relevant. Black people need the same kind of thing. But when the black student thinks in terms of relevance, what *he* finds at the college is not relevant to *him*. A white cat can take a history of art course dealing with sixteenth-century European art and find it relevant to him and to his culture. But it will not be relevant to a black person, who may say, "What am I taking this for?" and consequently not do as well. In the back of his mind, a white person will know that this is part of his thing, part of his culture; a black person will know this has no function to him in real terms. So, you have a contradiction.

Robinson: The concept of education needs to have a redefinition. My concept is that education should equip people to deal with reality. There's no other functional utility for the school except to teach people things which are useful. I gather that's why people started public schools in the first place—because society needs an educated citizenry. Well, if you view education as providing individual human beings with the tools that are necessary for them to survive and adjust to life, you go a long way away from the traditional idea of what a curriculum should be all about. It no longer becomes an arbitrary body of things that you have to know—to use a crude example, it's not in knowing how to use thee and thou the way Shakespeare did. The relevance question both on the public school level and the college level has to do with how well the educational process communicates ideas that have vitality and meaning for people's lives. I would argue that much of American education today isn't education at all, that it is simply pedantry.

YAM: You feel, then, that educators are locked into one view of reality?

Robinson: That's what's wrong with this particular society, the sort of pedantic "this is *the* way" assumptions that guide most American whites. At the BSAY symposium last spring Harold Cruse called it "cultural particularism," the idea that the Anglo-Saxon norm is not only a good norm but the *best* norm, and more than that, that every other norm must submit to it because it's Anglo-Saxon and white. We refuse to accept that; it's a fundamental kind of non-intellectualism. Education, then, must communicate real and vital things *to the people who are being taught.* Until that happens, you're going to continue to have the disoriented generation of white radicals, for example, who can't find any correlation between the America they're taught about—the George Washington cherry tree reality—and the realities they see around them. That's where the campus radicals come from; campus radicalism is a function of disorientation and when people get disoriented they start asking fundamental questions. Students now are asking what their education's all about and the educators can't tell them because they don't know. They refuse to assume responsibility for it, saying "It was here, and I just came to administer it." So you have a situation where the students say "My education is irrelevant to me," and the educators say "What do you mean?" and react with the how-dare-you-be-anti-intellectual approach mainly because they don't have an answer. Instead of having a friendly communication between interested intellectuals, you have an angry confrontation and you can see how campus rebellions get started. The system is really locked in; maybe it needs to be destroyed before it can be rebuilt.

YAM: Can we go back to talk for a minute about the ways Yale has changed in the last five years, and the changes you feel still have to be made?

Robinson: Freshman year I took American history. We saw blacks three times: the first time we saw them as happy slaves; next we saw them after the Civil War when they were wandering around confused and dazed, not knowing what to do; then we didn't see them until the sixties, when they started raising hell. This is an unacceptable view of history to me—it's a simplistic one. The changes? Now they talk about more than happy slaves and raising hell in the sixties. The end I see is the Afro-American studies program that we've been talking about—plus a fundamental change in the core of the education that's being offered here. Look at sociology, for example. There's an implicit view in sociology—a sort of balance model—that says that things that *are* are good because they're working. And you see in sociology a tendency to identify with what I would call the more oppressive aspects of American society because they're there and they work. Sociology talks in terms of a static, non-conflict model—if your demands to change things raise conflict then you're dysfunctional. And what we're talking about, frankly, is a change in the way the liberal arts curriculum here is organized, so that it corresponds more to reality. The reality in society is not non-conflict, but conflict. These are the sorts of changes we're talking about.

YAM: The curriculum aside for a moment, how do the social and environmental aspects of life at Yale stack up?

Thompson: The thing that struck me right off—I'm a freshman, and it's all fresh in my mind—was that Yale brings you right up against the white Anglo-Saxon tradition. I was put in a room with three white roommates. I'm straight from Harlem. I simply couldn't deal with those cats. Put in a situation like that which you can't handle, how do you deal with it? Blacks have a habit of either dropping out or doing badly academically at this place unless they can get together with other blacks. Black students want the help, guidance, and protection that can only come from other black students, and they want privacy. You don't want to be bothered with this constant "tell me about the problem" bit; one day a white student came up to me all serious and said: "Tell me about the black problem." I simply can't sit down and rap with this cat about the black problem, especially if 10 minutes later somebody else asks me the same thing. Sooner or later that would get to be your main thing, and you get the impression that the reason Yale brought you here was to be a guinea pig for the white kids.

deChabert: The black cat can't cope with that kind of thing because he has himself to cope with. Most black guys who come here are on their own for the first time, and when you're on your own it's the first chance you really have to develop any sense of self or self-consciousness. But when white people want to be tutored by you in terms of how you are related to them in the world situation, then it is a matter of you wasting your time. You realize it's hard enough to deal with yourself and other black people and to try to figure out your place in the world. A white person constantly asking to be educated into the black thing is in reality an imposition on your time. If you start to deal with white people, start to be a tutor or mentor or conscience for white people, you find after a while that you have ceased to be a mentor for yourself. And this is the essence of black consciousness: figuring out in your mind what you are to yourself and what you mean to the world in terms of its black population. When you have to throw that out to white people all the time it takes time away from self-development.

Nunn: I came to Yale because I wanted a top-notch education and I assumed I could get it here. But from the time I walked in the doors, I began to notice that implicit in the minds of white students (and also some of the administration and faculty) was the assumption that by coming to Yale I wanted "in," and that I meant to sever my ties with the black community. That just is not the case. Yet what I met here with the educational process and with the social process was the attempt to assimilate the black student totally, to cut off his ties with black America. The education is geared to make him as white as possible, the social structure is geared to make him as white as possible. The way it was evidenced to me was that the white kids I knew as a freshman and sophomore always used to ask me if I wanted to move into a white suburb. I couldn't understand that because I knew exactly what kind of community I wanted to live in: a black one. I have certain tastes, which mean that I don't want to starve and I'd like to make sure that the house I live in is comfortable, but at the same time I don't want to live in a white suburb. I want my kids to go to a black school, and I want them to look outside and see that the people walking down the street are black. The very fact that we black students identify closely as a group—perhaps we're the only really solid fraternity on this campus—should be evidence enough that there are things we want to retain, things that we hold dear.

Robinson: The basic issue here is why were we brought to Yale in the first place? I will argue that somewhere deep in the minds of the people on the admissions committee was the idea that they needed some diversity. It's sort of like when you're cooking you throw in some salt to make the food taste better. It's a fundamentally paternalistic conception, to assume that the functional utility for bringing black people here is to use them to broaden the horizons of the white students. It almost seems as if Yale said, "Let's get some Indians, a few niggers, keep the number small but have a few as spicing so you can have the whole pot taste good." I can't handle that; not very many other black people can handle it either. But some people might get the idea that talking this way implies that we're retreating into a certain negativism, that we're running away because we can't deal with it. That's not so. Our fundamental thing is a positive assertion: We refuse to be the spicing. We think there's much more to blackness than simply to make whiteness a little grey. We think that blackness in and of itself is good. We refuse to come here and lose our blackness by sort of helping out the white majority. In a sense, that would be asking a black student to come here and become deculturated. That's a hell of a process. And it's not something you ask anybody else to do. The desire for positive black identification is, quite frankly, a positive assertion that I have some identity that I intend to preserve. I'm not running away saying I can't deal with it. It's just that if you don't ask anybody *else* to do it, then don't ask *me* to do it.

YAM: The BSAY has been active in recruiting black students for Yale. On what basis do you talk to prospective applicants?

Nunn: I talk about Yale as I know it. There are two: there is a white Yale and a black Yale. There are positive attitudes I have toward black Yale in terms of social aspects, friendships, about what we do, about some of the fun and some of the real hard struggles that we've had. Then there is the other Yale which is white, which is the academic side of it. I don't intend to tell anybody that this is a haven for black students, that this is where you should come. I'm not at all sure that it is. I'm not even sure that I want my brother to come here. But you try to present people with "I think that Yale can offer a top-notch education because it can really challenge you." It can challenge you in terms of, say, developing a sound logical mind, which is essential really if you are going to keep yourself together as a black man on this campus. And that's a challenge that I think is very beneficial.

deChabert: I think a distinction should be made between paternalism and realistic assertion. Now, from the white point of view, to get a black person involved in the system of Yale education is paternalistic because intrinsic in the system is the assumption that the black person will come out a white/black person. Afro-American studies, on the other hand, represents a realistic assertion on the part of black students that there is something missing from Yale as it now exists which makes a white person less than a functioning person in this society. If Yale is to make a person a thinking person, a person who is discerning and able to recognize different things and different conditions, then an Afro-American studies major is essential—because before it existed Yale left out a large part of the people in the society, ignored their history, culture, economics, and so on. So black studies is an assertion that the world is more broadly based in humanity than just white people. To say that the world is based on white people and their culture is a paternalistic assertion.

Robinson: I want to suggest a basic difference between the way a black person conceives of Yale and the way whites here, particularly alumni, conceive of Yale. I keep getting the impression that alumni think the slogan "For God, For Country, and For Yale" means "God and Country Equal Yale." They view Yale as the epitome of all that is beauty and truth and light in America and that we should have some great allegiance to this institution. My conception of Yale is remarkably less laudatory. I view Yale as having a rather limited function and role for me: It can provide certain intellectual training and tools that I can use against the society which Yale supports. Many of the leaders who run this country come from Yale and it's obviously functional for those of us who have inclinations other than preserving this society the way it is to come here. Yale can do some things for blacks; one thing Yale *can't* do is provide inspiration for blacks. I don't think we're asking Yale to become black. The Afro-American studies program is going to be *Yale's* Afro-American studies program and we accept that Yale is going to be white. But being here can have a certain functional utility so long as you can survive with your blackness intact.

Nunn: Yes, you can become valuable to the black people, not in the sense of a leader, but as a resource with information on how the machine operates from the inside. I've heard the analogy that black students on white campuses are like spies from another world jotting down notes on what goes on. And in a way I *do* see myself as a sort of spy. I'm beginning to know Yale, its functions, its operations within the larger society. I don't see myself, quite frankly, as leading a revolution. But I do see myself as possessing valuable information which I can give to my black brothers, or to whoever is going to try to revolutionize this country and make it a really decent place for black people.

deChabert: I'd like to throw in something about this revolution thing because I know it's the *Alumni Magazine.* I assume that a lot of readers who talk about the separation and non-separation thing, the integration thing, wonder whether the separation that is wanted by "intelligent" or "responsible" black people is a permanent thing or a transitory thing. To me it seems essential that people understand that black people want to determine their own destinies, not for what's going to happen in the future, but for *right now.* Whatever comes out of black self-determination— whether it be an acceptance of integration or a recognition of the fact that the two races in this country can never be integrated— must be put on the shelf until it becomes necessary to make such a finalized decision. What is important is that black people right now are able to function as men and women in this country. If we choose to enter into an integrationist kind of thing with white people in the end, then that's our prerogative. If we don't, that's our right too. This is not the issue. The issue at hand is whether people are going to allow themselves to be sucked into the same kind of thing they've been sucked into for the last-I-don't-know-how-many years. It seems to me that at this time old people, young people, the middle-aged people—all kinds of black people have finally realized as a result of young black people's concern that they won't be sucked into this thing, and whatever comes out, ultimately, will be something for which they will face the consequences.

Robinson: Very few people have an idea of what integration really is about. It's not one culture swallowing up another and making it disappear. Integration implies a sort of mutualism, a diffusion where if you wanted to envision the society of the future it wouldn't be black and white, it would be tan. Unfortunately, when whites talk about integration they aren't talking about the tan model; they're talking about a white model, with black people becoming white. If you want to promote an integrated society, the first thing you have to accept is the essential duality that exists already between white and black. And furthermore, there's not going to be integration in any real sense until you have two groups (or maybe more) capable of standing independently on their own feet and freely choosing to do whatever they want to. Black people in this country are not in a position at this time to make such a choice: Anglo-Saxon racism has denied for a long time the true self-confidence that would allow that strength. You can't have sharing among unequal partners. You've got to have the psychological equality. You're going to have to accept the fact that before integration becomes possible in this society black people are going to have to be allowed to get themselves together.

YAM: The word racism has cropped up several times so far. What do you mean by it?

Robinson: How about substituting cultural particularism for racism?

YAM: Anything, then, that stands in the way of black self-determination?

Robinson: If one sat down and considered precisely what being white in this society means, I think you come to the essence of racism in America: to be white is to be non-black. That is the very best definition. If you look at it that way, everybody who defines himself as white in the society is a racist. What do you mean when you say I am a white American? It means that I'm not a black American. It means that I'm not different, I don't have that stigma. When you can begin to deal with that realization you can begin to see why black people have trouble identifying with a culture which defines itself as non-black. If you need confirmation of the essential racism of this society, look at your own Constitution. Look at the provision which provides for the proportional representation in the House of Representatives. You'll see that even in the Constitutions that are distributed today it says that black people are three-fifths of a human being. Being a whole American was defined as not being black.

Nunn: A racist in this country is anyone who would like to keep the power structure intact the way it is, and whose idea of extending equality to blacks is to co-opt them, sprinkling them here and there along the ladder in inconsequential positions. You see, I didn't buy "black capitalism" the very second I heard Richard Nixon talking about it. What he's talking about is, "Okay, we'll let blacks do the hiring and firing within their own areas." The very subtle thing underlying all this talk among whites about black capitalism is that the *real* power is still going to lie within the white establishment. Let us have power of hiring and firing of whites, have consequential power over them, just the way you have it over us, and then maybe we can start conversing politely over tea. Co-option assumes that when you offer the black man a bigger bone you've got him, he's your nigger for life. You give him an extra inch and you assume he's forever grateful to you for it. But the minute a black man starts thinking you've lost him forever. And we've started thinking.

YAM: Until now, the conversation has been largely about feelings. How do they translate into terms of political consciousness and action at Yale?

deChabert: We've dealt with Yale from an autonomous, independent black point of view, but one that has always fit easily into the University's intellectual criteria. In everything that we've done, we have thoroughly researched and programmed our plans of action. We have not had to go into any faculty or administration meeting and fall on our knees to ask for anything. We have always confronted them from a point of view which could be viewed by them as the point of view of an equal by virtue of the fact that we had done our homework. Stretching this out onto the political plane, black people are more and more beginning to understand that you can't tell somebody about the inequity of their system by just having a visceral reaction to that system. You have to have a program and a rational understanding of the way the system works to deal with them. When they cope with your objections it could again become a paternalistic sort of thing if they hand you a program that they worked out on their own. So I would say that the Black Student Alliance has made it very clear to Yale's administration and corporation that we are not begging them to do anything for us. We are simply coming in and telling them what's wrong with their system and telling them what they can do to make it better.

Robinson: Some white radicals at the *Yale Daily News* and some SDS types are upset because we don't want to cooperate and share our movement, telling them all that's going on. There was a pathetic column in the *News* not long ago asking, How come the Negroes are silent at Yale? How come they don't talk to us? They went on to threaten us: If you don't tell us now what you know we won't help in the future. That point of view is sort of the epitome of the sweet racist line, that is, to assume that they can be in on the planning of a black thing, that they can help it to function and succeed.

Nunn: I have an equal aversion to SDS. They need us, we don't really need them. The whole campaign which SDS raises against racism isn't really genuine because they look at blacks as a catalyst for their revolution; from what little I know about chemistry, the catalyst starts the chemical reaction and other things change but the catalyst never changes.

Robinson: I can't think of a more fundamentally racist conception than the idea that we are to be *used* by people to stimulate their rebellion. I'll be damned if I'm going to let them take things that are important to me and use them for themselves.

deChabert: We have no workable framework for white radicals at this time and in the foreseeable future. We feel that if there ever comes a time when we need the white radicals, regardless of our relationship with them over the past four or five years, if these people are sincere in their fights against oppression and what-not, they'll come over.

Nunn: To get to something more positive for a moment, you asked how we view Yale. I think that in working for the Afro-American studies major here we were very aware that if we could get something done here, we would help create the momentum to get things done other places. A principal concern of mine was that we might get some more conservative black administrators on black college campuses to realize that they had the real potential to do something even greater than we could ever hope to get accomplished at Yale. I saw the black studies major as something that had national importance. That's one thing that's pleased me in the four years I've been here; we've turned on something very positive.

Robinson: You can measure the significance of what we've achieved by the fact that our sister institution to the north has copied our program. Nonetheless, the view that we had while working on the program was that here was a chance to strike a blow, to begin to reform American education so it corresponds to reality. And that's the reason the program has been designed with as much care as it has, and I hope it has as much influence as it can have.

YAM: What are your summary views?

Thompson: Blacks at Yale are basically asking for the necessities of their lives. We need things that are more relevant to us, more black studies, more black students whom we can relate to on an individual basis, instead of trying to relate to the whole white world in general. And we need our privacy.

Robinson: Occasionally I detect some feelings from whites around here that the BSAY in the last analysis has copped out, because they don't see us doing anything, they don't hear any noises. I think that once again they're in the paternalistic bag: they assume that they have to know about it in order for it to be worthwhile. And that's trash.

deChabert: To close from my point of view, I think it's essential that people understand that we no longer believe this one nationhood or one countryhood American image. It has gone too far beyond that for anyone to assume that that will be the case in the near future, or indeed ever. Since white people have had their thing, they've run it to the disadvantage of black people, and many times to the disadvantage of other people too. Black people will not necessarily run their thing to the disadvantage of those white people, but they will run their thing *to* the advantage of their people. And this thought pervades not only the community; it runs through the minds of students on this particular campus and on campuses throughout the nation. It's an effort to cope with reality and an effort like this hasn't been made before.

Nunn: Closing for myself, I have a tendency to describe myself as a black student who coincidentally happens to be attached to a predominantly white student organization. I wear three-piece suits because I like them. I belong to a Yale senior society, and at the same time I'm always cognizant of the fact that my destiny is inextricably bound up with the destiny of all black people. So I know where my priority lies.

APPENDIX TO
PART FOUR

Women's Liberation

The women's liberation movement arose only at the tail-end of the sixties and, as of spring 1970, had not yet been the center of any major university conflict.* However, while it came later historically than Black liberation, the issue of women's liberation was posed in structurally similar terms. In both there was the basic material issue of discrimination—in admissions policies, for example. The two movements also shared a belief that culturally-imbedded patterns of subordinate behavior had to be overcome by a strong sense of collective identity. In both, therefore, there was a mix of economic and psychological concerns. Typically, the less militant factions in each movement confined themselves to the issues of economic discrimination, while the more radical emphasized the broader cultural problems as symptoms of the society's overall oppressiveness. Both were split between "integrationists" and "separatists." It may turn out that the move toward

* The one exception was the Marlene Dixon case at Chicago (see pp. 510–17) which also involved other issues such as student participation in tenure decisions and political criteria in faculty appointments.

greater co-education in universities will wane in time just as the movement for racial integration has weakened. Just as Black students have raised the issue of the Black university, so female students may begin to look at women's colleges as something other than an anachronism.

The following article from *The Old Mole* provides a general discussion of the ways in which the issue of women's liberation impinges on the university.

Article appearing in a collection entitled What Are We Complaining About?, *written by women staff members of* The Old Mole *and published March 1970. (No individual author identified.)*

Women and the University

Phi Beta Kappa key or no, she can expect to make anywhere from $85 to $110 a week.—*Boston Globe, July 27, 1969*

Yes, prior to 1968, girls were much more flexible. Now they're asking for a good deal more. And in many cases they just can't get it. I honestly don't know how some of them are going to survive.—*Elizabeth Welch, Careers for Women*

Girls really feel discriminated against. There's a great feeling of frustration, bitterness, and defeatism. A man's brain is saleable without skills. A woman needs skills and brains to be marketable. At the B.A. level a girl might just as well have graduated from kindergarten.—*Mrs. Lorraine Olson, dean of Hickox Secretarial School*

Oh, I've heard all the answers. "I don't want to sit behind a typewriter all day. I didn't go to college to do that."—*Mrs. Persis Blanchard, Women's Educational and Industrial Union.*

When a girl goes to college, she probably isn't sure what she wants, what kind of life she wants to lead. The college and guidance counselors have told her that college is a place where she can explore and define who she wants to be.

But a college or university is set up to define and limit women's lives—as an educational institution and as an employer, the university perpetuates women's subordinate roles.

When she first arrives at college, a girl notices that the authorities are nervous about her in a way that they are not nervous about boys. Most schools have curfews for freshman women in dorms, maintained with a system of sign-outs and permissions. Upperclass women may escape from these rules, but B.U.,* for instance, pressures girls to sign out when they leave the dorm, "for their own protection." The dorm rules limit women's freedom, and also say to women: you are somehow less able to live your own life than a boy.

Many schools also have special talks and seminars for women throughout the time they are at school, giving "advice" on dating, marriage, the problems of working mothers, etc. Although men date and marry, the school makes no such fuss about that. The assumption is that women automatically have a special responsibility for home and children—whether or not you have a "career" this is your main job. College may help you get a job, but by the attitudes of the college itself, anything you do with your life is a "second income," valid only as long as it doesn't interfere with being a wife and mother.

While establishing rules and advice courses on the problems of being a woman, the college provides no help for women who are trying to take control of their own lives. The health services refuse to give prescriptions for birth control devices, very few college health centers have staff gynecologists, fewer have female psychiatrists. Less obviously, many doctors will try to punish a woman for having a sex life by making nasty comments, refusing help, or even hurting her unnecessarily during examinations.

The college will not teach women how to protect themselves—almost nowhere is self-defense offered as a part of the regular physical education courses for women.

In spite of the wide range of courses in the catalog, a girl

* Boston University.

quickly learns that only certain majors and extra-curricular activities are "appropriate" for a woman. If she tries to major in something unfeminine, she will meet resistance from the professors themselves, and from male students who refuse to take her seriously, or warn her that brainy women are not attractive. The majors girls choose reflect this pressure.

The latest Northeastern senior class is typical:

Major	Men	Women
engineering	627	7
business	457	9
liberal arts:		
math	36	13
physics	20	0
chemistry	15	3
biology	41	13
medical tech.	0	23
psychology	29	17
sociology	21	41
political science	64	10
history	57	15
english	70	50
modern language	7	10
economics	32	1
education	65	67

Once in class, a girl hears women talked about as secondary, if they are discussed at all. History courses concentrate on people who have had power—they disregard working people, black people,—and women. A woman finds none of her own history in college, except maybe a week-long snicker about "suffragettes" in an American history survey course. Psychology courses based on Freud and Erikson tell her that a woman has an "incomplete ego" and isn't suited for accomplishing things; that women are nurturing and mothering, built around "inner space." Women's psychological problems come from "penis envy" (!)—a reluctance to accept their "natural" role.

If a woman can still decide to stay on in the university as a graduate student, she is less likely to be accepted in graduate school. Women receive less financial aid than men on all levels, although often just as many apply, and girls' grades are higher than boys' on the average. Women earn even fewer graduate degrees now than 30 years ago—about 30% of masters' degrees and Ph.D. degrees are earned by women.

If a woman decides to look for a job through the college placement office she is urged to be "realistic." Whether she is dropping out of Northeastern or graduating from Radcliffe, she finds that unless she is lucky enough to be trained for a traditional women's "service profession" (teaching, nursing), she had better forget about this "meaningful job" stuff and learn to type. She is a woman, and that makes her a secretary to American employers— her BA is nothing compared to the strength of that discrimination.

But a girl can learn that at college, too, the university itself is set up like any other corporation in America. It has a rigid hierarchy of power, salary, and prestige, and women are at the bottom of that hierarchy. The important administrators and almost all high ranking faculty members are men—the secretaries who type and answer their phones, the workers who serve their meals in the cafeteria—are women.

The university as an employer shows the same contempt for women as any other employer. One Harvard administrator explained, "These girls are dying to work at Harvard to meet Harvard men. We figure that's worth $10–$15 less on the paycheck each week"—so women at Harvard get paid very little.

The university is part of the chorus that tells women their main fulfillment is motherhood—but as an employer the university takes no responsibility for the day care of children whose parents work there. Only one school we know of, Emmanuel, offers paid maternity leave to its employees.

If a woman happens to make it onto the faculty, she is paid less (the national average is $1289/year less than male faculty), promoted less, and meets a general attitude of skepticism or hostility from men on the faculty. Harvard, of course, has no women full professors—the B.U. and Northeastern liberal arts faculties have 2 each.

Here are approximate figures for the Boston University liberal arts faculty:

Rank	Men	Women
professor	116	2
assoc. prof.	71	13
asst. prof.	101	19
instructor	31	12
academic administrators (deans, etc.)	9	0

The black and white radical student movements have challenged the university's claim that it is a neutral, ivory tower, and shown many ways in which universities maintain and aid oppression in America—from supporting war research to tearing down the neighborhoods of working people. Women are now learning that the university is an integral part of the system that tries to keep us "in our place" as wives and mothers, low-paid service workers—servants to men.

PART V

UNIVERSITY GOVERNANCE

Two demands—"due process" and "participation"—have dominated student protest against university governance. The demand for due process has been directed at university discipline, while the demand for participation has been focused primarily on institutional policy-making. One concerns judicial functions, the other legislative. The first is a question of student rights, the second of student power.

The drive to compel universities to follow due process in disciplinary proceedings began as part of a larger revolt against the university's *in loco parentis* role. Students objected to administration rules on visiting hours in dormitories, sexual relations, personal behavior, etc., and asserted that they had the right to do whatever they pleased. Except for small colleges and universities in conservative areas of the country, most schools have gradually, and peacefully, yielded *in loco parentis* control, at the behest of students and with the consent of the faculty.

However, at some universities where most *in loco parentis* regulations were relaxed, the disciplinary system itself continued to be paternalistic. This meant that often there were no written rules, or that rules were irregularly or capriciously enforced. When students were suspended or expelled, the administration did not have to present a full description of the charges and evidence against them. The students had no right to hearings in which they could call witnesses in their behalf or confront their accusers. If there was a hearing, it was usually conducted in secret. Counsel was rarely permitted, there was no protection against self-incrimination, and no fixed procedures existed for review or appeal.

University administrators defended such practices on the grounds that private institutions were not subject to the requirements of due process. They also argued that their decisions were more benign and flexible than would be the verdicts of a tribunal following legal procedures and interpreting formal regulations.

Besides, they said, universities did not have the resources to construct full-fledged judicial systems.

Student demands for due process found wide support in the academic community, and elsewhere. Several key court decisions were crucial in pushing universities in the direction of instituting formal procedures with at least minimal guarantees of fair play.

The drive for student participation, while aimed mainly at policy-making structures, was also directed at disciplinary systems. As with the demand for due process, the demand for participation in discipline drew on liberal rather than radical ideas. For example, students argued that administrators had no right to make, enforce, *and* interpret disciplinary rules, since this placed legislative, executive, and judicial functions in the hands of the same authorities, and thus violated the fundamental liberal concept of the separation of powers.

The question of participation in university governance was raised in two contexts. On the university-wide level, students generally sought a legislative body including both students and faculty that could override the administration. On the departmental level, students—usually graduate students—asked for joint governing structures; the demand in that context, however, represented a challenge to the faculty, not the administration. The issues were different on the university-wide and departmental planes. Institutional decisions, such as policies on military recruiting, are generally nonacademic. Departmental decisions, on the other hand, primarily involve curriculum, faculty appointments, fellowship awards, etc. In the latter case, the opponents of student participation maintained that students were not professionally competent to judge; in the former case, they raised other arguments—e.g., that students were transients and had no great stake in the university.

The demands for reorganization of university discipline and policy-making would probably never have been pressed if radicals had not precipitated crisis situations by demonstrating for other causes. SDS protested university discipline and policy, but after 1967 it never demanded or believed in structural reform. In fact, radicals in SDS denounced institutional reform as a diversion from the main issues. SDS argued that changing the university structure would change little of importance since American society, which created the problems, would remain untouched. When

SDS demanded due process in university discipline, it did so to protect its members from suspension, not to reform the disciplinary system. Structural or procedural changes had only an instrumental value for SDS. For the radicals a "reformed" disciplinary system was no more legitimate than an "unreformed" system if both punished students fighting for a just cause.

University reform, therefore, was not really the cause of SDS. It received support from some on the left, but its strength was the liberal center.

CHAPTER 14

Challenges to University Discipline

A general position paper on the role of students in the university endorsed jointly by the American Association of University Professors, the United States National Student Association (NSA), and several other national organizations opens this section. The statement is concerned primarily with such rights as freedom of expression in the classroom, freedom of association on campus, autonomy of student publications, and standards for due process in discipline. A brief section discusses, in general terms, student participation in institutional government.

The point of departure for student protest against university power was *in loco parentis* control, which reduced students to the status of children. The case against paternalism is presented here in a basic policy declaration of the U.S. National Students Association. From Purdue comes a typical instance of the issue. The dispute there revolved around statements made by the editor of the student newspaper. The administration, appalled at his language and his views, dismissed him from his position. Recounting the events which led to his ouster, the editor defends himself more with humor than outrage. He is answered in turn by a Purdue professor, Warren H. Hansen. Hansen describes his concept of the functions of a university education, posing as his basic question, "What is an educated person?" The gist of his answer is that education improves manners. "An educated person," he writes, "possesses a certain polish, a sophistication which others do not have. If he is male, he is a gentleman; if she is female, she is a lady." Despite Hansen's views, other faculty members supported the student editor and he was ultimately reinstated. In "The wider significance of the Columbia upheaval," Margaret Mead sketches the background of *in loco parentis* doctrine, and concludes that the decision by the administration to call in the police was the final recognition that students could no longer be treated as privileged children.

The rejection of *in loco parentis* doctrine posed new questions. If the university no longer had the extensive power of a parent over a child, in what areas did it still retain a right to impose discipline? A statement by the Wisconsin Students Association presented one position. In the students' opinion, the only basis for discipline is academic performance. When a student commits a violation of the law, it is the business of the government, not the university, to punish him. A Wisconsin faculty committee agreed that *in loco parentis* powers were not valid, but stated that there were areas other than academic performance where the university should maintain control. According to the faculty, acts—including violations of law—that endanger university functions, should be subject to university discipline. The charge has often been made, however, that prosecution by both civil and university authorities represents "double jeopardy." In reply to this argument, a student-faculty committee report from Cornell, written in September 1967, maintained that double prosecution results from legitimate "double jurisdiction," at least in certain cases. (An interesting fact about this report was that its signatories included both David Burak, the leader of SDS, and Professor Allan Sindler, chairman of the Department of Government, who were at the opposite poles of a political struggle at Cornell just eighteen months later.)

The relationship between university and civil authorities did not only involve the complicated question of jurisdiction. A separate issue arose when courts began to require universities to institute certain guarantees of fair play in disciplinary proceedings. One court ruling, presented here, spelled out minimum standards for due process in discipline, and suggested others which might be necessary in special cases. A resolution by the National Student Association demanded that universities go considerably farther in that direction.

The demand for due process challenged traditional university disciplinary systems, but did not attack the basic legitimacy of discipline. The documents in the last section here do just that. An editorial from the *Harvard Crimson* raises a series of issues, most importantly the political nature of disciplinary trials. Jack R. Stauder, a young faculty member who was disciplined at Harvard, defends his participation in the protests at that university in 1969. In a sharp debate with his court, Stauder rejects their arguments and their right to judge him.

Statement of a joint committee of the American Association of University Professors, U.S. National Student Association, Association of American Colleges, National Association of Student Personnel Administrators, and National Association of Women Deans and Counselors, June 1967. The statement was subsequently endorsed by many other professional bodies.

Joint Statement on Rights and Freedoms of Students

PREAMBLE

Academic institutions exist for the transmission of knowledge, the pursuit of truth, the development of students, and the general well-being of society. Free inquiry and free expression are indispensable to the attainment of these goals. As members of the academic community, students should be encouraged to develop the capacity for critical judgment and to engage in a sustained and independent search for truth. Institutional procedures for achieving these purposes may vary from campus to campus, but the minimal standards of academic freedom of students outlined below are essential to any community of scholars.

Freedom to teach and freedom to learn are inseparable facets of academic freedom. The freedom to learn depends upon appropriate opportunities and conditions in the classroom, on the campus, and in the larger community. Students should exercise their freedom with responsibility.

The responsibility to secure and to respect general conditions conducive to the freedom to learn is shared by all members of the academic community. Each college and university has a duty to develop policies and procedures which provide and safeguard this freedom. Such policies and procedures should be developed at each institution within the framework of general standards and with the broadest possible participation of the members of the academic community. The purpose of this statement is to enumerate the essential provisions for student freedom to learn.

I. FREEDOM OF ACCESS TO HIGHER EDUCATION

The admissions policies of each college and university are a matter of institutional choice provided that each college and university makes clear the characteristics and expectations of students which it considers relevant to success in the institution's program. While church-related institutions may give admission preference to students of their own persuasion, such a preference should be clearly and publicly stated. Under no circumstances should a student be barred from admission to a particular institution on the basis of race. Thus, within the limits of its facilities, each college and university should be open to all students who are qualified according to its admission standards. The facilities and services of a college should be open to all of its enrolled students, and institutions should use their influence to secure equal access for all students to public facilities in the local community.

II. IN THE CLASSROOM

The professor in the classroom and in conference should encourage free discussion, inquiry, and expression. Student performance should be evaluated solely on an academic basis, not on opinions or conduct in matters unrelated to academic standards.

A. Protection of freedom of expression

Students should be free to take reasoned exception to the data or views offered in any course of study and to reserve judgment about matters of opinion, but they are responsible for learning the content of any course of study for which they are enrolled.

B. Protection against improper academic evaluation

Students should have protection through orderly procedures against prejudiced or capricious academic evaluation. At the same time, they are responsible for maintaining standards of academic performance established for each course in which they are enrolled.

C. Protection against improper disclosure

Information about student views, beliefs, and political associations which professors acquire in the course of their work as instructors, advisers, and counselors should be considered confidential. Protection against improper disclosure is a serious professional obligation. Judgments of ability and character may be provided under appropriate circumstances, normally with the knowledge or consent of the student.

III. STUDENT RECORDS

Institutions should have a carefully considered policy as to the information which should be part of a student's permanent educational record and as to the conditions of its disclosure. To minimize the risk of improper disclosure, academic and disciplinary records should be separate, and the conditions of access to each should be set forth in an explicit policy statement. Transcripts of academic records should contain only information about academic status. Information from disciplinary or counseling files should not be available to unauthorized persons on campus, or to any person off campus without the express consent of the student involved except under legal compulsion or in cases where the safety of persons or property is involved. No records should be kept which reflect the political activities or beliefs of students. Provisions should also be made for periodic routine destruction of noncurrent disciplinary records. Administrative staff and faculty members should respect confidential information about students which they acquire in the course of their work.

IV. STUDENT AFFAIRS

In student affairs, certain standards must be maintained if the freedom of students is to be preserved.

A. Freedom of association

Students bring to the campus a variety of interests previously acquired and develop many new interests as members of the academic community. They should be free to organize and join associations to promote their common interests.

1. The membership, policies, and actions of a student organization usually will be determined by vote of only those persons who hold bona fide membership in the college or university community.

2. Affiliation with an extramural organization should not of itself disqualify a student organization from institutional recognition.

3. If campus advisers are required, each organization should be free to choose its own adviser, and institutional recognition should not be withheld or withdrawn solely because of the inability of a student organization to secure an adviser. Campus advisers may advise organizations in the exercise of responsibility, but they should not have the authority to control the policy of such organizations.

4. Student organizations may be required to submit a statement of purpose, criteria for membership, rules of procedures, and a current list of officers. They should not be required to submit a membership list as a condition of institutional recognition.

5. Campus organizations, including those affiliated with an extramural organization, should be open to all students without respect to race, creed, or national origin, except for religious qualifications which may be required by organizations whose aims are primarily sectarian.

B. Freedom of inquiry and expression

1. Students and student organization should be free to examine and.discuss all questions of interest to them, and to express opinions publicly and privately. They should always be free to support causes by orderly means which do not disrupt the regular and essential operation of the institution. At the same time, it should be made clear to the academic and the larger community that in their public expressions or demonstrations students or student organizations speak only for themselves.

2. Students should be allowed to invite and to hear any person of their own choosing. Those routine procedures required by an institution before a guest speaker is invited to appear on campus should be designed only to insure that there is orderly scheduling of facilities and adequate preparation for the event, and that the occasion is conducted in a manner appropriate to an academic community. The institutional control of campus facilities should not be used as a device of censorship. It should be made clear to the academic and large community that sponsorship of guest speakers does not necessarily imply approval or endorsement of the views expressed, either by the sponsoring group or the institution.

C. Student participation in institutional government

As constituents of the academic community, students should be free, individually and collectively, to express their views on issues of institutional policy and on matters of general interest to the student body. The student body should have clearly defined means to participate in the formulation and application of institutional policy affecting academic and student affairs. The role of the student government and both its general and specific responsibilities should be made explicit, and the actions of the student government within the area of its jurisdiction should be reviewed only through orderly and prescribed procedures.

D. Student publications

Student publications and the student press are a valuable aid in establishing and maintaining an atmosphere of free and responsible discussion and of intellectual exploration on the campus. They are a means of bringing student concerns to the attention of the faculty and the institutional authorities and of formulating student opinion on various issues on the campus and in the world at large.

Whenever possible the student newspaper should be an independent corporation financially and legally separate from the university. Where financial and legal autonomy is not possible, the institution, as the publisher of student publications, may have to bear the legal responsibility for the contents of the publications. In the delegation of editorial responsibility to students the institution must provide sufficient editorial freedom and financial autonomy for the student publications to maintain their integrity of purpose as vehicles for free inquiry and free expression in an academic community.

Institutional authorities, in consultation with students and faculty, have a responsibility to provide written clarification of the role of the student publications, the standard to be used in their evaluation, and the limitations on external control of their operation. At the same time, the editorial freedom of student editors and managers entails corollary responsibilities to be governed by the canons of responsible journalism, such as the avoidance of libel, indecency, undocumented allegations, attacks on personal integrity, and the techniques of harassment and innuendo. As safeguards for the editorial freedom of student publications the following provisions are necessary.

1. The student press should be free of censorship and advance approval of copy, and its editors and managers should be free to develop their own editorial policies and news coverage.

2. Editors and managers of student publications should be protected from arbitrary suspension and removal because of student, faculty, administrative, or public disapproval of editorial policy or content. Only for proper and stated causes should editors and managers be subject to removal and then by orderly and prescribed procedures. The agency responsible for the appointment of editors and managers should be the agency responsible for their removal.

3. All university-published and financed student publications should explicitly state on the editorial page that the opinions there expressed are not necessarily those of the college, university, or student body.

V. OFF-CAMPUS FREEDOM OF STUDENTS

A. Exercise of rights of citizenship

College and university students are both citizens and members of the academic community. As citizens, students should enjoy the same freedom of speech, peaceful assembly, and right of petition that other citizens enjoy and, as members of the academic community, they are subject to the obligations which accrue to them by virtue of this membership. Faculty members and administrative officials should insure that institutional powers are not employed to inhibit such intellectual and personal development of students as is often promoted by their exercise of the rights of citizenship both on and off campus.

B. Institutional authority and civil penalties

Activities of students may upon occasion result in violation of law. In such cases, institutional officials should be prepared to apprise students of sources of legal counsel and may offer other assistance. Students who violate the law may incur penalties prescribed by civil authorities, but institutional authority should never be used merely to duplicate the function of general laws. Only where the institution's interests as an academic community are distinct and clearly involved should the special authority of the institution be asserted. The student who incidentally violates institutional regulations in the course of his off-campus activity, such as those relating to class attendance, should be subject to no greater penalty than would normally be imposed. Institutional action should be independent of community pressure.

VI. PROCEDURAL STANDARDS IN DISCIPLINARY PROCEEDINGS

In developing responsible student conduct, disciplinary proceedings play a role substantially secondary to example, counseling, guidance, and admonition. At the same time, educational institutions have a duty and the corollary disciplinary powers to protect their educational purpose through the setting of standards of scholarship and conduct for the students who attend them and through the regulation of the use of institutional facilities. In the exceptional circumstances when the preferred means fail to resolve problems of student conduct, proper procedural safeguards should be observed to protect the student from the unfair imposition of serious penalties.

The administration of discipline should guarantee procedural fairness to an accused student. Practices in disciplinary cases may vary in formality with the gravity of the offense and the sanctions which may be applied. They should also take into account the presence or absence of an honor code, and the degree to which the institutional officials have direct acquaintance with student life in general and with the involved student and the circumstances of the case in particular. The jurisdictions of faculty or student judicial bodies, the disciplinary responsibilities of institutional officials and the regular disciplinary procedures, including the student's right to appeal a decision, should be clearly formulated and communicated in advance. Minor penalties may be assessed informally under prescribed procedures.

In all situations, procedural fair play requires that the student be informed of the nature of the charges against him, that he be given a fair opportunity to refute them, that the institution not be arbitrary in its actions, and that there be provision for appeal of a decision. The following are recommended as proper safeguards in such proceedings when there are no honor codes offering comparable guarantees.

A. Standards of conduct expected of students

The institution has an obligation to clarify those standards of behavior which it considers essential to its educational mission and its community life. These general behavioral expectations and the resultant specific regulations should represent a reasonable regulation of student conduct, but the student should be as free as possible from imposed limitations that have no direct relevance to his education. Offenses should be as clearly defined as possible and interpreted in a manner consistent with the aforementioned principles of relevancy and reasonableness. Disciplinary proceedings should be instituted only for violations of standards of conduct formulated with significant student participation and published in advance through such means as a student handbook or a generally available body of institutional regulations.

B. Investigation of student conduct

1. Except under extreme emergency circumstances, premises occupied by students and the personal possessions of students should not be searched unless appropriate authorization has been obtained. For premises such as residence halls controlled by the institution, an appropriate and responsible authority should be designated to whom application should be made before a search is conducted. The application should specify the reasons for the search and the objects or information sought. The student should

be present, if possible, during the search. For premises not controlled by the institution, the ordinary requirements for lawful search should be followed.

2. Students detected or arrested in the course of serious violations of institutional regulations, or infractions of ordinary law, should be informed of their rights. No form of harassment should be used by institutional representatives to coerce admissions of guilt or information about conduct of other suspected persons.

C. Status of student pending final action

Pending action on the charges, the status of a student should not be altered, or his right to be present on the campus and to attend classes suspended, except for reasons relating to his physical or emotional safety and well-being, or for reasons relating to the safety and well-being of students, faculty, or university property.

D. Hearing committee procedures

When the misconduct may result in serious penalties and if the student questions the fairness of disciplinary action taken against him, he should be granted, on request, the privilege of a hearing before a regularly constituted hearing committee. The following suggested hearing committee procedures satisfy the requirements of procedural due process in situations requiring a high degree of formality.

1. The hearing committee should include faculty members or students, or, if regularly included or requested by the accused, both faculty and student members. No member of the hearing committee who is otherwise interested in the particular case should sit in judgment during the proceeding.

2. The student should be informed, in writing, of the reasons for the proposed disciplinary action with sufficient particularity, and in sufficient time, to insure opportunity to prepare for the hearing.

3. The student appearing before the hearing committee should have the right to be assisted in his defense by an adviser of his choice.

4. The burden of proof should rest upon the officials bringing the charge.

5. The student should be given an opportunity to testify and to

present evidence and witnesses. He should have an opportunity to hear and question adverse witnesses. In no case should the committee consider statements against him unless he has been advised of their content and of the names of those who made them, and unless he has been given an opportunity to rebut unfavorable inferences which might otherwise be drawn.

6. All matters upon which the decision may be based must be introduced into evidence at the proceeding before the hearing committee. The decision should be based solely upon such matters. Improperly acquired evidence should not be admitted.

7. In the absence of a transcript, there should be both a digest and a verbatim record, such as a tape recording, of the hearing.

8. The decision of the hearing committee should be final, subject only to the student's right of appeal to the president or ultimately to the governing board of the institution.

In Loco Parentis

From the Basic Policy Declarations *of the U.S. National Student Association.*

No Paternalism

FACT:

The contemporary doctrine *in loco parentis* has its basis in certain late nineteenth century U.S. Court decisions which ruled that the university could impose no sanctions upon a student which a parent could not impose upon his children. Thus, this concept was originally conceived as a restriction upon the university in its dealings with students. Today, however, this theory is used as the basis for establishing the university as paternal guardian over the moral, intellectual and social activities of the student. From the tradition of *in loco parentis* come these conceptions: the student need not be directly involved in the formation of the general university policies and the administration may circumscribe the perimeter of a student's interests, speech and thought, personal and group associations, and actions. In addition to its effect upon the individual student, the university, operating within the framework of *in loco parentis,* may and does establish certain restrictions on the operation of the student government, the student press, and other student organizations.

In this regard, USNSA has commented critically on arbitrary expulsion of students, certain limitations on student government, press censorship, mandatory requirement of membership lists, restrictive regulations on speakers, suppression of access to information, and other problems relating to academic freedom and the social sources of repression. USNSA has not previously examined, however, the ways in which *in loco parentis*, as a theory, determines the attitude of administrations toward students and the ways in which it conditions the response of the individual student in asserting his own social and academic freedoms. . . .

PRINCIPLE:

USNSA continues to affirm the belief that the university must not restrict those freedoms of thought, association and action which are simultaneously the prerequisites of a fully democratic social order and personal development. The vision toward which we strive is that of a democratic university in which all share certain rights of participation in matter of common concern, and of freedom of inquiry, association, and development, and where paternalism is replaced by fellowship in the company of scholars.

USNSA endorses the following statement of Committee "S" of the AAUP:

"Free inquiry and free expression are essential attributes of the community of scholars. As members of that community, students should be encouraged to develop the capacity for critical judgment and to engage in a sustained and independent search for truth."

Likewise, USNSA supports the following ACLU statement on "Academic Freedom and Civil Liberties of Students in Colleges and Universities":

The relationship between the educational institution and its students must be viewed in the light of the function of the college or university: to transmit to the student the civilization of the past, to enable him to take part in the civilization of the present and to make that civilization of the future. In this great pursuit, the student must be viewed as an individual who is most likely to attain maturity if left free to make personal decisions and to exercise the rights, as well as shoulder the responsibilities, of citizenship on and off the campus.

DECLARATION:

USNSA condemns the tradition of *in loco parentis* and the educational habits and practices it justifies.

In loco parentis doctrine permits arbitrary and extensive repression of student pursuits and thereby impairs the total significance of the university as a center for the conflict of ideas.

Equally important are the effects of *in loco parentis* doctrine on the changing student. Paternalism in any form induces or reinforces immaturity, conformity, and disinterest among those whose imagination, critical talent and capacities for integrity and growth should be encouraged and given opportunity for development.

Insofar as *in loco parentis* doctrine removes responsibility for personal decision-making from the individual student, it distorts and weakens a significant phase of the educational process. The unexamined acceptance of authority which is often appropriate to the child-parent relationship must be replaced in the universities by the encouragement of a critical and dialectical relationship between the student and his community. The range of inquiry within or beyond the classroom must not be restricted out of paternal considerations but must be opened out of educational ones.

USNSA calls on faculties and administrations to open the universities to fuller and more meaningful student participation in those university and community affairs which shape student life and development. These include the content of the curriculum, in such social disciplines as is necessary to maintain order in the classroom. The process of education does require some minimal level of order and discipline.

However, those forms of discipline which can be justified on the basis of this formula are few and scarce, and the danger is great that illegitimate paternalism will be confused with proper control. It is the responsibility of all students to attempt to clearly delineate the equal responsibility of those academic administrators charged with the establishment of such policy to justify, individually, each attempt to impose any sort of order upon the academic community.

USNSA calls upon American students to seek not only an end to formal campus restrictions which prohibit legitimate freedoms, but also to seek the instruments with which to generate a community where men are linked by a common commitment to learning, not segregated by the atmosphere which paternalism fosters.

Article by William R. Smoot, II, editor of The Purdue Exponent, *student newspaper, Purdue University, November 21, 1968.*

The Unmaking of an Editor

Anything is possible—at Purdue University. A three-car train can chug its way across the middle of the campus. The President can continually hose the legal channels of students and faculty—and get by with it; a student editor can average five crank letters a day—two will be appeals for his soul's salvation, one an accusation of sexual mania, signed with name and phone number; students can ask a veteran civil rights lawyer what his stand is on open housing or inter-racial dating. If the world would only watch we could become the capital of entertainment—starring us all. But as it is, it's only we who watch ourselves. Which can be very interesting—as it was for me to watch the process of my position unraveling, the unmaking of an editor.

It started, in the manner of a storybook, on my twenty-first birthday—July 16, and I was speaking on student unrest to the local Rotary Club, and I probably caused more unrest than I discussed. Several administrators were present, including club song leader Mallett, who, to everyone's orgasmic delight, belted out "I-want-a-girl-just-like-the-girl-who-married-dear-old-Dad." I stored my laughter inside to be discharged at a more socially appropriate time. My speech seemed to have the same general effect as pouring sand in their underwear. Even the seasoned administrators seemed upset that I had the audacity to bear the hallmark of Purdue while criticizing authoritarian administrators, an immoral foreign policy, and a segregated Lafayette.

I somehow rated with *Lafayette Journal and Courier* editor John C. Scott a 27-inch column which began by observing I made the group "grateful that there are more Rotarians than there are Smoots," and ended by suggesting I have a picnic with the John Birch Society.

It seemed I had begun to make waves, or rather people like Mr. Scott had begun to make them for me.

Then there came my speech at the Green Guard ice cream social, reported in the *Journal and Courier* as a "free love speech" which made me wonder if maybe I hadn't spoken to some other group. The subsequent shock tremor ran all through the midwest. Reporters called for quotes, Indianapolis wanted me for television, professors had instant joke material, and Dean Roberts invited me for coffee in his office. I took mine with sugar while he tried to say sex and ice cream don't mix or something. He said his phone had rung off the hook with calls of protests, not to mention the fact that I had grossed out house-mothers and deans of women. He said it was not the content of the speech that mattered, but its effect—a remark that was not nearly as important as the philosophy from which it was derived.

It was about a week later that I learned at least two high-school administrators had expressed dismay over the nature of *Exponent*'s content and saw a boycott by local advertisers as a way out. My Rotary speech was mentioned, as was the content of the summer issue. Meanwhile, a student anti-Exponent petition came and went and an official in the alumni office told several students that I was a Communist and a sex maniac. I remarked in return that if one had to be a maniac I guessed a sex maniac was probably the best kind.

Then came the lull before the storm. Things were generally peaceful. Even the *Journal and Courier* got off my back, though Ralph Kramer of the *Indianapolis News* quietly reported.

Next, the sit-in against the CIA, and the *Exponent* was reporting, rather than creating the excitement, and that was as it should be.

While I was having eggs one morning I nearly laid one as the now infamous "Notes from a Black Book" column leaped at me from the editorial page. It sounded a little worse each time I read it, so I quit after three. It struck me that the column was fairly well done, hilariously funny, and gross as hell. I was beginning to have enough of a feel for Purdue and the zoo that surrounds it to know I'd have a few phone calls about that one.

And I did. The first was from Dr. Hicks, who said he was on his way over, which was extraordinary, to say the least, that the Executive Assistant to the President run over to see me at eleven in the morning. He seemed to regard the printing of the column as a crisis of the highest degree, and he strongly urged that we apologize for it. We talked about related and unrelated topics awhile, ending with the grape boycott in support of California grape-pickers.

That afternoon the senior staff agreed on an editorial apologizing to those who had had their sensibilities offended but affirming our justification in printing it. In the next two days I had several phoned threats, one by a student who identified himself as Bob Bradshaw. The others remained anonymous and I suggested to them we schedule the beating in order to have a reporter and photographer cover the action.

It was in a conversation with Dean Roberts that week that I began to realize the administration's extreme concern over the reactions of alums and others outside the university. It seems I had gained the dubious distinction of creating more furor at Purdue than Roberts had ever remembered in his 17 years here. We discussed the dilemma of editorial freedom versus alumni donations and legislature funds and both agreed that the question could well come down to whether you're willing to pay a million dollars for telling it like it is, and in the manner you want to tell it.

Then the Student Publications Committee swung into non-action, recommending a probationary period for me as editor as a result of the Cabbell column. The *Journal and Courier* came to life again in what was supposed to be a news story linking dirty signs at a football game to myself and Professor Gass. Though flattered by the association (to Gass, not the signs), I hardly regarded the connection a valid one.

Several alums had written letters of protest after the Cabbell column, but the 21 karat hose came when an alum called promising to see to it that I got fired stating he had the capital power to do it. I politely ran through my short freedom of expression speech, then he reaffirmed his promise and hung up. Hung up was right, I thought.

When the trustees came to town for their November meeting they were evidently upset about the *Exponent*. At their Tuesday night dinner meeting, an informant in the room has reported, they were discussing the paper and passing around not only Cabbell's controversial column, but also an *Exponent* editorial critizing the Krannert and engineering schools for a lack of emphasis on ethical and moral considerations. I find this particularly interesting in the light of administrative claims that it was "dirty" words, not editorial policies, that prompted my firing. Also being passed around the table was a copy of "Willie Masters' Lonesome Wife," a new book by Prof. Gass, about whom the Trustees spoke negatively on Wednesday for his activities with the *Exponent*.

It has been widely rumored that the Trustees asked [President] Hovde to expel me from school. Although one person in the dean's offices has confirmed this, he was not present at the meeting. Thus, it is still an undocumented rumor, and it should be regarded as such.

On Thursday morning the fatal poem was published in the *Exponent*'s literary magazine supplement, and when Hovde's plane landed at the Purdue airport, several vice-presidents were there to meet him. According to several airport employees, these administrators had several copies of Thursday's *Exponent* with them. The men met in a room at the airport, and it is believed that there the decision to fire me was made.

Early Friday morning administrative secretaries called my senior staff to inform them of an urgent meeting in the trustees' room at 11:00 a.m. I answered my phone shortly after nine as I was sitting over breakfast and my French book, sugar crisp and *Arsène Lupin,* and I was told to be in Roberts' office at 10:30. I informed the secretary that I rather had my heart set on attending my medieval philosophy class for the first time in a week, but she said the meeting was "extremely urgent."

So I walked into his office at 10:30 and was handed a notice of firing. The good Dean told me he would be glad to discuss the matter later, but was in no position to do so then. After being informed that I was not to attend the eleven o'clock meeting. So I left the office, and with it any hope that anything short of revolution could ever change Purdue.

I returned to the office to think, await my staff and the struggle that was to follow. And convinced that, indeed, at Purdue anything is possible.

Letter to The Purdue Exponent *from Warren G. Hansen, Associate Professor, School of Pharmacy, Purdue University, December 4, 1968.*

The University—House of Truth

AN OPEN LETTER TO THE EDITOR OF THE EXPONENT, THE STUDENT BODY PRESIDENT, ALL ACTIVISTS, AND IDEALISTS, GREEKS, AND THE UNCONCERNED.

Dear Editor:

I wish to begin by identifying myself as one of those professors who last spring was honored by his students as being "most popular." I start this way only because it has been implied in the *Exponent* that professors who rate well in students' eyes would be in complete agreement with all of the numerous protests, dissents, and demands that have been made during the last few weeks. This implication is not correct, and I feel strongly that a different point of view needs to be presented.

To put things in perspective, let us re-examine something that seems to have been forgotten in recent weeks—the basic functions of a university. A university—any university—has two basic functions. These are: (1) the promulgation of truth and (2) the search for new truth; in other words, teaching and research. As an ancillary activity to these basic functions, the university renders public service, chiefly in the form of consulting. It is important to note that it is not the function of the university to implement the information it transmits or generates.

Implementation is the function of other structures of our society: the political structure, the industrial structure, the business structure, the community structure. In recent years the university has come to be a major influence on the activities of other structures of society for a variety of reasons. It supplies trained people to carry out the functions of society, and it supplies information, both indirectly and directly, which is useful to society. However, it is to be repeated, the university is not responsible for the implementation of its information; the university does not make a god of itself and pass moral judgements on society.

The educated person, who is capable of fulfilling a meaningful and effective role in the activities of society is the chief product of the university's functions. That Mr. Editor is you, and the other 23,700 students who avail themselves of the facilities of this campus. Let us ask, therefore, a basic question: What is an educated person?

The educated person is many things at once. The most obvious of these is this: He has at his immediate disposal a body of information and/or technological skills which he can use directly in the performance of a job, by which he earns his (or her) livelihood. It is usually assumed that the job or profession which an educated person takes or enters is more rewarding both financially and in other ways than a job which would be available to a person without higher education. This is the basic reason that most students are here. There are only two basic forces which motivate people: reward and punishment, and the most powerful of these is reward. The job which awaits at graduation is the most basic of the rewards of education.

Other aspects of an educated person, while less obvious, are even more important than the basic skills involved in earning a livelihood. An educated person is mature. He is an adult. As such, he is capable of managing his personal life in an intelligent and, it is to be hoped, a creative fashion. He approaches his problems with the polished inner resources of his mind, rather than with the raw savagery of his animal instincts. He recognizes that as he grows in experience, his personal limitations may diminish and that his personal capabilities may expand. But he comes also to recognize that at no time in his life is he without limitations. Recognizing this, he realizes that most problems, most issues, do not lend themselves to instant solutions! He is aware that problem solving or issue resolving, is basically a process of trial and error.

An educated person does not become mature all at once. The matriculating freshman is not instantly transformed at registration time from an adolescent into an adult by some process of magic. The transition is gradual. The sophomore may believe that he knows everything worth knowing, and that he has the resources to solve all problems, if only those stupid middle-aged people riding the top of the Establishment would let him. The mature person has come to realize how much he does not know, and this should translate personally into a kind of intellectual humility. He realizes that he does not have all the resources necessary to solve problems instantly, or to resolve issues with quick dispatch. For most young people this transition from adolescence to maturity is an adventure, an experience which is joyful and exciting; for a few it is painful; for some (and these are the unfortunate ones) it is boring. A very few just never make it.

An educated person possesses a certain polish, a sophistication which others do not have. If he is male, he is a gentleman; if she is female, she is a lady. He has the inner resources of thought, attitudes, and vocabulary that he does not need to be vulgar, offensive, or shocking in order to make a point. I used to take my car to a certain mechanic for periodic repairs. When he would describe what he had done to my car, he would use an assortment of pungent four letter words and frequent references to the reproductive organs to illustrate his work. If I would take my wife with me to pick up the car, it was almost impossible for him to tell me what he had done. He did not know other descriptive language, yet he was enough of a gentleman that he knew his descriptions would offend a lady, and this he did not wish to do. It was easy enough to tolerate his language, because he had no education; he didn't know anything different! He was a CLOD, but at least he had the instincts of a gentleman. To this observer, the remarks made by the Editor early this year to the Freshman women were remarks characteristic of a clod, and devoid of the instincts of a gentleman. Somewhere along the line an education failed to make its impact! An ability to use one's mother tongue in a tasteful, elegant manner is the mark of an educated person! . . .

We have heard much in recent weeks about rights; we have heard nothing about duties or obligations. The educated person knows that these are intimately interrelated. He knows that if he is to receive a right, he obligates himself to grant the same right to each other person: He knows that an orderly functioning society must impose both constraints and obligations. The truly educated person does not feel called upon to demand the right to go to class in bare feet, or to use four letter words in public discussion. The question of whether bare feet might be construed lewd ought never to have come up. Of course bare feet are not lewd; they are simply inappropriate. One does not ordinarily attend church in a swim suit, a funeral in shirt sleeves, or apply for a new job in a sweat shirt and blue jeans. When one hears demands for rights of this sort, it is difficult to take them seriously. . . .

From an article by anthropologist Margaret Mead in Columbia University Forum, *Fall 1968.*

The Wider Significance of the Columbia Upheaval

The events at Columbia mark the end of a very long epoch during which students have been treated as wards of academic institutions, a position that joins special controls with special privileges and immunities from the civil authorities. . . . Under the traditional English and American system, students, whether they belong to the privileged classes or are permitted, by scholarship or menial work, to enter the cloistered halls designed for the privileged, are treated as academic novices toward whom the university acts *in loco parentis*, and the students have been subject to the authority of their teachers, as they are also subject to the authority of their parents. Every detail of their lives—where they sleep, what they eat, what they wear—has been, and to some extent still is, subject to college authority. Their less privileged age mates who go out to work become almost full adult members of the working world, but students remain in tutelage, socially privileged, but politically and economically in the position of minors who are supported by parents or given just enough to subsist on by grant-giving authorities. In the past they were expected not to marry, and if their wild oats were sown too publicly they were expelled. Going to college was, and still is, regarded as a privilege, and those who do not obey the rules can be "sent down" (in the English phrase) or "kicked out" (in the American). The college was, and still is, treated as if it were a little autonomous kingdom, situated on the best high ground, paying no taxes, and often enough barely giving aid and comfort to the theological and economic dissenters from the majority views of the surrounding community. In return for the continued protection and teaching offered by the college, students were expected to surrender part of their freedom as young adults; but they were also permitted considerable license, in the form of pranks, destruction of college property, defamation of sacred symbols, such as Alma Mater, importation of live stock into the classroom, organized cruelty to one another in the form of hazing, interclass ritual battles (only brought to a halt in the cases of severe maiming or death), initiation rituals rivaling those of savage tribes, cheating on a grand scale, and occasional forays into the town, where traditional town and gown conflicts were reflected in conflicts with the police. The police were expected to treat students with the gentleness their high status and tender years merited. Above all, in return for their protected state and license for fun and games, they were expected to be apolitical, and not, like some European and most South American students, to get mixed up in active politics.

Meanwhile, the whole face of the United States has changed. Half of our student-age people are in some kind of higher education and many of them are entirely state supported. In public institutions, instead of the old boards of trustees, custodians of endowments, there are governing boards subject to local political pressures. Study goes on far beyond the undergraduate college, which was once the preparation for academia, for a profession, or for a privileged life. Higher education is no longer a privilege or even a right. It is an arduous requirement laid on young people by the standards of employment in the society. Hundreds of thousands of students are husbands and wives, fathers and mothers, and wage earners who are attempting to carry the double load of study, still conceived of as an ivory tower activity, and full economic participation. Yet all students, those who are wage earners and those who are being supported by parents and scholarships in a nominal prolongation of childhood, are still set apart by their student status from full participation as members of society. Furthermore, although there is a draft that treats young men of 18 as ready to fight, there are also voting laws that deny them the vote and laws in most states that forbid anyone under 21 years of age, even veterans, to buy a glass of beer. The moralists, who have lost out in regulating the private lives of mature adults, still attempt to regulate the private lives of young adults by treating the late teens as an extension of childhood.

It is against this anomalous status that students are demonstrating and rioting, although the causes of rioting are variously defined: demands for the admission of members of minority groups; against dismissal or for retention of a professor; against classes on Good Friday; against the presence of Dow Chemical; against recruiting for the Marines; or just "general discontent." In this state of discontent, disturbances are triggered by any slight episode or by the organized disruptive behavior of small groups of the left or right. And every institution in this country is ripe for some kind of disorder. In some, the administration may have enough leverage to keep ahead of trouble; in others the students themselves have had the wisdom to anticipate the necessary changes (as when Cornell students voluntarily asked that the university no longer interpose its paternalistic arms between them and civil authorities). As in any potentially revolutionary situation, there are sporadic outbreaks, panicky and belated reforms, fumbles for leadership and, within the English speaking world, minor changes that are treated up to the last minute as unbearably revolutionary and destructive to our entire system as well as tremendous changes that are called minor adjustments.

The event that led to the involvement of Columbia students— undergraduates, graduate students, Teachers College students,

students in the professional schools and in General Studies—as well as the young faculty who identified with the students, *vis à vis* the heads of their departments, was the dramatic revocation of the university's traditional claim to protect and discipline its own students when the administration called in the police. This reversal was made more dramatic by the long period of waiting, the sense of a power vacuum, the formation of an interim and an *ad hoc* faculty group, and the appropriate and often heroic attempts of the faculty to protect students from one another, from the administration, and from the police. A compact as old as the university system was broken. Students were treated like ordinary disrupters of the peace, trespassers, vandals, despoilers of private property, breakers and enterers, and this at the initiation of the university authorities. This brought outraged accusations of incredible brutality, far exceeding the outcry raised when three Negro students were shot dead at South Carolina State University in Orangeburg. Although the students at Columbia suffered few serious injuries, the sense of the overwhelming brutal power of the police was due to this sense of outrage at a broken compact.

But the compact needs to be abrogated. It is no longer appropriate to treat students as a privileged and protected group who, in return for this special station, abstain from political activity of any sort, submit to the regulation of their private lives, and risk expulsion for every sort of minor infraction of a set of outmoded rules. It is time we have the 18-year-old vote and recognize that students are making a valuable contribution in the economic and social life of the country by learning some of its more demanding skills. Furthermore, we must increasingly take into account the many students at universities who are not young adults, but middle-aged men and women who are returning for refresher courses or for completely new careers. Thus it becomes totally unbearable to identify studentship with the prolongation of childhood.

Today's students should no longer be dependent on their parents—those whose parents have any funds—nor should they be dependent on scholarships grudgingly doled out after a means test. They should be given full economic status, the status of an adult who is expected to marry, who works and has a Social Security number and may become a member of a trade union; someone who may get a mortgage and a telephone, buy furniture on time, and can, if necessary, collect unemployment insurance. Under the guise of privilege and protection, we have been penalizing our student population, separating them from participation in the affairs of the real world and impairing their capacity to understand that world.

There is a bizarre inverse correspondence between student groups and that other locus of rioting and destruction of property in today's America, the ghetto. The inhabitants of the ghetto are underprivileged, where the students are overprivileged, hungry where the students are well fed, living among dirt and rats instead of in subsidized dormitories. But still there is a resemblance. As long as ghetto dwellers were docile, respectful, and accepted submissively their second-class political and economic status, they too were allowed license—within their black communities—which would not have been permitted outside. As long as they fought only among themselves, cheated or stole from one another, took out their frustrations on one another, the dominant white community interfered very little, except, sometimes, "to fix" a case for a Negro who did come in conflict with the law. This is a kind of bitter caricature of the way in which colleges and universities have been able to intervene on behalf of students who got into trouble with the police. Black adults and student adults alike have been treated as less than responsible, have been permitted to indulge in violent behavior as long as it was circumscribed and confined to their own territory. Too often, during the ghetto riots of the last three years, I have heard the comment, "Well, if they want to burn down their part of town, let them."

Demonstrations, civil disobedience, and inappropriate public behavior have been the perennial recourse of those who, lacking political power, seek to enter the world of the politically and economically privileged. German peasants during the Reformation, Quakers quaking in the streets, Buddhist monks who have forsaken their posture of peaceful noninvolvement, nuns who have come out of their cloistered walls, or housewives storming the House of Commons, all these are instances of groups that have resorted to various forms of unusual public behavior to attract attention to wrongs newly seen as wrongs, wrongs often so new that they had not yet been named.

Two generations ago, when women were fighting for the right to vote, they resorted to similar kinds of behavior—marches, hunger strikes, chemicals in mail boxes, tying themselves to the pillars of the White House, and throwing themselves down in the path of mounted police. Whenever a group that has been required to be docile, segregated, submissive, undemanding, and unparticipating, glimpses the possibility of wider participation in the society, we may expect phenomena like these demonstrations to call attention to their plight. And especially when the wider society has permitted limited license, we may expect violent contrast as combatants overflow the limits of violence and challenge the complacency and safety of the larger society.

The fumbling, hesitation, contradictions, and confusion at Columbia in the period between the Tuesday when an associate dean was taken hostage and the Tuesday morning a week later when the police were called in, were overdetermined by the presence of not one but two explosive groups, the students and the inhabitants of Harlem. Fear of one reinforced fear of the other. At the same time, the contrast between the two was reinforced by the greater self-discipline of the Black Power group who are in all this in deadly earnest and cannot afford the ebullience that still characterizes campus radicals, who have been protected by the university *in loco parentis.*

The issue of the gymnasium is a symbol of the town and gown difficulties of a great landowning institution like Columbia, situated on the heights like the castles of old, while the poor live down in the valley. Here, as in the relations between students, the university, and the larger society, there is need for a new set of relations between the boards that control these giant educational corporations and the deteriorating slum communities that surround them. The gymnasium had been intended as a good-will gesture, but it was a gesture, like that made by the students who made honest attempts to tutor children in Harlem. A "gesture" is no longer the answer. Just as boards of trustees must become more responsive to the will of the faculty and to the current student body within the institutions for which they hold responsibility, so also boards of trustees of tax-exempt private institutions must find ways of responding to the needs and wishes of the other institutions and the residents of the communities in which they are situated. One of the problems in the Columbia area is that there are too few ordinary, householding citizens who can voice such needs emphatically. Mammoth institutions too easily become slum landlords, and in so doing they lose both the confidence and the recognition of the people who live in the surrounding slums, against whom they close their high iron gates. The day is past for town and gown opposition, both the traditional opposition between students, the townsmen and the police and the headlined opposition between educational institutions and the ordinary residents of the town.

But the student body has not, I believe, quite realized the meaning of the changes that will come. They demand more participation in the institutions in which they are currently privileged or condemned to study in years of incarceration away from the real work of the world.

At present their demands are inchoate and, in many cases, either articulately destructive or simply unrealistic. For example, giving students the right to hire and fire professors is as inappropriate as if the passengers on a single voyage demanded the right to fire the captain in mid-ocean or midflight. They will want to think through carefully, and in consultation, just which are the university activities in which student control and student autonomy and initiative are important. Perhaps all responsibility for their nonacademic lives should be vested in the students. Do they want this? They will need to recognize just what it will mean to be treated like other citizens, subject to the same rules and the same penalties, unsupervised but also unprotected. They will need to decide on the kinds of university policies they think should be reported and explained to them; on the kinds of situations in which they can be observers and those in which they can be consultants, working with faculty, administration, and trustees. What should be their knowledge of and their voice in such matters as the policy of the university toward Selective Service, tax exemption, acquisition or sale of land, disciplining or encouragement of articulate dissent, payment of employees, treatment of unions, the management, building programs, and community relations? When they begin to make socially responsible demands, they will almost immediately acquire the education in real life which they complain the university denies them. . . .

Jurisdiction

Resolution of the Wisconsin Students Association (WSA), adopted October 12, 1967.

Resolution on University Jurisdiction

No University agency, student or otherwise, should pass or enforce regulations which protect or punish any student or organization violating a law of Wisconsin or the United States. It should be remembered that a student is a citizen and responsible to civil law whether he has committed an offense on or off campus. Civil law would be expected to be enforced on campus and no repetition of legislation on the use of drugs, alcohol, gambling or in the areas of civil rights and liberties need be made.

In no case should an individual or organization be subject to more than civil action; that is, it should in no way affect his status as a student. The status of a student shall be affected only by his ability to participate in classroom activity.

When a student has been apprehended for the violation of a law of the community, the state, or the nation, the University will not request or agree to special consideration for the student because of his status as a student. The University may only take sanctions against the student based on his academic participation.

The University may provide for a student whatever counseling, psychiatric, and medical facilities it has at its disposal (counseling does not include University sanctions such as probation or expulsion). However the University may not dismiss a student for anything other than his academic performance; nor may they review his status because of his breaking of a civil or criminal law (e.g., involvement with drugs).

From the report by the Ad Hoc Committee on The Role of Students in the Government of the University of Wisconsin (The Crow Committee), February 6, 1968.

Reply

We endorse much of the [Wisconsin Students Association] statement. The University should not ordinarily intervene in the individual activities or conduct of a student. There are many matters of individual student behavior as to which no University agency, student or otherwise, should attempt to make regulations or enforce discipline. . . .

However, the view that whenever *any* civil law applies to the conduct, the University must *never* impose its own discipline, goes too far. There must be exceptions where serious danger to University functions and processes is involved. In this connection, indeed, the student position, as it has been presented to us, is somewhat ambivalent. On the one hand, they assert that they want to be exclusively under civil rather than University authority. On the other, they do not appear to be asking for the logical extension that the campus and dormitories be regularly patrolled by the Madison police (or possibly campus police enforcing state law), who would presumably also be the first resort in any on-campus disorder or other conduct violating civil law. Individual student views vary. Indeed, without having the benefits of a detailed poll, we really wonder how many students would prefer being taken to criminal court for lesser offenses which might otherwise result in no more than a semester of disciplinary probation.

We are aware that some members of this faculty and of the administration think that University discipline should continue to apply to individual student misconduct because such discipline has educational and corrective value ("It's for the good of the student"). Some also think University discipline is appropriate because students should be expected to adhere to some higher standard of conduct than that enforced by the larger community upon its citizens in general. . . . While some members of the committee feel nostalgia for the relatively recent days when such views prevailed, we [believe] . . . that formal enforcement of these hopes and expectations as such is not feasible. With vast numbers of students in the University, many thousands of them married or over 21 or both, in the normal situation all students should be treated as young adults, expected to obey all the laws of the larger community and subject only to the same enforcement and punishment procedures as other citizens.

Therefore, in ordinary situations, we concur . . . with the general movement away from the University's playing a role *in loco parentis.* The off-campus behavior of a student as an individual in ways that do not represent a continuing threat to the welfare of others in the University community should not be a matter for University disciplinary action. Further, we think that the same proposition would hold even if the particular behavior should happen to occur within the geographical limits of the campus. Individual conduct on campus can be dealt with by campus police, who have the power to make arrests for violations of state laws. In addition, University authorities can deal with such conduct by bringing complaints against offending individuals to the attention of the Dane County District Attorney.

As stated previously, the ultimate WSA position that whenever civil law applies to student behavior, the University has no rights whatever to use disciplinary sanctions, is too absolute to be acceptable. There is a point at which it would not be feasible, nor would it be fair to the University community as a whole, for the University to fail to use its disciplinary powers.

The following are guidelines as to when University officials should have the discretionary authority to impose University discipline. . . .

1. . . . Intentional student conduct which seriously damages or destroys University property justifies imposition of University discipline. What about minor damage to, theft of, or defacing of University property? A complaint can be made to the civil authorities, but that course may be unwise in most such cases. We suggest that in such cases, the University should not assert the power of probation, suspension, or expulsion, but has and should assert the power to require the student culprit to pay for any needed repair, cleaning, replacement, or the like, and to withhold awarding of academic credit pending such payment. Such a procedure should be adequate for the lesser property damage cases. Within the spirit of those guidelines, we would expect appropriate University administrators to make the decision as to whether a given incident of property damage requires disciplinary action or merely compensation.

2. Likewise, student conduct which clearly indicates a serious continuing danger to the personal safety of other members of the University community will justify University discipline, including removal of the student from the University community by expulsion. The narrow scope of this category of conduct should be understood. One incident of even quite violent antisocial behavior by a student would not, in the Committee's view, justify University disciplinary action without clear and satisfactory evidence that the incident indicated a serious continuing danger to other members of the University community. It should be clear, however, that University authorities would be expected to bring such behavior to the attention of civil authorities.

3. The third category of conduct is still more difficult to state

with precision. [A previous faculty report] refers to conduct which is "unduly disruptive of the educational process." One example in that report is cheating on exams, which of course must be subject to University discipline; we do not understand the WSA position to be otherwise. But "disruptive" conduct includes a wide range of other conduct, depending on how one defines disruption and how one defines "educational process." Recent events only reinforce the Committee's belief that University power over conduct of this kind must be examined and restated with great care.

(a) We are agreed that at least some kinds of intentional conduct which affect University functions and processes must be subject to University discipline.

(b) In general, we think University discipline is proper only when the intentional student conduct involved has clearly and seriously obstructed or impaired a University function or process. We use here the phrase "intentional student conduct" with the hope that it will not be misconstrued. What must be "intentional" is the conduct itself; this does not require proof that the conduct was "intended" to have the consequence of a clear and serious obstruction or impairment of a University function. For example, a student who loses control while driving his car and crashes into a University building where a class is in progress, forcing the class to adjourn, might be very careless but would not be guilty of intentional conduct. On the other hand, students who mass at the entrance to a classroom, preventing students from getting to class, are engaging in intentional conduct. Their argument that their *intention* was not to obstruct the class, but only to protest the draft (or celebrate a Rose Bowl invitation), would in our view be irrelevant.

(c) Some conduct poses especially difficult problems because the conduct is politically inspired and, up to a point, represents an expression of the right of free speech and dissent which both the Constitution and our own University traditions not only permit but cherish. The right to speak out, to dissent, and to associate with others in doing so, does not however mean the right to forcibly stop the lawful activities of others. When student conduct, even though related to dissent or other political expression, clearly and seriously obstructs or impairs a University function or process, the University must be free to use its disciplinary powers as one means to stop the impairment and discourage future impairment.

(d) We emphasize "clear and serious obstruction or impairment," knowing that these words may be asserted by some to have the same vice of vagueness now claimed to corrupt words like "unduly disruptive." The words are general, indeed, but in the context of this discussion we do not regard them as vague. But as a further safeguard, we assert that we mean them to restrict sharply the kinds of conduct which fall properly within this category. It is our recommendation that in applying this standard, the University explicitly accept the burden of proving by clear and convincing evidence not only that the claimed misconduct occurred, but also that it was of the gravity and significance implicit in the general words we have offered. It follows that we cannot accept the suggestion made by some that the University is powerless to use its disciplinary processes unless it spells out a lengthy, detailed, and specific list of acts of prohibited conduct. We do not understand "due process" or any other constitutional imperative to require this of the University, but it may be that the promulgation of some sort of "Student Code" would be an aid in University disciplinary matters.

From the report of the faculty-student Commission on the Interdependence of University Regulations and Local, State and Federal Law (The Sindler Committee), Cornell University, September 27, 1967.

Distinguishing Code Enforcement and Law Enforcement

The separation of University disciplinary authority or Code enforcement from law enforcement raises many vexing and perhaps controversial implications of our position. Some of the more central problems are discussed below.

A. The mislabeled problem of "double jeopardy"

"Double jeopardy," which is proscribed by the U. S. Constitution, protects a person from being tried twice for the same offense. It is not considered the same offense, and hence, the protection does not apply when the person's action constitutes several offenses tried by one jurisdiction or separate offenses against different jurisdictions for which he is tried by those jurisdictions. Technically, then, the responsibility of students to the University and the civil society, wherein the same misconduct could be punishable by both, occasions no double jeopardy.

It is more appropriate to speak of "double jurisdiction," which is an unalterable condition for students, as for faculty and staff, who are subject to general laws just like everyone else, and to University rules as well. The spirit of double jeopardy, rather than its literal presence, is perhaps germane to invoke if one jurisdiction simply duplicates the regulations of the other and the student's misconduct is automatically punished by both. Such would obtain if the student were routinely punished by the University for the offense of being convicted of law violation.

Our proposals clearly dissociate University discipline from law violations as such, and hence, fully eradicate any aspect of double jeopardy. The student whose misconduct has resulted in conviction for law violation has the same standing as the student whose misconduct has not: in either case, disciplinary proceedings may be instituted only if the misconduct is shown to have adversely affected a specific University interest. As a practical matter, the student serving a sentence in prison is incapable of simultaneously continuing his Cornell education. But then his departure from the University comes not from the addition of University punishment to that of society, but from the exclusive action of society, i.e., his imprisonment.

While our proposals deny automatic imposition of University sanctions on a student because of his criminal conviction, they permit University review of such events to determine if specific Cornell interests have been damaged, i.e., to determine if the Code has also been violated. As discussed earlier, we expect sparing rather than routine reliance on this provision, because dismissal of a student from Cornell should be based on the harm to clear University interests his presence would cause.

B. Diverse outcomes under double jurisdiction

The double jurisdiction governing student misconduct, like all double jurisdictions that involve dissimilar standards, can produce diverse results only partly modifiable by enforcement methods. As a typical example, one not peculiar to the Cornell-Ithaca situation or to the standard we propose, consider the different outcomes of what might appear to be much the same misconduct when University jurisdiction is delimited to the "University community." Suppose a student stole a radio, this being the first time he had stolen anything or had committed any offense against the law.

1. If he stole from another member of the University community, then no matter where the theft took place, a Code violation has occurred.

(a) If the police apprehended the student, public officials would have disposition of the case, and the University could subsequently punish the student for a Code violation.

(b) If the University apprehended the student, it could turn the matter over to the police, and then follow the procedure set forth in (1,a); or it could handle the matter exclusively as a Code violation.

2. If he stole from someone not a member of the University community, then no violation of the Code has occurred, and public officials have exclusive jurisdiction.

As a matter of practice, we would expect the University not to impose Code punishment under its option in (1,a), and to handle the matter entirely as a Code offense under its option in (1,b).

Exercise of these enforcement options can modify, but not eliminate the diversity of outcomes. Nor is the diversity a special function of our standard of "University community"; comparable results would obtain by use of an off-campus/campus line of distinction. The basic reason for the varied results may be illustrated as follows. If the two jurisdictions were identical in their offenses, and each routinely imposed punishment for violations regardless of jurisdiction, then the outcomes would be uniform. The student petty thief, in the preceding example, would be simultaneously a Code violator and a law violator, and would be punished by both the University and the community.

Our proposals are grounded on defining the University's jurisdiction and interests much differently from those of the community. Like citizens under state and nation, then, students are separately accountable to the two different authorities of Cornell and society, each with its own set of interests, offenses, sanctions, and enforcement processes. The consequence is that an instance of student misconduct will be associated with different outcomes, depending upon which jurisdiction's interests are involved, which has apprehended the student, and which is considered paramount or exclusive in its handling of the matter.

C. The university posture toward law: Setting the problem

This Report leans heavily on the proposition that Cornell should carefully distinguish its responsibility for student conduct from the task of general law enforcement, which rests with the community. We believe this distinction is vitally necessary to promote the educational mission of the University, and in no way implies University support or approval of student violation of law, or University indifference to the occurrence of student law violation.

It should be apparent that a university cannot require a student to break the law as a condition of his satisfying educational requirements. A student would be well advised to reject his professor's requirement that he had to learn by personal experience, through his apprehension for law violation, the feelings of those arrested, booked, jailed, tried, etc. It is perhaps no less apparent—though not so invariably practiced—that a university should not, in effect, deprive a student of a constitutional right as a condition of his meeting its educational standards. For example, a university should have no disciplinary authority over a student legitimately exercising his right to picket peacefully in the non-university community, so long as the student did not claim, without authority, to represent the university. Finally, a university should not discipline a student for activity which the society does not punish, subject to the important qualification that discipline to protect the legitimate special interests of the university is altogether acceptable. Thus, a university can impose the gravest sanctions on a student for cheating at an examination (not a civil offense at all) or for willful disruption of a classroom (at worst, a minor civil offense).*

* There is a slowly developing body of case law in support of these and many of the subsequent points made here, but the doctrines are insufficiently formed to warrant reliance on them, especially in connection with private universities. For other reasons as well, we prefer to talk in this Report in terms of sound policy, rather than of legal compulsions.

Generally speaking, a university has the authority to punish student activity in violation of the law. The question before the Cornell community—and the central task of this Commission—is the determination of whether, and under what conditions, the University should exercise that authority. The basic position we have advanced carefully differentiates Cornell's responsibility for student misconduct from that of society, and confines the former to misconduct damaging its special interests as an educational community, defined independently of the law.

The full implications of our position for the University's posture toward law are suggested by considering three important and hard problems:

1. When the University must deal with student activity that violates both the Code and the law, to which jurisdiction should it assign the matter?

2. How should the University cooperate with public officials in investigations of students on behalf of law enforcement?

3. When the University is made aware of student activity which is in violation of law, but not in violation of the Code or of the University's interests, what action should the University take? *

D. The university posture toward law: Determining jurisdiction for student misconduct violating both code and law

When community officials apprehend a student for law violation . . . the University offers assistance to the student and cooperation with the officials, though not to the point of agreeing to substitute its discipline for the penalties of society.

When University officials apprehend a student for activity in violation of the Code and the law, we believe that all but very serious breaches of the law should be handled internally as a Code violation. It cannot be denied that such a practice tends to shield students from the ordinary consequences of their unlawful actions. We envision an effective system of University justice, in-

---

* The phrase, "or of the University's interests," is intended to cover situations where the illegal activity is obviously damaging to the University community, but the Code happens not to include an applicable provision. Since University discipline is confined to Code violations, the existence of such situations would call for rapid addition to the Code or, if warranted, emergency University action or community police action.

cluding the imposition of meaningful sanctions when merited. Experience suggests, however, that students will more often prefer to face University discipline than society's justice, which is a relevant measure of the shielding effect of the practice we recommend.

Our proposal, therefore, rests on factors which, in our judgment, thoroughly offset the defect just discussed. Perhaps the best way to indicate those factors is to ask what the alternatives to our position are. It would seem that either Cornell itself must be engaged in law enforcement within the University community, or that Cornell must expect to operate amidst the persistent and widespread presence within the University community of police and other law enforcement officials. We believe neither situation is compatible with the educational goals of Cornell or the maintenance of student-university relations based on trust and good will. We have concluded, therefore, that Cornell should expect to exercise jurisdiction over students it apprehends whose conduct violates both Code and law, excepting those serious breaches of the law which should be assigned to the civil authorities.

The determination of offenses serious enough to merit University assignment of the offender to the civil jurisdiction is a matter of judgment which the Commission has not explored and, hence, offers no position. Whatever the boundaries agreed to, grey areas will remain. In the words of an official of another university: "We tried for four years to delineate clearly which cases should be sent downtown and which should be handled on campus, without any success at all." We do urge that the University community be informed about the boundaries decided on, and that the decision reached on instances falling in the grey area be made not solely by the Code administrator, but in conjunction with the Vice-President for Student Affairs and the Dean of the Faculty.

It would be quite wrong to leave the impression that the University can act unilaterally in assigning students to its exclusive jurisdiction whose behavior violates the law as well as the Code. While there is no reason to believe that the community wants to police the campus any more than the University would welcome such policing, the fact remains that responsibility for law enforcement falls on public officials, not the University. As a matter of law and good sense, then, community law enforcement officials must and should be involved in understandings and procedures jointly worked out with the University and periodically reviewed by both. For example, the determination of what serious law violations are assignable to the civil jurisdiction obviously involves the judgment and cooperation of law enforcement officials. Again, since University enforcement of a Code violation is predicated on no subsequent community prosecution of the same offense as a law violation, the need for a working understanding with the appropriate public officials is apparent.

If the exercise of University justice were made the basis for subsequent public prosecution of a student, the disciplinary system would be profoundly altered in meaning. Under the working relationships we anticipate, no student should have to refuse to cooperate in University proceedings for fear of self-incrimination in connection with later community action. If a student does refuse, he is within his rights, but his status in the University might be placed in jeopardy by his action.

By means of such sensible and sensitive arrangements, Cornell and the community can satisfy their separate and common interests, with respect for the welfare of students.

E. The university posture toward law: Cooperating with public law enforcement with respect to student misconduct

Adoption of the principles and operating policies advocated thus far in the Report would help keep to an acceptable minimum University involvement in law enforcement with respect to students. There will, nonetheless, be times when public officials request University cooperation in a particular investigation. While the University often will be willing or feel obliged to accommodate such requests, care should be taken to assure that its cooperation does not damage student confidence in the University. As one extreme example, Cornell should never consider permitting activity within the student body of undercover agents or of invasion of privacy by wire-tapping, bugging, etc. Since the possible forms of cooperation are many and varied, we confine our comments to one illustration which permits raising some basic problems.

Campaigns to enforce a law within the general Ithaca community, including Cornell, presumably would originate with the city.

(On occasion, Ithaca officials might be loath to countenance lawful but disapproved activity by Cornell students conducted downtown. In such circumstances, the University should not hesitate to use its good offices to protect student exercise of citizen freedoms off the campus.) The University's response to Ithaca's request for its cooperation would turn on weighing the not always complementary factors of promoting the interests of the educational community and maintaining effective relationships with Ithaca officials. Assuming Cornell opted for cooperation, we would strongly urge that the University try to keep its involvement in law enforcement as such to the minimum. When, however, circumstances do not permit Cornell to adhere to this preferred position, we emphasize the following operating rule: *Just as soon as University-student relations are cast in a law enforcement context, students should be made aware of that context of University inquiry at once.* (The details of the conduct of a law enforcement investigation are governed, of course, by law and judicial standards.)

Our concern for adherence to this rule rests only partly on the fear that its violation might well result in a denial of the student's rights as a citizen or in the production of evidence inadmissible in court, or both. Our greater anxiety is that University indifference to the rule may unintentionally nurture student mistrust of the University, with consequences damaging not only to the regulation of student conduct, but to all facets of the University-student relationship.

We think this is no idle fear, as evidenced by the difficulties stemming from the dual role assigned the Proctor as part of the University's cooperation in law enforcement on the marijuana problem. Although operating in this matter primarily as a University official with respect to Code violations, the Proctor was also charged with the responsibility of transmitting to local law enforcement officials information and evidence concerning significant traffic in marijuana. The nature of that assignment inevitably led to student confusion, resentment, and ill will because the University failed to distinguish sharply between its (and the Proctor's) Code enforcement and law enforcement roles.

Nor do we think we exaggerate the harm which could follow failure to adhere to the principle advocated. Mutual good will and trust should undergird University-student relations, perhaps most especially in the sensitive areas of regulation of student conduct.

It seems imperative, therefore, that students be able to assume that when they cooperate with University officials for purposes of investigations of Code violations, they will not later be dismayed to learn they were cooperating unwittingly in the quite different matter of law enforcement. If University actions make such an assumption chancy—meaning that a student cannot be sure with which jurisdiction and for what purposes he is being asked to cooperate—then students may choose not to cooperate at all and to demand, instead, a formal judicialization of every stage of Code enforcement. Such a change, together with the underlying shift in student perception of the University from trusted ally to mistrusted adversary, would inaugurate a new and bleak period of student-University relations.

Admittedly, it is easier to assert the cogency of the principle than to assure adherence to it in every instance. A particularly vexing problem occurs when the University or community jurisdiction of an offense cannot be determined until the investigation is well under way. We have attempted to provide a partial answer through procedure, by assigning control of those investigating student misconduct to the Code administrator, so as to build in a sensitivity to the problem that might otherwise be lacking. But there is no denying that some circumstances will not permit as early and tidy a separation of Code and law enforcement roles as called for by the principle.

When such a troublesome situation arises, we recommend that the University publicly acknowledge the difficulty and indicate that the possibility of its being considered primarily as a law violation must remain open until further information is secured. This may thin the yield from the investigation on some occasions, but it assures the continued respect of students for the University. Given such a difficult situation, the University might well come in for some criticism, no matter what its decision. But if student respect obtains, criticism will neither derive from nor contribute to erosion of the mutual good faith that lies at the heart of an effective University-student relationship.

F. The university posture toward law: Student misconduct within the university community which violates law but not the code

Relatively few varieties of student conduct within the University community are likely to involve law but not Code violation;

probably most would relate to political protest and advocacy. A suitable example to dissect can be had by reworking elements of the campus dispute last spring over the solicitation of pledges to burn draft cards. We keep intact the fact that the activity at the table in the Straight lobby violated the terms of a federal law. The alleged unconstitutionality of that law is of no relevance to our treatment of the topic under discussion, and hence is excluded from consideration in this section. We alter the fact that the SCARB * constitution required a proscription of such activity as detrimental precisely because it was forbidden by the laws of the United States. Let us assume, instead, that no Code offense hinges on law violation as such.

The Code we advocate matches the assumption just made. Under that Code the University decides all questions of disciplinary jurisdiction by assessing whether the conduct adversely affects the educational community. If, for example, the solicitation was conducted so as to disrupt classrooms or libraries, discipline could—and should—be imposed. If we assume that the actual solicitation took place in orderly fashion in the Straight lobby, then we would conclude that no invasion of University community interests occurred and no basis for University discipline existed. (Actually, factors other than the manner of conducting the illegal activity would be appraised to determine whether University interests were harmed. We omit reference to these other factors now because their inclusion would not change our judgment on the incident in question.)

Our conclusion on the absence of University jurisdiction means that enforcement of the law against the illegal activity is left up to public officials. This does not mean that the University must remain mute. It would be entirely appropriate, for example, for the University to take public positions advising the students of the probable illegality of their actions and clearly dissociating itself from any implied support of this particular violation of law or from any general principle of law violation.

The Commission is aware that the position here advanced may subject the University to criticism and pressure from external and perhaps internal sources as well. Yet we believe the position advocated is the only one consistent with the basic premises and guid-

* Scheduling, Coordination, and Activities Review Board.

ing principles set forth in this Report. There seems little choice, therefore, but to impose on the University the burden of persuading its constituencies to understand the proposition that the non-identity of the jurisdictions of Cornell and society may lead occasionally to a situation of student law violation on campus which is entirely within the general community's jurisdiction to enforce. If, as is likely, such situations are associated with political dissent, the University would have another explanatory theme congenial to any institution of higher education concerned with the maintenance of academic freedom.

Due Process

From an order by the Federal District Court for the Western District of Missouri, en banc, 1968.

On Student Discipline

Memorandum on Judicial Standards of Procedure and Substance in Review of Student Discipline in Tax-Supported Institutions of Higher Learning

Definitions

"Education" as used herein means tax-supported formal higher education unless the context indicates another meaning.

"Institution" and "educational institution" as used herein mean a tax-supported school, college, university, or multiversity.

"Mission" as used herein means a goal, purpose, task, or objective.

Introduction

. . . The following memorandum represents a statement of judicial standards of procedure and substance applicable, in the absence of exceptional circumstances, to actions concerning discipline of students in tax supported educational institutions of higher learning.

Relations of Courts and Education

Achieving the ideal of justice is the highest goal of humanity. Justice is not the concern solely of the courts. Education is equally concerned with the achievement of ideal justice. The administration of justice by the courts in the United States represents the people's best efforts to achieve the ideal of justice in the field of civil and criminal law. It is generally accepted that the courts are necessary to this administration of justice and for the protection of individual liberties. Nevertheless, the contributions of the modern courts in achieving the ideals of justice are primarily the products of higher education. The modern courts are, and will continue to be, greatly indebted to higher education for their personnel, their innovations, their processes, their political support, and their future in the political and social order. Higher education is the primary source of study and support of improvement in the courts. For this reason, among others, the courts should exercise caution when importuned to intervene in the important processes and functions of education. A court should never intervene in the processes of education without understanding the nature of education.

Before undertaking to intervene in the educational processes, and to impose judicial restraints and mandates on the educational community, the courts should acquire a general knowledge of the lawful missions and the continually changing processes, functions, and problems of education. Judicial action without such knowledge would endanger the public interest and be likely to lead to gross injustice.

Education is the living and growing source of our progressive civilization, of our open repository of increasing knowledge, culture and our salutary democratic traditions. As such, education deserves the highest respect and the fullest protection of the courts in the performance of its lawful missions.

There have been, and no doubt in the future there will be, instances of erroneous and unwise misuse of power by those invested with powers of management and teaching in the academic community, as in the case of all human fallible institutions. When such misuse of power is threatened or occurs, our political and social order has made available a wide variety of lawful, non-violent, political, economic, and social means to prevent or end the misuse of power. These same lawful, non-violent, political, economic, and social means are available to correct an unwise, but lawful choice of educational policy or action by those charged with the powers of management and teaching in the academic community. Only where the erroneous and unwise actions in the field of education deprive students of federally protected rights or privileges does a federal court have power to intervene in the educational process.

Lawful Missions of Tax-Supported Higher Education

The lawful missions of tax supported public education in the United States are constantly growing and changing. For the purposes of this analysis, it is sufficient to note some of the widely recognized traditional missions of tax supported higher education in this country. Included in these lawful missions of education, the following are summarized:

1. To maintain, support, critically examine, and to improve the existing social and political system;

2. To train students and faculty for leadership and superior service in public service, science, agriculture, commerce and industry;

3. To develop students to well-rounded maturity, physically, socially, emotionally, spiritually, intellectually and vocationally;

4. To develop, refine and teach ethical and cultural values;

5. To provide fullest possible realization of democracy in every phase of living;

6. To teach principles of patriotism, civil obligation and respect for the law;

7. To teach the practice of excellence in thought, behavior and performance;

8. To develop, cultivate, and stimulate the use of imagination;

9. To stimulate reasoning and critical faculties of students and to encourage their use in improvement of the existing political and social order;

10. To develop and teach lawful methods of change and improvement in the existing political and social order;

11. To provide by study and research for increase of knowledge;

12. To provide by study and research for development and improvement of technology, production and distribution for increased national production of goods and services desirable for national civilian consumption, for export, for exploration, and for national military purposes;

13. To teach methods of experiment in meeting the problems of a changing environment;

14. To promote directly and explicitly international understanding and cooperation;

15. To provide the knowledge, personnel, and policy for planning and managing the destiny of our society with a maximum of individual freedom; and

16. To transfer the wealth of knowledge and tradition from one generation to another.

The tax-supported educational institution is an agency of the national and state governments. Its missions include, by teaching, research and action, assisting in the declared purposes of government in this nation, namely:

To form a more perfect union,
To establish justice,
To insure domestic tranquility,
To provide for the common defense,
To promote the general welfare, and
To secure the blessing of liberty to ourselves and to posterity.

The nihilist and the anarchist, determined to destroy the existing political and social order, who directs his primary attack on the educational institutions, understands fully the mission of education in the United States.

Federal law recognizes the powers of the tax-supported institutions to accomplish these missions and has frequently furnished economic assistance for these purposes.

The genius of American education employing the manifold ideas and works of the great Jefferson, Mann, Dewey, and many others living, has made the United States the most powerful nation in history. In so doing, it has in a relatively few years expanded the area of knowledge at a revolutionary rate.

With education the primary force, the means to provide the necessities of life and many luxuries to all our national population, and to many other peoples, has been created. This great progress has been accomplished by the provision to the educational community of general support, accompanied by diminishing interference in educational processes by political agencies outside the academic community.

If it is true, as it well may be, that man is in a race between education and catastrophe, it is imperative that educational institutions not be limited in the performance of their lawful missions by unwarranted judicial interference.

Obligations of a Student

Attendance at a tax supported educational institution of higher learning is not compulsory. The federal constitution protects the equality of opportunity of all qualified persons to attend. Whether this protected opportunity be called a qualified "right" or "privilege" is unimportant. It is optional and voluntary.

The voluntary attendance of a student in such institutions is a voluntary entrance into the academic community. By such voluntary entrance, the student voluntarily assumes obligations of performance and behavior reasonably imposed by the institution of choice relevant to its lawful missions, processes, and functions. These obligations are generally much higher than those imposed on all citizens by the civil and criminal law. So long as there is no invidious discrimination, no deprival of due process, no abridgement of a right protected in the circumstances, and no capricious, clearly unreasonable or unlawful action employed, the institution may discipline students to secure compliance with these higher obligations as a teaching method or to sever the student from the academic community.

No student may, without liability to lawful discipline, intentionally act to impair or prevent the accomplishment of any lawful mission, process, or function of an educational institution.

The Nature of Student Discipline
Compared to Criminal Law

The discipline of students in the educational community is, in all but the case of irrevocable expulsion, a part of the teaching process. In the case of irrevocable expulsion for misconduct, the process is not punitive or deterrent in the criminal law sense, but the process is rather the determination that the student is unqualified to continue as a member of the educational community. Even then, the disciplinary process is not equivalent to the criminal law processes of federal and state criminal law. For, while the expelled student may suffer damaging effects, sometimes irreparable, to his educational, social, and economic future, he or she may not be imprisoned, fined, disenfranchised, or subjected to probationary supervision. The attempted analogy of student discipline to criminal proceedings against adults and juveniles is not sound.

In the lesser disciplinary procedures, including but not limited to guidance counseling, reprimand, suspension of social or academic privileges, probation, restriction to campus and dismissal with leave to apply for readmission, the lawful aim of discipline may be teaching in performance of a lawful mission of the institution. The nature and procedures of the disciplinary process in such cases should not be required to conform to federal processes of criminal law, which are far from perfect, and designed for circumstances and ends unrelated to the academic community. By judicial mandate to impose upon the academic community in student discipline the intricate, time consuming, sophisticated procedures, rules and safeguards of criminal law would frustrate the teaching process and render the institutional control impotent.

A federal court should not intervene to reverse or enjoin disciplinary actions relevant to a lawful mission of an educational institution unless there appears one of the following:

1. a deprival of due process, that is, fundamental concepts of fair play;

2. invidious discrimination, for example, on account of race or religion;

3. denial of federal rights, constitutional or statutory, protected in the academic community; or

4. clearly unreasonable, arbitrary or capricious action.

Provisional Substantive Standards
in Student Discipline Cases
Under Section 1983, Title 42

1. Equal opportunity for admission and attendance by qualified persons at tax-supported state educational institutions of

higher learning is protected by the equal privileges and immunities, equal protection of laws, and due process clauses of the Fourteenth Amendment to the United States Constitution. It is unimportant whether this protected opportunity is defined as a right or a privilege. The protection of the opportunity is the important thing.

2. In an action under Section 1983 issues to be determined will be limited to determination whether, under color of any statute, ordinance, regulation, custom or usage of a state ("state action"), a student has been deprived of any rights, privileges, or immunities secured by the Constitution and laws of the United States.

3. State constitutional, statutory, and institutional delegation and distribution of disciplinary powers are not ordinarily matters of federal concern. Any such contentions based solely on claims of unlawful distribution and violation of state law in the exercise of state disciplinary power should be submitted to the state courts. Such contentions do not ordinarily involve a substantial federal question of which the district court has jurisdiction under Section 1983. This rule does not apply, however, to actions based on diversity of jurisdiction under Sections 1331, 1332 or 2201, Title 28, U.S.C.

4. Disciplinary action by any institution, institutional agency, or officer will ordinarily be deemed under color of a statute, ordinance, regulation, custom or usage of a state ("state action") within the meaning of Section 1983, Title 42, U.S.C.

5. In the field of discipline, scholastic and behavioral, an institution may establish any standards reasonably relevant to the lawful missions, processes, and functions of the institution. It is not a lawful mission, process, or function of an institution to prohibit the exercise of a right guaranteed by the Constitution or a law of the United States to a member of the academic community under the circumstances. Therefore, such prohibitions are not reasonably relevant to any lawful mission, process or function of an institution.

6. Standards so established may apply to student behavior on and off the campus when relevant to any lawful mission, process, or function of the institution. By such standards of student conduct the institution may prohibit any action or omission which impairs, interferes with, or obstructs the missions, processes and functions of the institution.

Standards so established may require scholastic attainments higher than the average of the population and may require superior ethical and moral behavior. In establishing standards of behavior, the institution is not limited to the standards or the forms of criminal laws.

7. An institution may establish appropriate standards of conduct (scholastic and behavioral) in any form and manner reasonably calculated to give adequate notice of the scholastic attainments and behavior expected of the student.

The notice of the scholastic and behavioral standards to the students may be written or oral, or partly written and partly oral, but preferably written. The standards may be positive or negative in form.

Different standards, scholastic and behavioral, may be established for different divisions, schools, colleges, and classes of an institution if the differences are reasonably relevant to the missions, processes, and functions of the particular divisions, schools, colleges, and classes concerned.

8. When a challenged standard of student conduct limits or forbids the exercise of a right guaranteed by the Constitution or a law of the United States to persons generally, the institution must demonstrate that the standard is recognized as relevant to a lawful mission of the institution, and is recognized as reasonable by some reputable authority or school of thought in the field of higher education. This may be determined by expert opinion or by judicial notice in proper circumstances. It is not necessary that all authorities and schools of thought agree that the standard is reasonable.

9. Outstanding educational authorities in the field of higher education believe, on the basis of experience, that detailed codes of prohibited student conduct are provocative and should not be employed in higher education.

For this reason, general affirmative statements of what is expected of a student may in some areas be preferable in higher education. Such affirmative standards may be employed, and discipline of students based thereon.

10. The legal doctrine that a prohibitory statute is void if it is overly broad or unconstitutionally broad does not, in the absence of exceptional circumstances, apply to standards of student conduct. The validity of the form of standards of student

conduct, relevant to the lawful missions of higher education, ordinarily should be determined by recognized education standards.

11. In severe cases of student discipline for alleged misconduct, such as final expulsion, indefinite or long-term suspension, dismissal with deferred leave to reapply, the institution is obligated to give to the student minimal procedural requirements of due process of law. The requirements of due process do not demand an inflexible procedure for all such cases. "But 'due process,' unlike some legal rules, is not a technical conception with a fixed content unrelated to time, place and circumstances." Three minimal requirements apply in cases of severe discipline, growing out of fundamental conceptions of fairness implicit in procedural due process. First, the student should be given adequate notice in writing of the specific ground or grounds and the nature of the evidence on which the disciplinary proceedings are based. Second, the student should be given an opportunity for a hearing in which the disciplinary authority provides a fair opportunity for hearing of the student's position, explanations, and evidence. The third requirement is that no disciplinary action be taken on grounds which are not supported by any substantial evidence. Within limits of due process, institutions must be free to devise various types of disciplinary procedures relevant to their lawful missions, consistent with their varying processes and functions, and not an unreasonable strain on their resources and personnel.

There is no general requirement that procedural due process in student disciplinary cases provide for legal representation, a public hearing, confrontation and cross-examination of witnesses, warnings about privileges, self-incrimination, application of principles of former or double jeopardy, compulsory production of witnesses, or any of the remaining features of federal criminal jurisprudence. Rare and exceptional circumstances, however, may require provision of one or more of these features in a particular case to guarantee the fundamental concepts of fair play.

It is encouraging to note the current unusual efforts of the institutions and the interested organizations which are devising and recommending procedures and policies in student discipline which are based on standards, in many features, far higher than the requirements of due process.

Joint Statement on Rights and Freedoms of Students. [See above, pages 405–14.] . . . University of Missouri, *Provisional Rules of Procedure In Student Disciplinary Matters.*

Many of these recommendations and procedures represent wise matters of policy and procedure far above the minimum requirements of federal law, calculated to ensure the confidence of all concerned with student discipline. . . .

From the Basic Policy Declarations *of the U.S. National Students Association.*

Due Process

I. PROCEDURAL DUE PROCESS

Preamble:

In recent years, certain colleges, university administrations and student judiciaries summarily disciplined students, denying them basic rights. At some universities there has been a refusal to give students specific reasons for their punishment, while others have construed amorphous regulations rendering an apparently innocent act in violation of university policy. Students have been prosecuted by university authorities for activities also subject to civil and/or criminal prosecution.

Principle:

USNSA affirms that the basic protections available to citizens under American jurisprudence should be available to all students charged with violating regulations within university communities. Where state law provides that the President or the board of trustees of the university are to have the ultimate disciplinary power, USNSA urges that the President or board of trustees delegate their authority.

Declaration:

Student due process rights should include, but not be limited to, the following:

a. To a clear statement of the types of actions that shall be considered violation of university regulation;
b. To a statement which delineates and makes public maximum punishments that may be imposed for specific violations of regulation;
c. To a published statement from the university administration of the protections available to students;
d. To adequate advance notice of particular charges;
e. To assistance in obtaining the testimony of witnesses necessary to defense;
f. To be tried before an impartial trial body where any member of the trial body may be challenged for cause. In no case shall the trial body include, or be appointed by a person who has brought charges or who is engaged in bringing charges;
g. To free choice of counsel;
h. To be prosecuted by someone other than a member of the trial body;
i. To testify on one's own behalf, or remain silent without any presumption of guilt;
j. To call witnesses in one's own behalf;
k. To cross-examine all prosecution witnesses;
l. To rely on rules of evidence in accord with the principles of American jurisprudence;
m. To be free from the possibility of another trial where one is acquitted, from being punished after having been acquitted by any trial body, or from receiving a greater punishment than that decided upon by the initial trial body;
n. To be furnished, upon the request of the defendant, a record of the proceedings before any judicial body;
o. To appeal a conviction to a higher body or challenge the fairness of a punishment before a higher body;
p. To be free from punishment by university officials for a violation of civil law while one's case is pending before civil courts, except where a clear and present danger may justify a temporary measure;
q. To be free from punishment by university officials for a violation of civil law where there is no clear relationship between the illegal act and the educational objectives of the university;

r. To be informed of the rationale behind a punishment;
s. To be free from punishment as an individual for the actions of other members of the group to which that individual belongs;
t. To the right to an open hearing and the right to a closed hearing at the defendant student's request.

II. SUBSTANTIVE DUE PROCESS

Preamble:

Many colleges and universities have regulations similar to the following: "The University assumes that its undergraduates will conduct themselves as responsible citizens, and therefore reserves the right to dismiss any student or group of students whose conduct, on or off the campus, is unbecoming to a . . . student or reflects discredit on the institution of which he is a member."

This policy can be applied by members of the university only through subjective, personal interpretation as to what constitutes improper student conduct. These criteria of subjective interpretation create problems of fluctuating standards as applied by the university and, as a result, confuse the student as to what constitutes an infraction at a given time and place.

In the application of a university's policies, basic student rights have often been violated. Frequently a university administration and student judiciary have resorted to this type of regulation to punish students for actions merely distasteful to itself.

Principle:

USNSA asserts that no contractual agreement with a university should abrogate a student's right to due process. This right is not satisfied simply by procedural safeguards. The right of due process is fulfilled only when the substance of the university regulation does not infringe upon the following fundamental rights:

1. Freedom to participate in political, religious, and social action groups, on or off the campus;
2. Freedom to express political, religious and social ideas, either written or spoken;

3. Freedom to engage in responsible criticism;
4. Freedom to pursue knowledge through free and open inquiry within the academic community;
5. Freedom to petition for redress of grievances.

Declaration:

USNSA strongly recommends that all universities respect these unalienable rights in this statement in the enforcement of any campus regulation.

The Radical Challenge to Discipline

Editorial in The Harvard Crimson, *student newspaper, Harvard University, January 6, 1970.*

There Can Be No Punishment

It would be more pleasant if everyone at Harvard accepted the same basic system of social and political values. Then the whole community could discipline the few who transgress against the general will.

This is not the case at Harvard today. The socio-political goals which divide the community are in many senses as great as those which bring it together. No appeal by Faculty members or Young Americans for Freedom can paper over the division on the basic goals of the community. Many feel, quite rightly, that the daily study can only come while the University is making strides toward achieving justice in its relations with those students and workers within the community and those without. If the University does not meet the just demands of these groups, then Administration activity will be interrupted by those seeking change.

According to the Constitution of the Commonwealth of Massachusetts, all power is given to the Corporation and all intra-university power is derived from it. This small group of men administer a large financial trust—a billion dollar holding company. The members of the corporation naturally seek to defend this trust against those who challenge its policies.

The Corporation and its Administration have chosen to interpret the interruption of the normal administrative routine as an attack on scholarship and academic freedom. Students and Faculty members should recognize the serious nature of this red herring. No classes or research were affected by demonstrations this Fall. The scattered instances of class disruption last Spring, during a voted university-wide strike, were not sanctioned by any group. Academic freedom has not been at stake during the demonstrations of 1969. Ernest R. May was not obstructed on November 19 because of his well-known views on American diplomatic history. He was obstructed, perhaps unwisely, because he had identified himself with the University's racist employment policies by speaking at a news conference on November 11 with the University Personnel Director to "explain" the painters' helper issue. No classes are taught in University Hall, the Faculty Club, or the Gund Hall construction site.

The Committee on Rights and Responsibilities, like the Committee of Fifteen last Spring, has accepted the rationale of the Corporation and its Administration for punishing those students who have disrupted this historic University. As the Committee's news release said, such obstructive demonstrations "can substantially impede the work of members of the University and contribute to a general atmosphere of intimidation."

In this divided community, the Committee has accepted the rules and definitions set up by one side; it punished those who violated those rules. Ordinary discipline is political punishment when it is carried on by one party, based on its set of political values, against another party in a polarized community.

The Committee on Rights and Responsibilities and the majority of the Faculty which have accepted the Administration's argument that obstructive demonstrations are an attack on academic freedom are acting unwittingly in the interests of the Corporation and its Administration. The Committee punishing those who were protesting the Corporation's racist practices and immoral employment practices is perpetuating those practices.

In order for the Faculty or the Committee to assume a neutral position, the Administration would have to be subject to discipline. Neither the Code nor the Committee is designed to prosecute the Corporation and the Administration. The Faculty would have to establish legal power over the Corporation in order to punish it. This would require a change in the Constitution of the Commonwealth of Massachusetts, a very unlikely event.

The people who were punished before vacation and those who are scheduled to be punished in the next few weeks have been organizing against racist employment practices, against a Defense Department-funded computer project which will serve to carry on future wars like Vietnam, and ultimately against the Corporation and its billion dollar trust invested in numerous racist companies around the world. The students who put their futures on the line were right in their actions.

Those who believed in changing the Corporation's policies on ROTC, expansion, and Black Studies, and believe now that racist employment practices should be changed, must not be deceived by a disciplinary committee acting in the interests of the Corporation. Students should join together in opposing these political punishments.

The students who accept the Corporation as benign should take a close look at the extremely political nature of the punishments and the apparatus which made them. Any concern for academic freedom and legal procedures of the Administration has been sacrificed to insure that those who have attacked the Corporation most strongly will be kept from other students. The Committee on Rights and Responsibilities transgresses its own professed beliefs in order to make its very political punishments.

Though all-white juries have been found unconstitutional in the civil courts, the all-white Committee on Rights and Responsibilities feels qualified to discipline black students acting against racism. This white racism can't be eliminated by token appointments. As long as this community cannot agree on the meaning of racism, there is no hope of establishing a disciplinary body which can discipline across racial boundaries.

The University feels that it has found a solution for some of the more than 75 students who participated in the November 19th demonstration in University Hall. Virtually all the students in the demonstration participated by linking arms, obstructing Dean May, chanting, and keeping him from carrying on official business (a telephone call). But May charged only 25 of the students with these crimes. And in May's opinion, in fact, some of the charged students were guilty of more than chanting and linking arms, some of lesser offenses. A few including the chairman of SDS and the leaders of the painters' helper campaign, were charged with all counts—from "entering the Office of the Dean of Harvard College without invitation" to "intervening with . . . the freedom of movement of the Dean of Harvard College by bodily resisting his efforts to depart from his office." Others were charged with lesser counts; many were not charged. It is significant that those students with the most serious charges were the leaders of SDS and a few freshmen who had been very active in radical politics.

Dean May has said that the other 50 students couldn't be identified. There is evidence to indicate that this isn't the case. Barbara Slavin, who testified at her trial before the Committee, reported that every person in the University's photographic evidence had a letter or number next to his or her head. Some of those clearly visible toward the front of the pictures were not charged, though Miss Slavin thought they were known to the Administration. For the most part these people were new to radical politics. Why wouldn't the Dean not want to charge all those he possibly could? The University realizes that if it charged too many, the students community would object. Instead the radicals are kicked out in small groups, and others are given stiff warnings so that they will be suspended after the next demonstration.

This is not to say that those students who weren't charged will not be punished for the demonstration in the future. The Committee on Rights and Responsibilities said in its report on those disciplined in the November 19 demonstration that the harassment of Dean May was more serious in several of the cases because they had harassed May in earlier demonstrations when no charges had been brought. This is in violation of laws of jurisprudence, as well as the Code of Rights and Responsibilities, which state that a suspect can only be charged and found guilty for crimes with which he has been charged.

The trials themselves are as "intimidating" as anything Dean May felt in the nasty November 19 demonstration. They are closed meetings, where only witnesses and one person for counsel are permitted. Three policemen escort each of the defendants through four sets of locked doors on the way to the trial. Each set of doors is carefully unlocked in front and then locked behind the defendant before the next set is opened. No press is allowed, even if the defendant asks for his testimony to be made public. Virtually all those charged in the political demonstrations of the past year have asked that the trials be open. The Bill of Rights guarantees "a speedy and public trial, before an impartial jury" in all civil trials, but apparently the Harvard Faculty which approved the Code on Rights and Responsibilities and the by-laws of the present committee did not feel that such safeguards were needed at Harvard.

Even if the proceedings were made public, they would continue to violate the impartial jury clause of the Bill of Rights. The Committee consists of three students, three Faculty members, and three representatives of the Administration. The last three are paid by the Corporation to handle the business affairs of the University.

The Faculty members of the Committee were elected to the Committee of Fifteen last Spring. One of these men—all are men —told Miss Slavin who was attempting to present her defense by applying the Code to the Corporation's responsibilities, "I wrote that section of the Code; I know what it means. Your interpretation is not what I meant." It is an interesting separation of powers between legislator and judge which governs Harvard discipline. Another of the Faculty representatives told one *Crimson* reporter recently he would always accept the story of a dean about an incident when choosing between the dean's testimony and an SDS member's testimony. "The SDS member would bend the truth to serve his political ends," he said. This jury is far from impartial.

As for the student members, it must be remembered that the Code of Rights and Responsibilities and the Committee were established after a one-hour discussion in the Faculty meeting when few students were on campus last June. There was no consultation with the student body—no attempt to move through all the "democratic channels" in the community. The three student representatives were chosen by those students who were selected from the lottery of those elected from the Houses last April. These hastily conducted elections barred students involved in the University Hall turmoil and permitted no statement of qualifications or political views. They were, as the CRIMSON pointed out at the time, elections in name only. The students were denied any grounds for choice. The three students on the Committee now represent what can only be considered the ultimate in indirect non-election. Unfortunately, it would make little difference if the students were elected by a direct election next week, for a majority, three administrators and two Faculty members, is enough to convict and sentence on the Committee.

Appeals can only be made to the Committee itself. These appeals can [be], and have been, summarily dismissed. The joint appeal of the November 19 demonstrators was dismissed the day it was made because of "insufficient grounds" for appeal. The appeals system reinforces the Committee's procedural injustices. Without any system of review, the Committee's closed and "secret" deliberations are relatively insulated from criticism.

The punishments are as objectionable as the supposedly democratic procedures behind the Committee. Students who are suspended must prove that they have left the "Harvard community" for the entire period before they are readmitted. The "community" has been liberally defined; one Harvard student suspended last Spring for a semester has not been readmitted because he has remained in the Harvard "community." He is living in Boston and organizing for SDS at Northeastern.

Those who deny political repression at Harvard should ask themselves why students engaged in local radical activity should be denied readmission when their formal term of suspension ends. Why are these students never to be permitted to speak on campus without "formally" being readmitted? Is it not curious that virtually all of the SDS leadership both from last Spring and this Fall have been suspended or dismissed? and that the leaders of the November Action Coalition at Harvard and OBU * were charged a week before Christmas?

By creating the illusion that the Committee of Fifteen was acting as an impartial jury, rather than a committee to punish those who had demonstrated against the Harvard Administration last Spring, the Faculty and its Committee were acting as agents of the Corporation. The Faculty and the Committee had accepted the Corporation's analysis of the actions—that students and Faculty had violated the rules of the community in the demonstrations. There was no procedure for charging, much less disciplining, those who called the police last Spring; and, there is no procedure for disciplining the Corporation for continuing its racist employment practices. The Committee on Rights and Responsibilities is perpetuating these injustices. Its racist, unconstitutional, and very partial character is not a coincidence but an unwitting reflection of the interests of the Administration.

Only when the Corporation can be suspended and criminally prosecuted for its racist policies, when it appears on campus, will

* Organization for Black Unity.

it be possible to construct a legitimate disciplinary body for this community.

Statement by Dr. Jack R. Stauder, Department of Social Relations, to Joint Committee on Charges Against Certain Officers of Harvard University, July 28, 1969.

We Will Fight to Win

President Eliot of Harvard once said, "The scab is an American hero."

President Lowell exempted students from exams to serve in the militia used against the textile strikers at Lawrence in 1912.

In 1969 President Pusey defended ROTC on the grounds that the role of the American military around the world is basically good and justified by "destiny."

These have not been accidental statements of petty men—they have come from public spokesmen of the American ruling class, a small group of men who own and control the large corporations, the U.S. government, and the universities—including Harvard. They derive their profits and power from the exploitation of working people all over the world. They are the men who sit on the Harvard Corporation and who use Harvard to further their personal interests and those of their class. They use ROTC to train students to put down popular rebellions from Detroit to Vietnam —rebellions against the daily oppression millions of people face at the hands of these men and their class. They evict black and white working people from their homes in Cambridge and Roxbury to make way for expansion which can only serve the ruling class—for political science institutes and research hospitals catering to the rich. Harvard's expansion is only part of a general plan to convert Cambridge into a center for imperialist research— research into perfecting weapons and improving counter-insurgency techniques for use against the people of the world.

This spring Harvard students waged a sharp struggle against these ways in which Harvard attacks working people at home and abroad. As President Pusey says, I openly "encouraged and participated" in this struggle, which clearly threatens the interests of those who rule Harvard. It is not surprising therefore that the Administration has called me before a handpicked committee which will undoubtedly find me guilty of "misconduct" and recommend "discipline"—either a warning or quite possibly a firing.

My "misconduct" is joining the fight against the ways Harvard serves imperialism, practices racism, and attacks the working class.

My case does not arise in isolation: for participating in the same struggle eighteen students have been thrown out of the University, numerous others admonished, one student sentenced to a year in jail, and a number of teaching fellows and another faculty member have had their jobs threatened. It is necessary to fight back hard against this attempted intimidation and repression—which is aimed not so much at a few individuals, but rather at the thousands of students at Harvard who during the struggle this spring came to the realization that ROTC should be abolished and Harvard expansion stopped.

That the few men who run Harvard are afraid of the student body is shown by how they have chosen to exercise repression: in my case, as in all others, through private star-chamber proceedings with punishments announced after the normal school year was over and students had gone home. But these students will return in the fall, and in their eyes the Corporation and the Administration will have been increasingly isolated and exposed by their attempts to punish the leadership of the struggle against ROTC and expansion.

Our struggle is just, and no punishment is justified, regardless of procedure. I am not opposed, however, to answering questions about my "conduct" and presenting my "case," as President Pusey has asked me to do before this committee. But for me to do this, two conditions would be necessary: that any "hearings" be public and that they be held in the fall when all interested students and faculty could attend. I would welcome such an opportunity to explain why I and others took such actions as we did—though I believe our reasons are already clear to most persons at Harvard.

If the Administration and Corporation were not afraid of Harvard students and faculty they would accept the kind of hearing I suggest. I believe they will not accept such a hearing. So I appear today simply to submit this statement and to reaffirm our intention. We will not be intimidated. We will stay and fight. And we will fight to win.

From the report of the Joint Committee to the Harvard Corporation on Charges Against Certain Officers of Instruction of Harvard University, September 8, 1969.

The Case of Jack R. Stauder

This committee finds that Dr. Stauder was present in University Hall at 5:00 A.M. on April 10, 1969, that his presence there at that time was with the full knowledge that it was unlawful and that he deliberately remained there until arrested by the police, thereby identifying himself with those students and others who had engaged in and were continuing to engage in unlawful acts. As to his encouragement of such acts, we have heard no direct evidence that he personally participated in the planning of the occupation, or that he overtly or expressly urged others to participate. But it is evident that any officer of the University who publicly participates in such misconduct, by that act alone likewise encourages participation of others. As an officer of instruction Dr. Stauder's admitted presence in the building represented in itself an encouragement to and support of the acts that occurred there, including physical violence and threats of violence to officers of administration and the rifling of the University's confidential files. In such circumstances the duty of an instructor is to dissuade students from persisting in such acts. The contrary act—that of remaining in University Hall after all present had been forbidden to do so by officers of the University—called into question the gravity and authority of these warnings and encouraged some to remain who might otherwise have departed.

In the absence of any explanation of his actions and in the light of Dr. Stauder's refusal to answer any of the Committee's questions—a refusal which is not based on any pending legal proceedings, since Dr. Stauder paid his fine and did not appeal his conviction—we find that the charges made in President Pusey's letter that Dr. Stauder "encouraged and participated in the forcible occupation of University Hall on April 9, 1969, and remained in the building on April 10th after having been forbidden to do so by officers of the University" have been fully sustained. The testimony given under oath and subject to cross-examination by witnesses who appeared in the criminal proceedings at which Dr. Stauder was represented by counsel, together with the testimony of the Dean of Harvard College that he saw Dr. Stauder in University Hall prior to the arrests and after the warnings to vacate the buildings, are, we think, sufficient evidence to support these findings.

This Committee is unanimously of the view that Dr. Stauder's participation in and encouragement of the forcible occupation of University Hall constitutes "grave misconduct" in the meaning of the Third Statute of the University. By virtue of an instructor's acknowledged responsibilities, such activity constitutes grave irresponsibility toward the collegial community of which he professes to be a member. Moreover, it represents a singularly irresponsible abdication of a teacher's obligations to students. By encouraging students to persist in such activity—even, indeed, by failing to take positive action to dissuade them—a teacher thereby places such students as look to him for counsel and example in both legal and disciplinary jeopardy.

The disruptive act of participating in the seizure of a University building, when carried out by a student, must, in the words of the Committee of Fifteen, be "severely judged." Depending on the nature of their involvement and their previous disciplinary record, if any, the students who were found to have participated in the unauthorized occupation of University Hall received discipline ranging from a warning to formal dismissal by the Faculty of Arts and Sciences. When such an act is performed by an officer of instruction, it must be judged all the more severely. Those who display by their acts an unwillingness to accept the canons of free discussion and democratic choice as the guiding principles of university life show themselves to be so fundamentally at odds with the nature of a university committed to learning that they cannot, without the showing of important mitigating circumstances, have a place on its faculty.

Dr. Stauder's participation in and encouragement of the seizure of University Hall expressed approval of an act that was thoroughly antipathetic to the foundations of the University community. Members of this University have always had the right to express their views and to press for action on matters of concern to them by any and all means appropriate to a free academic institution. These means include the right to join and organize political groups and associations, to convene and conduct non-disruptive meetings on all public and political issues, and to express, advocate and publicize opinions. But the possession of these rights imposes the duty to respect the freedom of others to move, speak or listen. And any teacher who engages in activities such as the forcible occupation of a University building, or the disruption of University functions, or the physical obstruction of academic or administrative processes, is violating these rights and has no proper place in a free university.

This Committee is also unanimously of the view that Dr. Stauder's failure to explain fully his misconduct to a duly constituted body engaged in disciplinary proceedings is "neglect of duty" in the meaning of the Third Statute of the University. A teacher's responsibilities in this regard were set forth in President Pusey's letter of July 7 to Dr. Stauder, asking him to appear at a hearing before this committee on July 28: "Since the responsibilities of an individual holding a teaching appointment are greater than those of a student, your involvement in an event like the forcible occupation of University Hall is a particularly grave matter which you have a professional responsibility to explain." When Dr. Stauder appeared before this committee on July 28, he simply read a prepared statement, refusing to answer any questions or to discuss, in any way, his alleged misconduct. When offered another opportunity to appear before the committee, in order to present substantive reasons for postponement, Dr. Stauder failed even to acknowledge the communication from the committee and did not appear on August 6 for discussion or explanation of his involvement in the forcible occupation of University Hall.

It should be clearly understood that in making this judgment we are not referring to Dr. Stauder's expressed attitude toward this committee nor to his unmannerly behavior on the one occasion when he appeared before it. Our concern is not with Dr. Stauder's style but with his failure to meet the responsibilities which he assumed when he accepted appointment as instructor in the Harvard Faculty of Arts and Sciences. His failure to explain or discuss his misconduct, it must be emphasized, constitutes implicit contempt of that entire Faculty. The Faculty of Arts and Sciences accepted the President's announced intention to discuss with the faculty members of the Committee of Fifteen what disciplinary procedures were to follow the findings of fact reported by the Freund Committee. Those faculty members—all elected by their colleagues—unanimously endorsed the form of this joint committee. Moreover, they elected from among themselves three faculty members to serve on the committee—as, in effect, representatives of the Faculty of Arts and Sciences. Such a faculty participation in disciplinary proceedings has traditionally and historically been, at Harvard as at other universities, a means whereby a faculty safeguards the rights of its members and preserves the integrity of its profession. By refusing to appear, for serious discussion, before a committee so constituted, Dr. Stauder has failed to fulfill his obligations both to his colleagues and to standards of academic integrity and freedom.

This committee, therefore, unanimously recommends that Dr. Stauder's present appointment as instructor in social anthropology be immediately terminated and that the Corporation not ask the Board of Overseers to consent to his recommended appointment as lecturer on social anthropology for two years, ending June 30, 1971.

In so recommending, this Committee seeks to make clear that Dr. Stauder's actions in participating in and encouraging the forcible occupation of University Hall, and his subsequent refusal to explain such misconduct to a duly constituted committee are each of them adequate and reasonable grounds for immediate termination of an appointment as an officer of instruction at Harvard University. We hope that the Corporation will make unequivocally clear that any such conduct by anyone holding a corporation appointment will hereafter invariably be deemed grounds for immediate termination of that appointment.

We believe, however, that there are reasons why Dr. Stauder's connection with the University should not, at this time, be finally and completely severed. In the light of what has occurred at Harvard since the McNamara incident, it would be fair to take into consideration that for some of the younger members of the faculty, the responsibilities which go with a corporation appointment as an officer of instruction have been obscured by the failure to take disciplinary action in cases where faculty participation in or encouragement of disruptive activities were widely believed to have occurred. Moreover, through a desire to be scrupulous in the protection of Dr. Stauder's rights, this Committee has postponed action in his case until it is too late for him to make other arrangements for the academic term which is about to open.

We, therefore, unanimously recommend that he be given an appointment as Instructor in Social Anthropology for one year beginning July 1, 1969, at the same salary which he had been receiving during the past academic year. We further unanimously recommend that he be suspended from all teaching privileges for the first term of the academic year. This will afford a period during which Dr. Stauder will have an opportunity to demonstrate by his conduct that he is prepared to accept the responsibilities which go with an appointment as an officer of instruction in this University. If, at any time, during the period of this appointment, Dr. Stauder should be found by the appropriate fact-finding body to have engaged in any activities warranting disciplinary action against him, we unanimously recommend that his appointment be immediately and finally terminated.

From the statement by Jack R. Stauder to the Harvard Faculty, Harvard University, October 7, 1969.

Statement to the Harvard Faculty Concerning my Firing

On September 8 the Harvard Corporation fired me from my three-year appointment as instructor in Social Anthropology, and denied my department's request for a superseding two-year appointment as lecturer. The Corporation's action was quite clearly taken for political reasons, and although several teachers were not re-hired at Harvard during the 1950's because of their former membership in the Communist Party, my case is the first one in recent times to raise the question of political firings at Harvard. My firing also raises in a sharp way the political issues of last spring—issues which remain with us. . . .

Part I. Events Over the Summer: Procedural Questions

The Faculty elected the Committee of Fifteen to do several things, including recommending discipline for students involved in the spring events. The Faculty later accepted the Committee's recommendation that 18 students be thrown out of Harvard. As this recommendation was not made public until the Faculty meeting at which it was accepted, there was no chance to discuss the recommendation beforehand, and very little opportunity for discussion of it at the meeting itself—one dissenting speech was allowed before voting.

In this manner, behind a façade of "democracy"—because the Committee of Fifteen had been elected from among candidates who approved of its disciplinary purposes—the Faculty put its stamp on what the Administration clearly desired: to isolate for punishment a few students within the much larger number who participated in the spring events and who supported the SDS demands. The punishment of this smaller number could serve two purposes: to intimidate the rest of the student body and to foster the Administration's myth that the massive protest at Harvard last spring was attributable to a small hard core of "wreckers" who somehow managed to manipulate everyone else into following them. I believe that the Faculty's acceptance of the Committee of Fifteen's recommendations, and even its setting up of the Committee, were wrong. I believe no punishment of any of the students was justified, for reasons which I will later go into, in connection with the justice of my own punishment.

In any case the Faculty never gave to the Committee of Fifteen a mandate to discipline or to legitimate discipline against faculty members involved in the spring events. No faculty committee was elected for this purpose, as AAUP procedures would require. In fact, the question of discipline for faculty members was never substantially considered or discussed at a Faculty meeting. When asked at the last Faculty meeting of the year what the Administration intended to do, President Pusey replied in a vague manner that proper procedures would be followed and the Committee of Fifteen would be consulted. No discussion ensued, and faculty sentiment on the matter was in no way ascertained. . . .

If the Faculty played no part in my firing, what part was played by the AAUP and its guidelines? Although dubious about any possible help the AAUP could provide me, I called their local representative to inform him of my case. I found he had from the beginning been in "consultation" with the Corporation, and in fact had helped to devise the firing procedures which were being used! Far from being concerned to "protect" my "rights", he was in fact engaged in protecting the cover of legitimacy the Corporation wished to give its procedures. . . .

I personally do not believe that any particular set of procedures can guarantee truly democratic or just decisions. For instance, I do not believe that any punishment of those who participated last spring in the anti-ROTC, anti-expansion struggle, would be justified, regardless of procedures. The nature of Harvard expansion and ROTC is that they threaten people outside of Harvard, and in fact serve the interests of only a relatively few people while attacking the lives of many. The facts and reasoning behind this analysis can be argued. How one reacts to these issues furthermore depends on one's fundamental political attitudes, and where one perceives one's interests to lie. But because the policies of ROTC and expansion chiefly affect people outside the University, no University procedure can be devised which would guarantee "democratic" decisions on these questions. Therefore no University procedure could be devised which could "democratically" decide as to whether or not the opponents of ROTC and expansion were justified in taking the actions they did. . . .

The Corporation set up the Joint Committee without the Faculty's prior knowledge or approval. And the recommendations of the Joint Committee were acted on by the Corporation well in advance of the first Faculty meeting of this term, so that the Faculty would be presented with a *fait accompli.*

Although I regarded the Joint Committee as illegitimate in purpose, I did appear before it as requested. There I read a statement which explained my position and requested an open hearing in the fall when students and faculty members could be present, and could make known their opinions. In making this offer, it seems to me that I came much closer to respecting the ideals of "free discussion" and "democratic choice" than did the Joint Committee, which despite its declaration that these are "guiding principles of university life," proceeded to deny my request for open "free discussion" of my case with students and faculty able to participate. To compound their hypocrisy, the Joint Committee then recommended I be fired on the basis of my "unwillingness" to accept the "principles" they were clearly so unwilling to accept in practice!

I should make it clear that I do not believe that "free discussion and democratic choice" are in fact guiding principles in university life. The actions of the Joint Committee and the Corporation confirm my disbelief that these "principles" really apply in how the University is run.

The stated reasons of the Joint Committee for refusing to accept my offer to discuss my case fully at an open, fall hearing, were two: (1) that such an open meeting would be "unprecedented," and (2) that a university committee could not "protect" itself from "disruption or harassment." The first reason ignores the fact that the procedures the Joint Committee was in fact operating under were themselves "unprecedented," as were in many respects the cases before it. The second reason, I think, comes nearer the truth as to why the Joint Committee would not consider a postponement or an open hearing. This Committee is afraid of the "community" it purports to speak for. Though we have all seen that the University can call upon all sorts of powers —from within and without—to "protect" its functions by enforcing order, nevertheless the Joint Committee was quite clearly afraid to hold their hearings in public or in the fall, because they were apparently afraid of any manifestation of student or faculty opinion about my case, before they had achieved their object. The procedures I suggested—though obviously closer to their supposed standards of "free discussion" and "democratic choice"— were unacceptable to the Joint Committee (and no doubt also to the Administration and Corporation) because they would have made more difficult or impossible what the Joint Committee was set up to do: to fire me.

In other words, far from being "fair", "democratic", "neutral", or from safeguarding my supposed rights, or from representing the will of the Faculty, the vaunted elaborate procedures by which I was fired were quite clearly nothing more than a convenient mechanism by which the Corporation achieved its object. The Corporation must have been quite conscious and calculating about this, and for reasons of their own the faculty members of the Committee of Fifteen and a representative of the AAUP lent themselves completely to the Corporation's will.

None of the actions of the Corporation or its Joint Committee in my case should be surprising or shocking in retrospect to anyone who has followed closely the handling of the ROTC and expansion issues by the men who run the University. Radicals' analysis of the power relationships and class nature of the University has been confirmed time and again. The Overseers and Corporation hold ultimate power, and make use of the Administration and a few individuals within the Faculty to achieve what the Corporation and Overseers see as in their interests, and in the interests of their class, the men who control the U.S. government and the large corporations. The Faculty at Harvard has no real power, except over arrangements (like the Afro-American Studies Department) which do not threaten the interests of the class of men who sit on the Corporation and the Board of Overseers. It is clearly against the interests of these men to have on the Harvard Faculty persons who fight against policies important to them. Therefore it was seen as politically necessary for them to fire one faculty member as an example to others so that they should see the consequences of seriously opposing the men who run Harvard. I was chosen to be the example, as I had openly participated in the struggle against ROTC and expansion.

One final point concerning procedures in my case: the Report of the Joint Committee attempts to convey the impression that I refused their request to appear at a second hearing, and that I refused to explain or discuss seriously the charges brought against me. I was requested to appear at the first hearing and did so. I was *not* requested to appear at the second hearing—rather, the Committee (in Mr. Marbury's letter of July 28) offered me "a further opportunity" to appear at a second hearing "provided that a written request for such a meeting is received from you." It was therefore open to me to request or not my own appearance at the second hearing. I chose not to make such a request, but I did not refuse any request by the Committee.

In any case, despite misrepresentations by the Joint Committee in its statement of July 28, AAUP recommended procedures do not require a faculty member to appear before, or disclose information to, a disciplinary committee. Yet in my case the Joint Committee tried to use these grounds to justify my firing.

Such procedural questions I regard as beside the point, but as some persons feel they are important and as they provide another example of how the Joint Committee attempts to mislead faculty opinion, these examples should be clarified. . . .

Part II. Political Issues Raised by My Case

˙The issues raised by my firing include both the political issues behind the occupation of University Hall and also the issue of political firing itself.

The Report of the Joint Committee evades the original, substantive issues—the issues of ROTC and Harvard expansion—but quite clearly poses the issue of political firing. My firing is explicitly intended as a precedent. The reasons the Committee gives to justify my firing are meant to provide a rationale for firing in the future other faculty members who dare to support the student movement, or any movement, taking militant action against University policies. My firing therefore can be seen as an attempt to intimidate other faculty members and to inhibit their political activities.

Let us look at the specific arguments of the Joint Committee. They find that I "encouraged and participated in the forcible occupation of University Hall"—a charge I have never denied. This act was not only "unlawful" (i.e. considered "trespass" by the courts) but was also "grave misconduct" because it allegedly constituted "grave irresponsibility toward the collegial community" including "irresponsible abdication of a teacher's obligation to students." . . .

The Joint Committee's argument is that my action encouraged students to follow me into the same action and thereby get into trouble. This argument reveals a patronizing attitude towards students. Students who participated in the occupation of University Hall, whether or not they were "encouraged" by my presence there, were themselves quite aware of the risks they were taking and the commitment they were making. Their decision to participate was their own—and it is insulting to them to continue to maintain, as the Administration and its apologists constantly do, that students in University Hall were somehow manipulated or lured irrationally into an act with which they did not agree politically.

The Joint Committee's Report also insults and threatens faculty members in general. Not only is it "grave misconduct" for a faculty member to participate in an act such as the occupation of University Hall, the Report proclaims, it is misconduct to *encourage* students in such acts, "even, indeed, by failing to take positive action to dissuade them"! "In such circumstances the duty of an instructor is to dissuade students from persisting in such acts."

The threat is clear: the vast majority of faculty members did not attempt to dissuade the masses of students who occupied University Hall and who "disrupted" the University by going on strike. Indeed, many faculty members supported the students in various ways. The criteria used by the Joint Committee to fire me could just as well have been used to justify the firings of many more faculty members.

That the Corporation has not at this time chosen to fire others can be attributed to the fact that more firings are not yet seen as necessary: my case can be used as an exemplary warning to other faculty members of what can be done to them if in the future they "encourage" or "fail to dissuade" student actions against the Administration and Corporation. In other words, faculty members are being pressured by the Administration and Corporation to act in the latter's interest: to become agents of political control over students, to become in effect policemen. This is the "free discussion and democratic choice" the Corporation promotes: to keep one's job, one has to act in the Corporation's interest. A teacher must hold down his students when their demands and struggles threaten the Corporation's interests.

Thus it is clear what the Joint Committee means when it accuses me of "irresponsible abdication of a teacher's obligation to students." This strange charge makes sense if re-worded as "irresponsible abdication of a teacher's obligation to the Corporation." For I was indeed "irresponsible" to the Corporation: I joined thousands of others in opposing University policies on ROTC and expansion, and with hundreds of others I took the militant action that was necessary to effectively challenge these policies. I was in no way irresponsible to the majority of students who demonstrated that they wanted these policies changed. Students and faculty members, on the whole, do not benefit from the University's policies on ROTC and expansion; and the people who suffer from them—black people, working people, Vietnamese and other Third World peoples—are those to whom we *were* responsible in taking the acts we did in occupying University Hall and in striking. This "responsibility," I believe, justifies those actions and justifies "irresponsibility" towards the Corporation and Administration—a few men whose interests conflict with those of most people.

The Joint Committee's Report carefully omits consideration of these issues. It poses the question instead in a deliberately narrow frame of reference: in terms only of "the University community," as if we were an island, an ivory tower independent of the real world, the rest of the world. Moreover, it is assumed that in this "community" we are all equals with the same "rights" and "responsibilities" and that we share a unity of interests.

I maintain that this frame of reference is not only totally misleading but dangerous: it masks and defends practices which in fact hurt many people—primarily people outside of the Harvard "community." For the University is in fact very much part of the real world.

Let us look closely at the Joint Committee's rationalization of why I do not belong at Harvard:

Dr. Stauder's participation in and encouragement of the seizure of University Hall expressed approval of an act that was thoroughly antipathetic to the foundations of the University community. Members of this University have always had the right to express their views and to press for action on matters of concern to them by any and all means appropriate to a free academic institution. These means include the right to join and organize political groups and associations, to convene and conduct non-disruptive meetings on all public and political issues, and to express, advocate and publicize opinions. But the possession of these rights imposes the duty to respect the freedom of others to move, speak or listen. And any teacher who engages in activities such as the forcible occupation of a University building, or the disruption of University functions, or the physical obstruction of academic or administrative processes, is violating these rights and has no proper place in a free university.

In what sense is Harvard a "free university"? The Report points out that students and faculty members have a few "rights," namely "the right to join and organize political groups and associations, to convene and conduct non-disruptive meetings on all public and political issues, and to express, advocate and publicize opinions." Of course, members of the Administration, Corporation and Board of Overseers have these "rights" too—as well as superior financial resources "to express, advocate and publicize" *their* opinions. But aside from the disparity of resources at our disposal, are we all then equals in our "rights and responsibilities"?

The answer is obvious. Students, faculty, the people of Cambridge, people elsewhere—we can express, press "appropriately," join, organize, convene, conduct, advocate, publicize as much as we are able. But only the Corporation and the Board of Overseers have the "right" actually to decide and implement the policies Harvard pursues. They do not and will not share this "right" with anyone. And despite whatever motions of "consultation" are gone through, despite whatever Student-Faculty-Overseers committees are set up, one need not be cynical to suppose that Harvard policy never runs and never will run opposed to the interests directly represented on the Corporation and Board of Overseers. In fact one can assume, and observe, that Harvard policy consistently serves these interests—the interests of the large corporations, the U.S. government and allied organizations. The class of men who control these institutions also control the universities.

What if the interests of this ruling class are fundamentally opposed to those, for instance, of the working people of Cambridge and Roxbury threatened by Harvard expansion; or to those of the Vietnamese, black people, etc., whose struggles for liberation are threatened by an army with ROTC-trained officers? What if students and faculty members in the "university community" identify their own interests with those of black people, Vietnamese, Cambridge working people, and try to support these people by fighting against Harvard policies which threaten them?

In this case, the model of "community" breaks down. In terms of "rights" the Corporation, Overseers, and Administration have all "rights" (i.e. power) to act as they please to implement their "opinions" and satisfy their interests. Students and faculty have no "rights" except to voice their "opinions." Because their "rights" as ordained by the Joint Committee do not include the right to take militant action to fight harmful policies of the Corporation when such action might be the only way to defeat such policies, students and faculty are condemned to ineffectiveness.

In this situation the Corporation, Board of Overseers and their Administration retain their monopoly on the "right" to use force: to evict people from their homes, to train officers for the army, to bring in police to attack students occupying buildings, to throw students out of school and to fire a teacher for fighting back against University policies.

In other words, so-called "rights" in the "university community" boil down to a power relationship: the University is organized as a class institution, with a small group of men at the top who use their position to serve not only themselves but also the ruling class from which they come. They hold essentially all legal power to govern, and they have all the power of the State behind them to enforce their "rights." The only real power students, faculty members, workers and others have is the power to resist by fighting back: by taking militant action if necessary. The exercise of this power from below is of course not recognized as a "right" by the class of men who exercise power from above. They have the power to define "rights." And so the Joint Committee has defined "rights" as it has, and coated them with sugary cant about "community" and "a free university."

The free university the Corporation and Adminstration want is a university they are free to rule as they want, in their narrow interests—a university where others are not free to interfere with their policies. It is freedom for a small class of men to act and profit at the expense of others.

It is true that I have not respected the "freedom" and "rights" of the Administration and Corporation. In occupying University Hall we certainly interfered with the freedom and right of the deans to carry on business as usual there. By violating this "freedom" and "right" we did disrupt the functioning of the University. This disruption was necessary to bring pressure to bear on the men who rule Harvard. This pressure was exercised on behalf of two sets of demands: (1) to abolish ROTC and (2) to stop Harvard expansion and rent-gouging. The "freedom" and "right" of the Corporation to continue these policies must be balanced against other rights and freedoms: the rights of Cambridge working people to remain in the city they built and live in, and the rights of Vietnamese, black people and peoples elsewhere to be free from suppression by the U.S. military and its ROTC-trained officers. It was the freedoms and rights of these people for which we were fighting when we occupied University Hall. We took their side against the Harvard Corporation and the class it represents and serves. Whose rights are more important? Whose rights are just? The "rights" of the businessmen and their administrators who run Harvard University, or the lives of the masses of people who are hurt by Harvard policies? This is the basic issue underlying my firing.

The Administration and its apologists try in every way possible to avoid or obscure this basic issue, but it remains. It explains why I acted as I did, why I was fired, why I am convinced we were right to occupy University Hall, and why any punishment is wrong for what was a just and necessary action.

* * * * *

HISTORICAL NOTE: In 1835 Charles Follen, a professor of

German literature, was fired by the Harvard Corporation for his activities in the anti-slavery movement. In the years up until the Civil War numerous other faculty members at Harvard were denied reappointment or promotion for their anti-slavery activities.

CHAPTER 15

Participation and Power:
Should the University
Be Restructured?

If there was one idea that expressed the essence of New Left philosophy in the mid-1960s, that idea was "participatory democracy": people should have a meaningful voice in the decisions that vitally affect their lives. This concept originally served SDS as the keystone of its ideals, the logic behind its immediate demands, and the basis for its internal organization. Although SDS never rejected participatory democracy as an ideal, during the late sixties it became increasingly suspicious of participation as an immediate goal and also began to downgrade it as an organizational principle. But as SDS dropped its initial drive for student power and participation, the cause was taken up by more moderate students, who seemed to gravitate to positions SDS had only recently deserted.

In 1966, the slogan "student power" was born at Berkeley in conscious imitation of the slogan "black power." In October of the following year, the Collegiate Press Service distributed two statements on student power, one written by Edward Schwartz, soon to be President of the National Students Association, and one by Carl Davidson, who presented the viewpoint of SDS. The right responded to the call for activism with charges that "student power" was a disguise for left-wing designs. In a 1967 leaflet from Wayne State University, one right-wing critic of SDS told students to spurn demands for participation in university decisions. "We were invited to this campus by the Michigan taxpayer," the student declared. "Let us honor that invitation."

By 1969 SDS was no longer raising demands for a student role in institutional governance. Positions had shifted so that now it was SDS that called "student power" a trick. The radicals saw participation as an attempt by the establishment to co-opt them into running the system. Structures might be altered, but not enough to change the functions performed by the university for corporations and the military. This is the basic argument of the leaflet by Mike Prokosch of Harvard SDS written during the 1969 strike at that university.

The position of the reformists was that students and faculty constituted the legitimate university community and that it was only democratic, therefore, for them to determine policy through bipartite legislative and judicial structures. "What could be more American, more democratic than that?" J. P. Jordan of Columbia wrote. "It is based on Montesquieu and Madison, not Marx or Mao." Mike Wallace put the case simply: "A community of scholars should be controlled by scholars."

Several objections were raised to the reformist demand for bipartite student-faculty control. Some questioned whether students and faculty were the only group with a legitimate claim to power, while others doubted that students were competent enough to play a significant role. The issues of legitimacy and competence were both raised by Charles Frankel, a professor of philosophy at Columbia and Assistant Secretary of State for Cultural Affairs under President Johnson. Frankel contended that outsiders merit representation in university governance and that the role of the trustees is legitimate. He also maintained that egalitarian ideals that are valid in society are not transferable to the university since there are "acceptable procedures" in the university for determining who is competent to make decisions.

Students should be given a voice in university decisions, but not a vote, according to John McDonough, a Stanford law professor. Rejecting the view that everyone ought to participate in the decisions that affect them, McDonough pointed out "that we do not let the patients manage the hospital; we do not let clients manage the law firm; we do not let the passengers manage the airlines; and we do not let the consumers manage a business enterprise." McDonough saw two different conceptions of the university and left little doubt about which one he prefered: "Will we accept the students' view of the University, essentially as a kind of democracy in the councils of which they are entitled to at least equal representation? Or will we take the view that the University is essentially an educational enterprise, organized and run by the trustees, administration and faculty, which any student can take or leave, as he sees fit, but which is not entitled to participate in managing while he is with us?"

A different response to student demands came from Kingman Brewster, Jr., president of Yale University. Brewster suggested that universities should give students not representation, but accountability. As a first step, he recommended that his own term as president be limited to seven years.

Most of the supporters of student representation have based their arguments on democratic principles. A more pragmatic justification for student participation in university governance, however, saw questions of principle as irrelevant. "The politicians of early nineteenth-century England did not regard as reasonable the claims of the working class to the vote and to political representation," Philip Oldham wrote. Yet the politicians yielded, and so should the universities, according to Oldham, because students are an interest group that ought to be accommodated.

The demand for student participation in decisions on faculty hiring and tenure has excited more intense opposition than the demand for participation in university policy making. In all but a very few cases—one notable exception being Harvard's Afro-American studies department—the demand has been refused. At the University of Chicago, the issue arose with particular force when a woman assistant professor of sociology, Marlene Dixon, was denied reappointment. According to protesters, the decision was made because of her sex and her radical political leanings. Hence the controversy involved not only the issue of student participation, but also women's liberation and the political character of the faculty.*

We open the Chicago debate with a statement by the administration reasserting the authority of the faculty in educational mat-

* For text of student demands, see Appendix to Volume II.

ters, while granting students an advisory role. Next is a broadside by the radical New University Conference challenging the view that academic appointments are based on objective, neutral standards and supporting the students' demand for a voice in decisions, "not as a 'concession' to students or merely as a democratization of the university, but as an intellectual necessity."

An editorial from the *Chicago Maroon,* the student paper, admits that students have limitations as participants in academic decisions, but states that they are "really the only ones who can evaluate teaching very well" and should, therefore, be regularly consulted on faculty appointments. Finally, a statement by a group of protesters explains the reasoning behind their demand for equal power in the hiring and rehiring of faculty: "While students are perhaps less competent than faculty to judge according to narrow academic criteria, they are more competent to judge teaching ability, and to assess relevance of scholarship to current and future social concerns."

After the protesters had occupied a university building, 37 of their number were expelled. In the end, Chicago did not rehire Marlene Dixon, nor did it grant the demand for a student role in faculty hiring.

Student Power

Two statements on Student Power written in 1967 by Edward Schwartz and Carl Davidson, and distributed by the Collegiate Press Service in October of 1967 to represent the views, respectively, of the U.S. National Students Association and Students for a Democratic Society.

He Who Must Obey the Rule Should Make It
By Edward Schwartz

My comments will be necessarily brief, but the point should be clear—student power means, not simply the ability to influence decisions, but the ability to make decisions. The days when two students, hand-picked by the administration, could sit on a college-policy committee for seven months, only to endorse a report having little to do with student demands, should end. Student power involves the organizing of all the students, not just the elite; it involves the participation of the students, not just the elite.

The educational premise behind demands for student power reflects the notion that people learn through living, through the process of integrating their thoughts with their actions, through testing their values against those of a community, through a capacity to act. Education which tells students that they must prepare to live tells infants that they learn to walk by crawling. College presidents who invoke legal authority to prove educational theory—"if you don't like it, leave. It's our decision to make."— assume that growth is the ability to accept what the past has created. Student power is a medium through which people integrate their own experience with a slice of the past which seems appropriate, with their efforts to intensify the relationships between the community within the university.

Let this principle apply—he who must obey the rule should make it.

Students should make the rules governing dormitory hours, boy-girl visitation, student unions, student fees, clubs, newspapers, and the like. Faculty and administrators should advise—attempt to persuade, even. Yet the student should bear the burden of choice. They should demand the burden.

Students and faculty should co-decide curricular policy.

Students, faculty, and administration should co-decide admissions policy (they did it at Swarthmore), overall college policy affecting the community, even areas like university investments.

Student power brings those changes, and in the latter cases, it means that the student view will be taken seriously—that it will be treated as a view, subject to rational criticism or acceptance, not simply as "the student opinion which must be considered as the student opinion—*i.e.,* the opinion of those lesser beings in the university."

Student power brings change in the relationships between groups within the university, as well as change in attitudes between the groups of a university. It renders irrelevant the power of factions outside a university who impose external standards on an internal community—Trustees, alumni.

Student power should not be argued on legal grounds. It is not a legal principle. It is an educational principle. Students who argue for "rights" usually fail to explore the reasons for rights. In a university, a right should spring from a premise of education, not a decision of a court, although the two may coincide. Student power can suggest a critique of education.

Most students don't want student power. They are too tired, too scared, or too acquiescent to fight for it. That, too, is a student decision. Those with potential power may choose to ignore it—even those who have decided not to decide have made a decision.

Yet, abdication of responsibility, or transferral of authority to other people inhibits individual and collective growth. Students who accept other people's decisions have diluted their desire to question, to test themselves, to become through being. They create walls between their classroom material and their lives, between their inner and outer selves. Acquiescence is boring, even humiliating. Education should be neither.

Student power is threatening to those who wield power now, but this is understandable. A student should threaten his administrators outside of class, just as bright students threaten professors inside of class. Student power ultimately challenges everyone in the university—the students who must decide; the faculty and administrators who must rethink their own view of community relations in order to persuade.

People who say that student power means anarchy imply really that students are rabble who have no ability to form community and to adhere to decisions made by community. Student power is not the negation of rules—it is the creation of a new process for the enactment of rules. Student power is not the elimination of authority, it is the development of a democratic standard of authority.

Students who ignore student power ignore themselves. They are safe, respectable, but emasculated. Ultimately, they can be dangerous. Later in life, they wield power in the way in which it was wielded upon them—without any standard to govern it save that of power.

The standard of the university should encourage a democratic temperament, not an authoritarian elite. That's the point of student power.

Student Power: A Radical View
By Carl Davidson

What can students do?

Organizing struggles over dormitory rules seems frivolous when compared to the ghetto rebellions. And white students are no longer wanted or necessary in the black movement. Organize against the war? Of course. But we have pride in being a multi-faceted movement, organizing people around the issues affecting their lives.

Change your life. The war hardly affects most students. In some sense, we are a privileged elite, coddled in a campus sanctuary. Draft resistance tables in the student union building—the arrogance of it all. We organize students against the draft when the Army is made up of young men who are poor, black, Spanish-American, hillbillies, or working class. Everyone except students. How can we be so stupid when we plan our strategies?

Students are oppressed. Bullshit. We are being trained to be oppressors and the underlings of oppressors. Only the moral among us are being hurt. Even then, the damage is only done to our sensitivities. Most of us don't know the meaning of a hard day's work. . . .

Student power! Classes are large and impersonal. Reduce the size of the class in counter-insurgency warfare from 50 to 5. Students and professors should "groove" on each other. We want to control student rules, tribunals, and disciplinary hearing "ourselves." One cop is so much like another.

Student radicals cannot leave the campus because they might lose their 2-S deferments. Organize in the white community. What white community can be organized by an organizer with a 2-S?—Hippies, students, and middle class suburbanites. What sections of the white community are exploited and oppressed?—The poor and the working class. That's where we're at, brothers and sisters.

Yet, there is a student movement. Something is afoot on the nation's campuses. What can we do with it?

We have to look at the university more carefully, but, at the same time, keep it in its proper perspective. The university is connected structurally with the larger society. Nevertheless, we cannot build socialism on one campus. Most attempts in reforming the university have ricocheted immediately against the necessity of transforming the society as well.

Which is as it should be. Our analysis of the university as a service station and job-training factory adjunct to American corporate capitalism would hardly be relevant otherwise. If this is the case, however, where do student politics fit into the picture?

In the past few years, the student revolt has been primarily directed against the form of our education: i.e., class size, grading, participation in rule-making, etc. We have emphasized these aspects over and above the "content" and "ends" of our "training"; and, as a result, we have failed in eliciting a seriousness and sense of direction in our work.

Being a student is not an eternal condition. Rather, we are a flow of manpower with the need of being whipped into shape before entering a lifelong niche in the political economy. While this process has precious little to do with education, there is nothing wrong with it in itself. I have no objection to the "training" of schoolteachers. And our knowledge factories do an effective job of that.

Rather, my objectives focus on how they are being trained and for what ends. Perhaps the implications of these questions can be seen if we examine an institution like student government.

My objection to student government is not that it is "unreal" or "irrelevant." Quite the opposite. Student government is quite effective and relevant in achieving its purpose. Beginning in grade school, we all went through the "let's pretend" process of electing home room officers. In high school, student council was the name of the game. And so on into college.

Throughout it all, none of us ever doubted the fact that forms of our self-government had any power. We all knew the teacher, or the principal, or the administration, or the regents had the final and effective say-so in most of our affairs.

But think about it for a minute. Did not the process effectively achieve its purpose?

We learned to acquiesce in the face of arbitrary authority. We learned to surrender our own freedom in the name of something called "expertise."

We learned that elections should be personality-oriented popularity contests; that issues with which we ought to be concerned should only be the most banal.

Most of all, we learned about "responsibility" and "working inside the system." Was all of this not an adequate preparation for "life in the real world?" Are national, state, and local elections any different?

The farce of it all is only evidenced by comparing the reality of our political lives with the ideals we are given to revere. Even so, we were also taught to smirk at "idealism."

We learned our lessons well, so well in fact, that some of us

have embraced a cynicism so deep that the quality of our lives has
been permanently impaired. Perhaps a majority of us have been
castrated by the existing order; a generation's young manhood
and womanhood manifesting nothing beyond the utter destruction of seriousness. Give a flower to a cop. Join the marines and
be a man. James Bond is the fraternity man of the year.

Student government reeks of the worst aspect of this syndrome.
Because of that, it may be a good place for initiating on the campus the movement for human liberation already in progress off
the campus.

We have no blueprints. Only some guidelines. Administrators
are the enemy. Refuse to be "responsible." Have more faith in
people than in programs. Refuse to accept the "off-campus-on-
campus" dichotomy. Finally, demand seriousness by dealing with
serious issues—getting the U.S. out of Vietnam, getting the military off the campus, enabling people to win control over the quality and direction of their lives.

In short, make a revolution.

*Leaflet distributed in the spring of 1967 by Counterthrust, a right-wing student
organization at Wayne State University.*

Student Power Is a Farce

Our University is being treated to the insanity of Left-Wing students demanding the run of the University. This situation would
be hilarious if it were not for the fact that so many intelligent students are allowing themselves to be taken in and used by the Left.
Wayne students are told by the Left that "student power" merely
means more democracy on campus. This is an outright lie! "Student power" is a left-wing catchword symbolizing campus militancy and radicalism. In actuality, the Left-wing, spearheaded by
the SDS (Students For a Democratic Society) want to radically
alter the university community. A "student power" movement is
a necessary first step in the formation of student unions (controlled and dominated by the Leftists).

In a leaflet issued by Carl Davidson, head of the SDS Great
Plains Regional Organizing Committee, plans for student power-
unions are discussed. The leaflet is entitled "Toward a Student
Syndicalist Movement." * The initial section of the leaflet is a

* For text, see Vol. II, pp. 98–107.

condemnation of the present university system. The Leftists charge a sinister plot by private enterprise to train students for jobs at taxpayers' expense. Evidently it never occurred to the SDS that private enterprise is also the biggest single taxpayer for schools. But, of course, that would require a little thought on the part of the SDS which they have already demonstrated they are incapable of. Students who obey university rules and regulations are labeled as the creators of situations like Watts, Mississippi, and Vietnam (in other words, racists and warmongers).

The byword of student power-union advocates is Radicalism. As they say in their leaflets, "we allow ourselves to be intimidated by the word 'Responsible'. We spend more energy assuring our Deans that we don't have another Berkeley than we do talking with students about real issues". Frankly, Wayne students should demand of Chuck Larson and his pea-brained cohorts assurances that Wayne will not be another Berkeley.

Fraternities and student Governments will have no place in student power-unions since both are considered allies of the status-quo and thus useless. It is clearly evident that no self-respecting Greek could give support to a student power-movement.

Student power-union plans call for a list of demands on the University with a time limit set for meeting them (as is now the case on the Wayne Campus). If the demands are not met, mass demonstrations, sit-ins and a general strike will be probably used. If the power-unions succeed, then Leftist plans call for (A) demands upon each professor at the beginning of each quarter that students participate in shaping course contents, (B) organization of students to work out counter-curriculums, mainly because students shaped it rather than on its merits, and (C) mock trials of the Deans for "crimes against humanity."

As responsible Wayne students, we cannot allow our University to be used by the Leftists for their narrow purposes. We were invited to this campus by the Michigan Taxpayer to receive an education. Let us honor that invitation.

Chuck Larson, who just a few short weeks ago chaired the disgusting "War Crimes Hearings" at which American soldiers were "indicted" as "murderers," should be impeached from his position as Chairman of the Student-Faculty Council. Larson has demonstrated, beyond any doubt, that he is incapable of being a responsible student leader.

From a leaflet by Mike Prokosch, Harvard-Radcliffe SDS, April 1969.

Structural Reform and Concrete Demands

Many students, though sympathetic to our eight demands, have criticized us because we have not added structural reform to them. How, they ask, can we stick to a small set of concrete demands which will not change the institutions that caused the underlying problems?

We have stuck to our demands for good reasons. Our strategy in maintaining them is based on a view of the University that differs radically from the view of structural reform's advocates. The Corporation's actions of the last six days support our conception.

Power and Interests at Harvard

It's crucial to realize that Harvard is run by and for powerful business interests—the Corporation. "The principal governing board of the University" whose consent is required for "all changes in policy or in the University statutes" (*General Catalogue,* 1966–67) is six men and Pusey who presently hold one chairmanship, 3 presidencies, and 33 directorships in major corporations. . . . These businessmen's final say over all University policy ensures that Harvard will serve the interests of the country's ruling elite, of which they are prominent members. We see this in a description of Harvard's functions:

• Undergraduates are trained for places in the country's ruling elite, for professional roles which support that elite. Pusey thinks, for example, "it's terribly important that ROTC be kept here. I personally feel it's terribly important for the United States of America that college people go into the military." (*Crimson,* March 20, 1969) College-graduate officers maintain a class structure in the Armed Forces that keeps them operating smoothly in the interests of men like those on the Corporation. Pusey's conception of ROTC is very revealing.

• Much of Harvard's faculty is a brain trust for the government. Men like Henry Kissinger and Arthur Smithies travel around the world trouble-shooting for the Administration. . . .

• Briefly, the various departments of natural and social sciences mix scholarly and applied research to serve business and the government. The University's over-all function of research, to which education is subordinated (professors are researchers first and only then teachers), implements government and business policies that are accurately called imperialist. Government and university personnel, interchangeable in such places as the Center for International Affairs, the Russian Research Center, and the East Asian Research Center, commute between Washington and Cambridge to unify theory and practice in such fields as national development and social control. The government depends on free access to this expertise for carrying out its domestic and foreign policies of social manipulation.

Those are the purposes for which Harvard is run. Its housing policies in Cambridge support them, against the interests of Cambridge's working-class residents. When Harvard puts up new buildings to expand its research facilities, housing goes. The housing (Peabody Terrace, Mather House) it erects for University members destroys working-class neighborhoods and drives the residents, unable to pay for new homes at current market prices, out of the city. When Harvard wants to empty one of its properties so it can expand onto the site, it raises rents and lets the property deteriorate (as at University Road). Tenants can only move. Since Harvard constantly buys property for future buildings, speculators acquire housing and jack up rents, while letting it run down (since they expect to be bought out soon). Landlords can extort high rents because Harvard directly and indirectly attracts large numbers of high paying middle-class people, and because Harvard's expansion has decreased the housing supply. Indeed, Harvard sees its (with MIT's, NASA's etc.) transformation of Cambridge into a middle-class community as a desirable goal. Such a community would not just be a more congenial setting for a University. "A Cambridge whose entirely middle-class citizens worked in Harvard's and other corporations' research centers will be a richly funded complex grinding out programs (and the technical means) to suppress black rebellions, worker and student struggles, and insurgency in the American empire." . . . In other words, driving the working class from Cambridge supports and amplifies Harvard's own functions.

In its function and its practice we have seen Harvard acting in certain specific interests—those of the country's ruling elite—against the interests of all other sectors of the population. In Cambridge the working class is most blatantly hurt. The events of the last five days, however, show that *anyone* who gets in the way of those interests will be run over. . . .

Even the Faculty, when it got in the Corporation's way, was pushed aside. Dean Ford's ROTC letter to Pusey* does not even consider the possibility of executing the Faculty's proposal as formulated. It is devoted to getting around it and retaining ROTC, in the Corporation's interests. Harvard is run in those interests. Its stated ideals of scholarship and free enlightened inquiry must be seen in the context of this function—serving and training the country's ruling elite against the interests of all other sectors of the population.

What Are You Going to Do About It?

Well, say proponents of restructuring, if Harvard is run that way we should change its ruling bodies—appoint committees to regulate Harvard's relations with the community . . . or even put the Corporation under the control of a student-faculty senate . . . But that is naive. The Corporation simply will not vote itself out of power. Its members assumed their positions because Harvard's functions are vital to their interests. They will close the University sooner than let these functions escape their control and cease. Besides, they gain great influence from their positions in a billion-dollar Corporation and great personal prestige from heading a key university and research center. Our power is not yet great enough to force them out, though it is strong enough to force them to grant specific demands.

But there are innumerable ways for apparent reforms to leave power in Corporation hands and policy in ruling-class interests. We cannot . . . assume the Corporation's benevolence. . . .

Moreover, a strategy for reform which puts restructuring foremost can be used by the Corporation. The ways to restructure are infinite, and debate over them infinitely lengthy and confusing.

* For text, see pp. 286–89 of this volume.

Negotiations to achieve a new structure tie students to existing power relations. Besides distracting them from their real aims and their essential opposition to the Corporation's interests, it legitimates the new structure. But the new structure could pass policy as reactionary as the University's present practices. It simply doesn't make sense to channel a movement for real social change into work with such uncertain payoffs. The reality of power, what gets done, is what we must attack—not power's form. And in fact, the Corporation has already started the process of co optation. Its new committees, like the Overseers' coming consultations with "faculty, students, administration and others as appropriate" "to investigate in detail the events of the last week at Harvard," will postpone and ultimately preclude, rather than speed, real change in Harvard's policies.

And time is extremely important. If we wait for the New Harvard to take form, the Old Harvard will continue to screw Cambridge *and us*. While we wait our strength will ebb. Confused and divided by the complex ties and secret negotiations of restructuring, we will lose the base for a movement for real change. Restructuring could ameliorate dormitory life and curriculum, but it won't help the people of Cambridge and of the world whose interests Harvard's functions directly oppose. To use our movement for small improvements in our own condition, while ignoring the vital interests of all these others, is not only elitist; it is stupid. It splits us from them and prevents us from ever allying for general social change.

What we *should* do is to work for concrete demands. The Corporation will clearly meet them or not; no compromise or negotiations are involved. It's true that winning them will not in itself stop Harvard from initiating new, equally bad policies two weeks later. But in winning them we will build a movement that will prevent Harvard from doing this. In working for the good of all, we cannot let ourselves get entangled in institutions run by and for those whose interests oppose most people's welfare. *All of us* who believe in social justice must build a movement *independent* of such institutions as Harvard. Only thus will we change the policies of the men who run the Corporation and the country. Join us —we will win.

Student-Faculty Control

From a letter to the editor of the New York Times, *written by J. P. Jordan of the Students for a Restructured University, Columbia University, May 14, 1968.*

For Democracy in Universities

. . . I am a graduate student at Columbia—never a member of the Students for a Democratic Society, not one of those who occupied buildings, and over thirty. I am by now completely nauseated by irrelevant preachments on the limits of civil disobedience in a democracy.

Where democratic means are available, we use them, as in the McCarthy campaign. But American colleges and universities (with a few exceptions, such as Antioch) are about as democratic as Saudi Arabia.

If, as most liberals admit, civil disobedience was justified in Mississippi, where the forms of democracy were combined with the facts of oppression, it is *a fortiori* justified in academic institutions which lack even the semblance of democracy.

We have among us a few Maoists, Trotskyites, and other exemplars of what Lenin called "an infantile disease." But most of us who support the strike at Columbia are simply fighting for what Americans fought for two centuries ago—the right to govern ourselves.

Everyone agrees that the functions of a university are education and research. The people who perform those functions are faculty and students. Ergo, faculty and students are the university. Others—trustees or typists, presidents or plumbers, deans or groundskeepers—perform functions useful or even necessary, but strictly ancillary.

Admittedly, by a legal fiction the trustees are the university, as by another the stockholders are General Motors (I'd like to see them build one car). But fictions should be adjusted to facts, not vice versa.

Since faculty and students are in fact the university, they should govern it—not on a one-man, one-vote basis, which would always allow students to outvote faculty, but through bipartite legislative and judicial bodies of faculty elected by faculty and students elected by students. Let administrators confine themselves to administering, and trustees to managing the university's investments—something they understand.

What could be more American, more democratic than that? It is based on Montesquieu and Madison, not Marx or Mao. That liberal politicians like Hubert Humphrey, liberal cartoonists like Herblock, liberal newspapers like *The Times,* seem totally incapable of understanding such basic and obvious applications of principles they have long professed can hardly promote trust in the "liberal establishment."

Internal document of the Strike Steering Committee, Columbia University, written by Mike Wallace, for the Reconstruction Committee, May 1968.

Restructuring at Columbia

The Strike seems to have convinced every group on campus of at least one thing: that Columbia is badly in need of "restructuring." Students, faculty, employees, administrators, and trustees—all are agreed that "restructuring" is in order. But what does "restructuring" mean? That the administration grant the College Faculty the privilege of electing their own Dean? That the administration establish some more tripartite committees? That the administration institute new judicial procedures which violate basic rights of due process? Will next year bring some shuffling of the bureaucracy which will leave basic power relationships untouched? The Strike Committee thinks this will be the case. We feel that for many, "restructuring" means rearranging, readjusting, retouching: making the minimum number of minimal changes that will allow the University to resume "normal functioning."

Real change at Columbia must take two things into account: the impact of society upon the university, and the deeply undemocratic nature of Columbia as currently constituted.

The internal structure of the university cannot be separated from the university's social and political function in American society. National imperatives have warped and corrupted the academic community: many of the policies we have been fighting originated outside the university and cannot be altered by internal reforms. For example, a society that devotes half its resources to warfare cannot help distorting academic priorities: by funneling tagged money via military contracts into secret research, by co-opting the university into complicity with aggression via membership in the IDA [Institute for Defense Analyses], by inducing the academic community to train military personnel, accept a branch of the military intelligence on its campus, and serve as a recruiting station for the armed forces. With the passing of time the University has come to accept such activities as right and proper: its values have been bent to conform to those of the country at large. It has become complacent about its complicity. Finally, the University comes to adopt national patterns in its own relations with its own neighbors. America's arrogance and imposition of its values become Columbia's arrogance and imposition of *its* values in Morningside Heights and Morningside Park. Thus the relationship between society and academia is a subtle and far-reaching one: the ownership of Columbia by assorted Board Chairmen and real estate interests is just the grossest manifestation of this interaction. Change at Columbia, therefore, to some extent must wait upon changes in American society.

Yet it is not impossible for change to begin here and now. But it must be based upon a correct understanding of the nature of power relationships within the university; and thus an understanding of how basic the alterations must be to be effectual. Columbia is a corporation. A Board of Trustees owns it. An Administration controls it. Faculty are hirelings, whose complacency is purchased by granting them de facto control over strictly academic matters. The students are clients. They have no power whatever. The whole structure is sugared over with a soothing façade of committees and consultations; its skeleton of force and cops is revealed only at crisis moments. This is absurd. This is a perversion of what an academic community should be. Any changes that do not completely alter this state of affairs are worse than meaningless.

A community of scholars should be controlled by scholars. The direction of American Universities by outsiders, representatives of the affluent community, is a historical accident, a diversion from European patterns of student or faculty control. In the seventeenth and eighteenth centuries, trustees were functional; they are no longer so. Trustees are strangers to Academia; their values are the values of the business or professional world. It is absurd for these outsiders to govern a community perfectly capable of governing itself. It is dangerous for spokesmen of corporate

America to preside over an institution which supposedly acts as a major source of criticism of that America. And it is unnecessary for them to do so: their supposed function of funneling money into university treasuries could be done far more effectively by professional endowment managers.

Faculty and students should run Columbia, with the participation of those who are affected by University policies. Democratic structures should be established to effectively represent their views, and these structures should be the governing bodies of the University. Columbia needs talented, creative men to staff its bureaucracy, to propose plans for the future, to take charge of the mechanics of institutional life. But administrators should ever be subservient to Faculty and Students. They should be the people who carry out and execute previously arrived-at policy decisions. There is simply no reason for allowing the President of the University to wield the enormous powers he now does. Autocratic Presidents are as anachronistic as trustees.

In a restructured Columbia, there must be a totally new relationship between the university and its neighbors, and between the university and its employees. Both should have a major say in making decisions that affect them. The community of the affluent has been given the right to dictate university policy, while the real community, our neighbors, have no rights beyond desultory consultation. This must be changed.

In a restructured Columbia there must be established rigorous judicial procedures that would protect the rights of the accused. An informal, paternalistic, nonlegalistic relationship between deans and students may once have been workable, when a "framework of trust" existed; it is no longer so. We have seen what happens to the "framework of trust" when Students issue real challenges to the Administration. We have learned once again that arbitrary power can never be rested safely anywhere. At a time when university discipline can be equivalent to a death penalty, we insist on the establishment of the most rigid safeguards.

From an article by Professor Charles Frankel, Department of Philosophy, Columbia University, in Saturday Review, *November 2, 1968.*

The Trustees in Perspective

There is a fundamental respect in which the administrators of a university are in a different position from the managers of a company. The university administrators cannot create a total plan of work, define jobs within it, and then assign individual workers to them. Of course, now that labor unions have the power they have, managers cannot do this as easily as they once could either. But the difference between their position and that of university administrators is still very great. The product of a factory is a corporate product to which individuals contribute. The product of a university is many separate, individual products, for which the corporate arrangements provide protection and support, but for which the individuals have basic responsibility.

. . . The right of a citizen of the larger society to vote just as the next man can, without regard to hierarchy, is based on the premise that, where the major policies of the state are concerned, where the nature of what is good for society is at issue, only extreme inadequacies, like illiteracy or a criminal record, are disqualifying. The basic reason for this view is that there are no reasonably defensible general procedures by which the citizenry can be divided into the class of those who know enough to have an opinion worth counting or an interest worth expressing, and the class of those who don't.

In contrast, while universities are democratic organizations in the sense that individuals have a broad array of personal rights within them, and that there is a play of opinion inside them which has a massive effect on their evolution, they are not democratic organizations in the sense that majority rule applies to them. For within a university there are acceptable procedures by which people can be graded in accordance with their competence, and grading people in this way is essential to the conduct of the university's special business. The egalitarian ideal does not apply across the board in universities any more than it does in any other field where *skill* is the essence of the issue. To suggest that it should apply is to make hash of the idea of learning. If there is a case to be made for student participation in the higher reaches of university government, therefore, it is a case that is not based upon *rights,* but upon considerations of good educational and administrative practice.

Does this imply that the government of colleges and universities by trustees is a good system? No; but it helps to put this system in perspective. The case which is generally presented against trustee control of universities mixes truths with exaggerations. It is true that most trustees tend to be preoccupied with other matters than education, that they are inaccessible to teachers and students, and that a dispiriting number of them have reached an age and station in life calculated to protect them against fresh ideas. It is not surprising, therefore, that professors and students are sparing in the confidence they lavish on trustees. The government of American universities by boards of trustees is not an example of government by the consent of the governed.

However, neither is it an example of tyranny. The powers of trustees are severely limited by custom and law, and by the realities of a university. In any well-established university, trustees normally leave educational decisions to the faculty. One of their primary educational functions, indeed, is simply to provide the educational community of the university—its students and faculty—with protective insulation. The trustees throw their mantle of influence and respectability around it, deflecting and absorbing criticisms and denunciations, and thus guarding the community's freedom. Indeed, it is doubtful that faculties and student bodies could by themselves, in many parts of the country, and without the help of trustees, successfully defend their autonomy, even assuming that their economic problems could be solved. It is odd that trustees should be attacked as though their presence was in contravention of academic freedom. Their presence is usually a condition for it.

Still, it can be asked whether this form of government is the best form for a college or university. Trustees (or regents) do make educational decisions, even if most of these are only indirect. They allocate resources, do more for one field of learning than for another, and make arrangements affecting the relation of the university to the larger society which affect the daily lives of teachers and students. Would it not be better if trustees continued to do their work of finding the money, but surrendered the other powers they exercise to the people who really constitute the university—namely, its students and teachers? Obviously, it is doubtful that many trustees would accept this proposal that they should supply the money but keep quiet about the way it is used. Just to see where the argument goes, however, let us imagine that trustees have a capacity for self-immolation not conspicuous in most human beings. Would it be a good thing for them to retire from the scene?

Not entirely. They are the buffers of the university against external pressures. As we have seen, an educational institution requires such protection. Most organizations, furthermore, benefit from having a lay group of critics with deep commitments to them, who are nevertheless not part of their daily operations. In addition, since universities must maintain relations with the surrounding society, they require people on their board of governors who have interests and experience in that society. And it is always well to remember that though education, like the law, is in part a professional business, it is also everybody's business. If students have a stake in what happens to them, by the same token, so do their parents and so do lay members of the community. In courts of law, juries are not composed of professional lawyers. On the university scene, the outsider, though he should not have as decisive a place as a juror has, also deserves to be represented.

Yet these same considerations call for change in the composition of most boards of trustees. They call, equally clearly, for changes in the manner in which they communicate with the communities they govern. Boards of trustees ought to have more younger people on them, and poorer people. They ought to have recent graduates, not only older ones. They ought to have people who have not yet arrived, not only those swollen with success. The surrounding neighborhood should, if possible, be represented. That is not always easy to arrange because there are so often disagreements about who is "representative" of whom. But if it can be done without creating quarrels that did not exist before, then it should be done. And students and faculty members either should be represented on the board or assured of regular consultation with it. . . .

In the end, we are discussing not matters of right and justice, but matters of political wisdom. Trustees will not know what they should know unless they mix with the people who can tell them. The community they govern will not understand why the trustees have made the decisions they have, and will not have confidence in these decisions, unless it has its own trusted emissaries to keep it in touch with the board. Faulty communication is the heart of the political problem in the American universities that are having trouble today. Demands for "student power" and "faculty power," so interpreted, are more than justifiable.

From an article in the Stanford Daily, *April 21, 1966, by Professor John R. McDonough, School of Law, Stanford University.*

The Role of Students in Governing the University

Some students appear to hold the view that what is fundamentally wrong with American universities in general and Stanford in particular is that a university is very largely run or governed by a bureaucracy known as the Administration. The Administration is perceived as either inadvertently or malevolently making a large number of unwise decisions relating both to educational policy and to standards of student conduct.

Both students and faculty are regarded as being largely subjugated by the Administration and required to conduct themselves in ways that are antithetical to the true values and purposes of a University.

The ultimate solution proposed for this regrettable state of affairs is the establishment, as the premier governing and policy-making entity within the University, of a kind of unicameral legislature in which faculty and students would be equally represented.

Another view held by many students—which seems to be a variation of or exception to the notion just expressed—is that students should have sole power and responsibility for fixing standards for student conduct.

The students who hold these views are currently making demands for recognition, autonomy and participation in decision-making which will move the University immediately in the direction, and ultimately to the realization of the goals they have set. Their strategy and tactics seem currently to be taking two major directions.

First they are endeavoring to organize the student body, both undergraduate and graduate, into a monolithic political constituency. Thus, we have witnessed in recent years the emergence of the Legislature of the Associated Students of Stanford University as the preeminent organ of student political action. LASSU has asserted, and both the ASSU presidents and the student judicial councils appear to have accepted, the view that LASSU is predominant in the student political structure.

During the current year LASSU has been asserting influence over various student entities, boards and enterprises which were formerly quite autonomous, thus further consolidating the Legislature's ascendancy in the student realm.

Second, the activists are demanding student membership in various decision-making entities with the University community. The LASSU has recently asserted that students should be given voting memberships on the various Presidential committees appointed by Dr. Sterling and on the several committees appointed by the Executive Committee of the Academic Council. LASSU has also asserted that both students and faculty members should be voting members of committees of the Board of Trustees. And two weeks ago *The Daily* suggested that there should perhaps be student members of the Board of Trustees itself.

To date, it should be noted, these demands have been for representation, as distinguished from *adequate* representation—a voice, rather than enough votes to give students control or even to constitute a significant voting block. But I have little doubt that once the principle of the right to participate were established, it would be followed by a demand for something at least approaching equal representation.

How ought the rest of the University community to respond to this conception of the Great University Society?

It seems to me that the other University constituencies have no duty to accede to these demands merely because the students are making them—that we are entitled and, indeed, bound to ask if and why changes of this magnitude in the governance of the University ought to be made. What, then, is the case to be made for such enhancement of student participation in University decision-making?

Let me at this point draw a sharp distinction, to which I will return later. It may well be that at least many decisions made within a University community would be sounder decisions if the people making them took the trouble to consult students before the decisions are made, both to ascertain relevant facts and to learn what the attitudes of the students are toward the matters under consideration.

But the students are not asking alone for the right to be consulted by University decision-makers; they are asking also to participate in the process of judgment and decision itself.

The question presented, then, is whether and why students should have a right to decide or substantially to influence decision not alone by persuasion but by sheer voting strength.

One conceivable answer to this question is that students should be permitted to decide because they are simply better qualified to make sound decisions than faculty members and administrators —or, to put the matter in a somewhat more conciliatory way, that at least a substantial number of decisions which students were able to influence by their sheer voting strength would be, to that extent, sounder decisions.

Is such an assertion persuasive? What, if any, are the students' qualifications for the decision-making role they seek? What do they have to offer, either absolutely or as compared with the faculty members and University administrators in whose hands the power of decision now rests?

Presumably, all would agree that a first-quarter freshman is hardly qualified for this role. Presumably, the students would argue that a last-quarter senior is qualified—and that he became qualified at some point (perhaps quite early) during the intervening period. But, are even the ablest and most perceptive students adequately equipped in terms of education, experience, or maturity to decide difficult questions of University policy? And, are the ablest and most perceptive students those we are talking about?

As a practical matter, it seems to me, we are talking about those students who gravitate to positions of power in campus politics, not all of whom have, in the past, proved to be outstandingly able, well-educated, experienced or mature. Is this group really qualified to displace, *pro tanto*, a portion of those now having decision-making power in the University?

Perhaps the student activists would answer this question with a ringing affirmative—they are no less self-confident than the rest of us. I do not believe, however, that they base their claim primarily on their superior capacity to do the job. Rather, I think that they, if pressed, would respond by asserting that the primary reason why students should participate in making decisions is because they are affected by them. Much student thinking about this matter appears to be based on the assumption that University decision-making ought to be regarded as an essentially democratic process in which the students are entitled to be represented simply because they are there—a kind of application to academia of the principle: "one man, one vote." To them, what is wrong with present University decision-making is that it is government without representation, insofar as the students are concerned.

Is this assumption about the nature of a University well founded?

It would be too harsh an answer, perhaps, to respond to the students by pointing out to them that we do not let the inmates run the asylum. But it may not be too harsh and it may be relevant to point out that we do not let the patients manage the hospital; we do not let clients manage the law firm; we do not let the passengers manage the airlines; and we do not let the consumers manage a business enterprise. Is a University community really analogous to a civic community? Or is it, correctly perceived, much more a kind of ongoing educational enterprise, in relation to which students are essentially in the position of patrons or consumers?

To take the enterprise view of the matter is not to deny to students the right to make decisions—and in doing so to affect substantially both the decisions of others and the course of events within the University. It is, however, to suggest that the student's power to decide is essentially the patron's or consumer's traditional power to exert leverage upon any enterprise—that is, his power to decide initially to go elsewhere or to decide to discontinue his patronage if and when he becomes dissatisfied with what the enterprise has to offer. This is a remarkably effective power, but it is a vastly different thing from the power to manage the enterprise, which is what the students are seeking.

Here, then, as I see it is the heart of the matter: Will we accept the students' view of the University, essentially as a kind of democracy in the councils of which they are entitled to at least equal representation? Or will we take the view that the University is essentially an educational enterprise, organized and run by the trustees, administration and faculty, which any student can take or leave, as he sees fit, but which is not entitled to participate in managing while he is with us?

Of course, this is not to suggest that a polar view of the matter is necessary or even desirable. Various accommodations and arrangements may and ought to be made in developing a viable University community—accommodations and arrangements which may vary considerably from one University to another.

But, it seems to me, there is a fundamental issue about the essential nature of a University and of students in relation to it which must be perceived, faced and decided in order to provide both a context in which, and a rationale upon which particular decisions can be made. Unless and until the University does think this issue through, it will not be in a position to respond intelligently to particular requests or demands. Nor will it be able rationally to determine where ultimately to draw the lines in allocating powers and functions among its several constituencies.

It is not without hazard, in this day and age, to question the assumption that a University is essentially a democratic community of which the student body is a major constituency. To argue that a student's tuition entitles him, not to a share of voting stock in the University enterprise but essentially to the right to take or leave what the University holds out by way of an educational opportunity, could precipitate angry reaction.

The easier course is to try to find palliatives and expedients by which to surmount immediate crises rather than to challenge the students' fundamental assumptions. Whether that is the wise and responsible course to pursue is, however, another matter.

Now, to return to the point which I reserved earlier. In responding to the students' demand for a role in decision-making I believe that we might usefully make a distinction, familiar to lawyers, between the right to participate in the making of decisions and the right to be heard before important decisions are taken by duly-constituted decision-making bodies. In society at large the power to make various kinds of legally binding decisions, whether legislative, administrative or judicial, is delegated to relatively few entities. Such entities are usually representative in only a very general and remote sense of the individuals whose lives, liberty, rights or property are significantly affected by the decisions they make.

On the other hand, by law and tradition, legislative, administrative and judicial decision-makers accord a right to be heard to those whom their decisions will affect. This is done both to assure that each decision made will be a fully informed one and to enhance the acceptability of the decision to those who will be governed by it.

I believe that this kind of procedure ought to be used in University decision-making more often than it has been in the past. Students often have valuable information to contribute. They may have ideas and insights which ought to be taken into account. And decision-makers ought often to be aware of and give weight to student attitudes simply to reach sound, workable and fair decisions.

This is not to suggest that students should be heard prior to all University decision-making. Offhand, for example, I see no reason to elicit their views on the University's endowment investment policy or on the appointment of new faculty members or on radiological hazards control. Decisions in all of these areas will affect students, among others. But the contribution which students could make, if heard, is simply not commensurate with the complications engendered by hearing them.

To implicate students in the decisional process does, of course, complicate it. Perhaps the major complication arises out of the relative shortness of the student's tenure at the University.

First, it tends to give any problem, in the eyes of the student, a greater urgency than the problem intrinsically has. The student activist will typically be involved as such only during his last year or, at the most, his last two years. He tends to demand action and accomplishment while he is on the scene. He is impatient with the more deliberative approach of other constituencies.

Second, relatively short student tenure means a high rate of turnover, which in turn means that each new group of students must be educated—taken patiently over ground long familiar to other constituencies in order to provide the background, insights and perspective which are crucial to wise decisions. This requires not only much time but no little patience and endurance.

Third, and pehaps most important, the student's relatively brief tenure means that he will not have to live with the decision; indeed, that he will often be gone even before it is put into effect. Yet, nothing is more conducive to thoughtful decisions than the knowledge that mistakes are costly and that the decision-makers, among others, will have to pay for them.

Once the decision has been taken that students ought to be heard prior to particular kinds of decisions, one means of providing such a hearing is to include students among the members of the decision-making body, such as a Presidential, Academic Council or Trustee committee. But, if and when this is done students ought, I believe, to be *ex officio* rather than voting members of such committees, in order to make it clear to them as well as others that they are advising, assisting and advocating rather than deciding.

Moreover, it should be left for each committee to decide for itself whether it chooses to avail itself of this particular mechanism of communication with the students, or would prefer to have student consultants, to hold hearings, or to adopt other modes of communication. . . .

From a speech to the Yale Political Union by President Kingman Brewster, Jr., Yale University, September 24, 1969.

Accountability

The main thrust of most current reappraisals and proposals concerning how a university should be run have supposed that there should be a broader and more "democratic" participation by students in the decisions of the faculty.

They also seek a broader and more democratic participation by both faculty and students in decisions traditionally reserved to the administration and trustees. The central issue in the ensuing debate has been how far this participation should be broadened, and how democratic the selection of participants should be.

Even if we could knock most radical participatory democrats and most reactionary traditional autocrats off their extreme perches, however, there does remain a fundamental choice of emphasis which must be made, and which is really receiving almost no attention at all.

I have done no more than hint at it timidly in the past because I was not sure where I came out. Now I am. I am convinced that representation is not the clue to university improvement, indeed that if carried too far it could lead to disaster. I am, rather, now convinced that accountability is what we should be striving for.

I happen to think that in a world in which ideas and policies and institutions have a high rate of obsolescence, on many matters the young are more perceptive, wiser if you will, than their elders. On the other hand, experience has its claim. And in a self perpetuating institution the claims of continuity have to be weighed against the claims of "now."

From time to time the opportunity for spokesmanship in the name of student opinion will be seized by a wholly unrepresentative group.

So assumption No. 1 which has led me to the conviction that broader sharing of responsibility for ultimate academic decisions is not the primary thrust of useful university reform is: the majority is not sufficiently interested in devoting their time and attention to the running of the university to make it likely that "participatory democracy" will be truly democratic.

Assumption No. 2 is that most students would rather have the policies of the university directed by the faculty and administration than by their classmates.

So, I am now convinced that the political symbolism of participatory democracy is an illusion when applied to many of the academic and financial decisions which direct an academic institution.

The answer to the legitimate student demand for great individual self-determination is wider and wider latitude for academic as well as personal choice, including the choice of whether and when to stay at the institution, now inhibited by an outrageous Selective Service System.

The answer to the legitimate student demand to have protection against incompetent and unresponsive administration is not formal representation in all matters. It is administrative accountability.

The first requirement of accountability is disclosure. Those affected by policies and decisions cannot hold those who make them to account unless there is full and adequate public access to the record of the process by which the decision was made.

The second requirement of accountability is the right of petition by those affected by decisions. There has to be a legitimate, easy and reliable way in which critical opinion can be generated and communicated. Informal access through a variety of channels is the best way to do this in a relatively healthy situation.

The third essential element if accountability is to be real is some regular, understood process whereby reappraisal of the competence of administration and the community's confidence in it can be undertaken without waiting for a putsch or rebellion.

For a couple of years now I have been toying with ways in which the president might be made more accountable to those whose lives and professional circumstance he crucially affects. While I do not think that his power can be fully shared by any legislative process, I do think that his own tenure should be at risk if he is to enjoy the latitude of executive decision which the job requires.

In thinking through the question of the president's responsibility in the case of a disruptive confrontation, I concluded that the power to act on the spot should not be stultified; but that in spite of all the risks of Monday-morning quarterbacks on the faculty, the president should submit his actions to review and should, if necessary, make the issue one of confidence.

The principle of executive accountability as the price which must be paid for the exercise of executive discretion has, up to now, been formally limited to the power of the trustees to fire the man they hired as president. This is a terribly limited and inhibited power, since it cannot be exercised without running contrary to the expectation of a lifetime tenure.

The essence of the problem is that, while there is legal accountability to the trustees, there is no orderly way in which those most significantly affected by maladministration can invoke trustee action within a measurable time, without open challenge to the stability of the institution and the integrity of its processes.

It seems to me that the only way this problem can be solved is to require the periodic, explicit renewal of a president's tenure. I happen to think that ten or twelve years or so is about enough anyway, although there is no generalization valid for all times and places and people.

I think Yale would be better off if it were understood that the trustees would make a systematic reappraisal and explicit consideration of the president's reappointment at some specified interval. This might be seven years after the initial appointment, perhaps at a somewhat shorter interval thereafter. I would urge the trustees right now to consider adoption of such a policy.

This would mean a termination of my present appointment a year from June and an explicit judgment about the wisdom of my reappointment by that time. Under present circumstances the effect would be to make the office more attractive not only for initial appointment but also for continuation in it. . . .

I make these somewhat radical proposals because while I do respect and share the dissatisfaction with a governance which seems free to ignore the will of the governed, I think that the sharing of faculty and administrative power with students on a widely dispersed democratic basis would be a disaster for our kind of academic institution.

From a letter by Philip Oldham to the editor of the New Leader *in response to an article by John Roche, published November 24, 1969.*

Students as an Interest Group

It is true, of course, that if the teachers do not know more than their students, then there is no purpose whatsoever to the university, and that therefore no academic institution can be a democracy. Yet in a sense, this is true of any institution. We all have only one vote, but we obviously do not and cannot have equal influence in the state. Nonetheless, politicians have the sense to keep the essentially oligarchic nature of our democracy to themselves. The more intelligent politicians attempt to accommodate demands made by radically disaffected groups (like blacks and antiwar protesters) who, despite their minority status, are capable of upsetting the stability of our social and political institutions. . . .

Students increasingly view themselves as an interest group within academia. It is debatable, and also essentially irrelevant, whether this is justifiable. The politicians of early 19th-century England did not regard as reasonable the claims of the working class to the vote and to political representation. Who knows if in a hundred years the protestations [against student participation] will not seem equally absurd?

Let us remember that the first universities of medieval Europe were corporations of students, not of faculties or of trustees. . . . Of course, the educational conditions of the 13th century do not really exist now, yet we should not forget that the achievements of these schools were quite impressive, even by today's standards.

Student Participation in Faculty Hiring: The Marlene Dixon Case

Statement by the academic deans, University of Chicago, January 21, 1969.

For Student Consultation

The relevance of student views on educational matters is clear. Students can bring to an understanding of academic issues knowledge that is outside the direct experience of the faculty, viewpoints that may counteract attitudes or unexamined premises that age and institutional factors tend to perpetuate in a university, and ideas that may have escaped even the most inventive of faculties.

Faculties within this University have always recognized, of course, the pertinence of student views in educational discussions, and through informal channels have availed themselves of this resource. They have taken into account student judgments and ideas on a wide range of academic matters, including programs, requirements, and the performance of faculty members. Decisions on such matters have often been importantly influenced by what has been learned from students.

Recognizing that the purpose of student consultation is to improve the quality of education at the University of Chicago, and believing that this purpose is best served by rational discussion and regular communication, we urge adherence to the following principles with respect to student participation in the processes by which academic policies are determined:

1. The most appropriate and most productive modes of eliciting student views, and indeed the extent to which these views can contribute to the wise governance of the University, will vary from area to area within the University, depending upon the size, traditions, and procedures within each area and the nature of the problems with which it is confronted at particular times in its development. Accordingly, the kind of student participation should reflect the educational situation within each Division, School, or other academic unit of the University.

2. We endorse the policy of the President to encourage the election within each academic unit (including, where relevant, de-

partments or degree-recommending committees) of a student council or advisory group to meet regularly with a committee of the faculty. We urge the several faculties to develop these arrangements into significant instruments of educational policy. Although no single instrument or mode of faculty-student communication should be seen as exclusive or as sufficient in itself, we believe that the existence of such councils can (1) provide continuity and responsibility in student counsel, (2) deepen student understanding of educational problems confronting the University, and (3) offer accessible channels for the expression of diverse student opinion.

3. Recommendations on academic appointment are the responsibility of the several faculties. In reaching decision on such a recommendation, the extent to which student appraisal of the effectiveness of a faculty member is taken into account should be determined by the particular faculty making the recommendation. Use of the evidence provided by student appraisals is wholly consistent with the established appointive processes of the University. To enhance the objectivity of this evidence, the faculties should inform themselves of student appraisals of individual instructors on a continuing basis rather than in the context of an immediate decision. This procedure should be an institutionalized part of the process.

4. In making use of the consultative processes described above, or any others, each faculty as a Ruling Body remains responsible under the University Statutes for the determination of academic policies within its jurisdiction.

Broadside distributed by the University of Chicago New University Conference, a radical faculty organization, January 1969.

The Dixon Case

Marlene Dixon has not been rehired. We are told that the decision was based on professional competence and was independent of her being a woman, holding radical ideas, and participating in radical causes. We do not believe it. In our view the central issues raised by this firing are as follows:

1. Can faculty members who actively participate in radical political movements and who openly criticize university policies ex-

pect to remain in social science departments at the University?

Most faculty seem to believe that such activities ought to be ignored by those responsible for decisions concerning hiring and promotion and that, as a general rule, they *are* ignored. Still, the principle of confidentiality concerning such decisions prevents the community from verifying whether claims of political neutrality are honored in practice. Since it was only in the recent past that radicals as a matter of course were barred from university faculties, we feel it incumbent on the Gray Committee to fully investigate the possibility that political bias was a factor in the Dixon case. (They could, for example, ascertain whether the faculty involved in the Dixon decision agreed with the opinion recently expressed by a tenured social scientist who denied political prejudice but said that "anti-types" such as Staughton Lynd should be barred from the faculty.)

2. Do existing standards for academic appointment and tenure operate to exclude or inhibit the development of radical scholarship in the social sciences?

We think they do. Most social scientists believe that if not all individuals, at least the profession, acts in an objective, value-free way. But what is objective sociology? The prevailing theories, the relevant questions, the legitimate techniques vary so greatly from country to country that we are left with the impression that, in practice, objectivity is a community of bias. Prevailing social theory and analysis rests on ideological foundations which presume the legitimacy and humaneness of the American state and America's international policies. Senior faculty members in the social sciences are likely to be those who helped create and elaborate the complacent ideological underpinnings of the disciplines—how can they be surprised when they are not trusted to make objective judgments about the work of those who challenge these traditions?

It is not necessary to challenge the *subjective* honesty of social science faculty. In truth they are the best qualified to judge, by the accepted standards of the craft, the practitioners who accept their norms and aspire to join them. But what of challenges from outside the craft? What of those who do not measure up, not because they cannot, but because they reject the measure? What of those whose search for the truth leads them to retool, to study rather than rush into print. . . . The disdain of the empiricist for utopians, of the cynic for crusaders, of the detached (whose intellectual activity is often almost a game) for those in whom the passionate commitment to change motivates the scholarly effort results in a new situation in which even the honest application of a profession's accepted standards is unjust to young dissident scholars, narrows the scope of individual departments to particular schools, or excludes from serious consideration ideas that are the live issues on a world scale.

Dissident ideologies may require the development of a new methodology; existing advanced techniques, as powerful as they are in dealing with micro-sociological questions, may have little practical application to major problems of central concern to our society. In developing new methods, radicals have to cope with data that are not only difficult to get but also deliberately hidden or distorted. They have to learn how to use their experience as participants in political struggle to enlighten their theory without distorting it. They often have to sacrifice precision (which passes for accuracy) to retain scope and depth.

The screening out of radical scholars, the coercion to conform to the accepted styles of work and of "career development" results in loss to the science, the university, and the students as well as to the direct victims of the discrimination. Sociology renounces the social critical promise and withdraws to the domain of irrelevance or complicity. Students are excluded from the exciting intellectual adventure of the New Left—the rethinking of theory and method, often in the context of experiments in pedagogy and group effort.

But who is to judge? To take the decision out of the exclusive control of the senior faculty may mean to weaken technical judgments and bibliographical insights. But students, less trained in the details of the trade, are also less bound to its traditions, and at least as competent to evaluate relevance. Therefore, we support the student demand for a voice, not as a "concession" to students or merely as a democratization of the university, but as an intellectual necessity.

The problem will not be solved by new committees with so many votes for each party or by a set of rules designed to guide judgment. Political biases will continue to influence professional decisions and result in discrimination. We must oppose that discrimination and challenge those biases.

Editorial in The Chicago Maroon, *student newspaper, University of Chicago, January 28, 1969.*

Some Questions

Two weeks ago the Committee of 85, the radical coalition generated by the Marlene Dixon case, issued its demand that students be given equal power in the hiring and firing of faculty. Since then this has been repeated a number of times, along with the demand that Mrs. Dixon be rehired, but it has never been elaborated. Presumably the idea is to have as many students on the "personnel" committees of the various departments as professors. The students would have the same number of votes as the faculty, and thus an effective veto.

The Committee of 85 has, so far, not explained how much the students would do on such committees. Would they simply approve or reject the appointments the faculty might make? Or would students elected to the committees (they would be *elected?*) be required to read the literature pouring out from other campuses, and their own departments? And if they weren't required to prepare themselves as the faculty does before deciding appointments, then how could they be expected to arrive at half-way intelligent decisions; and how could the professors up for reappointment be expected to accept them? And what assistant professor would submit to a decision by students on whether he was worthy for reappointment or tenure?

Someone might interpose here: But what's the difference between students saying to an assistant professor that his scholarship is not good enough and the faculty saying it? The difference is that the students just haven't gotten as far into the discipline; they haven't had the experience in the "profession." They are still looking around, they are still reading their way through the basic material in a field, still sorting out theories. Students really don't have the time to keep up with all the new work that is being done in a field, and they don't have the knowledge to judge it very critically.

Well, the question might be raised, how do you insure that a department does not become overpopulated with one particular school of thought, how do you stop the tenured faculty from appointing only *their own?* The answer is: that is why you have deans. They are the people who are supposed to make sure that departments are free and growing, and that the divisions are open to new disciplines. And if the deans are somehow in cahoots with the reigning department cliques? Then there is the dean of the faculties. (And the precedent is fairly strong for deans of faculties —provosts, as they used to be called—to send recommendations for appointments back for reconsideration.) And if the dean of the faculties is corrupted, there is the president.

But to return to the issue, the immediate faculty appointments: the *Maroon* has already come out for student participation in the hiring and firing of professors, because we think teaching is an integral part of the scholarship at the University of Chicago . . . and students are really the only ones who can evaluate teaching very well. The paper proposed that the student councils should have as part of their official function consulting on faculty appointments. There should be such councils in every department and every division, and they should be elected by their constituent students. Ideally, the consulting would take place all the time (or at least every week), rather than in the month before appointments are made. It would not work to put a notice on the bulletin board that such and such a professor was up for reappointment, so everybody send in their comments. (If we were that professor, we would probably head for the nearest think tank.) The councils should make an effort to collect student opinion of professors, but the opinion should be honest, and unbiased by the fact that the man is being considered for reappointment or by political heat.

That is our plan. If it had been effective over the last year, we don't know if Marlene Dixon would have been reappointed, but we would have known that at least her qualities as a teacher would have been taken into account. Whether this plan is feasible remains to be seen; we are waiting to hear criticism of it. And we are still waiting to hear the plan of the Committee of 85.

From a statement issued by the Ad Hoc Steering Committee during the first stage of a student sit-in at the University of Chicago, January 30, 1969.

Rehire Marlene Dixon

We need to make clear what we are doing and why we will continue to clarify our position as our action develops.

To explain the "why" of our action we must review the events of the last three weeks that have brought us here: the facts of the Marlene Dixon case, the painstaking efforts of the students to open the university to substantive discussion of their positions, and the reactions of the administration and faculty.

Full understanding of our position also depends upon our analysis of what the university is and what interests it serves.

To make clear the "what" of our action we must show that we have no alternative, but to sit in, in order to achieve our demands. We emphasize that by sitting in we do not intend to "close down" the university. We want to continue the process, begun in the last three weeks, of fighting for an open university at Chicago.

Who rules the university?

The University is commonly portrayed as a neutral haven, separable from the rest of the society, within which knowledge is pursued. We maintain that this is a comfortable self-serving illusion which bears little resemblance to its true nature and function.

This institution is primarily a research organization. It is dominated by the graduate departments—guilds of male scholars who are more interested in professional expertise than in critical knowledge; more concerned with training other scholars then with educating men. The College has become a prep school for graduate or professional work.

Within such a situation students are of very little intrinsic importance. They are valuable insofar as they provide the raw material for this process of scholarly reduplication. Their opinions of faculty members and of the education they receive are irrelevant.

Research specialization not only operates against students and teachers. It also has a built-in political and intellectual bias. The function of most research is to provide quanta of information within pre-existing frameworks rather than to critically examine the frameworks or construct new ones. Those scholars who have larger concerns or heterodox and radical points of view are automatically weeded out.

It is not merely a matter of chance that these frameworks tend to be positivistic, "apolitical," and non-dialectical. The University does not exist in an economic vacuum. It requires funding—especially government funding—and the government quite naturally invests in education in terms of its own self-interest. It wants trained manpower and information it can use. It has discovered that the social sciences are as valuable to it as the physical and biological sciences.

Most scholars are only too happy to comply. Not only can they receive large grants for their research, but they can flatter themselves with grandiose illusions that they constitute a new mandarin caste. Yet these scholars are the servants, not the wielders of power. They have become little more than intellectual clerks, alienated from themselves and their labor, whose quest for knowledge has become transformed into the production of a mental commodity which serves to maintain the status quo.

The university is not an intellectually open ivory tower which is threatened by radicals who try to involve it in social and political questions. It is ideologically narrow, and it is already very much socially and politically committed. We are unhappy with the nature of that commitment. For the effective function of the university has become to serve corporate capitalism through the production of trained manpower and research data.

Marlene Dixon refused to serve this function.

The demands formulated by the Committee of 85, and ratified by the evening meeting January 29 which approved the sit-in, are (1) that Marlene Dixon be rehired immediately both to the Committee on Human Development and to the Department of Sociology, and (2) that students share equal power with the faculty in hiring and rehiring decisions.

Why these demands? The demand for the rehiring of Marlene Dixon is basic and non-negotiable. We suspect that Mrs. Dixon was fired either as an act of discrimination against women or as an act of political suppression. Any response short of rehiring Mrs. Dixon is no response at all. That she be hired to both departments involved will help to counteract the ideological imbalance in the sociology faculty and ensure that her professional status will be in no way reduced. The demand for equal student-faculty power grounds the Dixon case in a general principle of broader application. While students are perhaps less competent than faculty to judge according to narrow academic criteria, they are more competent to judge teaching ability, and to assess relevance of scholarship to current and future social concerns. In the words of a New University Conference leaflet, this demand is essential not only as "a democratization of the university, but as an intellectual necessity."

PART **VI**

THE EDUCATIONAL PROCESS

We have observed that the political demands of the student movement are contained within the context of the larger youth movement directed against many other aspects of modern culture. In the university, the cultural side of the movement has been reflected in the demands for reform of the educational process.

Of course, the demand for educational reform is not new; nor are most of the current specific recommendations. What is noteworthy is how these demands are now intertwined with a political movement.

CHAPTER 16

Relevance and Professionalism

At the 1969 convention of the American Philosophical Society, one radical wrote on the blackboard: "When critical philosophers point their finger to reality, orthodox philosophers study the finger. Power to the people."

That succinctly sums up the radical attack on professional academic work. To the ideal of professionalism, radicals counterposed the ideal of relevance. Two sets of values came into conflict.

The case for relevance is presented here by Louis Kampf of MIT, who described the primary academic role of the radical faculty as the "development of an alternative culture." The Sociology Liberation Movement, a group composed mostly of graduate students and junior faculty, claimed that in the name of professionalism sociologists "have willfully turned from the problems of our time" and performed research for the powerful interests of American society.

Criticism of liberal academic ideals has also come from the right. Allen Brownfeld, writing in a "journal of conservative thought," demands a renewed emphasis on "cultural continuity."

Marvin Levich made a strong defense against these charges,

arguing that "the ideology of relevance" was incompatible with "intellectual integrity."

From a speech by Professor Louis Kampf, associate professor of literature, Massachusetts Institute of Technology, to the Modern Languages Association, September 1968.

The Radical Faculty—
What Are Its Goals?

What are the radical faculty's goals for society? They are no different from those of any radical or socialist or anarchist. I think they have been stated clearly by André Gorz, in his important book, *Strategy for Labor:*

> Economically, it [Socialism] can mean nothing but collective ownership of the means of production, that is to say the end of exploitation. But socialism is also more than that: it is also a new type of relationship among men, a new order of priorities, a new model of life and culture. If it is not all this also, it loses its meaning. This meaning, to define it in one sentence, is: the subordination of production to needs, as much for *what* is produced as for *how* it is produced. It is understood that in a developed society, needs are not only quantitative: the need for consumer goods; but also qualitative: the need for a free and many-sided development of human faculties; the need for information, for communication, for fellowship; the need to be free not only from exploitation but from oppression and alienation in work and in leisure.

Gorz's words can serve us as a basic text. We radicals know that, since men must not be mere means of production, our first task is to eliminate the inhumanities and contradictions inherent in property relationships. For only their elimination will give us the freedom to envision a new man and a new culture.

Such social objectives have some clear implications for colleges and universities. Rather than detail a complete program—a task which, in any case, ought to be a basic component of any education—I shall make a few related suggestions.

1. Admission policies should not be geared toward getting the

"best" students for any given institution but toward finding the institution which will be best for the student. It should be recognized that the "best" students are almost invariably the economically privileged.

2. We radicals want a university which does not stress professionalization—hideous word!—at the expense of the student's human faculties and natural talents. He must be given the opportunity of developing these at his own pace and by his own methods.

3. The university should become a place where students and faculty can pursue their cultural and social needs as ends in themselves. Ordinarily, the fulfilment of these needs is constrained by the university's master, the social system. We must begin our search with an inquiry into that system, an inquiry which must be allowed to challenge the system—and the university—itself.

4. Our goal is a university which transcends the obsessive inwardness of the quest for personal fulfilment: that is, a university which makes students and faculty aware of their social role. The notion of absolute individual freedom is one more ideological trap set by the system. For it allows us an easy escape into a private universe dissociated from our social role.

Capitalism, of course, typically transforms collective needs into individual ones. The academy encourages this transformation—with notorious success—by its brutal stress on individual accomplishment (read competitiveness). Students and faculty who are well attuned to the academy's schedule of rewards, therefore, learn to carefully plan and rationalize their work with a view toward squeezing the most out of the system, or even beating it. There is a pathos in the attempt, for it is doomed to failure; the very failure to understand the social function of one's own competitiveness leads to inevitable defeat at the hands of the system.

Only when students and faculty begin to understand their roles as producers will they be capable of developing their individual roles in terms of commonly—not privately—attained freedoms. Rather than learning to beat the system, we must learn to direct our work toward those individual satisfactions which will benefit the whole. But the powers that be know that if we stopped cutting each other's throats, we might, figuratively, cut theirs.

So once more, what is the meaning of these goals if we consider the actualities of power? Does the radical faculty have any power at all? It does, to a degree. This is at least indicated by your desire to listen to my harangue. However, whatever strength we have does not so much derive from our own organizing efforts as from the contradictions of American higher education. I shall merely allude to a few.

Deans, presidents, members of corporations never seem to tire of humanistic rhetoric; yet higher education is used for the wider reproduction of labor. They pay lip-service to the traditional notion of the critical intellectual; yet the system rewards professionalism and bourgeois accommodation. They encourage the tacit assumption that education is the province—even the property—of students and teachers; yet both the latter know that they are alienated from the products of their labor. Most insidiously, they have encouraged their faculties to think of higher education as an instrument of social mobility and amelioration when, in fact, it generates new class hatreds to replace the old, and leads students to view their teachers as agents of social oppression.

The contradictions are also apparent in broader social terms. Industrial capitalism has created a set of needs which it cannot meet, because they do not relate to the concept of economic man and the latter's goal of individual consumption. Our presence in this city reminds us that industrialism has destroyed the natural environment, thus giving rise to real—indeed desperate—collective needs. Those needs cannot be met by our present social and political structures, because they contradict the criterion of profitability.

The needs should be familiar to you: air we can breathe without risking lung cancer; housing and city planning which addresses itself to building a humane environment and which is not reserved for the economically privileged; services such as nursery schools, clinics and transportation; and, perhaps most importantly, the development of communities having enough cohesion to address themselves—freely and in their own terms—to matters of culture and group leisure. All these needs are fundamentally biological and natural; yet they can be dealt with only by cultural and institutional means, by the imaginative collective use of our resources. I feel safe in saying that none of these needs will be met. They will not be met because they contradict the economic imperatives of our system.

In our society's failure to resolve the contradictions fathered by these needs the university has played an important role. Most obviously, departments of planning, architecture and economics rarely encourage—except in their rhetoric—students and faculty to explore what the real needs of the community are. Academic security and prestige, not to speak of comfortable grants, come to those who meet the demands of their profession. The dangers of the professionalism that academic life encourages—especially to social scientists and planners—should be obvious. Academics tend to reduce any complex human activity to the construction of abstract models. Build a more elegant model, and academic success will be your meed.

Left to itself and separated from the rest of the world, such activity would be harmless enough, though extravagantly wasteful. But any profession sees itself as an elite, as experts whose models should be humbly admired by the ignorant and fervently institutionalized by those in power. The models may involve monstrosities like counterinsurgency or urban renewal or planned unemployment or atomic warfare, but who can show concern for such human trivia or community needs when the rationality of one's model—one's very expertise—guarantees the correctness of the enterprise?

Any professional elite will almost invariably sell its expertise to those with economic and institutional power; further, it will shape the very nature of its field to the demands of established institutions. The contradictions of industrial capitalism are thus reinforced by the dynamic of professionalism. Are there departments of social science which encourage their students and faculty to work as equals with those constituencies and communities that most desperately need them?

But something curious has been happening with the young. Some of them, to everyone's surprise, have taken the humanistic rhetoric of the academy seriously. Consequently, they have become nearly incapable of living with the contradictions of capitalism and the hypocrisies of the professions available to them. Many students are engaged in an almost frantic—often desperate —search for alternate careers and for alternate models of consumption—for a way of life in which production is subordinated to human needs, and activity is not simply geared to production.

This search should, of course, be an integral part of higher education. Scholarship, instead of bending students toward exclusively professional concerns, should be the servant of self-discovery. If so, it must begin with an inquiry into its own nature and into the institutions which are engaged in its administration. But for scholarship to perform such a function, scholars will have to reclaim the traditional role of the critical intellectual; further, they will have to establish its centrality for academic culture. Clearly, for this to occur, we shall need a cultural revolution on our campuses. Yet this revolution is necessary for your own survival; if it is to be suppressed, I have little doubt that your institutions will blow apart or at least crumble.

The primary academic goal, then, of radical faculty is the development of an alternate culture. As industrial capitalism generates more elaborate bureaucratic structures, the need for autonomous bodies making decisions democratically becomes increasingly urgent. We radicals want universities and colleges to be such bodies. . . .

Statement by the Sociology Liberation Movement, 1968.

Knowledge for Whom?

The values, beliefs and formal affiliations of the field of sociology bind it too closely to the governing structures and the powerful interests in our society.

—Posing as disinterested scholars, we perform policy research for the powerful organizations in our society, providing them with the knowledge they need to influence or control their "problems." We have placed our expertise at the disposal of the establishment, letting the development of our field be guided by the needs of those who can pay for our time. In the name of value-neutrality, we have failed to contribute equally to the efforts of the poor, the powerless or the disorganized to control or influence the power-holders.

—In our attempts to share the prestige of "science" we have pursued the development of "scientific" methodology at the expense of meaningful content and have developed "scientific" theories at the expense of a knowledge of society. We have wilfully turned from the problems of our time, and he who interests himself in a confrontation with reality is dismissed as a "mere journalist."

—In our attempts to adopt the prestige of professionalism we have restricted entry to our field, isolated our discipline from others, and enforced conformity to the mainstream as the price of professional success. The interests of the professional hierarchy have worked against meaningful innovation in methods, theories, and areas of study.

—The liberal conservative bias of our "theory" exaggerates consensus, ignores conflict, and assumes that everything can be settled with a little communication, a little patience, and a lot of good will. This is more of a prayer than a theory, reflecting not reality but the hopes of our own social class.

—In the illusion that we can be responsible members of society and yet above its petty quarrels, we have abstained from our moral duty to speak out against the forces of repression in our society. The reactionary nature of our government becomes "beyond the scope of our field." But silence means consent, and by not speaking out we are speaking up for the status quo.

SOCIOLOGY WILL NOT CHANGE UNLESS SOCIOLOGISTS CHANGE IT
JOIN THE SOCIOLOGY LIBERATION MOVEMENT!

From an article by Allan C. Brownfeld, member of the faculty and Ph.D. candidate at the University of Maryland and editor of The New Guard, *publication of Young Americans for Freedom, in* Ideas, *Spring-Summer 1969.*

The Challenge to Cultural Continuity

Many in the New Left criticize the university for being "too political" today, for being too closely tied with the Pentagon, with the nation's war policies, and with government and large foundation grants. While such criticisms are, in many instances, the same ones which were made by more conservative critics of the concept of federal aid to education, the fact remains that the New Left seeks a "political" university, only with a different kind of politics. In neither instance is real education provided. . . .

Students are demanding that education be made "relevant." Often they claim that the colleges and universities are far removed from the needs of society, that their four years of undergraduate learning is essentially cloistered unreality.

Yet, the question of what is truly "relevant" with regard to education is not quite so simple. Neither is the question of what kind of education best prepares students to cope with such practical problems as race relations, urban renewal, war, and poverty. . . .

What do students mean when they raise the question of relevance? Relevance to what? What they ought to mean, perhaps, is "relevant to wisdom," though many think only of "relevance to current affairs." The notion of "adjustment to modern society," however, may not be relevant to what we have traditionally called higher learning. In his novel, *Scott-King's Modern Europe,* Evelyn Waugh's hero learns by a summer's experience of modern society that it would be infinitely wicked to teach young men to adjust to the modern world. Russell Kirk notes that "to adjust to the age of the mass state, of the concentration camp, the secret police and injustice triumphant, would be sin and shame. The higher learning is not meant to inculcate conformity to passing fad and foible, nor necessarily to present domination and powers. It is intended, rather, to reveal to us the norms, the enduring standards, for the person and the republic. Adjustment to abnormality is ruinous policy."

Modern technology alters so rapidly that, as Peter Drucker has pointed out, the college and university cannot possibly keep abreast of industrial methods. What higher education should do is discipline the intellect so that it may be applied in future productive processes as to many other matters. The truly relevant things in a college are the permanent things, in T. S. Eliot's phrase. They are the body of knowledge not undone by the machinations of the modern world. Is such an education "relevant?" Dr. Kirk states that "If a formal education does not bear at all upon our personal and social difficulties today, of course it is a sham and worthless; in that, the students of the New Left are quite right. But no modern authors are more genuinely relevant than are Plato and Augustine today. Preoccupation with the passing pageant is merely the sort of 'relevance' which the big commercial bookclubs sell; and college and university were not endowed for that purpose."

Another basis for calling modern education "irrelevant" is that, in many instances, it has discouraged students from original thinking. Modern education has as its aim, as Erich Fromm pointed out in *Escape From Freedom,* ". . . to teach the individual not to assert himself. Already the boy in school must learn 'to be silent' not only when he is blamed justly but also has to learn, if necessary, to bear injustice in silence." Fromm notes that "Another closely related way of discouraging original thinking is to regard all truth as relative. Truth is made out to be a metaphysical concept, and if anyone speaks about wanting to discover the truth he is thought backward by the 'progressive' thinkers of our age. Truth is declared to be an entirely subjective matter, almost a matter of taste."

Fromm states that the result of this relativism "which often presents itself by the name of empiricism or positivism or which recommends itself by its concern for the correct usage of words, is that thinking loses its essential stimulus—the wishes and interests of the person who thinks, instead it becomes a machine to register 'facts.' "

In many respects the kind of education which best prepares young people for dealing with what appears to be the earthshaking problems of today—crime, violence, bigotry—is to understand the causes of such problems by studying the history of man, for, in a sense, we have seen most of this before, even if in different circumstances and surroundings. Education, to be relevant, should attempt to make us aware of the wisdom of the ages so that we may build upon it and not simply spend our lives seeking things which have already been discovered.

Many today argue that the world has changed to such a degree that the truths enunciated in the past are no longer either applicable or valid to the twentieth century. Today, they argue, we have mass transportation, air pollution, and narcotics addiction. What this means, says Dr. Elton Trueblood, the distinguished Quaker philosopher, is ". . . that we cut ourselves off from the wisdom of the ages . . . It means that if this is taken seriously we are really an orphan generation that takes itself far too seriously, that is too much impressed with changes which may be only superficial. And of course, if this is true of our generation, there is no reason why it will not be true of another generation. Therefore, whatever we gain would naturally be rejected by our descendants. No civilization is possible this way. Contemporaneity when it is a disease is a very damaging disease, because it destroys the continuity of culture."

The concept that "you can't trust anyone over 30," that the wisdom of the past is irrelevant to the present and to the future, that the university's role is simply as a power-broker in an effort to achieve practical solutions to every-day problems, all of these represent a challenge to the concept of civilization and continuity.

The New Left is reacting against a modern educational system which has abandoned its task of spreading the values of Western civilization to the new generation. . . . The educational system fashioned by liberal educators has failed at its very root. It has not even managed to stimulate respect for itself. Those who recognize the faults in the present system and the danger of those who seek to destroy that system and replace it with something far worse, must act to preserve not only the institution of the university but something far more important. What lies in the balance are the values which mankind has striven so long and hard to attain. Santayana has said that those who do not learn from the past are condemned to repeat its mistakes. At this perilous period of man's history we cannot afford to repeat such mistakes. The continuity of culture which is now under attack must be preserved, and those who seek to preserve it must, in a short time, come to grips with this challenge.

From a speech by Professor Marvin Levich, Department of Philosophy, Reed College, given at the Association of American Colleges in Pittsburgh, January 1969.

The Ideology of Relevance

The question is . . . "What should be the impact of the ideology of relevance on humanistic studies?" I will proceed as follows: First, I will provide what will have to be a crude statement of some traits of the ideology that bear directly upon the content and intellectual role of humanistic studies in higher education. I will say of these traits that at bottom they are clearly and dangerously anti-intellectual and, on the assumption that the humanistic studies are not, that they pose a threat to them. Then I will refer to some features of humanistic studies that make them special targets, and likely victims, of the threat. I will finally maintain, unfashionably, that there is nothing much to be done in the face of the threat than to stand firm.

I pass now to the nature of the ideology, the first trait of which I shall call that of "external justification." It is to be found in the literature of the New Left and on the lips of many of our students, and it is expressed in the currently voguish question, "What is the relevance of a liberal arts education, what is the relevance of this or that course in the curriculum, what is the relevance of teaching this or that course in this or that way?" The context of the question is most frequently one in which the curriculum or some element of it is under attack and where it is held that our society is beset with near-fatal maladies for which the courses or curriculum under consideration are not, but should be, palpable remedy.

In the context of its asking, the question requires that courses be justified in the light of some showing to the effect that the giving of them will contribute to the amelioration or elimination of political and social evil. I call it "external justification" because it requires that what is done in a college is to be judged in respect of its effect upon the social order and, further, in respect of those effects that are external to, or independent of, the properties of education or learning, *per se.*

There are, of course, some things the doing of which we justify in this way. We take a bus because it gets us somewhere, not because of any value in the bus ride itself. (At least, that is why I take a bus.) We take an aspirin because it reduces our fever, not because the taking of it has any merit, *per se.* That is another way of saying that if aspirins did not succeed in reducing our fever, we would stop manufacturing and taking them. The anti-intellectualism of the view at issue lies in the fact that it leads us to talk about education as we do buses and aspirins, to try to find the cultural Florida which will justify the trip, the social fever which will justify swallowing the pill.

But, of course, the pursuit of learning is not at all like this. The properties which make it what it is are identical with those which make it of value to the society in which it is pursued. If it is successful, the students who pursue it learn what is true and what is not, and how to find it out, and learn further that there are different ways of finding it out according to subject-matter, and different degrees of certainty which, depending upon the subject-matter, they can attach to their findings. If we think that society is the better for having in it people who have learned these things, then education is relevant to society. If we don't, we talk of destinations and fevers.

This is why I find the question about the relevance of education to be so clearly anti-intellectual. There is an answer to the question. I have just given it. And the answer will be rejected as unresponsive exactly to the extent that knowledge and understanding, *per se,* are rejected as valueless. Since those who pose the question do find this answer unresponsive, I have no doubt that the asking of it already reflects a repudiation of the intellectual life. One particularly good way of finding out what a person means by a question is to find out what he will be prepared to accept as appropriate answer.

This is why I maintain that what I have called the "trait of external justification" relegates intellectual inquiry, and therefore its institutional setting, to the role of morally neutral instrument to be used, modified or rejected, as we do any instrument, according to the purpose for which we take it up and of which it is the logical servant.

Now to a second and related trait of the ideology of relevance, one that I shall call "tactical redescription." On this trait, some of the fundamental qualities of education are redescribed as being less than morally neutral, as being of positive disvalue. The influential source in this case is Marcuse. The qualities in question are dialogue, toleration and coming to conclusions in the light, and not in advance, of evidence and appropriate argument. Dialogue has to do with the fact that intellectual inquiry is necessarily public in character, its conclusions being couched in symbols that have public meaning, its methods of establishing them being testable in some way against experience. Toleration has to do with the fact that those who seek the truth are men, therefore fallible, and that, as a result, the intellectual arena must be one in which the widest possible scope is provided for argued dissent. The third of my fundamental qualities is, I think, self-explanatory.

Now, on the ideology of relevance, all these features are redescribed as tactical instruments which our society uses for the purpose of protecting itself against the possibility of radical incursion. By always calling for analysis in advance of action, by insisting that judgment be withheld until the evidence is in, by requiring that all the viable alternatives be weighed, the intellectual enervates radical actions and preserves the vested interests of a society of which he is at once protector and beneficiary. Educational institutions, therefore, because built around these factors, are the most powerful of the weapons which a conservative society uses in the interests of defeating the radical. The first and last mistake which a radical can make, therefore, is to allow himself to be drawn into the form of intellectual exchange in which these factors are operative. He stops acting, starts talking, and he is lost.

To take this position is by definition to be anti-intellectual. The very attributes which are constitutive of the nature of intellectual inquiry are redescribed as tactical weapons so powerful and debilitating that the radical must reject them out of hand if he is to get on with his work. . . .

I turn finally to the question of what is to be done about this, and I will give you an answer that I am absolutely certain you will regard as being as silly as it is drab. The answer is "Nothing." Let me explain. I do not mean to suggest by it that what is now being done within humanistic studies is perfect, that there are no new topics to be considered, no new problems to be investigated, no new methods to be contrived which refine, supplement or replace what is already being done. Nor do I think it necessarily evil to have courses in black history or the literature of revolution. What I do think is that there are no changes of this kind, large or small, that can at once satisfy what is demanded by the ideology of relevance and preserve the intellectual integrity of the material presented.

Suppose, for example, courses multiplied in the problems of contemporary America and of the world. Suppose we examine the music of the blues as it expressed these problems, the poetry of Tuli Kupferberg as it communicated them, the arts of "pop" and "op" as they embodied them, and added some work in history to tell us how it all came about. If we read something as old as the Iliad we would use it to raise the question of whether Achilles would have ridden round the Pentagon as he did the walls of Troy. It could be said, fairly, that there is nothing wrong and a good deal that is right in the intellectual scrutiny of our society, and even in engaging in a comparative analysis of the role of heroism in the Homeric and the modern world.

The curriculum might be skewed, but there have also been times when it was skewed wrongly in the other direction. The important thing is to treat the subjects properly, and since that can be done, a little imbalance in the curriculum is a small price to pay for a regimen of topics that will be able to re-engage the interests of our students. Perhaps so. Given my curriculum as described, I can think of worse things that have been done in the name of education.

My point, however, is something different. It is that whatever we did, we couldn't make the courses good enough, or bad enough, to satisfy those who want them. Not good enough, because they are asked for in the expectation that there is some course of studies which, if followed, will have the effect of over-turning the values of those who partake of them and of the society of which they are part, and further, that all this is to happen at once. There is no such course of studies. That is, there is nothing that we can do that will be good enough.

They could also not be bad enough. For according to reasons I have already given, it is not enough to simply present contempo-rary, "relevant" materials. The ordering of them by the standard canons of logic and evidence, the dispassionate scrutiny of their features—the very things, you will recall, which enervate action—will be as objectionable as courses in which the materials them-selves would be exclusively traditional.

What is wanted, I believe, is nothing less than capitulation. And if that means that everything of intellectual worth in human-istic studies has to be sacrificed to the great God Relevance and converted into a political vehicle, that will not be a problem. For those who perform the sacrifice will not think that anything of worth is being lost. They would of course preserve the label "In-tellectual Inquiry," for what is wanted is the prestige of that exer-cise and not the inconveniences involved in its actual practice. I believe it to be a capital mistake to think that we can give a little bit, that the bulk of work in humanistic studies will remain unim-paired, and that after a while, because the ideology of relevance is only a passing fad, it will all go away and we will return to our books, remembering fondly those few romantic hours before the barricades. Half a crumb does not satisfy a very large mouth. It stimulates the appetite.

I have to say that I am not very hopeful that institutions of higher learning will stand their ground. That is because, for the first time, the anti-intellectual attack on the academy is coming from those with whose substantive aims many, perhaps most, in-tellectuals sympathize. If we gave in to McCarthy or Velde, it was because we were afraid, not because we shared their political ob-jectives. But most of us do agree that the war in Vietnam is a predatory adventure, that our government and major political parties have become increasingly immune to the sentiments of those they purportedly represent, that the conditions of the urban ghettos are execrable and the exploitation of the black man shameless. And because academics so strongly sympathize with the political goals of the relevance ideologists, they cannot bring themselves to reject the demands which the latter make on higher education—out of fear that by rejecting the educational demands they will be thought of as having repudiated the political goals.

These are strong words. I am afraid that some may find them offensive. But I say them because I think them to be true. I say them because I think that those of us who value humanistic studies, and indeed all of higher education, now have something to fight for, and against, and that unless we are clear about what is involved in the fight and respond with honor, we will be aiding those who think rather less of the academy than do we in the business of its dismantling. And if that, unhappily, were to happen, we would then no doubt hail what we have accomplished, in the rubbery phrases of educational statesmanship, as "a creative and imaginative experiment in higher education."

CHAPTER 17

Authority and Democracy
in the Classroom

Radical critics have challenged not just the content of liberal education, but its form as well, maintaining that authoritarian learning patterns emasculate students, blunt their energies and imagination, and prepare them for authoritarian patterns of government and social behavior. The critics have argued that all too often schooling produces no genuine education but rather one long exercise in pleasing teachers and carrying out instructions. In *The Student as Nigger,* a classic indictment of formal education, Jerry Farber made precisely this point: "[Students] haven't gone through twelve years of public school for nothing. They've learned one thing and perhaps only one thing during those twelve years. They've forgotten their algebra. They're hopelessly vague about chemistry and physics. They've grown to fear and resent literature. They write like they've been lobotomized. But, Jesus, can they follow orders!" *

Michael Rossman, a leader of the Free Speech Movement at Berkeley in 1964, has been another fierce exponent for radical change in classroom authority relations. In an interview in

* Farber's essay unfortunately had to be withdrawn from this chapter. Rights for republication were not available from the publisher.

Change magazine in 1969, Rossman answered a charge by Morris Abram, President of Brandeis, that he was copping out by ignoring the electoral system with these words: "You give me control of what happens in the classroom, baby, you let me write and speak and touch people in such a fashion that it changes classroom relations and basic authority relations, and I'll give you the entire electoral system. You aren't going to have a chance: I'm going to have your kids. And I'm going to make your kids able to talk to each other in such a way that they're capable for the first time of coping with democracy on a mass scale. You're just messing around with the surface of social change." *

One of the techniques that Rossman and others have used in trying to overcome existing patterns of classroom interaction is described in the first article reprinted below. The technique is a "learning game" in which students and an organizer act out the roles of "good student" and "good teacher." In the process, they analyze their own actions as characteristic responses of people performing those classroom roles. This self-analysis produces tension and "role-confusion" as the players become more acutely aware of their own inauthenticity and "role-conditioning." Finally, the game breaks down, each engaged participant emotionally shaken. But even then the group finds it has not escaped the classroom authority structure, for whenever "the organizer tries to contribute his knowledge or feelings, the geometry of control snaps back into existence." Nevertheless, Rossman sees the game as a valuable "deconditioning" experience which forces the players "to realize that their social performance as a 'good student' has little to do with whatever *being* a good learner actually means to each individual."

The effort to democratize the classroom and create a more informal, less structured mode of authority has met strong criticism from many educators, including some sympathetic to radical politics. Robert Brustein, dean of the Yale Drama School and a signer of the "Call to Resist Illegitimate Authority," † decried what he

* Whether educational reform is revolutionary is a question that has provoked intense disagreement among radicals. For an answer to Rossman, see Jo Anne Wallace, "Behind the Free University Crisis," pp. 235–242, Vol. II. For more on the general subject of classroom authority, see "A Dialogue on Classroom Disruption," pp. 57–61, Vol. II.

† See above, pp. 188–90.

saw as a mistaken application of democratic ideals to the educational process and a trend toward idolization of the amateur as a cultural model. Brustein contended that "the concept of professionalism is being vitiated by false analogies. Because *some* authority is cruel, callow or indifferent (notably the government in its treatment of certain urgent issues of the day), the Platonic *idea* of authority comes under attack."

In reply to Brustein, Eric Bentley interpreted his colleague's remarks as a turn toward "defensive conservatism." Brustein answered that his feelings on the war and other social issues were unchanged, but that he questioned whether the tendency of radical students "to concentrate on the purification of the universities" would lead to a resolution of those larger problems.

Mimeographed article by Michael Rossman, educational reformer, September 1969.

The Totalitarian Classroom—
A Learning Game

Among the many learning games which young free-lance educators are now introducing on campuses is one called Totalitarian Classroom. It depends on the depth to which students (and teachers) have been blindly conditioned to play the social game "good teacher/good student" which dominates formal education. T.C. is in fact a deconditioning game against this, and its players experience a painful and illuminating perspective on the roles and processes through which they normally move.

The Totalitarian Classroom begins when its organizer announces to a group of from twelve to twenty innocents:

"I want to lead you in a learning game. Whoever plays Totalitarian Classroom with me must follow a small set of rules and roles, which form a stage. Inside this stage, let's try to hold a real discussion of a specific subject: how people act out their parts in the classroom game called 'good student.' First I want to describe the few rules and roles of our own game, and ask you to agree to them. Then we'll start the discussion itself; maybe we can carry it on to consider what the 'good student' game has to do with good learning, if anything.

"The two rules come from assuming that everyone's a 'good

student.' That means he's independent, critical, he has his own unique viewpoint. So I'm always free to ask any of you to express a view that differs from one just given by someone—you can extend him, contradict him, whatever. And likewise, a 'good student' is in command of the material and can make connections between its parts. So I can call on anyone to explain the connection between any two points other people have previously made."

Of course, the organizer need have no idea whether such points are in fact connectible: that's not his problem. He doesn't mention this, but goes on to ask for volunteers to play three standard "good student" roles.

"One way to present yourself as a 'good student' is to display your command of the material. Another is to brown-nose, to agree with the teacher. But you can also win points by creative disagreement in the classroom game. So we'll want a Scribe, to take absolutely verbatim notes. And a Yes man. When I ask him, about any statement, 'Is that right, Mr. Yes?' his job will be to say, 'Yes, that is right,' and then *explain why*. Likewise we'll want a No man, whose job will be to say, when asked, 'No, that is wrong,' and then explain why. Is all this clear?"

"Are the rest of us supposed to play roles?" someone asks.

"No. No one else should try to play-act a role. Everyone is free to respond as who they are—even the three people who'll volunteer to play these formal roles that are the game's stage, even they should respond as themselves except when I call on them specifically in role. As ourselves, let's try to keep the discussion as real and substantive as we can. I'll try to use the two rules in this way too."

He calls on these few roles and rules at will, to punctuate or speed up the game, as well as to advance the discussion: they are the formal trace of his control (which extends far beyond them in fact) and they create a stage for theater. With practice, simply establishing their power is sufficient, and the game may be brought to its desired effect while calling on them rarely.

Typically the volunteers for Yes and No man depend on these strategies naturally. As discussion develops, other players will also assume them unconsciously. The organizer exposes this, after first using them to guide the discussion as he pleases. Often no one will volunteer as Scribe. Insisting that verbatim transcription is essential—which is almost true, since the richest examples of "good student" performance lie in the precise words people choose for their responses—the organizer drives the group into a democratic election to burden someone with the job. Later he pokes the Scribe with questions, illustrating how impossible it is to think or respond during the process of recording material for playback.

When the discussion begins, the organizer is in total control, no matter how gently or jovially he may have introduced T.C. He is marked as the Expert, bankrolled with specialized Knowledge, the Man Who Knows What Should Happen. He does nothing to inflate or dispel the illusion, but leads the game through its three phases. In the first, by asking questions and giving hints, he gets people to describe in detail the ways in which "good students" act out their roles in the classroom theater.

"Very well. What are some ways that people project themselves as 'good students' in the classroom?"

"They come to class on time." "They hand in their homework."

"Yes, yes. Some others."

"Eye contact with the teacher is very important—so is volunteering information." "Coming up to him after class to talk about something."

"What about the way people look? You—how do you look, when you've just been asked a question you can't answer but you don't want the teacher to know you haven't thought about it?"

"I sit up straight and wrinkle my forehead, searching—maybe he'll speak first."

"And you?"

"I lean forward a little and look earnest, and try to talk about something else . . ."

"And you?"

Soon the discussion reveals that different choices of where to sit, of posture, dress and expression, of complaisant or sarcastic attitude, and so on, are rich elements in a variety of styles of projecting oneself to a teacher and class as a 'good student.' The organizer leads the group on, to recognize reinforcing elements and to complete strategies.

"What might go with sitting in the back row and looking out the window, to project a whole 'good student' image?"

"Missing a lot of classes but seeing the professor in his offices, maybe not during regular hours."

"You, I don't know your name, can you give me an independent opinion? No? Well, you next to her, can you?"

"Being casual with your homework, but sparkling on the final."

"You—what's the connection between the last two answers? Explain."

"Both times you're showing that you know what's important."

"Very good! This strategy will work with every teacher, is that right, Mr. No?"

"No, that is wrong, it'll only work with some."

"Because?"

"Because some teachers are uptight about petty detail."

"In other words, what's important is what *they* think's important. I take it you use this strategy yourself?"

"Something like that."

"All right. So it's clear different strategies work with different teachers, and different classes too—they're part of the audience too. Now who can say why? What determines whether a projection of yourself as 'good student' will be successful, besides skill?"

"If it helps the teacher play his own role well, if it complements his role."

"Is that right, Mr. Yes?"

"Yes, that is right, because then it satisfies his image of himself, it feeds his ego."

"Is that your real opinion, or your role speaking?"

"Yes" (after some hesitation).

"Then does the image or role of a 'good student' necessarily resemble the image of the 'good teacher' he's facing?"

"No."

"Can you give an example? . . . Can anyone?"

"What about the freak in class, and the scholarly professor who translates the freak's occasional insights—which of course *he* recognizes—so the rest of the dull class can understand them?"

"That'll do."

Soon the group is fully caught up in the roles and rhythms of an academic seminar. From here T.C. passes easily into its second phase of *reflexive theater*, of play which comments upon its own performance.

"How long do you think it takes to figure out what a teacher expects from you, what 'good student' roles you can play with him? Someone: how long?"

"Maybe like three weeks."

"Anyone think the time is shorter? You do, huh. How short?"

"Oh, you can tell where most teachers are at within the first day or so."

"Tell him why you think it isn't three weeks."

"The way he talks about midterms and homework. How he's dressed, whether he wants to bullshit a bit or get right down to the subject. Things like that."

"Why did you say that looking at me, when I asked you to explain it to him?"

"Because . . . I don't know."

"Did that explanation make sense to you, do you see why three weeks is too long an estimate?"

"Yes. I can see that it starts right at the beginning. Like whether the teacher asks the class questions about themselves."

"Wait . . . what is there about what he just said, that is a presentation of himself as 'good student'?"

"He admits his mistake."

"Anyone have a better answer?"

"He not only admits it, he shows he's learned by adding something new."

"Right on! Now go back. When I asked five of you how you looked when trying not to show you didn't know the answer to a question, everyone gave a different answer—showing they were individual, that's very good. But everyone answered in words. No one demonstrated the look itself, even though you know how many words a picture's worth. How come you didn't?"

"You wanted us to answer in words."

"How do you know? As a matter of fact, I was hoping someone wouldn't. Someone else?"

"I think it's because you're articulate."

"How is that a 'good student' response?"

"He was uncertain and afraid you'd tell him he was wrong, so he took care to qualify it."

"Right. But I think he's right. Can you go on? I mean, how does my being articulate work?"

"What do you mean?"

"I mean . . . No, let's get at this a different way." (The organizer changes ground whenever he wants; he is in control and need never appear at a loss for words.) "The other side of the 'good student' game is the 'good teacher' game. So: in what ways have I been presenting myself as a 'good teacher' here?"

"You seem to know what you're doing." "You care what people say, and try to draw them out."

"Thanks for feeding my ego. Something more impersonal?"

"Well, first, you stand at the front and you're always moving, that way we have to focus on you. Secondly, you look people in the eye—that's how you call on them to speak, too. Third, you keep trying to probe deeper for answers. Fourth, . . ."

"Stop right there. Can someone tell me: how is he projecting himself as a 'good student,' what elements is he projecting?"

"I'm not playing 'good student.' "

"I don't think you're trying to. But I'm not asking you. Someone else?"

"He volunteered." "He's observant and original."

"Something less trivial."

"He said 'first, second, third . . .' "

"Right on! How is that a presentation of himself as a 'good student'?"

"It shows he has an orderly mind."

"Do you *always* say 'first, second, third . . .'?"

"No."

"Why did you say it here? How did I cue that response?"

"You speak like that, even though you don't say the numbers."

"Hmmm . . . in what way was that a presentation-of-self-as-good-student?"

"He gave you a sharp answer, even though it might have displeased you personally."

"How do you know that strategy's a good one to choose with me?"

"Because of how long your hair is."

"Yes, I pride myself on my tolerance. But I talk like a pedant still, so he knows to give a pedantic answer, right?"

The players, and the organizer himself, have been deeply conditioned. They cannot discuss the game without at the same time playing it. While trying to keep the discussion unfolding with substance and logic, the organizer calls constant attention to the way people act out the only roles they know how to assume in a context of directed and goal-oriented learning. Pressure and pain mount in this second phase, sometimes amazingly. The players become confused and frustrated, as they struggle to keep going with responses whose conditioned nature someone may at any time eagerly and accurately point out. Asked, "Is that you speaking now, or a role?" they often complain in anguish that they do not know.

The group gives them no help. Initially curious and open, its members are withdrawn with anger and closed. Sharp questions have goosed them impatiently through the organizer's program of knowledge, making them feel slightly stupid. Fellow members have vied to tear their answers down or give better ones. Reward now means simply to be left alone; punishment, to be called upon by the finger of Authority to answer, isolated and uncertain. Only the Teacher's Pet is at ease. (I have seen no one, however skilled, manage to avoid generating a Pet relationship with at least one player while directing T.C. The conditioning runs deep.)

The organizer's absolute control is only reaffirmed when he points out gently the scornful violence he has been doing to individuals, their willingness to accept it, and the usual fact that no one has faced or addressed another player directly, or defended or supported another against attack. People try to break past their role-confusion, but cannot: the organizer skillfully co-opts any argument or objection to further the game itself, using the "let's talk about it, why are you doing what you're doing?" routine. The pressure goes up and up, until someone breaks—perhaps into tears or by slamming out of the room. Either response says, in pain and anger, "I won't play your game any longer." One is an act of defeat, the other of rebellion and perhaps of liberation. The organizer declares the Totalitarian Classroom game ended, and asks people to talk about the experience and their feelings within it.

And its third phase begins. In the second, trapped in the game they were discussing, the players struggled with the real pain of being unable to transcend their *individual* conditioned roles. In the third, the agony continues. For, though all have now said, "Let's stop playing this game"—and perhaps symbolized this by shifting from a classroom seating to an informal circle—they find they are playing the game still, *as a group.*

Among themselves, they can begin to discuss the experience in informal democracy. But when the organizer tries to contribute his knowledge or feelings, the geometry of control snaps back into existence. He does not want the role of Teacher any more, and says so; but the group finds with dismay that it cannot treat him otherwise, nor help him leave his very real personal imprisonment in the role.

Partly this is because they all have a large burden of anger for him that cannot be discharged by rational discussion—partly, because he still has unique expertise, and they know no other means of receiving it than by way of an Expert and in a way which reasserts totalitarian control over the group's context and process. All find that the context must be broken completely to permit a fresh start in a healthier game. From this point on, an extended workshop in learning can fruitfully proceed through a nonverbal game session dealing with the release of anger, and then into discussion and games aimed at training for an alternate style of teaching/ learning interaction, radically nonauthoritative and noncoercive.

A full Totalitarian Classroom takes about two hours. Well-run, it leaves its players shaken, acutely conscious of the social game structure of classroom interaction and of its destructive qualities (which are merely emphasized into visibility in T.C.). They are also left to realize that their social performance as "good student" has little to do with whatever *being* a good learner actually means to each individual—a question which most realize they have not actually examined.

As a learning game, T.C. depends on two characteristic dissonances. The first comes from its nature as a hybrid form. Seminars proceed by intellectual reaction to intellectual process; encounter forms, by emotional response to emotional process. But T.C. proceeds by intellectual analysis of the emotional process of intellectual analysis of an emotional process. The tension or dissonance of thus combining two ways of knowing opens people to both. A similar dissonance comes from T.C.'s nature as reflexive theater. For here the rules of the play of learning are on stage as part and focus of that play—rather than agreed upon and never mentioned, as in the theater of the standard classroom. The players are thus forced to a doubled consciousness—within the play, and of the play *as play,* simultaneously—which painfully opens a new way of seeing.

If this bears family resemblance to, say, Brecht's theories about "alienation" in the theater, that is not surprising. T.C. was designed by a young English professor at the University of Illinois— Neill Kleinman—who was deeply involved with the study of modern theater and reflexive forms. Neill played T.C. twice and described it to me. I ran three sessions as part of the Educational

Reform workshop at the 1968 NSA Congress, and played and taught it on individual campuses such as Sonoma State College and Denison University. Like most of our learning games, thereafter it spread quickly and anonymously. Students at Antioch and in Pennsylvania used it to help build orientation programs; when I visited the University of Michigan four students who had been leading T.C.'s described their individual variations; student government kids at San Diego State are practicing it upon their faculty. Its propagation testifies to its flexible strength and impact, and also to our eager need for new games and forms—of deconditioning and new creation—that will help us learn what we need to know.

Article by Professor Robert Brustein, Dean, School of Drama, Yale University. Rebuttal by Professor Eric Bentley, Department of English, Columbia University and answer by Brustein. In The New Republic, *April 26, 1969, and May 17, 1969.*

The Case for Professionalism
by Robert Brustein

In such a state of society [a state of democratic anarchy], the master fears and flatters his scholars, and the scholars despise their masters and tutors; young and old are alike; and the young man is on a level with the old, and is ready to compete with him in word and deed; and old men condescend to the young and are full of pleasantry and gaiety; they are loth to be thought morose and authoritative, and therefore they adopt the manners of the young. . . .

Plato, *The Republic,* Book VIII

Among the many valuable things on the verge of disintegration in contemporary America is the concept of professionalism—by which I mean to suggest a condition determined by training, experience, skill, and achievement (by remuneration, too, but this is secondary). In our intensely Romantic age, where so many activities are being politicalized and objective judgments are continually colliding with subjective demands, the amateur is exalted as a kind of democratic culture hero, subject to no standards or restrictions. This development has been of concern to me because of its impact upon my immediate areas of interest—the theater and theater training—but its consequences can be seen everywhere, most conspicuously in the field of liberal education. If the amateur is coequal—and some would say, superior—to the professional, then the student is coequal or superior to the professor, and "the young man," as Plato puts it in his discourse on the conditions that lead to tyranny, "is on a level with the old, and is ready to compete with him in word and deed."

As recently as five years ago, this proposition would have seemed remote; today, it has virtually become established dogma, and its implementation is absorbing much of the energy of the young. Although student unrest was originally stimulated, and rightly so, by such external issues as the war in Vietnam and the social grievances of the blacks and the poor, it is now more often aroused over internal issues of power and influence in the university itself. Making an analogy between democratic political systems and the university structure, students begin by demanding a representative voice in the "decisions that affect our lives," including questions of faculty tenure, curriculum changes, grading, and academic discipline. As universities begin to grant some of these demands, thus tacitly accepting the analogy, the demands escalate to the point where students are now insisting on a voice in electing the university president, a role in choosing the faculty, and even a place on the board of trustees.

I do not wish to comment here on the validity of individual student demands—certainly, a student role in university affairs is both practical and desirable, as long as that role remains advisory. Nor will I take the time to repeat the familiar litany of admiration for the current student generation—it has, to my mind, already been sufficiently praised, even overpraised, since for all its intrinsic passion, intelligence, and commitment, the proportion of serious, gifted, hardworking students remains about what it always was (if not actually dwindling for reasons I hope soon to develop). I do want, however, to examine the analogy which is now helping to politicize the university, and scholarship itself, because it seems to me full of falsehood.

Clearly, it is absurd to identify electoral with educational institutions. To compare the state with the academy is to assume that the primary function of the university is to govern and to rule. While the relationship between the administration and the faculty does have certain political overtones, the faculty and administration can no more be considered the elected representatives of the student body than the students—who were admitted after voluntary application on a selective and competitive basis—can be considered freeborn citizens of a democratic state: the relationship between teacher and student is strictly tutorial. Thus, the faculty member functions not to represent the student's interests in relation to the administration, but rather to communicate knowledge from one who knows to one who doesn't. That the reasoning behind this analogy has not been more frequently questioned indicates the extent to which some teachers are refusing to exercise their roles as professionals. During a time when all authority is being radically questioned, faculty members are becoming more reluctant to accept the responsibility of their wisdom and experience and are, therefore, often willing to abandon their authoritative position in order to placate the young.

The issue of authority is a crucial one here, and once again we can see how the concept of professionalism is being vitiated by false analogies. Because *some* authority is cruel, callow, or indifferent (notably the government in its treatment of certain urgent issues of the day), the Platonic *idea* of authority comes under attack. Because some faculty members are remote and pedantic, the credentials of distinguished scholars, artists, and intellectuals are ignored or rejected, and anyone taking charge of a classroom or a seminar is open to charges of "authoritarianism." This explains the hostility of many students towards the lecture course—where an "authority" communicates the fruits of his research, elaborating on unclear points when prodded by student questioning (still a valuable pedagogical technique, especially for beginning students, along with seminars and tutorials). Preferred to this, and therefore replacing it in some departments, is the discussion group or "bull session," where the student's opinion about the material receives more attention than the material itself, if indeed the material is still being treated. The idea—so central to scholarship—that there is an inherited body of knowledge to be transmitted from one generation to another—loses favor because it puts the student in an unacceptably subordinate position, with the result that the learning process gives way to a general free-for-all in which one man's opinion is as good as another's.

The problem is exacerbated in the humanities and social sciences with their more subjective criteria of judgment; one hardly senses the same difficulties in the clinical sciences. It is unlikely (though anything is possible these days) that medical students will insist on making a diagnosis through majority vote, or that students entering surgery will refuse anaesthesia because they want to participate in decisions that affect their lives and, therefore, demand to choose the surgeon's instruments or tell him where to cut. Obviously, some forms of authority are still respected, and some professionals remain untouched by the incursions of the amateur. In liberal education, however, where the development of the individual assumes such weight and importance, the subordination of mind to material is often looked on as some kind of repression. One begins to understand the current loss of interest in the past, which offers a literature and history verified to some extent by time, and the passionate concern with the immediate present, whose works still remain to be objectively evaluated. When one's educational concerns are contemporary, the material can be subordinated to one's own interests, whether political or aesthetic, as the contemporary literary journalist is often more occupied with his own ideas than with the book he reviews.

Allied to this problem, and compounding it, is the problem of the black students, who are sometimes inclined to reject the customary university curriculum as "irrelevant" to their interests, largely because of its orientation towards "white" culture and history. In its place, they demand courses dealing with the history and achievements of the black man, both in Africa and America. Wherever history or anthropology departments have failed to provide appropriate courses, this is a serious omission and should be rectified: such an omission is an insult not only to black culture but to scholarship itself. But when black students begin clamoring for courses in black law, black business, black medicine, or black theater, then the university is in danger of becoming the instrument of community hopes and aspirations rather than the repository of an already achieved culture. It is only one more step before the university is asked to serve propaganda purposes, usually of an activist nature: a recent course, demanded by black law students at Yale, was to be called something like "white capitalist exploitation of the black ghetto poor."

On the one hand, the demand for "relevance" is an effort to make the university undertake the reparations that society should be paying. On the other, it is a form of solipsism, among both black students and white. And such solipsism is a serious threat to that "disinterestedness" that Matthew Arnold claimed to be the legitimate function of the scholar and the critic. The proper study of mankind becomes contemporary or future man; and the student focuses not on the outside world, past or present, so much as on a parochial corner of his own immediate needs. But this is childish, in addition to being Romantic, reflecting as it does the student's unwillingness to examine or conceive a world beyond the self. And here, the university seems to be paying a debt not of its own making—a debt incurred in the permissive home and the progressive school, where knowledge was usually of considerably less importance than self-expression.

In the schools, particularly, techniques of education always seemed to take precedence over the material to be communicated; lessons in democracy were frequently substituted for training in subjects; and everyone learned to be concerned citizens, often at the sacrifice of a solid education. I remember applying for a position many years ago in such a school. I was prepared to teach English literature, but was told no such subject was being offered. Instead, the students had a course called *Core*, which was meant to provide the essence of literature, history, civics, and the like. The students sat together at a round table to dramatize their essential equality with their instructor; the instructor—or rather, the coordinator, as he was called—remained completely unobtrusive; and instead of determining answers by investigation or the teacher's authority, they were decided upon by majority vote. I took my leave in haste, convinced that I was witnessing democracy totally misunderstood. That misunderstanding has invaded our institutions of higher learning.

For the scholastic habits of childhood and adolescence are now being extended into adulthood. The graduates of the *Core* course, and courses like it, are concentrating on the development of their "life styles," chafing against restrictions of all kinds (words like "coercion" and "co-option" are the current jargon), and demanding that all courses be geared to their personal requirements and individual interests. But this is not at all the function of the university. As Paul Goodman has observed, in *The Community of Scholars*, when you teach the child, you teach the person; when you teach the adolescent, you teach the subject through the person; *but when you teach the adult, you teach the subject.* Behind Goodman's observation lies the assumption that the university student is, or should already be, a developed personality, that he comes to the academy not to investigate his "life style" but to absorb what knowledge he can, and that he is, therefore, preparing himself, through study, research, and contemplation, to enter the community of professional scholars. In resisting this notion, some students reveal their desire to maintain the conditions of child-hood, to preserve the liberty they enjoyed in their homes and secondary schools, to extend the privileges of a child- and youth-oriented culture into their mature years. They wish to remain amateurs.

One can see why Goodman has concluded that many of the university young do not deserve the name of students: they are creating conditions in which it is becoming virtually impossible to do intellectual work. In turning their political wrath from the social world, which is in serious need of reform (partly because of a breakdown in professionalism), to the academic world, which still has considerable value as a learning institution, they have determined, on the one hand, that society will remain as venal, as corrupt, as retrogressive as ever, and, on the other hand, that the university will no longer be able to proceed with the work of free inquiry for which it was founded. As an added irony, students, despite their professed distaste for the bureaucratic administration of the university, are now helping to construct—through the insane proliferation of student-faculty committees—a far vaster network of bureaucracy than ever before existed. This, added to their continual meetings, confrontations, and demonstrations—not to mention occupations and sit-ins—is leaving precious little time or energy either for their intellectual development, or for that of the faculty. As a result, attendance at classes has dropped drastically; exams are frequently skipped; and papers and reports are either late, under-researched, or permanently postponed. That the university needs improvement goes without saying. And students have been very helpful in breaking down its excesses of impersonality and attempting to sever its ties with the military-industrial complex. But students need improvement too, which they are hardly receiving through all this self-righteous bustle over power. That students should pay so much attention to this activity creates an even more serious problem: the specter of an ignorant, uninformed group of graduates or dropouts who (when they finally leave the academic sanctuary) are incompetent to deal with society's real evils or to function properly in professions they have chosen to enter.

It is often observed that the word *amateur* comes from the Latin verb, to love—presumably because the amateur is motivated by passion rather than money. Today's amateur, however, seems to love not his subject but himself. And his assault on authority—on the application of professional standards in judgment of his intellectual development—is a strategy to keep this self-love unalloyed. The permanent dream of this nation, a dream still to be realized, has been a dream of equal opportunity—the right of each man to discover wherein he might excel. But this is quite different from that sentimental egalitarianism which assumes that each man excels in everything. There is no blinking the fact that some people are brighter than others, some more beautiful, some more gifted. Any other conclusion is a degradation of the democratic dogma and promises a bleak future if universally insisted on—a future of monochromatic amateurism in which everybody has opinions, few have facts, nobody has an idea.

Defensive Conservatism
by Eric Bentley

Today the conflicts of interest are so acute, and the concomitant feelings of hostility so strong, that, at many points, "dialogue" is fruitless and a mockery. But as between Robert Brustein and myself these conditions do not obtain. We are old friends and have labored in the same vineyards. I suppose that the question now is whether being a Dean is forcing him into solidarity with other Deans, which in turn would mean a break with his old friends and co-workers.

I should, however, make it plain that I agree with what I take to be the main point of his declaration, "The Case for Professionalism," which is that up to now the student left has failed to understand university education and maybe all education. Let me restate the point in my own way, and with my own provincialism —Columbia, not Yale, as the center of the universe. The Student Afro-American Society wants its undergraduate members to control admission to Columbia of all students with what is called black skin, even though no group or groups of students controls admission of students with what is called white skin. There is a valid criticism of the old principle of admission involved, namely, that it confused cultural superiority with class superiority, but it has not been made clear what the new principle will be, except perhaps a preference for militant and malcontent attitudes. (I am *for* such attitudes but . . .) Students for a Democratic Society differ with their black brothers on nearly everything, and specifically on admission to Columbia. What they want is that anyone from the four high schools nearest Columbia should be allowed to enter the university without test or question. In which manner universities that previously had entertained the notion of being national institutions would have to settle down to being community colleges, modestly continuing the work of the high school at the end of the block. On such terms, they would be able to keep all their faculty mediocrities, while losing all teachers of real eminence. SDS leaders themselves, admitted to Columbia through their own academic excellence, would find themselves outside the gates. And so on. This whole way of thinking is absurd and incidentally bears no relation to any revolutionary America of the future. Under a revolutionary regime, national institutions would remain national. Columbia would be made more elitist, not less. And a very good thing too. A higher degree of selectivity is really needed, not a less, even if with some different *ways* of making the selection. (I admit that SDS's position is sanity itself compared with positions taken by some of the Yippies. Abbie Hoffman has proposed burning down all high schools, a very funny idea indeed—and he aims to be funny—because, in the past, though they have sometimes burned their enemies, revolutionaries have always kept buildings intact—for their own use. But then Abbie regards Sirhan Sirhan as a freedom fighter.)

So much to establish that I believe Robert Brustein has a good solid point. The question is whether this entitles him to take off in a new direction. Not long ago he signed a "Resist" statement* which endorsed not only legal forms of opposition to the Vietnam war but illegal ones. Surely Vietnam is not unique? Is not an exception to all rules? The Resist people certainly don't think so, and have subsequently issued other statements, including one that ends with the avowal: "We therefore find ourselves engaged in an effort to reconstruct American society by deliberately going outside of the existing political system." How about that? Can American *education* be reconstructed without going outside existing academic politics? Many of us doubt it, and it may be of interest that a liberal, nonradical Columbia professor, Amitai Etzioni, has recently recommended that the principal "outside," extra-legal

* For text, see pp. 188–90.

device of campus disputes—the sit-in or occupation—be recognized as legitimate, as strikes have been in labor-management disputes.

That, I think, is the main issue. My friend Robert does not say where he now stands on it, and I might have just sat back and waited for him to explain himself on some future occasion were his present article not dotted with epithets, phrases, ironies, sarcasms, and above all exaggerations, which suggest that he is going over to the enemy. What are we to make, for example, of his vision of a future in which "everybody has opinions, few have facts, nobody has an idea"? It strikes me as a description of [Columbia] Low Library as run by Grayson Kirk and David Truman. Or of all the Russias until Lenin came along. It has no special relevance to present-day radicals. Or: "that sentimental egalitarianism which assumes that each man excels in everything." No such egalitarianism pervades student meetings: sometimes, as the tide of misanthropy rises, I wish it did. Or: "The familiar litany of admiration for the current student generation." Is "litany" a fair word here? I mean: can admiration legitimately be *avoided?* What the students have done is to come out of the coma of the Joe McCarthy era and even help America to come out of that coma.

I would not pick on phrases if they were not infused, as is Robert's whole article, with a defensive conservatism that, to my mind, has no concrete content. "All this self-righteous bustle over power." "In our intensely Romantic age, where so many activities are being politicalized . . ." One would like to interrupt at such a point and ask if he has forgotten *why* politics became so all-pervasive and *whose fault* it was? And whether things, in this respect, mustn't get worse before they can get better? But the very first phrase of his whole article contains what turns out to be the premise of the whole presentation: "Among the many valuable things on the verge of disintegration in contemporary America is . . ." Ah, so America did have integrity and integration until yesterday? Did have professionalism until it was upset by the amateurs? The implied philosophy is pure conservatism, and I call it "without concrete content" not only because one cannot point to any such phase preceding "disintegration," but also because I can only see Robert's present stance as something sheer Deanship must have pushed him into. Whether or not I am right about this, I would maintain that to abandon political radicalism in order to combat educational amateurism would be to empty out the baby with the bath.

Mr. Brustein replies . . .

My friend Eric Bentley has responded to what was intended to be an impersonal analysis of the eroding effect of student radicalism on the function of education with an argument which forces me into personal testimony and defense. Such is the intensity of today's quarrels, as he suggests himself, that old friends are pressed into public confrontations.

To Mr. Bentley's assertions that I am "going over to the enemy" or abandoning "political radicalism" or engaging in "defensive conservatism," I must reply that I remain the man I always was—this may, indeed, be the source of our disagreement. As long ago as the fifties, when Eric Bentley was sniffing out "pseudo-radicalism" in American plays and productions (*pace* "The Missing Communist" and elsewhere), my major concern was with the defense of free artistic expression, and the alteration of any institutions that inhibited or blocked this expression (*pace* my "Madison Avenue Villain" and elsewhere). I am not by nature an ideological animal. I was originally attracted to scholarship through a love of art, and a respect for those men who were capable of speaking the truth, even when it was awful or unfashionable. The substance of my writings (and the theme of *The Theatre of Revolt,* as anyone knows who has read past the title) concerns the doubleness of great drama and the complexity of life, and so I have always felt a revulsion from monolithic thinking from any quarter.

Therefore, I do not love political radicalism for its own sake, and I deplore the kinds of thinking that expresses itself in terms of "enemies" and "sides." Since I was only a child in the thirties, I have no vestigial nostalgia for the conflicts of that period; since I was not particularly political in college, I do not feel compelled to relive my student radicalism today. In consequence, I do not share the current reflexive assumption that radical movements are necessarily more humane or more compassionate than other movements. I hear the SDS affirm this, but I see no evidence in fact. When I hear of a Columbia history professor having his arms pinioned by students about to occupy a building and being hit in the face with a club, or of the gentle lady president of Radcliffe being terrorized by students protesting a minor disciplinary action, I do not automatically think of the courteous Marxism espoused by Brecht, but rather of the bully tactics used by the Nazis (before they came to power) against the educational institutions of another corrupt liberal regime, the Weimar Republic. (Yes, the police use these tactics, too, when pulling out students—and should be banned from the campus for the same reason.) The SDS, and its supporters, always emphasizes its idealism when defending such actions; but I imagine National Socialism had idealists too (it was, after all, a partially *socialist* movement). Anyway, as a student of Ibsen and Shaw, Eric should be a little more skeptical of actions taken under the name of "idealism."

I loathe the Vietnam war, and I continue to support the Resist movement in its efforts to end that war. My question is whether the assault on the universities is helping to end the war—or to deflect the nation's attention from it. With university news getting such prominence these days in the media, the atrocities in Vietnam get elbowed off the front page, and so does the attention of the legislators who begin to pour their energies into making laws against disruption. It is obvious that the ROTC is an extension of the military on the campus, and I personally believe that it has no place whatsoever in the university, but I sincerely wonder how important this issue is in the order of priorities. While the great ROTC controversy of 1969 occupies the campus activists at Yale (and elsewhere), the Olin Mathison plant (and others) just down the street continues to pour out armaments that will be sent to Vietnam. While the university is being closed down, the munitions plants continue on twenty-four hour shifts, unnoticed, untouched, unaffected by student protesters.

Of course the university has been impure in its relations with the government; of course its expansion into slum communities has left many homeless; of course many professors have been mentally isolated from the vital concerns of the day. And these are issues that require varying degrees of radical reform. But it is also true that the university has been at the center of Vietnam resistance, that it has been in the forefront of enlarging educational possibilities for all the people of the nation, and that it has been attracting (until recently) some of the best and most effective minds in the country. To concentrate on the purification of the universities to the exclusion of concluding the war and solving urban problems is to play right into the hands of those who would perpetuate the conflict and maintain the ghettos. If I had an SDS-type mind, I would begin to suspect a conspiracy between the radical students and the Pentagon. As it is, I will satisfy my-self with psychological rather than political explanations. The as-sault on the universities sometimes looks less to me like honest idealism than a grownup version of the bully game called "get the guy with the glasses." (I notice one of my correspondents offering to use a club against any lecturer he found engaged in military re-search. One of the studies that should be conducted by students and faculty alike is to what extent American violence has brutal-ized people on all sides of the political spectrum.)

My article was an implicit demand on people not to polarize dumbly into unthinking positions, but to keep alert to brutality wherever it may appear. In some nonpolemical, nonpolitical cor-ner of his mind, Eric Bentley must have realized that the "valua-ble things on the verge of disintegration" I referred to were not the social or political institutions that he (and I) may find want-ing, but rather the kinds of conditions that were able to produce a Faulkner, a Fitzgerald, a Hemingway, an O'Neill, an Eliot, a Robert Lowell, an Edmund Wilson, a Lionel Trilling—in other words, the various consolations provided by art and intellect that are now in danger of being obliterated by clenched fists and clenched minds. The kind of thinking and writing being inspired by our current situation frankly appalls me: I do not think it is in-apposite to observe how few legitimate works of art and intellect have been produced by the radical young, for all the ferment of the past three years (admittedly, I do not count rock music). I seem to remember that the French revolution wasn't very impres-sive in its cultural achievements either, apart from Delacroix—and man cannot live on revolution alone.

He cannot live on "relevance" alone either. My very simple point was that in order to become a doctor and help the sick of the ghettos, you must first study "irrelevant" subjects like com-parative anatomy and organic chemistry. In the same way, you must give yourself up to the seeming irrelevancies of the past in order to be relevant to the present. Otherwise, you will be con-demned to repeat the errors of history, as the saying goes—and as we seem to be doing at the present moment. Clearly, the system is not working, and I share a profound sense of disturbance about it. But I do not believe it can or should be improved by violence, and the eagerness of the radical young to escalate their actions to their irrational rhetoric makes me worry whether the society they would substitute would not be worse than the one we now have.

What we need are ideas, not romantic gestures, and the current situation is preventing ideas from being formulated.

A last word. I must be very careful—indeed, everyone must be careful—not to generalize wildly about students. They are an incredibly diverse and various group of people. My quarrel is with radical students of the SDS persuasion; all others I can reason with. I believe in students, as must surely be obvious from the fact that I am continuing in my present academic post. The temptation these days to withdraw from the academy into private life is simply overwhelming; if I am not mistaken, Eric Bentley is yielding to this temptation himself (let us hope temporarily). But I still believe that the dialogue we are conducting can best be held *inside* the university—so long as that institution is permitted to function and survive.

NOTE TO THE READER

If you know of any good documents we've missed, please send them to us, care of Random House.

The Editors

IMMANUEL WALLERSTEIN of the Department of Sociology at Columbia University was very active in the events leading up to, during, and after the Columbia revolt of 1968. He was chairman of the Faculty Civil Rights Group (1966–69), a member of the Steering Committee of the Ad Hoc Faculty Group (April 1968) and the first Executive Secretary of the Executive Committee of the Faculty formed on May 1, 1968. Author of *University in Turmoil: The Politics of Change* (1969), he has also written many books and articles on contemporary Africa.

PAUL STARR, twenty-one, was an undergraduate at Columbia during the 1968 revolt. A co-author of *Up Against the Ivy Wall,* a narrative of the rebellion, he served as editor-in-chief of the *Columbia Daily Spectator* from March 1969 to March 1970. He is now a graduate student in social theory at Harvard.